STRUCTURE AND GROWTH OF PHILOSOPHIC SYSTEMS
FROM PLATO TO SPINOZA

II

PHILO

VOLUME II

PHILO

FOUNDATIONS OF RELIGIOUS PHILOSOPHY
IN JUDAISM, CHRISTIANITY, AND ISLAM

BY

HARRY AUSTRYN WOLFSON

NATHAN LITTAUER PROFESSOR OF HEBREW LITERATURE
AND PHILOSOPHY IN HARVARD UNIVERSITY

VOLUME II

THIRD PRINTING
REVISED

CAMBRIDGE · MASSACHUSETTS

HARVARD UNIVERSITY PRESS

1962

CONTENTS

VOLUME II

CHAPTER IX

41214

CHAPTER X

Philo's impugnment of "the laws of cities" as man-made and not in accordance with nature, 187. — His contention that the Law of Moses, because it is divinely revealed, is the only natural law in the true sense of the term, 189. — The Law of Moses allusively compared by Philo with the *Laws* of Plato, 194. — Philo's answer to the question raised in Greek philosophy as to how happiness or virtue is to be acquired, 196. — Revelation as a corollary of the conception of God as a free agent, 199.

(*a*) *Classification of Commandments and Virtues* — Philo's fourfold classification of the laws of Moses, three traditionally Jewish, and one based upon the classification of the philosophic virtues with which the Mosaic laws are identified by him, 200. — Various attempts by Philo to classify the virtues, resulting in the threefold classification of intellectual, moral, and practical, 202.

(*b*) *Intellectual Virtues and Actions* — The eight scriptural presuppositions as intellectual virtues, 208. — Actions recommended by certain laws conceived as having for their purpose the inculcation of intellectual virtues, 210. — The intellectual virtues together with their corresponding actions described in their totality as the virtues of wisdom, piety, godliness, holiness, and faith; Greek and Jewish elements in Philo's treatment of these virtues, 211. — Faith as a virtue of strictly Jewish origin: its special meaning, 215.

(*c*) *Moral Virtues and Actions* — The four cardinal virtues, prudence, courage, temperance, and justice, and the virtues of humanity (*philanthropia*), fellowship, concord, equality, grace, mercy, and nobility: Greek and Jewish elements in Philo's treatment of these virtues, 218. — Actions recommended by certain laws conceived as having for their purpose the inculcation of moral virtues, 221. — The Stoic "forethought" and "assent" required by Philo in the performance of right actions as the equivalent of the rabbinic "intention" and "joy," 223.

Control of actions and control of emotions, 225. — The treatment of the tenth commandment as dealing with the control of the pure emotion of desire in native Jewish tradition and in Philo, 226. — Philo's diatribe against the emotions and the rabbis' diatribes against the evil *yeṣer*, 229. — Similarity and difference between Philo on the one hand and Aristotle and the Stoics on the other in their treatment of the emotion of desire, 231. — "Continence" as the virtue opposed to the vice of "desire," 235.

IV. Prayer, Repentance, and Study as Virtues 237

(a) *Prayer* — Prayer as a virtue of strictly Jewish origin, 237. — Philo's terminology of prayer, 239. — His treatment of the relation between prayer and sacrifice, 241. — Silent prayer and audible prayer in native Jewish practice, in Greek practice, and in Philo, 248.

(b) *Repentance* — Repentance as a virtue of strictly Jewish origin: Greek philosophic sentiments about repentance, 252. — Various conceptions about repentance in Philo and in native Jewish tradition, 256. — Question as to the relative merit of the penitent and the perfectly righteous in native Jewish tradition and in Philo, 258.

(c) *Study and Teaching* — The study and the teaching of the Law as virtues based upon Mosaic commandments, 259. — Question as to the relative importance of the study and the practice of the Law in native Jewish tradition and in Philo, 261. — Formulation of this question by Philo in terms of the Greek philosophic problem as to the relative importance of the contemplative and the practical life, 262.

(d) *Deeds, Words, Intentions* — Additional fifth classification of the commandments into those relating to deeds, those relating to the spoken word, and those relating to right thoughts and right feelings, i.e., the heart, 266.

V. The Definition of Virtue 268

Analysis of the Aristotelian and Stoic definitions of virtue and the resulting three differences between them, 268. — How Philo must have found the three implications of the Stoic definition unacceptable to Judaism, 270. — How Philo adopted the Aristotelian definition of virtue, but still found use, in a limited sense, for the Stoic definition, 272. Philo's new use of the Stoic term "eupathy," 275. — The use of the terms "light," "heavy," and "intermediate men" in Philo and native Jewish tradition, 277.

VI. The Reward of Virtue 279

The problem of virtue and its reward in Greek philosophy and Judaism, 279. — Various answers to the question of the suffering of the righteous and the prosperity of the wicked in Greek philos-

CHAPTER XIV

CONTENTS

between pagan Greek philosophy and philosophy since the seventeenth century, 444. — General survey of the common problems and principles of that intermediate or mediaeval type of philosophy, 445. — Philo the founder of that type of philosophy; Spinoza its overthrower, 457.

PHILO

FOUNDATIONS OF RELIGIOUS PHILOSOPHY IN JUDAISM, CHRISTIANITY, AND ISLAM

VOLUME II

CHAPTER IX

KNOWLEDGE AND PROPHECY

I. Sensation, Reason, and Prophecy

THE PSYCHOLOGY of Philo is essentially Platonic, though in his description of the faculties of the soul he uses Stoic vocabulary and occasionally also Aristotelian vocabulary.[1] The soul, or to be more exact the rational soul, has an existence prior to the body and when placed in the body it continues to exist as something distinct from the body. But unlike Plato's soul, as we shall see, it did not possess a knowledge of its own which it forgot upon its entrance into the body and to regain which it had to reëducate itself by the instrumentality of the body. Its knowledge begins upon its entrance into the body. Through the instrumentality of the body it acquires the knowledge of sensation and from that lowest form of knowledge it rises to higher forms.

There is in Philo no formal classification of the various types of knowledge. In the places in which he happens to touch upon the subject he mentions only two types of knowledge, sensation and mind ($\nu o \hat{v} s$),[2] or sensation and thought ($\delta \iota \acute{a} \nu o \iota a$),[3] or sensation and reason ($\lambda o \gamma \iota \sigma \mu \acute{o} s$).[4] These two types of knowledge are considered by him as being dependent upon each other. With regard to the dependence of reason upon sensation, he says that it is impossible to apprehend the intelligible world or any other existing being which is incorporeal "except by making corporeal objects our starting-

---

[1] Cf. above, I, 389.

[2] *Leg. All.* I, 11, 29; cf. Leisegang, *Indices*, under αἴσθησις, 4.

[3] *Conf.* 26, 133; cf. Leisegang, *loc. cit.*, 3; cf. also "sensation and the power of thinking ($\delta \iota a \nu o \eta \tau \iota \kappa \grave{\eta} \delta \acute{v} \nu a \mu \iota s$)" (*Leg. All.* II, 7, 23, and II, 8, 24).

[4] *Praem.* 5, 28; cf. Leisegang, *loc. cit.*, 5.

point," 5 for the visible world is "a kind of gate (πύλη τις)" to the intelligible world.⁶ Similarly, with regard to the dependence of sensation upon reason, referring to the Stoic eightfold classification of the faculties or parts of the soul, he says that "were a man to do away with the eighth, mind, which is the ruler of these . . . he will paralyze the seven also; for they are all strong by sharing the strength and vigor of the mind." ⁷ In this he is merely reëchoing the view common to Plato, Aristotle, and the Stoics. All of them, in different ways, believed in the existence of a reciprocal relation between sensation and reason.

But, just as to him God is above the Logos immanent in the world,⁸ so he also argues that God is above the mind immanent in man, and God it is who directs the activities of that mind. Just as God, on implanting in the world a Logos, did not abdicate His power to govern the world,⁹ so also, on implanting a mind in the human body, He did not abdicate His power to govern the processes of human knowledge. And he constantly reminds the reader that it is God who is directly the cause of the processes of sensation and reason. "He is a shallow thinker," says Philo, "who supposes that in strict truth anything whatever derives its birth from the mind or from himself," ¹⁰ meaning thereby Protagoras, to whom all the functions of the soul are due to the soul itself which resides in the body or to the body which houses the soul.¹¹ Nay, "it is God who brings about birth," ¹² that is to say, it is God who, having created a soul with various potentialities, brings them out into actuality.¹³ "The mind," he says in another place, "imparts to the portion of the soul that is devoid

5 *Somn.* I, 32, 187.
6 *Ibid.*, 188.
7 *Deter.* 46, 168.
8 Cf. above, I, 327 ff.
9 Cf. above, I, 349, 429.
10 *Leg. All.* II, 13, 46.
11 *Ibid.*, 45. Cf. above, I, 167 ff.
12 *Ibid.*, 47.
13 Cf. *ibid.*, 44–45.

of reason a share of that which it had received by God, so that the mind was besouled by God, but the unreasoning part by mind." [14] But lest one think that God's direct share is only in the rational processes of the soul and not in its irrational processes, he explains in another passage that God has a direct share even in the process of sensation. "But neither has the mind power to work, that is, to put forth its energies by way of sense-perception, unless God send the object of sense as rain upon it." [15]

Not all the knowledge of reason or of the mind, however, is dependent upon sensation. In several passages Philo quite clearly indicates that there is another kind of knowledge of reason or of the mind which is not dependent upon the senses. In one place he says that nature bestows "on mind, as on a mighty king, (a) through the senses as its bodyguards, all the things which are perceptible by the senses; (b) without them, all those things which are apprehensible by reason." [16] In another place he says that while sense-perception observes only "the surface of things visible," the mind (διάνοια) " (a) penetrates through the depths of corporeal things, accurately observing their whole contents and their several parts, (b) surveying also the nature of things incorporeal, which sense is unable to descry." [17] Combining these two passages we get the view that the knowledge of the mind, as distinguished from the knowledge of sensation, is subdivided into two parts, namely, (a) the knowledge of the mind through the senses, and this consists in the knowledge of the constitution of corporeal things and all their parts in their relation to each other, and (b) the knowledge of the mind without the agency of the senses, and this consists of the knowledge of "things incorporeal," that

---

[14] *Ibid.* I, 13, 40.
[15] *Ibid.* I, 11, 29.

[16] *Spec.* III, 20, 111.
[17] *Virt.* 3, 12.

is, the ideas. These two types of the knowledge of the mind are also suggested in a passage in which he describes two kinds of mind, one which gains its knowledge of God "from created things" and another which, rising itself above creation, "obtains a clear vision of the uncreated One." [18] The latter kind of knowledge of God is called by him "the great mysteries," [19] in contradistinction to the former kind of knowledge of God which he calls the "lesser mysteries." [20]

This distinction between two kinds of knowledge of the mind is to be discerned also in a passage in which he enumerates the following three types of knowledge: (1) knowledge of things seen "by the eyes of the body"; (2) knowledge of things which "the soul beholds by its own agency without the assistance of any other," that is, without any assistance from sensation, and this is the knowledge of the "intelligible things" (τὰ νοούμενα) which are "a light to themselves"; (3) knowledge of "the sciences" (ἐπιστῆμαι) which we learn when "the mind applies its eyes which never close or sleep to the doctrines (δόγμασι) and propositions (θεωρήμασι) set before it and sees them by no borrowed but a genuine light which shines forth from itself." [21] In this passage, it will be noticed, the last two types of knowledge are contrasted with the first type in that they are both knowledge of the mind, but the difference between them, though not clearly stated, would seem to be that in the case of the second type the object of knowledge is the "intelligible things," that is, the ideas, whereas in the case of the third type the object of knowledge is the "doctrines and [geometrical] propositions" which are ultimately derived from sensation. In another passage, Philo mentions again two main types of knowledge, that of reason (λογισμός) and that of sensation (αἴσθησις), describing

[18] Leg. All. III, 33, 100; cf. Abr. 24, 122.   [20] Abr. 24, 122. Cf. above, I, 47 ff.
[19] Ibid.   [21] Mut. 1, 4–5.

the former as dealing with intelligible things (νοητά) the end of which is truth (ἀλήθεια) and the latter as dealing with visible things (ὁρατά) the end of which is opinion (δόξα).[22] In this passage, in the light of a classification we shall quote from Plato, it is not impossible that under the knowledge of "reason" which deals with "intelligible things" Philo means to include the two types of knowledge of the mind mentioned in the other passages, namely, the knowledge of the ideas and the knowledge of the sciences which is ultimately based upon sensation.

We thus have in Philo a general twofold division of knowledge subdivided into three. (A) Knowledge of the senses, consisting of (1) sensation and opinion. (B) Knowledge of the mind, consisting of (2) rational knowledge, such as a knowledge of the various sciences which ultimately rests on sensation, and of (3) the knowledge of the ideas which does not rest on sensation at all.

Now, on the whole, this classification of the various types of knowledge reflects a composite view of many statements of Plato, which may be reduced to the following scheme of classification. Knowledge is either of the (A) visible (ὁρατόν) order or of the (B) intelligible (νοητόν) order.[23] The former consists of (1) sensation (αἴσθησις) and opinion (δόξα).[24] The latter consists of (2) science (ἐπιστήμη),[25] whereby he means the mathematical sciences, including geometry, astronomy, acoustics, and harmonics, as well as, in fact, all the other sciences which must begin with certain visible images,[26] and of (3) the knowledge of the ideas.[27] But, in Plato, the high-

---

[22] *Praem.* 5, 28.
[23] *Republic* VI, 509 D.
[24] Aristotle, *De Anima* I, 2, 404b, 23–24; Plato, *Timaeus* 52 A.
[25] *De Anima, loc. cit.*, 22; *Timaeus* 37 C.
[26] *Republic* VI, 510 B–511 A; VII, 526–527.
[27] *Ibid.* VI, 511 B–C.

est kind of knowledge, the knowledge of the ideas, comes, according to the *Republic*, through dialectics [28] and, according to other dialogues, through recollection.[29] In Philo, however, dialectics as a method of arriving at a knowledge of the ideas is never suggested.[30] Nor is there in his writings any suggestion of recollection in the Platonic sense of the recollection of the ideas. There are only three references to recollection in his writings, and none of them, as may be gathered from the context, is used in that Platonic sense. In one place he says: "The advance from forgetfulness necessarily involves recollection, and recollection (ἀνάμνησις) is akin to learning (μαθήσεως). For what he has acquired often floats away from the learner's mind, because in his weakness he is unable to retain it, and then emerges and starts again. When it flows away we say he is in a state of forgetfulness, and when it returns we call it a state of recollection. Surely then memory (μνήμη) closely corresponds to natural excellence and recollection to learning." [31] This statement, indeed, contains references to Plato's statements about learning being recollection [32] and about the difference between memory and recollection,[33] but it does not deal with the recollection of the ideas which were forgotten at the time the soul entered into the body; it deals rather with the recalling to memory of something we have acquired and then forgotten during our lifetime. In another place he refers to "the saying that learning is recollection." [34] This again is a reference to Plato,[35] but from the context it is quite evident that it

---

[28] *Ibid.* VI, 511 B ff.

[29] *Phaedo* 72 E–76; *Phaedrus* 249 C; *Meno* 80 D ff.

[30] Cf. *Agr.* 3, 13; 31, 140; *Plant.* 27, 115; *Congr.* 4, 18; *Mos.* II, 7, 39, where he uses the term "dialectic" in its strictly Aristotelian and Stoic sense.

[31] *Mut.* 16, 100–101.

[32] *Phaedo* 72 E; *Meno* 81 D.   [34] *Praem.* 2, 9.

[33] *Philebus* 34 A–C.   [35] Cf. above, n. 32.

does not refer to the Platonic theory of the recollection of the ideas but rather to his own view that none of the human achievements is a discovery by man's own power but that all of them were implanted by God in nature at the time of creation for men later to discover. In a third place, describing the gifted nature of Moses and how he anticipated all the instruction of his teachers, he says that "his seemed (δοκεῖν) to be a case rather of recollection (ἀνάμνησις) than of learning (μάθησις).[36] Though the contrast between "recollection" and "learning" in this passage reflects again Plato's statement that "our learning (μάθησις) is nothing else than recollection (ἀνάμνησις)," [37] still from the very statement that only the learning of Moses seemed to be recollection, and even that learning only *seemed* to be recollection, it is quite evident that he does not share Plato's view that all learning is recollection and that the highest kind of knowledge, the knowledge of the ideas, is attained through recollection (μνήμη).[38] Philo's highest kind of knowledge, the knowledge of the ideas, is therefore neither the dialectics nor the recollection of Plato. What he means by that kind of knowledge must be determined by what he says about it in various places.

A suggestion as to what he means by his third class of knowledge may be found in an implied threefold classification of knowledge in a passage in which he gives an allegorical interpretation of the verse "Now the giants were on the earth in those days." [39] In this story, he says, Moses wishes to show that "some men are earth-born, some heaven-born, and some God-born." [40] The earth-born are defined by him

---

[36] *Mos.* I, 5, 21.   [37] *Phaedo* 72 E.
[38] *Phaedrus* 249 c.   [39] Gen. 6: 4.
[40] *Gig.* 13, 60. For the expression "earth-born" and "heaven-born," see *Republic* X, 619 c–d: τῶν ἐκ τοῦ οὐρανοῦ ἡκόντων τῶν ἐκ τῆς γῆς.

as those "who are hunters after the pleasures of the body." Pleasure is elsewhere connected by Philo with sensation.[41] The heaven-born are defined by him as those "who are men of art and scientific knowledge and devoted to learning; for the heavenly portion of us is our mind." This quite obviously refers to the second type of knowledge. The God-born, or, as he also calls them, the men of God, are defined by him as those who "have risen wholly above the sphere of sense-perception and have been translated into the world of the intelligible and dwell there registered as freemen of the commonwealth of ideas, which are imperishable and incorporeal." This, again, quite obviously refers to what we have called his third type of knowledge. Now these God-born men, or men of God, who have attained the third stage of knowledge are said by him to be "priests and prophets," with the implication that the third type of knowledge is what Scripture calls prophecy. Here, then, Philo identifies his third and highest kind of knowledge, the knowledge of the ideas, with prophecy, thus substituting the term prophecy for the Platonic term recollection. For Plato never describes recollection by the term prophecy. He calls it philosophic frenzy,[42] but never prophecy. The term prophecy is reserved by him as description for that kind of frenzy which inspires divination or the prediction of the future.[43] Prophecy as a substitute for Plato's highest type of knowledge is also implied in Philo's statement that "the holy books of the Lord are not monuments of knowledge (*scientiae*) or of vision (*videndi*), but are the divine command and the divine Logos," [44] that is to say, they are not based upon scientific knowledge or sensation but rather upon prophetic revelation. When Philo, therefore, describes that which Plato would call recollection

[41] *Leg. All.* II, 18, 73–74.
[42] *Phaedrus* 249 D; *Symposium* 218 B.
[43] Cf. below, p. 14.
[44] *Qu. in Gen.* IV, 140; cf. below, p. 189.

or philosophic frenzy as prophecy, there must be some reason
for it. What that reason is we shall now try to discover.

II. The Four Functions of Prophecy

We have reason to believe that Philo had learned about
prophecy from Scripture before he became acquainted with
it in his reading of Homer and Plato and the Stoics, and that
his own ultimate views on prophecy, like all his religious
views, were formed from certain basic conceptions derived
from Scripture and reshaped and restated in terms borrowed
from philosophy. We must therefore first try to find out
what basic conceptions of prophecy he may have gathered
from Scripture.

To begin with, prophecy as depicted in Scripture must have
appeared to him as the power to predict the future. Jacob,
in his prophetic spirit, is pictured in Scripture as telling his
children that which shall befall them in the end of days.[1]
Moses, in his prophetic capacity, is depicted in Scripture as
making predictions about the successful outcome of the
crossing of the Red Sea,[2] about the coming down of manna
from heaven,[3] and about the future of each tribe.[4] Samuel,
in his capacity as a prophet, is represented as a seer who can
foretell the future.[5] The prophets in the early history of
Judah and Israel are pictured as diviners who foretell the
outcome of sickness or rebellion or war.[6] All the later prophets prophesy about the future of nations and the world.[7]
Divination is thus the first characteristic of prophecy which
Philo could have gathered from Scripture.

Second, prophecy as depicted in Scripture must have also

[1] Gen. 49: 1.
[2] Exod. 14: 13–14.
[3] Exod. 16: 4–7.
[4] Deut. 33.
[5] I Sam. 9: 6–9.
[6] Cf. I Kings 5: 1–14; 22: 7–28.
[7] Cf., e.g., Isa. 15; 17; 19; Jer. 46–51; Ezek. 25–32.

appeared to him as the power to know what rites are to be performed and what prayers are to be offered in order to propitiate God and to avert some evil which God has inflicted upon people. Abimelech is told by God in a dream concerning Abraham: "For he is a prophet, and he shall pray for thee, and thou shalt live." [8] In the wilderness, when a plague began among the people of Israel, Moses as prophet told Aaron as priest to take the fire-pan and lay incense thereon and make atonement for the people and, when that was done, the plague was stayed.[9] Later, at the time of David, when the Lord sent a pestilence upon Israel, Gad, who is described as a prophet,[10] came to David and told him to rear an altar unto the Lord in a certain specified place [11] and, when that was done, "the Lord was entreated for the land, and the plague was stayed from Israel." [12] Again, when Jeroboam's hand was "dried up," a certain "man of God," [13] who is described as a "prophet," [14] prayed for him "and the King's hand was restored him, and became as it was before." [15] And so prophecy, as portrayed in Scripture, meant the power to know by what prayer or sacred rites one can propitiate God.

Third, prophecy as depicted in Scripture must have appeared to Philo as the power to receive from God certain communications by which men were to be guided in their life. This is the main burden of all the prophets from Adam to Malachi. Adam was told what to eat and what not to eat; [16] Noah was similarly told what to do and what not to do; [17] Abraham received a communication from God ordering him to establish a certain custom which was to be fol-

[8] Gen. 20: 7.
[9] Num. 17: 11–13.
[10] II Sam. 24: 11.
[11] *Ibid.* 24:18.
[12] *Ibid.* 24:25.

[13] I Kings 13: 6.
[14] *Ibid.* 13:18.
[15] *Ibid.* 13:6.
[16] Gen. 2: 17–18.
[17] Gen. 9: 1–7.

lowed by his descendants.[18] But the outstanding example of this type of prophecy is the revelation of a complete and comprehensive system of law through Moses, who is proclaimed as the greatest of prophets. And not only the laws but also the poetry found in Scripture are divinely inspired. Miriam, when she took a timbrel and sang a song unto the women who went out after her with timbrels and with dances, is described as "the prophetess." [19] Deborah, the authoress of a song,[20] is also described as a "prophetess." [21] David, in his last words as psalmist, says of himself: "The spirit of the Lord spoke by me, and His word was upon my tongue." [22] And so prophecy as portrayed in Scripture meant to Philo the revelation of the laws and poetry contained in Scripture.

Fourth, prophecy as depicted in Scripture must have also appeared to him as the power to know things which cannot be perceived by the senses. That there are things unperceived by the senses which a prophet may see or may aspire to see is clearly maintained throughout Scripture. God and angels make their appearance to certain persons. Moses prays to be shown the "glory" of God,[23] which evidently refers to something which cannot be seen by the ordinary senses. God is said to have shown to Moses "the pattern of the tabernacle, and the pattern of the instruments thereof" in the likeness of which he was to build a tabernacle and to make its instruments.[24] The pattern was evidently something that could not be seen by the ordinary senses. Then also Isaiah [25] and Ezekiel,[26] by virtue of their being prophets, see visions which men who are not prophets cannot see. And so prophecy as portrayed in Scripture meant to him the

[18] Gen. 17: 10.
[19] Ezek. 15: 20–21.
[20] Judges 5.
[21] Judges 4: 4.
[22] II Sam. 23: 2; cf. also I Sam. 16: 13.

[23] Exod. 33: 18.
[24] Exod. 25: 9; Num. 8: 4.
[25] Isa. 6: 1 ff.
[26] Ezek. 1: 1 ff.

power to see things which were imperceptible to the ordinary senses.

On his becoming acquainted with Greek philosophy, Philo could not help noticing that these four powers which in Scripture are ascribed to prophecy correspond exactly to the four kinds of inspiration which Plato calls frenzy (μανία). According to Plato, there is first the frenzy of the diviner, which produces the art of divination (μαντική), whereby the Pythia and others have foretold future events.[27] Second, there is the frenzy of the priest, which by some oracular power finds a way — through prayers, the service of God, purifications, and sacred rites — to release men from disease and other ills.[28] Third, there is the frenzy of the Muses, which is the source of the songs of poets and the laws of statesmen and kings.[29] Fourth, there is the frenzy of the philosopher, which consists in the recollection of the ideas that cannot be perceived by the senses.[30]

But Philo could not have failed to see an important terminological difference between the four kinds of prophecy in Scripture and the four kinds of frenzy in Plato. In Scripture, the Greek term "prophet" used in the Septuagint as a translation of the Hebrew term *nabi'* applies to all the four powers alike; in Plato, as well as in Greek literature in general, the term prophet is used only in connection with the frenzy of divination. None of the other three kinds of frenzy are described as prophecy.[31] With regard to the enactment of

[27] *Phaedrus* 244 B.
[28] *Ibid.* 244 D–E. This kind of frenzy is not definitely described by him as that of a priest. But priests are generally taken by him to have charge of the service of God. (Cf. *Statesman* 290 C.) Hence this may be described as the priestly frenzy. Chrysippus, however, includes this kind of ritual function under divination (cf. Cicero, *De Divinatione* II, 63, 130).
[29] *Ibid.* 245 A; *Meno* 99 D.
[30] *Ibid.* 249 D ff.
[31] In early Greek history prophets or soothsayers were not priests, though in

laws, which is of special interest to us in our present study, Xenophon in his reports of the conversations of Socrates says definitely that it does not come within the sphere of divination or prophecy, or of any oracle revealed by the gods. The gods, he says, have implanted in us the faculty of reasoning and the power of speech whereby we are enabled "to enact laws and to administer states," and that it is only "in so far as we are powerless of ourselves to see what is expedient for the future" that "the gods lend us their aid, revealing the issues by divination to inquiries, and teaching us how to obtain the best results." [32] "What the gods have granted us to do by help of learning, we must learn; what is hidden from mortals we should try to find out from the gods by divination," [33] and that which is hidden from mortals and must be found out by divination is that which has reference to consequences which cannot be foreseen.[34] Similarly Cicero, in his analysis of the Greek conception of prophecy or rather divination, says explicitly that moral philosophy, duties to parents, and the management of the state — in short, all those teachings which constitute the Mosaic law and which according to Philo were revealed by God through a prophet — are not within the province of divination or prophecy.[35] Indeed there were popular beliefs among the Greeks that certain laws came from God — Plato refers to Minos, the founder of the Cretan laws, as having been guided by the oracles (φῆμαι) of Zeus, and to the Lacedaemonian laws as having come from Apollo [36] — but still the term prophet is

---

later times Greek priests gained control of soothsaying by having their subordinates practice it (cf. P. Gardner and F. B. Jevons, *A Manual of Greek Antiquities*, 2nd ed., 1898, pp. 253–254). In Egypt, however, during the Roman period, prophets were also priests (cf. G. A. Deissmann, *Bible Studies*, pp. 235–237). Cf. below, p. 342.

[32] *Memorabilia* IV, 3, 11–12.
[33] *Ibid.* I, 1, 9.
[34] *Ibid.* I, 1, 6–8.
[35] *De Divinatione* II, 4, 10–11.
[36] *Laws* I, 624 A–B; cf. *Minos* 320 B.

not applied to those who have received the laws from the gods. Similarly, the expression νόμοι πυθόχρηστοι does not mean that these laws were revealed by God through a prophet; it only means that the god gave his approval to laws made by men.[37]

Thus the term prophet as used in the Greek translation of Scripture has a wider meaning than the same term used in Greek philosophy. It includes all the four types of frenzy or inspiration enumerated by Plato, the divinatory or prophetic frenzy, the ritualistic or priestly frenzy, the poetical and legislative frenzy, and the philosophical frenzy. It is in this wider scriptural sense of the term, as including these four functions, that Philo uses the term prophet.

This use of the term prophet as including four distinct functions, though not formally stated by Philo, is clearly brought out by him in his description of the achievements of Moses.

In Scripture, Moses is described not only as prophet,[38] but also as one who commanded a law to the people [39] and as king [40] and as priest.[41] The description of Moses as king and as priest is dwelt upon also in post-Biblical Palestinian literature.[42] With these native Jewish views in mind, fortified undoubtedly also by Greek conceptions as to the relation of priesthood to kingship,[43] Philo describes Moses as king, lawgiver, priest, and prophet.[44] Of these four titles, the first two,

---

[37] Cf. Xenophon, *Lacedaemoniorum Respublica* VIII, 5.

[38] Deut. 34: 10.   [39] Deut. 33: 4.

[40] Deut. 33: 5: "And he was King in Jeshurun." The Hebrew commentators differ as to whether "he" refers to God or to Moses (cf. Rashi, Ibn Ezra and Naḥmanides). *Midrash Tehillim*, on Ps. 1:1, § 2, p. 2a, however, takes it to refer to Moses.

[41] Ps. 99: 6.

[42] Cf. below, pp. 326, 337.

[43] Cf. Goodenough, *By Light, Light*, pp. 181–182, 190.

[44] *Mos.* II, 1, 2–7; *Praem.* 9, 53–56; also philosopher in the sense of king (*Mos.* II, 1, 2), following therein Plato, *Republic* V, 473 D (cf. Badt in *Philos Werke* and Colson, *ad loc.*).

lawgiver and king, are only two phases of the same function, both having to do with law, one enacting it and the other enforcing it. That the titles lawgiver and king here are considered by Philo as only two phases of the same function may be indirectly gathered from a passage in which he compares the inseparability of the "union of these four faculties" in Moses to the inseparable union of the Graces.[45] Now of the Graces he says elsewhere that they are three in number.[46] There are, therefore, only three titles, lawgiver, priest, and prophet. As for these three titles, it can be shown that the term "prophet" is used by Philo not as something distinct from lawgiver and priest but rather as a general term under which lawgiver and priest are to be included. This may be gathered from certain passages in which he discusses the functions of Moses as prophet and as priest. In one passage, after having completed his discussion of Moses as king and lawgiver and priest, and announcing his intention of dealing with Moses as prophet,[47] he divides his treatment of Moses as prophet into three parts, two of which describe Moses' activities as lawgiver,[48] thus indicating clearly that under prophet he includes lawgiver as one of its subdivisions. The legislative function of the prophet is also to be found in his statement concerning Moses that to enact fresh laws "is the task of one . . . who has received from God a great gift — the power of expressing (ἑρμηνείαν) and'of revealing in a prophetic manner (προφητείαν) the sacred laws." [49] In another passage, in which he deals with Moses as priest, he still continues to call him prophet [50] and describes him as being "armed with prophetic knowledge," [51] thus indicating clearly that under

[45] *Mos.* II, 1, 7.
[46] *Abr.* 11, 52–54.
[47] *Mos.* II, 35, 187.
[48] *Ibid.*, 188–191.
[49] *Mut.* 22, 126. On the meaning of the two Greek terms, ἑρμηνεία and προφητεία, cf. below, pp. 41–43.
[50] *Mos.* II, 16, 76.
[51] *Praem.* 9, 56.

prophet he includes priest as another one of its subdivisions. This inclusion of priest under prophet may be also discerned in his statement that "the true priest is at once also a prophet," [52] and still more so in his description of matters relating to the high priesthood of Moses as matters "of the high priesthood of the prophet." [53]

From all these passages we gather that in his description of Moses as lawgiver and priest and prophet he does not mean that Moses performed three functions which were distinct from each other; he rather means that Moses whose chief description in Scripture is that of prophet was not a prophet in the ordinary sense of the term prophet as used in Greek, namely, a diviner, but he was a prophet according to the wider sense which that term has in Scripture, namely, a prophet who by virtue of his being a prophet is also priest and lawgiver.

But besides priest and lawgiver, the prophet in Scripture, as we have seen, is also one who possesses the power of divination and the power of perceiving incorporeal things which are beyond sense-perception. Accordingly we should expect that Philo, in his description of Moses as prophet, should mention not only his powers as priest and lawgiver but also his powers as diviner and as one who perceives incorporeal things. This is exactly what he does. In two passages, where he ostensibly describes Moses as priest or as prophet, we shall try to show that he is really describing the four functions of Moses as a prophet in the scriptural sense of the term, corresponding, as we have said, to the four kinds of frenzy enumerated by Plato.

In one passage, ostensibly dealing with Moses as prophet in the sense of priest, Philo ascribes to him two functions.

[52] *Spec.* IV, 36, 192.   [53] *Mos.* II, 50, 275.

First, as a prophetic priest, Moses was to know the sacred rites (ἱερά) and divine service (θεοῦ θεραπεία) by means of which he was to avert evil from the people and to attain good for them,[54] and by means of which also he was to bring the thanksgivings of the people when they did well and their prayers and supplications when they were sinful.[55] This quite obviously corresponds exactly to the propitiatory function of the prophet as described in Scripture, and to the second type of frenzy as described by Plato. Second, as a priest, says Philo, one of Moses' duties was to build and furnish a sanctuary.[56] But, being not merely a priest but a prophetic priest,[57] he had a direct vision of the idea of that sanctuary and its furniture as it existed in the intelligible world of ideas, for "he saw with the soul's eye the immaterial forms of the material objects about to be made" [58] with the result that "the shape of the model was stamped upon the mind of the prophet [i.e., priest], a secretly painted or molded prototype, produced by immaterial and invisible forms." [59] In this passage, then, Moses as prophet is described as having the propitiatory power and the power to know things not perceived by the senses. In another passage, ostensibly dealing with Moses purely as a prophet, Philo ascribes to him again two functions. First, as a prophet, Moses was the vehicle through whom the Law was revealed, having come to him from God either at God's own initiative or as answers to questions asked by Moses.[60] Second, as a prophet, Moses possessed "the power of foreknowledge, by means of which he was able to reveal future events." [61]

From these two passages, then, we gather that under his

54 *Mos.* II, 1, 5.   58 *Ibid.*, 74.
55 *Praem.* 9, 56.   59 *Ibid.*, 76.
56 *Mos.* II, 15, 75.   60 *Mos.* II, 35, 188–189; cf. below, p. 39.
57 *Ibid.*, 76.   61 *Ibid.*, 190.

treatment of Moses as priest Philo has included two distinct functions of prophecy, the propitiatory and the visionary, and that similarly under his treatment of Moses as prophet he has included two other functions of prophecy, the legislative and the predictive. The prophecy of Moses is thus described by Philo as including all the four functions of scriptural prophecy, which in Plato are treated as four distinct types of frenzy.

Evidently in an effort to show that these four functions of scriptural prophecy are unlike the four distinct types of frenzy in Plato, he tries to show the inseparability of these four functions of prophecy from each other and their dependence upon each other. Speaking of Moses as king and lawgiver and priest and prophet, under which, as we have seen, he includes the four functions of prophecy, he says: "Beautiful and all-harmonious is the union of these four faculties; for, intertwined and clinging to each other, they move in rhythmic concord, mutually receiving and repaying benefits, and thus imitate the virgin graces whom an immutable law of nature forbids to be separated. And of them it may be justly said, what is often said of virtue, that to have one is to have all." [62] In Plato, there is no such mutual dependence between the four types of frenzy. The philosophic frenzy, for him, is quite distinct from the poetic frenzy: the former is above reason, the latter is below reason.[63] It is because of this mutual dependence between these four functions of prophecy that a knowledge of the propitiatory rites and of divine service, which primarily belongs to the prophet as priest, is treated by Philo as belonging also to the prophet as lawgiver, and all the sacred rites and divine services are treated by him as part of the laws revealed through Moses

[62] *Ibid.*, II, 1, 7.
[63] Cf. *Phaedrus* 249 B–D and *Ion* 534 A–E.

by virtue of his being a prophet in the sense of lawgiver.[64]
It is also because of this mutual dependence between these
four functions of prophecy and their inseparability from
each other that the general definition of prophecy given by
Philo is that which primarily applies to the prophet in the
sense of one who has the power to know things beyond
sense-perception. He thus says that by his prophetic gift
the prophet "might discover what by reasoning he could
not grasp," [65] or that "the wise man [i.e., the prophet] sees
God and His powers," [66] or that "priests and prophets" are
those who "have risen wholly above the sphere of sense-
perception and have been translated into the world of the
intelligible and dwell there registered as freemen of the commonwealth of ideas, which are imperishable and incorporeal," [67] or that "to a prophet nothing is unknown, since
he has within him a spiritual sun and unclouded rays to give
him a full and clear apprehension of things unseen by sense
but apprehended by the understanding." [68] Still, knowing
as he does that the characteristic difference between prophecy
as used in Scripture and prophecy as used in Greek literature is that in the former it means also the revelation of a
law, whereas in the latter it has not that meaning, he constantly emphasizes that point. In one place, after describing prophecy as that which "divines" (*divinat*), he adds "by
which oracles and laws are given from God." [69] In another
place, wishing to prove that Abraham was a prophet, he
says: "Indeed I see that he is a prophet and lays down law,
prophesying what things are to be and to be done, for law

---

[64] Cf. *Decal.* 30, 158–161; *Spec.* I, 12, 66–47, 256.

[65] *Mos.* II, 1, 6.

[66] *Immut.* 1, 3; cf. below, p. 32, on use of the term "wise man" in the sense of
prophet.

[67] *Gig.* 13, 61. Cf. above, p. 10.

[68] *Spec.* IV, 36, 192.   [69] *Qu. in Gen.* III, 9.

is an invention of nature and not of men. Since the mind beloved of God [in us] migrates and translates itself in another land outside all the land of sense, there it becomes possessed and prophesies." [70] The surnames by which he usually refers to Moses are (1) prophet and (2) lawgiver.[71]

It is as a result of this wider conception of the scope of prophecy that Philo departs from Plato in his classification of the types of knowledge. To Plato the highest type of knowledge, that which is superior to reason based upon sense-perception, is only philosophic frenzy, that frenzy during which the mind through recollection has a vision of the incorporeal ideas. The three other kinds of frenzy, even the frenzy of the statesman in enacting law, are to him of a lower grade of knowledge.[72] To Philo, however, prophecy in all its four functions constitutes what he considers the third and highest kind of knowledge. What to Plato and to other Greek philosophers is to be attained by philosophy is to Philo to be attained by prophecy. "For what the disciples of the most approved philosophy gain from its teaching, the Jews gain from their law and customs, that is, to know the highest and the most ancient cause of all things." [73]

III. The Three Types of Prophecy

We have thus seen how the four distinct types of frenzy enumerated by Plato are combined by Philo into four interdependent functions of prophecy, and prophecy in all its functions is placed by him as the highest grade of knowledge. Now knowledge must have a source whence it comes. In the case of his two lower grades of knowledge, Philo tells

---

[70] *Qu. in Gen.* IV, 90.
[71] See Leisegang, *Indices*, under προφήτης and νομοθέτης.
[72] Cf. Zeller, II, 1⁴, p. 594, n. 4 (*Plato*, p._176, n. 20).
[73] *Virt.* 10, 65.

us directly that their source is sense-perception.[1] In the case of the highest and third grade of knowledge, in those very same passages in which the lower grades of knowledge are said to have their source in sense-perception, this grade of knowledge is merely said to be independent of sense-perception. But if sense-perception is not its source and if recollection, too, is not its source,[2] what, then, is its source? The answer to this question is furnished by Philo in several other passages. In one group of passages he tells us rather vaguely that "a prophet has no utterance of his own, but his utterance comes from somewhere else, the echoes of another voice," [3] or that "nothing of what he says will be his own" for "he serves as the channel for the insistent words of another's promptings,"[4] or that "he is not pronouncing any command of his own, but is only the interpreter of another."[5] This vagueness, however, is removed in another passage where that "other" who prompts the prophet is identified with God. "For the prophet is the interpreter of God who prompts from within what he should say."[6] This on the whole reflects the conception of prophecy in Scripture as well as the conception of the various kinds of frenzy in Plato. In Scripture the prophet always speaks in the name of God,[7] and in Plato the various kinds of frenzy are described as a divine gift (θεία δόσις)[8] or as a divine dispensation (θεία μοῖρα).[9]

However, to say that the prophet is prompted by God from within as to what he should say does not explain fully the process of prophetic knowledge, any more than to say that everything that happens in the world is caused by God would

---

[1] Cf. above, p. 3.
[2] Cf. above, p. 8.
[3] *Heres* 52, 259.
[4] *Spec.* I, 11, 65.
[5] *Qu. in Gen.* III, 10.

[6] *Praem.* 9, 55.
[7] Cf. Deut. 18:18–22.
[8] *Phaedrus* 244 A.
[9] *Ibid.*, 244 C.

explain the processes of God's activity in the world. For in
man, no less than in the world, according to Philo, God acts
in a variety of ways. Sometimes he acts through agents, His
powers which are immanent in the world, and sometimes He
also acts directly in His own person.[10] We shall therefore
have to find out whether the process of prophecy, which to
be sure, like everything else in the world comes from God,
does also, like everything else in the world, come either indirectly from God or directly from God, or whether it comes
both indirectly and directly from God. On the whole, we
shall try to show that Philo enumerates three sources of
prophecy, namely, (1) the divine spirit, (2) God himself,
or, as it is also described by Philo, the voice of God, and
(3) angels, the first two of these being, according to Philo,
the sources of the prophecies of Moses, which are divided by
him into three groups.

(a) Prophecy through the Divine Spirit

Throughout Scripture, prophetic communications are said
to have their source in what is described as the "spirit of
God" or the "spirit of the Lord." It is this spirit of God
which "comes upon" the prophet,[11] or "comes mightily
upon"[12] him, or "falls upon"[13] him, or "descends and
rests on"[14] him, or "clothes"[15] him, or "fills" him,[16] or
"speaks"[17] by him. The prophet is also described, according to the Septuagint version, as one driven out of his senses
(ὁ παρεξεστηκώς), and as inspired (ὁ πνευματοφόρος).[18] Now, in
Plato, the various states of frenzy are said to be brought
about by divine inspiration (ἐνθουσίασις)[19] or possession

---

[10] Cf. above, I, 349, 376.
[11] I Sam. 19: 20.
[12] I Sam. 10: 6.
[13] Ezek. 11: 5.
[14] Num. 11: 25; Isa. 11: 2.

[15] Judges 6: 34; II Chron. 24: 20.
[16] Micah 3: 8.
[17] II Sam. 23: 2.
[18] Hos. 9: 7.
[19] Phaedrus 249 A.

(κατοκωχή),[20] and divination in particular is described by
him as a gift of God to "human thoughtlessness (ἀφροσύνη)"
which no man achieves "when in his rational mind, but only
when the power of his understanding is fettered in sleep or
when it is distraught by disease or by some divine inspiration." [21] Following his general method, Philo will combine
the "divine spirit," which according to Scripture is the
cause of prophecy, with the process of "divine inspiration"
or "possession" which, according to Plato, is the cause of
his various kinds of frenzy, and especially the frenzy of divination. Thus the process of prophesying through the divine
spirit will become with him identical with the process of
divine inspiration or divine possession in Greek philosophy.

The manner in which he combines the scriptural divine
spirit with the Platonic divine inspiration may be gathered
from several of his homilies.

First, he uses those Greek terms which describe the state
of frenzy as a description of prophetic visions in Scripture.
In his comment upon the verse "and it came to pass, that,
when the sun was going down, a deep sleep fell upon
Abram," [22] he takes the term ecstasy (ἔκστασις), which in the
Septuagint is used for the term "deep sleep," and explains it
as having four meanings. The fourth of these meanings,
that which Scripture uses in connection with Abraham's
prophetic vision, is described by him as "the divine possession (ἔνθεος κατοκωχή) and frenzy (μανία) to which prophets
as a class are subject,' [23] or as "the experience of the God-
inspired (ἐνθουσιῶντος) and the God-possessed (θεοφορήτου),"
which, he says, "proves him to be a prophet." [24] In many
other passages other Greek terms are similarly applied by

[20] *Ibid.*, 245 A.   [22] Gen. 15: 12.
[21] *Timaeus* 71 E.   [23] *Heres* 51, 249; 53, 264.
[24] *Ibid.* 52, 258; cf. *Qu. in Gen.* III, 9; *Spec.* I, 11, 65.

him to scriptural prophecy. Scriptural prophecy thus becomes with him a frenzy, an ecstasy, a divine possession [25] and an enthusiasm (ἐνθουσιασμός),[26] and the scriptural prophet becomes with him one who is thrown into a state of enthusiasm or inspired by God (ἐνθουσιῶν), or one who is possessed by God (θεοφόρητος).[27]

Then, just as he uses the Greek terms describing the state of frenzy as a description of scriptural prophecy, so he also uses the scriptural term "divine spirit" as a description of the Greek conception of frenzy. The Greek terms ecstasy, God-inspired, and God-possessed, all of which are used as descriptions of that which produces the state of frenzy, are explained by him as meaning the same as when Scripture says that the spirit of God came upon the prophet, or rested upon him, or fell upon him, or clothed him, or filled him, or spoke by him. Thus, in dealing with the prophetic experience of Abraham, while on the one hand he describes it after the Greek manner as a state of being possessed (κατασχεθείη), on the other hand he describes that state of being possessed, after the scriptural manner, as being due to "the divine spirit which was breathed upon him from on high." [28] Again, "when the intellect is inspired (*imbuitur*) with divine things," he says, "it receives the divine spirit" (*divinum spiritum*).[29] Thus the Greek expression "to be God-possessed" or "to be God-inspired" came to mean with him to have the divine spirit come upon one, or rest upon one, or fall upon one, or speak by one. It must, however, be remarked that the term "divine spirit" used by Philo in those passages where prophecy is the subject of discussion is to be distinguished from the term "divine spirit" used by him in other passages where the sub-

[25] Cf. above, n. 23.
[26] *Mos.* II, 45, 246; cf. above, n. 24.
[27] *Heres* 52, 258.

[28] *Virt.* 39, 217.
[29] *Qu. in Gen.* III, 9.

ject of discussion is the rational soul of man. The former is sometimes described by him more specifically as "the divine and prophetic spirit" (τὸ θεῖον καὶ προφητικὸν πνεῦμα)[30] or simply as the "prophetic spirit" (προφητικὸν πνεῦμα),[31] whereas the latter is used by him as the equivalent of that incorporeal and rational soul which God breathed into Adam as a breath of life.[32] Since, as we have seen, Philo does not believe in Plato's theory of recollection,[33] man's rational soul is not conceived by him as having any knowledge of its own; it has only a capacity for knowledge, and that capacity becomes actualized in either one of two ways: first, by data of the external world received through the senses which are transformed by its native power into rational concepts; second, by communications received from God through the divine spirit.

Finally, the scriptural resting of the divine spirit upon the prophet, which is now identified by him with what the Greeks call ecstasy, is described by him as a psychological process like that used in the description of ecstasy, but with the admixture of certain scriptural terms which he has already introduced into his own revision of Platonic psychology. There is in man, to begin with, an incorporeal soul, that divine spirit breathed by God into Adam, which incorporeal soul has a capacity for knowledge. Through the instrumentality of the body and the corporeal soul, that incorporeal soul acquires the data of the external world furnished to it by the senses, and by its native power it transforms these data of sense-perception into rational concepts. This constitutes what may be called the natural order of rational knowledge. It is the second of Philo's three stages of knowledge; it is a knowledge of rational concepts formed by the mind out of

30 *Fug.* 33, 186.   32 Cf. above, I, 394.
31 *Mos.* I, 50, 277.   33 Cf. above, p. 8.

the data of sensation. But when that incorporeal soul frees itself from the bodily influence, as well as from its own rational concepts which are based upon the impressions of bodily sensation, it becomes filled with the divine or prophetic spirit and through that spirit it receives a new kind of knowledge from God, a knowledge of things incorporeal. This constitutes what may be called the supernatural order of rational knowledge. Because prophetic knowledge, unlike the rational concepts, is entirely free from sensation, it is described by Philo also as unmixed knowledge (ἄκρητος ἐπιστήμη).[34] In other words, prophecy yields a new kind of knowledge, entirely independent of sensation, a knowledge imported from another region by the divine spirit and instilled into the rational soul of man, and therein it takes the place of those rational concepts formed by the rational soul out of the data of sensation.

This general theory is expressed by him in a variety of ways and with his usual loose use of terminology in many passages. In one passage, using the term "soul" for the rational soul and the term "reason" for the rational concepts which were formed by the rational soul out of the data of sensation, he says: "For no pronouncement of a prophet is ever his own; he is an interpreter prompted by another in all his utterances, when knowing not what he does he is filled with inspiration (ἐνθουσιᾷ), as the reason (λογισμός) withdraws and surrenders the citadel of the soul (ψυχή) to a new visitor and tenant, the divine spirit, which plays upon the vocal organism and dictates words which clearly express its prophetic message."[35] Similarly in another passage, dealing with the prophetic gift of Abraham, he uses the term "soul" for the rational soul, saying that when he prophesied "the divine spirit which was breathed upon him from on high made

[34] *Gig.* 5, 22.   [35] *Spec.* IV, 8, 49.

KNOWLEDGE AND PROPHECY   29

its lodging in his soul (ψυχή), and invested his body with singular beauty, his voice with persuasiveness, and his hearing with understanding." [36] In still another passage, using the term "mind" in the sense of that "reason" which consists of rational concepts derived from sensation and omitting the term "soul," that is, the rational soul, in which, according to the two preceding quotations, that "reason" gives place to the divine spirit, he says: "This is what regularly happens to the fellowship of the prophets. The mind (νοῦς) that is in us is evicted [from the rational soul] at the arrival of the divine spirit, but, when that departs, the mind returns to its tenancy, for mortal and immortal may not share the same home. And therefore the setting of reason (λογισμός) and the darkness which surrounds it produce ecstasy and inspired frenzy." [37] In this passage, we take it, the description of "reason" as mortal does not mean the same as when the irrational soul is described as mortal. [38] It is described as mortal only by comparison with the divine spirit, inasmuch as in contradistinction to the latter it is ultimately based upon sensation and the mortal part of man. In two other passages, using the term "mind" in the sense of the rational soul, he describes the process of prophesying as that in which the rational soul departs from all bodily associations and in its new state of bodiless existence becomes possessed by the divine spirit. He thus says: "Ecstasy, as the word itself evidently points out, is nothing else than a departure of the mind (*mens* = νοῦς) wandering beyond itself," for "when the intellect (*intellectus* = διάνοια) is inspired with divine things, it no longer exists in itself, since it receives the divine spirit within and permits it to dwell with itself." [39] In this passage the "itself" (*se*) be-

[36] *Virt.* 39, 217.   [38] Cf. above, I, 395.
[37] *Heres* 53, 265.   [39] *Qu. in Gen.* III, 9.

yond which the rational soul wanders and in which it no longer exists is that "self" of it which it becomes through its association with the body.[40] Again, "since the mind (*mens* = *νοῦς*) beloved of God [in us] migrates and transfers itself into another land outside all the land of sense, there it becomes possessed and prophesies."[41] In all these passages he is restating in a mixture of scriptural and philosophic terms Plato's statement, repeated also by later Greek philosophers, that "no man achieves true and inspired divination when in his rational mind."[42]

The "divine spirit" is thus that "other" which prompts the prophet to prophesy, corresponding to the traditional Jewish view that it is through the resting of the Holy Spirit upon them that the prophets receive the gift of prophecy,[43] the term "Holy Spirit" being used in post-Biblical Hebrew literature for the Biblical "spirit of God"[44] which Philo usually, though not always, refers to as the "divine spirit."[45]

But what is that divine spirit in the sense of prophetic spirit which is treated of by Philo as a sort of intermediary through which God communicates His message to prophets? No definite explanation of it is to be found in his writings. But inasmuch as the same term divine spirit is used by Philo as a designation of both the prophetic spirit and the incorporeal soul in man, there is no reason why we should not assume that the divine spirit in the sense of prophetic

---

[40] Cf. Plato *Ion* 534 B: "For a poet is a light and winged and sacred thing, and is unable ever to indite until he has been inspired (*ἔνθεος*) and put out of his senses (*ἔκφρων*), and his mind (*νοῦς*) is no longer in him."

[41] *Qu. in Gen.* IV, 90.

[42] *Timaeus* 71 E.

[43] Cf. *Sifre Deut.*, § 176, on 18.18, F, p. 1076; HF, p. 221; *Leviticus Rabbah* 15, 2.

[44] The term "holy spirit" occurs in Isa. 63: 10, 11; Ps. 51: 13(11).

[45] Besides "divine spirit" (*πνεῦμα θεῖον*) he uses also the expression "spirit of God" (*πνεῦμα θεοῦ*), both these forms being a translation of the Hebrew *ruʾaḥ Elo-him*.

spirit is of the same essential nature and of the same order of existence as the divine spirit in the sense of the incorporeal soul of man. The divine spirit in the latter sense, as we have seen, is a real incorporeal being created by God as an image of the idea of mind, which is one of the ideas constituting the intelligible world.[46] So also the divine spirit in the sense of the prophetic spirit, we may assume, is conceived by Philo as a real being created by God as an image of the idea of mind. The divine spirit in this sense is thus an incorporeal soul or mind. Being an incorporeal soul or mind, it is also like the angels who are similarly described as incorporeal souls or mind. But unlike the incorporeal souls in men and the angelic incorporeal souls, both of which are many, the incorporeal soul which is the prophetic spirit is only one, and it is one and the same divine spirit which rests upon all the prophets and through which God communicates His message to them. It is as a real being created by God after the order of angels such as Philo's "divine spirit" that the prophetic divine spirit is also conceived in native Jewish tradition, where it is better known as the Holy Spirit and Shekinah,[47] and it is also as such a being that the Holy Spirit started on his career in the history of Christian theology.[48] The divine spirit is thus a sort of angel. In Philo, therefore, there are three kinds of incorporeal souls or minds created by God as images of the idea of mind. First, the incorporeal souls which become incarnated in the bodies of men. Second, the incorporeal souls which never become incarnated in bodies, and as pure unbodied souls are known by the name of angels. Third, one

[46] Cf. above, I, 390.
[47] Cf. L. Blau, "Holy Spirit," *Jewish Encyclopedia*, VI, 448; "Shekinah," *ibid.*, XI, 259; G. F. Moore, *Judaism*, I, 437–438.
[48] Cf. H. B. Swete, "Holy Spirit," *Dictionary of the Bible*, II, 408, 411a.

unique incorporeal soul known as the divine spirit *par excellence* which has the sole function of acting as an intermediary of divine communications to men. And just as the incorporeal souls in man and the incorporeal souls which are angels are each called by Philo "Logos," [49] so also the incorporeal soul which is the divine spirit of prophecy could be called "Logos." While indeed Philo does not directly designate the divine prophetical spirit by the term "Logos," he identifies it with the scriptural term "wisdom," [50] which is the same as Logos.[51] He similarly uses the term "wise" (σοφός) as synonymous with prophet,[52] and the expression "divine Logos" (λόγος θεῖος) as a description of the prophetic revelations contained in Scripture.[53]

The divine spirit in the sense of the prophetic spirit is thus an incorporeal being which "comes upon" a man, or "falls upon" him, or "descends and rests on" him or "clothes" him, or "fills" him, or "speaks" by him.[54] But man must be prepared for this visit of the divine prophetic spirit, and he becomes prepared for it when that other "divine spirit" within him, his incorporeal soul or mind, detaches itself from all bodily influences and empties itself out of all bodily kinds of knowledge, whether sensations or rational concepts based upon sensations, with which it has become charged through its existence in the body. When that liberation from the body is achieved, the divine prophetic spirit comes and infuses into that other divine spirit in man a new kind of knowledge, prophetic knowledge, unmixed knowledge, a knowledge of things incorporeal. But such a state of com-

---

[49] Cf. above, I, 377, 393.   [51] Cf. above, I, 255.
[50] *Gig.* 5, 23; cf. Drummond, II, 216.   [52] *Gig.* 5, 22; *Immut.* 1, 3.
[53] *Mut.* 31, 169; *Somn.* I, 33, 190. This usage of Logos is based upon such expressions as "The word of God came upon the prophet" (I Kings 13: 20), in which the term "word" is often translated by λόγος without the article. Cf. below, p. 189.
[54] Cf. above, p. 24.

plete liberation from bodily influences can be attained by the ordinary run of man only on certain occasions and under special conditions. Therefore, the divine prophetic spirit is described by Philo as visiting man only periodically (ἐπιπε- φοιτηκότος)[55] and as abiding with him only for a while. "Though the divine spirit may stay a while in the soul, it cannot abide there," [56] for "nothing is harder than that it should abide for ever in the soul with its manifold forms and divisions — the soul which has fastened on it the grievous burden of this fleshy coil." [57] Only in the case of excep- tional men may the divine prophetic spirit abide forever in their souls, and such an exceptional man was Moses. With him it abided a very long time, and this for the reason that his virtuous nature was constant and was free from change and mutability.[58]

Prophecy through the divine spirit is thus one type of prophecy.

This type of prophecy through the divine spirit, which is characteristic of the prophecy of all the prophets, is also characteristic, according to Philo, of the "third" of the three groups of prophetic utterances into which he divides the prophecies of Moses.[59] What he calls the "first" group belongs to a different type of prophecy, and we shall deal with it in our discussion of prophecy by the divine voice. What he calls the "second" group does not constitute a new type of prophecy; it belongs to a combination of prophecy through the divine spirit and prophecy by the divine voice, and with this group, too, we shall deal in our discussion of prophecy by the divine voice.

The third group of prophecies of Moses are described

[55] Spec. IV, 8, 49; cf. above, p. 28.
[56] Gig. 7, 28; cf. 5, 19.
[57] Immut. 1, 2.
[58] Gig. 11, 47–49.
[59] Mos. II, 35, 189–190.

by Philo as those "spoken by Moses in his own person, when possessed (κατασχεθέντος) and carried away out of himself." [60] "Possessed by God" (ἐνθουσιῶδες) [61] and "possessed" (κατεχόμενος; [62] κατασχεθείς) [63] are the terms used by Philo in characterizing the source of this group of the Mosaic prophecies. These terms, as we have already seen, mean to Philo the same as the scriptural expressions of the coming or falling or descending or resting of the divine spirit upon the prophet or its filling the prophet. This becomes still more evident in his description of Moses' predictive prophecy concerning his own death, which quite obviously belongs to the third group of Moses' prophecies. In this description Philo uses the term καταπνευσθείς, [64] which undoubtedly was meant by him to be a reproduction of the scriptural expressions about the divine spirit coming down upon the prophet. The third group of the Mosaic prophecies, therefore, have the same source as the prophecies of all the other prophets, except for the following difference. In the case of all the other prophets, the divine spirit visits them only periodically, whereas in the case of Moses it abided, as Philo says, for a very long time. [65] Moses, therefore, could prophesy always, for the divine spirit was always upon him, and he did not have to wait for sudden flashes of prophetic inspiration. The Mosaic prophecies of this group are accordingly described by Philo as those which are "spoken by Moses in his own person," [66] or as those which "are assigned to the lawgiver himself: God has given to him of His own power (δύναμις), by means of which He is able to reveal future events." [67] Eight instances of this type of prophecy are cited by him: (1) At the

[60] Ibid., 188.
[61] Ibid., 191.
[62] Ibid., 49, 270.
[63] Ibid., 50, 275; 51, 288.
[64] Ibid., 51, 291.

[65] Gig. 11, 47; cf. above, p. 33.
[66] Mos. II, 35, 188.
[67] Ibid., 190; cf. above, p. 19.

Red Sea, Moses predicted the destruction of the Egyptians.[68]
(2) He told the people not to leave any of the manna till the
morning.[69] (3) He conjectured correctly that the seventh
day of the falling of the manna was the Sabbath.[70] (4) He
predicted that there would be no manna on the Sabbath.[71]
(5) In the story of the golden calf, Moses called out: "Whoso
is on the Lord's side, let him come unto me." [72] (6) He predicted what would happen to Korah and his followers.[73]
(7) He predicted what was to happen to each tribe.[74]
(8) He prophesied the story of his own death.[75] It will be
noticed that in all these instances there is no mention of
God having spoken unto Moses to say those things which he
is recorded to have said.[76] It is evidently because of this
omission that Philo characterizes all these utterances as
having been spoken by Moses "in his own person." It will
also be noticed that all these instances deal with predictive
prophecy or with prophecy which implies prediction.[77]

[68] *Ibid.*, 46, 251–252; cf. Exod. 14: 13–14.

[69] *Ibid.*, 47, 259; cf. Exod. 16: 19.

[70] *Ibid.*, 48, 263–265; cf. Exod. 16: 23. In Exod. 16: 5, God had only told him
that the people should gather on the sixth day a double portion. According to
Philo, while the people knew that the seventh day of the creation of the world was
the Sabbath, they did not know, before this utterance of Moses, when that seventh
day was. Cf. *Mos.* I, 37, 207.

[71] *Ibid.*, 48, 268; cf. Exod. 16: 25.

[72] *Ibid.*, 49, 272; cf. Exod. 32: 26. Cf. 270: "though perhaps they may be thought
to resemble exhortations rather than oracular sayings."

[73] *Ibid.*, 50, 280; cf. Num. 16: 5.

[74] *Ibid.*, 51, 288; cf. Deut. 33: 1 ff.

[75] *Ibid.*, 51, 291; cf. Deut. 34: 5–8.

[76] The only possible exception would seem to be Exod. 16: 23, which in the Hebrew
text reads: "This is that which the Lord hath spoken: Tomorrow is a solemn rest, a
holy Sabbath unto the Lord." But in the Septuagint this verse reads: "Is not this
which the Lord spoke, Sabbaths are a rest holy to the Lord?" According to the
Septuagint reading, then, the people were only told that Sabbaths are a rest, but
they were not told that the seventh day of the manna was Sabbath.

[77] Five of the eight examples cited by Philo are quite obviously predictions. The
following three examples require explanation. (1) Moses' ordering that the manna

Hence he describes this type of prophecy as that by which Moses "is able to reveal future events." [78]

(b) Prophecy by the Divine Voice

As a close student of Scripture, however, Philo must have known that the divine spirit is not the only means by which God communicates His message to the prophets. In the case of Moses, for instance, the common expression by which the divine communications to him are described is not that the divine spirit came upon him, but rather that God spoke unto him. That this speaking unto him is to be taken as something different from the prophetic inspiration of other prophets is quite clearly stated in Scripture when it says that to him, unlike other prophets, God has spoken "mouth to mouth" [79] or "face to face." [80] Such prophetic utterances of Moses, which in the Pentateuch are said to have been spoken by God unto Moses, constitute that which Philo designates as the first group of Mosaic prophecies and which are described by him as belonging to a different type of prophecy.

In his description of what he calls the first group of the prophecies of Moses, Philo says that they are those which are "spoken by God in His own person" (ἐκ προσώπου τοῦ θεοῦ).[81] This reflects the combined scriptural statements

not be left till the morning implies the prediction that it would breed worms (Exod. 16: 20). (2) His conjecture that the seventh day of the manna was Sabbath implies also a prediction, for it was later corroborated by God (Exod. 16: 28–29). Philo himself calls it "conjecture" (εἰκασία) and says that without the guidance of the "divine spirit" the mind could not have guessed right (Mos. II, 48, 265). (3) With regard to his summons to the people at the time of the Golden Calf, Philo himself says that "perhaps they may be thought to resemble exhortations rather than oracular sayings" (ibid., 49, 270).

[78] Mos. II, 35, 190.
[79] Num. 12: 8.
[80] Exod. 33: 11; cf. Deut. 34: 10; cf. Sifre Deuteronomy, § 176, on 18. 18, F, p. 107b; HF, p. 221.
[81] Mos. II, 35, 188.

"and the Lord *spoke* unto Moses *face* to *face* (ἐνώπιος ἐνωπίῳ), as a man *speaketh* unto his friend"[82] and "whom the Lord knew *face* to *face*" (πρόσωπον κατὰ πρόσωπον),[83] the Greek word for "face" in the second statement meaning also "person." This type of prophecy undoubtedly refers to all the utterances of Moses which are said to have been spoken by God unto Moses before they were delivered by Moses unto the people. In all these instances Moses receives the communication directly from God and the people receive it through Moses who is the prophet of God. How these utterances were "spoken by God in His own person" is not explained here by Philo.' But the explanation for it is to be found in his description of the revelation of the ten commandments on Mount Sinai. The ten commandments, according to him, were revealed to the entire people directly by God "in His own person," in the same way as, also according to him, all the other commandments delivered to Moses were revealed. "For it was in accordance with His nature that the pronouncements in which the special laws were summed up should be given by Him in His own person (αὐτοπροσώπως), but the particular laws by the mouth of the most perfect of His prophets."[84] Now elsewhere he says of these ten commandments that they were delivered by God "not through a prophet but by a voice (διὰ φωνῆς) which, strange paradox, was visible."[85] From this we may infer that to have been spoken by God "in His own person" means to have been delivered by God "not

[82] Exod. 33: 11.
[83] Deut. 34: 10.
[84] *Decal.* 33, 175.
[85] *Mos.* II, 39, 213. The description of "voice" as "visible" is based, of course, on Exod. 20: 18: "And all the people saw the voices." In *Decal.* 9, 33, however, Philo speaks of an "invisible sound," by which, of course, he means an "incorporeal sound." But the "visible" voice here he explains, in *Decal.* 11, 46, to mean an "articulate voice," to which he also refers in *Decal.* 9, 33; cf. below, p. 38.

through a prophet but by a voice." By a voice, then, we may assume, were delivered also to Moses those communications which according to Philo's description, were "spoken by God in His own person." What the nature of that voice was, as well as the condition of the people who heard that voice, is described by Philo in some detail.

Taking for his text the scriptural statement that at the revelation on Mount Sinai God answered Moses "by a voice" [86] and "spoke" [87] all the commandments, Philo raises the rhetorical question: "Did He do so by His own utterance in the form of a voice?" [88] Of course, God did not speak with a physical voice which needs "mouth and tongue and windpipe." [89] But still the story of the revelation on Mount Sinai is a historical event which is not to be denied and is not to be explained away. It did really happen; God really spoke to the people; the people really heard the ten commandments; but it was not physical speech by means of a physical voice and physical hearing. A special miracle, "of a truly holy kind," was wrought by God on that occasion. He bid an "invisible sound" ($\dot{\eta}\chi o\nu$ $\dot{\alpha}\acuteο\rho\alpha\tau o\nu$) to be created. That invisible sound was something incorporeal, something living, something rational, in fact, "a rational soul ($\psi\nu\chi\dot{\eta}$ $\lambda o\gamma\iota\kappa\dot{\eta}$) full of clearness and distinctness," and that "invisible sound" sounded forth an "articulate voice" ($\phi\omega\nu\dot{\eta}$ $\ddot{\epsilon}\nu\alpha\rho\theta\rho o\varsigma$) also incorporeal but described as "visible." [90] This "new miraculous voice" was set in action by the power of God which "breathed" upon it, and as a result thereof it created in the "soul" of each of those present a miraculous sort of "hearing," and this miraculous hearing of "the God-possessed mind" went forth to meet the "spoken words." [91]

[86] Exod. 19: 19.
[87] Exod. 20: 1.
[88] *Decal.* 9, 32.

[89] *Ibid.*
[90] Cf. above, n. 85.
[91] *Decal.* 9, 32–35.

The same, we may assume, was also true in the case of Moses, whenever God, according to Philo's description, spoke to him "in His own person."

According to this description, then, the process of receiving a revelation directly from God "in His own person," and not through the "divine spirit," falls into three stages. First, God creates a miraculous voice, which is a rational soul. Second, that voice, on being set in action by the power of God breathed upon it, creates in the soul of the prophet a miraculous hearing, whereby that soul of the prophet becomes a God-inspired mind. Third, through that miraculous hearing the prophet hears the spoken words of God. Especially significant is his description of the miraculous voice as a "rational soul." The "divine spirit," as we have tried to show, is also a rational soul.[92] It is undoubtedly this miraculous hearing created in Moses to receive the voice of God that Philo describes as a "new birth" or a "divine birth" in his statement that the "vocation of the prophet," that is, Moses,[93] was a second birth (δευτέρα γένεσις) or a divine birth (divina nativitas), which, in its miraculous character, is compared by him to the act of the creation of the world.[94] The expression "divine birth" means evidently the same as "God-born," which, as we have shown, refers to prophecy.[95]

Prophecy by the divine voice is what Philo calls the first group of Mosaic prophecies, in contrast to prophecy through the divine spirit, which he calls the third group.

A combination of these two groups of prophecy is characteristic of what Philo calls the second group of Mosaic prophecies. In all the prophecies of this group, Moses in his own person asks questions; God in His own person

<hr />

[92] Cf. above, p. 31.
[93] Exod. 24: 16.
[94] *Qu. in Exod.* II, 46; Harris, *Fragments*, pp. 60–61.
[95] Cf. above, p. 10.

answers him. Philo describes the prophecies of this group as those which "have a mixed character; for, on the one hand, the prophet asks a question under divine possession (ἐνθουσιᾷ), and on the other hand the Father, in giving the word of revelation, answers him and talks with him as with a partner." [96] The main point in this statement is that the questions were asked by Moses "under divine possession," that is, with the abiding of the divine spirit upon him, as in the third group of Moses' prophecies; and that the answers were given by God by His own spoken words or voice, as in the first group of Moses' prophecies. Thus in this group of the Mosaic prophecies the two groups of prophecy are combined. Four cases of this group of prophecy occur in the Pentateuch, and Philo mentions all of them. They are (1) the case of the blasphemer,[97] (2) the case of the Sabbath breaker,[98] (3) the case of the second Passover,[99] and (4) the case of the daughters of Zelophehad.[100]

The first and the second groups of Mosaic prophecies are contrasted by Philo according to two other distinctions. Prophecies of the first group are not only spoken by God "in His own person" but they are also spoken by Him "through an interpreter (ἑρμηνεύς), the divine prophet." [101] They are furthermore "too great to be lauded by human lips," for, in addition to their other inexpressible merits, "they are delivered through an interpreter, and interpretation and prophecy are not the same thing." [102] The second group of Mosaic prophecies, on the other hand, is that "in which the speaker appears under that divine possession in virtue of which he is chiefly and in the strict sense considered a prophet." [103] In these passages Philo quite ob-

[96] *Mos.* II, 36, 192.
[97] *Ibid.*, 36, 193–38, 208; cf. Lev. 24: 10–16.
[98] *Ibid.*, 39, 213–40, 220; cf. Num. 15: 32–36.
[99] *Ibid.*, 41, 222–42, 232; cf. Num. 11: 1–14.
[100] *Ibid.*, 43, 234–44, 245; cf. Num. 27: 1–11.
[101] *Ibid.*, 35, 188.
[102] *Ibid.*, 191.
[103] *Ibid.*

viously makes four statements. First, prophecy and interpretation are two different things. Second, in the second group of his prophecies, when he speaks under divine possession — that is, when he delivers to the people words communicated to him by the divine spirit and not those spoken to him directly by God in His own person — Moses is to be ₁called prophet in the strict sense of the term. Third, in the first group of his prophecies, when he delivers to the people words spoken to him directly by God in his own person, Moses is not a prophet in the strict sense of the term but only an interpreter. Fourth, the words spoken by God to Moses in His own person and delivered to the people by Moses only in his capacity as an interpreter are too great to be lauded by human lips. These references to prophecy and interpretation have puzzled students of Philo.[104] We shall try to explain them.

In Plato, reference is made to a distinction between a man who in a state of frenzy ($\mu\alpha\nu\epsilon\nu\tau\sigma$) sees visions ($\tau\dot{\alpha}$ $\phi\alpha\nu\epsilon\nu\tau\alpha$) and utters words ($\tau\dot{\alpha}$ $\phi\omega\nu\eta\theta\epsilon\nu\tau\alpha$) and a man who in his right mind ($\check{\epsilon}\mu\phi\rho\sigma\nu\sigma$) is the interpreter ($\dot{\nu}\pi\sigma\kappa\rho\iota\tau\dot{\eta}s$) of these visions and voices.[105] Plato himself applies to the former the term "diviner" ($\mu\dot{\alpha}\nu\tau\iota s$) and to the latter the term "prophet" ($\pi\rho\sigma\phi\dot{\eta}\tau\eta s$). There is, however, no rigidity about the use of these terms. In Greek, the term "prophet" is also used of persons who believed themselves to possess oracular power, and as such it is used in contrast to the term "interpreter" ($\dot{\epsilon}\xi\eta\gamma\eta\tau\dot{\eta}s$), which means a person who interprets oracles.[106] Even Plato himself uses the term "prophet" in that sense, when he speaks of the Pythia as a prophetess.[107]

[104] Cf. Gfrörer, I, 54–56; Goodenough, *By Light, Light*, p. 193, n. 70.
[105] *Timaeus* 71 E–72 B.
[106] Cf. Liddell and Scott, s.v.
[107] *Phaedrus* 244 B. Cf. Archer-Hind's note in his edition of the *Timaeus*, p. 267, on l. 16.

Philo, as is evident from his statement that "interpretation (ἑρμηνεία) and prophecy (προφητεία) are not the same thing,"[108] uses the term "prophet" in the sense of one who possesses oracular power, in contrast to one who only interprets oracles. Now in Scripture no distinction is made between the office of prophet, in the sense in which Philo uses it, and the office of interpreter. The same person who receives the message from God under divine inspiration also delivers it to the people in clear and understandable language. Every prophet in Scripture is therefore his own interpreter. He does not employ another person to interpret his message. Accordingly, when Philo, on many occasions, happens to deal with prophets, and these prophets are scriptural prophets, he takes care to tell his Greek readers, who are accustomed to the Greek usages of language, that "prophets are interpreters of God,"[109] meaning thereby that in Scripture there is no distinction between prophet and interpreter, for all prophets are interpreters of God, and not of oracles delivered by other prophets. And so also, in the passages here under consideration, he calls attention to the distinction in Greek between interpretation and prophecy, but at the same time he tries also to point out that no actual distinction between these two exists in scriptural prophecy.

In his description of the first group of Mosaic prophecies, he thus quite properly begins by saying that "God spoke in His own person through His interpreter, the divine prophet,"[110] that is, Moses, who was the prophet of God and heard directly the "voice" of God, and was himself also the interpreter of that voice. Then, wishing to show how difficult it is to praise with human lips the words "spoken

[108] Mos. II, 35, 191.
[109] Spec. I, 11, 65; cf. Deter. 12, 39; Immut. 29, 138; Mut. 22, 126; Spec. III, 2, 7; IV, 8, 49; Legat. 13, 99.   [110] Mos. II, 35, 188.

by God in His own person," that is, directly by the "voice" of God, he says that "they are delivered through an interpreter, and interpretation and prophecy are not the same thing," [111] that is, what we have in Scripture of this first group of prophecies is only that which has been transmitted to us in understandable language through Moses in his capacity as interpreter; it does not represent the original "voice" spoken by God "in His own person" and heard by Moses in his capacity as a prophet. God's own words, he says, "are too great to be lauded by human lips," [112] that is, they are inexpressible in human language.

Similarly, in his description of the second group of Mosaic prophecies, he says that it is that "in which the speaker appears under that divine possession in virtue of which he is chiefly and in the strict sense considered a prophet." [113] What he means is that it is chiefly and strictly in the sense of being under divine possession that the term "prophet," as distinguished from the term "interpreter," is used in Greek divination. When we recall that in his description of this second group of Mosaic prophecies he dwells upon the terms "foreknowledge" and the revelation of "future events" [114] and also that all his instances of this group of prophecies deal with predictions of the future,[115] the significance of this last statement as a reference to Greek divination and to the use of the term "prophetess" in connection with the Pythia [116] becomes all the more evident.

(c) Prophecy through Angels

We have so far discussed two types of prophecy which are mentioned by Philo, one which comes indirectly through the

---

[111] *Ibid.*, 191.
[112] *Ibid.*
[113] *Ibid.*

[114] *Ibid.*, 190.
[115] Cf. above, p. 35.
[116] Cf. above, p. 14.

divine spirit and another which comes directly by the voice of God. In his threefold classification of the prophetic utterances of Moses, we have also shown, Philo is really trying to classify the prophetic utterances of Moses, in accordance with their sources, into two classes: one coming directly from God and the other coming indirectly through the divine spirit. But, besides these two methods by which God communicates His message to prophets, there is, in Scripture, reference to a third method, and that is divine communications through the intermediacy of angels. Thus an angel is said to have appeared to Hagar,[117] to Abraham,[118] to Balaam,[119] to Gideon,[120] and to many other persons, and in each case the angel predicted the future, which is one of the functions of prophecy.

Now angels, according to Philo, are real beings, incorporeal souls, hovering in the air and in the heavens, identical with what the Greeks call demons, and from his description of the functions of angels in general and of the actual tasks they are said to have performed in particular we may gather that they are considered by him as intermediaries of what he calls prophetic communications. To begin with, among the functions he ascribes to them is that of ambassadors of God through whom "He announces whatever predictions he wills to make to our race." [121] Prediction, according to Philo, is one of the four functions of prophecy. Furthermore, when Sarah began to realize that the three strangers who had predicted to her the birth of a son were not ordinary human beings, she began to suspect that they were, as Philo says, "prophets or angels." [122] Angels, then, perform the same function as prophets, that of prophesy-

---

Gen. 16: 7–12; 21: 17–18.
[118] Gen. 18: 2–16; 22: 15–18.
[119] Num. 22: 22–35.
[120] Judges 6: 12–24.
[121] *Abr.* 23, 115.
[122] *Ibid.*, 113.

ing. Still further, the angel in his address to Balaam is made by Philo to utter the following words: "I shall direct your speech, prophesying (θεσπίζων) through your tongue all that shall happen, though you yourself understand nothing of it." [123] An angel is thus here explicitly said to be a source of prophecy. And so prophecy through an angel is, according to Philo, a third type of prophecy. If the question should be raised why in his enumeration of the groups of prophecies of Moses no mention is made by him of prophecy through an angel, the answer is quite obvious. There is no reference in Scripture of this type of prophetic revelation in the case of Moses. There is indeed a reference to an angel who appeared to Moses at the burning bush.[124] But that angel did not speak to Moses. The speech which followed after the appearance of that angel is ascribed to God himself,[125] and hence it belongs to those communications which are described by Philo as spoken by God "in His own person." Inasmuch as to Philo the angel acts as an agent of prophecy and performs the same function as a prophet, the term angel is sometimes taken by him to mean prophet, for, referring to the verse "Behold I send an angel before thee," [126] he says: "One must suppose that the angel mentioned a little before communicated the voice of God, for the prophet is the angel or messenger of the Lord, who is the real speaker." [127]

(d) Differences between the Three Types of Prophecy

If we now compare these three types of prophecy, we find that they have one element in common. They all come about by means of something like a rational soul. The "voice" of God is directly described by Philo as a rational

---

[123] *Mos.* I, 49, 274.   [124] Exod. 3: 2.
[125] Exod. 3: 4; cf. *Mos.* I, 12, 63 f.; *Fug.* 25, 141; *Mut.* 23, 134.
[126] Exod. 23: 20.   [127] *Fragmenta*, Richter, VI, 243 (M, II, 678). Cf. above, I, 418.

soul.[128] Angels are also directly described by him as rational souls.[129] As for the divine spirit, we have tried to show that like the divine spirit which God breathed into Adam it is also a rational soul. And still, despite the common element in these three types of prophecy, Philo distinguishes between prophecy by the "voice" of God and prophecy through the "divine spirit," and consequently, it may be inferred, also from prophecy through "angels," calling prophecy by the "voice" of God a direct kind of divine communication in which God speaks to the prophet "in His own person." [130] The "voice" of God must therefore have been conceived by Philo as a rational soul which carries the very words of God to that new kind of "hearing" which it created in the soul of Moses as well as in the souls of those who stood witness at the revelation of the ten commandments on Mount Sinai,[131] whereas the "divine spirit" and "angels" are rational souls which communicate God's message in their own words. Between the "divine spirit" and "angels" there is still another difference. Angels are many, and each angel is a messenger of God not only in imparting to men prophetic communications but also in performing other tasks, such, for instance, as bringing secondary goods or punishments.[132] The divine spirit, on the other hand, is one unique being whose only office is that of imparting prophetic knowledge to men.

His differentiation between the three types of prophecy has led Philo to lay down different sets of qualifications for the prophetic gifts of the various types of prophecy. That prophecy required certain qualifications is assumed in native Jewish tradition. In the Talmudic literature, according to

---

[128] *Decal.* 9, 33; cf. above, p. 38.
[129] *Conf.* 35, 176; cf. above, I, 367.
[130] *Mos.* II, 35, 188; cf. above, p. 37

[131] Cf. above, p. 38.
[132] Cf. above, I, 381–382.

one list, the qualifications for prophecy are wisdom, strength, riches, and high stature; [133] according to another list, they are study, strictness, zeal, integrity, abstinence, purity, holiness, humility, fear of sin, and piety.[134] To be of Jewish descent, however, is not considered a required qualification. Seven gentiles mentioned in Scripture, including Balaam, are said to have been prophets,[135] though certain distinctions are drawn between the prophecy of Israel and the prophets of other nations.[136] The Stoics are similarly reported as having said that only the upright man ($\sigma\pi o\upsilon$-$\delta\alpha\hat{\iota}os$)[137] or the wise man (*sapiens*)[138] can be a diviner. However, there is a difference between the Jewish and the Stoic view. According to the Jewish view, prophecy, like any act of individual providence, has in it an element of divine grace and selection, and the qualifications required are those which render men fit to be selected by God for the divine gift of prophecy. According to the Stoics, prophecy is a natural and necessary process,[139] and the qualifications required are those which render men naturally fit for the power of divination.

In accordance with these prevailing views, Philo also discusses the qualifications for prophecy. The wicked ($\phi\alpha\hat{\upsilon}\lambda os$) and iniquitous ($\mu o\chi\theta\eta\rho\acute{os}$) man, he maintains, can never be a prophet.[140] Prophecy is reserved only for the refined man ($\dot{\alpha}\sigma\tau\epsilon\hat{\iota}os$),[141] the wise man ($\sigma o\phi\acute{os}$),[142] the just man ($\delta\acute{\iota}\kappa\alpha\iota os$),[143]

[133] *Shabbat* 92a; *Nedarim* 38a.
[134] '*Abodah Zarah* 20b and M. *Soṭah* IX, 15, combined.
[135] *Baba Batra* 15b.
[136] *Genesis Rabbah* 52, 5; *Leviticus Rabbah* 1, 13.
[137] Stobaeus, *Eclogae* II, p. 114, l. 16 (Arnim, III, 605). The term $\sigma\pi o\upsilon\delta\alpha\hat{\iota}os$ literally means the same as the Hebrew term *zerizut* ("quickness," "zeal," "eagerness"), quoted above.
[138] Cicero, *De Divinatione* II, 63, 129. Cf. Pease's note in his edition.
[139] Cf. above, I, 352 n.   [140] *Heres* 52, 259.   [141] *Ibid.*
[142] *Ibid.; Immut.* 1, 3; *Gig.* 5, 23.   [143] *Heres* 52, 260.

and the genuine lover of wisdom (φιλόσοφος ἄνοθος).¹⁴⁴ With
these qualifications of refinement, wisdom and justice any
man is capable of attaining prophecy.¹⁴⁵ Still, while he does
not say so explicitly, there is no doubt that with his belief in
individual divine providence the attainment of prophecy by
those who are worthy of it is through an act of divine grace
and selection. No qualification of descent is specified by
him. Referring to prophetic knowledge as "pure knowledge," he says that "it is the pure knowledge in which
every wise man in all likelihood (εἰκότως) shares." ¹⁴⁶ Here
again the sharing in this "pure knowledge" by "every wise
man" is through an act of divine grace and selection.
Furthermore, inasmuch as every man possesses an incorporeal rational soul and inasmuch also as in no man is the
rational soul always completely submerged in bodily sensations, there is no man who does not occasionally get a flash
of the divine prophetic spirit. "Who indeed is so lacking
in reason (ἄλογος) and soul (ἄψυχος) that he never either
with or without his will receives a conception of the best?
Nay, even over the reprobate hovers often of a sudden the
vision of the excellent, but to grasp it and keep it for their
own they have not the strength. In a moment it is gone and
passed away to some other place, and from the habitation
of those who have come into its presence after wandering
from the life of law and justice it turns away its steps. Nay,
never would it have come to them save to convict those who
choose the base instead of the noble." ¹⁴⁷ The phrase "vision of the excellent" in this passage refers to the "spirit
of God" mentioned previously,¹⁴⁸ and that spirit of God,
as may be judged from the context, refers to the spirit of

¹⁴⁴ *Plant.* 6, 24.
¹⁴⁵ *Heres* 52, 260.
¹⁴⁶ *Gig.* 5, 22.

¹⁴⁷ *Ibid.*, 20–21.
¹⁴⁸ Cf. *ibid.*, 19.

prophecy.[149] In some respect this passage reflects Plato's statements that all men by their very nature have the capacity to regain the vision of the ideas for fleeting moments during their lifetime,[150] and that the soul by its very nature has the capacity of divination (μαντικόν τι).[151] But there is an additional element in it. These brief visitations of the divine prophetic spirit to the reprobates are not always altogether a natural act of necessity, they have an element of divine grace in them. They are the work of divine providence for the purpose of convicting the reprobates, of making them conscious of their wrong-doings and thereby causing them by their own free will to abandon the base and choose the noble.[152]

Scriptural prophecy through the divine spirit thus differs from the various kinds of frenzy or ecstasy or divine possession known among Greeks in that it has an element of divine grace in it. Commenting upon the name Hannah, which in Hebrew means "grace," Philo says that "without grace it is impossible to leave the ranks of mortal things or to stay forever among things imperishable."[153] What he means is that it is only by the grace of God that one can rise from the knowledge of things sensible to prophetic knowledge of things intelligible. He then goes on to say: "When grace fills the soul, that soul thereby rejoices and smiles and dances, for it is possessed with a frenzy (βεβάκχευται), so that to many of the unenlightened it may seem to be drunken, crazy and beside itself,"[154] for "with the God-possessed (θεοφορήτοις) not only is the soul wont to be stirred and goaded as it were into ecstasy but the body also is flushed and fiery . . . and thus many of the foolish are

---

[149] Cf. *ibid.*, 23 ff.
[150] *Phaedrus* 249 B–D.
[151] *Ibid.* 242 C.

[152] Cf. above, I, 437–438.
[153] *Ebr.* 36, 145.
[154] *Ibid.*, 146.

deceived and suppose that the sober are drunk."[155] The
Greek term used here by Philo for "possessed with a frenzy,"
it will be noticed, is βεβάκχευται, which literally means
"possessed with a Bacchic frenzy." Elsewhere Philo uses
this term in the sense of a frenzy which has been brought
on by one's own will (ἑκουσίῳ)[156] or which has been induced
by "unmixed wine" (ἀκράτῳ).[157] The reference quite evidently is to the festivals of Bacchus or Dionysus, at which
ecstasy or frenzy or divine possession was brought on voluntarily by the drinking of wine. Philo indirectly alludes
to this practice when he mentions "drunkenness" (μέθη) and
"drunken frolic" (παροινία) in his description of the manner
in which heathen festivals are celebrated.[158] The purpose
of his comment on the name Hannah, therefore, is to show
that the ecstasy which comes by the grace of God through
the divine spirit is not the same as that which is induced
voluntarily by strong wine in the cult of Dionysus. Though
resembling intoxication, it is really a sober ecstasy. It is
for this reason that elsewhere he describes this kind of
ecstasy as "a divine intoxication (θεία μέθη), more sober than
sobriety itself,"[159] or as "sober intoxication" (μέθη νηφά-
λιος).[160]

Every man and woman by virtue of their being endowed
with a rational soul may thus be chosen by divine grace for
the gift of that type of prophecy which comes through the
divine spirit. No qualification of descent is required, though
moral and intellectual qualifications may be required for the
permanency of the prophetic gift of this type. Similarly,
prophecy through an angel may come by divine grace to

---

[155] *Ibid.*, 147.
[156] *Ibid.* 31, 123.   [158] *Cher.* 27, 92.
[157] *Somn.* II, 31, 205.   [159] *Leg. All.* III, 26, 82.
[160] *Probus* 2, 13. For other implications of this expression, cf. H. Lewy, *Sobria
Ebrietas*, 1929.

any human being of whatever descent; and, inasmuch as this type of prophecy is always only of a temporary nature, even the qualification of moral and intellectual perfection is not required, as is evidenced by the instances of Hagar and Lot and Balaam. God may send an angel to any human being He chooses.

Not so, however, is that type of prophecy which comes directly from God, by the voice of God. In this there must be a certain qualification of descent. Commenting upon the verse in which Hagar says to the angel who has appeared to her, "Thou art the God that didst look upon me?" [161] he says: "for being Egyptian by descent she was not qualified to see the Supreme Cause." [162] Here then Egyptian descent disqualified one from attaining that kind of prophecy which comes directly from God. Complementary to this passage there is another passage in which, though he does not say that non-Jewish descent disqualifies one for this type of prophecy, he does say that Jewish descent especially qualifies one for it. Of the prophecies which were spoken to Moses by God "in His own person" he says that they "are absolutely and entirely evidences of the divine excellences, namely, of His graciousness and beneficence, by which He incites all men to noble conduct, and particularly the people which is dedicated to His service, for whom He opens up the road which leads to happiness." [163] By the "people which is dedicated to His service" he means here Israel, for Israel, Philo says elsewhere, is the best of races and is capable of seeing God,[164] and this capability of seeing God is based upon the habit of its service to God.[165] In this type of prophecy, then, the divine grace of prophecy is not given to

[161] Gen. 16: 13.
[162] *Somn.* I, 41, 240.
[163] *Mos.* II, 35, 189.
[164] *Congr.* 10, 51; *Post.* 26, 92.
[165] *Sacr.* 36, 120.

man by the mere fact of his being morally and intellectually
qualified for it; the qualification of Jewish descent is required. Elsewhere he tells us, as we have seen, that this
divine grace in the case of Moses is a free grace [166] and in the
case of the people of Israel it was due to the merit of the
Patriarchs.[167] This view, that the revelation of the Law was
a special gift to Israel, was by the time of Philo a common
belief among the Jews, as is evidenced from Sirach.[168]

This variety of meaning of the term prophecy as used by
Philo will throw light also upon the question whether Philo
differed or did not differ from Palestinian Judaism with regard to the doctrine of the cessation of prophecy. The emphasis laid by students of Philo upon his conception of the
universality of the gift of prophecy and upon his account of
his own personal experience of prophetic inspiration [169] has
created the impression that Philo did not believe in the cessation of prophecy.[170] But prophecy is a complex term, both
as used in Palestinian Judaism and as used by Philo, and
when we speak of the cessation of prophecy we must first
determine what type of prophecy is meant by such a cessation.

The cessation of prophecy which according to Palestinian
tradition took place upon the death of the last of the prophets,
Haggai, Zechariah and Malachi,[171] means that the kind of
prophecy which inspired the teachings contained in the
Hebrew Scripture came to an end, so that henceforth no
other teachings will have been inspired by the same kind of

---

[166] *Leg. All.* III, 46, 134–135.
[167] *Ibid.* II, 9, 33–34; cf. above, I, 450–455.
[168] Sirach 24: 8, 12.
[169] *Migr.* 7, 34–35; *Cher.* 9, 27; *Somn.* II, 38, 252.
[170] Cf. R. H. Pfeiffer, *Introduction to the Old Testament*, p. 67, referring to Gfrörer,
I, 46–68.
[171] *Yoma* 9b.

prophecy. This may be gathered from the distinction which Talmudic sources constantly make between Scripture and extra-scriptural writings [172] and the fact that every book included in Scripture was believed to have been inspired by the Holy Spirit.[173] We may also gather this from Josephus' statement that "from Artaxerxes (i.e., the Book of Esther) to our own time the complete history has been written but has not been deemed worthy of equal credit with the earlier records, because of the failure of the exact succession of the prophets." [174] Other forms of prophecy, however, did not disappear. Both in Talmudic literature and in Josephus there are references to predictive prophecy, attributed to an echo of a heavenly voice (*bat ḳol*, φωνή),[175] which in Josephus is loosely referred to as prophecy.[176] In Talmudic literature it is told how Hillel said that the people would know how to act on a certain occasion by the Holy Spirit,[177] how Gamaliel guessed by the Holy Spirit the name of a gentile whom he had never seen before,[178] and how, after three years of debate between the schools of Shammai and Hillel, a heavenly voice called out that the views of the school of Hillel should be accepted as law against those of the school of Shammai.[179] Thus according to Palestinian tradition, prophecy in the sense of prediction and in the sense of knowing things beyond sense perception and reason never ceased to exist. Moreover, the fact that, despite the cessation of prophecy, Maimonides claims to have discovered the hidden meaning of certain verses in the Book of Job by a

[172] *M. Shabbat* XVI, 1; *M. Sanhedrin* X, 1; *Tos. Yom-Ṭob* IV, 4.
[173] *BabaBatra* 14b–15a; *Magillah* 7a.
[174] *Apion.* I, 8, 41.
[175] *Soṭa* 33a; *Tos. Soṭa* XIII, 5; *Antt.* XIII, 10, 3, 282.
[176] *Antt.* XIII, 10, 7. 299–300; *Bell. Jud.* I, 2, 8, 68–69.
[177] *Tos. Pesaḥim* IV, 2.
[178] *Ibid.* I (II), 27.   [179] *'Erubin* 13b; *Yer. Berakot* I, 7, 3b below.

sort of prophecy[180] shows that the prophecy which ceased was a special kind of prophecy, that kind of prophecy which inspired the teachings contained in Scripture. This is exactly the view of Philo. The accounts of his own personal experience of prophetic inspiration [181] relate only to the attainment of a knowledge of things by inspiration when ordinary reasoning processes failed him. This is exactly what Palestinian rabbis still continued to claim for themselves. But there is no evidence that unlike Palestinian Jews he believed that that type of prophecy which gave Scripture its special character continued to exist. His assertion that all things written in the Pentateuch are divine revelations [182] and his references to the inspired nature of the other books of Scripture which he happens to mention [183] indicate that he assigned no such distinction to any other books written after the Scripture. With regard to the laws of Moses, his expression of hope, that is, of belief, that they are eternal,[184] clearly indicates that the prophetic inspiration which produced them came to an end. Indeed, he speaks of the Septuagint translation as having been done by its translators "as if they were divinely inspired" (καθάπερ ἐνθουσιῶντες) and he describes their work of translation by the term "prophesied" (προεφήτευον),[185] but so also the Palestinian rabbis sometimes did not hesitate to say that the Aramaic version of the prophets [186] and even the Septuagint [187] were done under divine inspiration.

---

[180] *Moreh Nebukim* III, 22.
[181] *Migr.* 7, 34–35; *Cher.* 9, 27; *Somn.* II, 38, 252.
[182] *Mos.* II, 35, 188.
[183] Cf. Gfrörer, I, 46–48.
[184] *Mos.* II, 3, 14; cf. above, I, 187.
[185] *Mos.* II, 7, 37; cf. Wisdom of Solomon 7: 27.
[186] *Megillah* 3a.
[187] *Megillah* 9a; *Masseket Soferim* I, 8 (ed. M. Higger, p. 82).

IV. Prophetic Dreams

There are thus, according to Philo, three sources of prophecy, God, the divine spirit, and angels. The first two sources
are explicitly distinguished by him in his analysis of the
prophecies of Moses; the third may be discerned in his discussion of angels. Now in Greek philosophy similar views are
expressed as to the sources of divination. Corresponding to
two of Philo's sources, namely, God and angels, there is the
statement attributed to the Stoics that divination comes
either from the gods or from demons.[1] Corresponding to the
remaining one of Philo's three sources of prophecy, namely,
the divine spirit, which, in the case of Moses, is described by
him as the power (δύναμις) of foreknowledge imparted by
God to him through the permanent abiding upon him of the
divine spirit, whereby he is able to reveal future events,[2]
there is the view ascribed to Chrysippus that divination is
"the power (vim) to see, understand, and explain pre-
monitory signs given to men by the gods."[3] But there is no
evidence that Philo was influenced, in his enumeration of
these three types of prophecy, by these non-Jewish sources.
The only formal enumeration of the sources of divination in
Greek philosophy is that in which, as quoted above, gods
and demons are mentioned. No such formal enumeration is
found in Philo, though, as we have shown, angels, which
correspond to demons, are undoubtedly considered by him a
source of prophecy. The only formal enumeration given by
him is his analysis of the prophecies of Moses into those

---

[1] Stobaeus, *Eclogae* II, p. 67, ll. 16–19; cf. Zeller, III, 1⁴, p. 352, n. 6 (*Stoics,
Epicureans and Sceptics²*, p. 378, n. 2).

[2] *Mos.* II, 35, 190; cf. above, p. 34.

[3] Cicero, *De Divinatione* II, 63, 130; cf. also I, 32, 70; I, 49, 110; II, 11, 26. See
A. S. Pease's notes in his edition.

"spoken by God in His own person" and those "spoken by Moses in his own person when possessed by God," that is, through the divine spirit.[4] And such a classification of the sources of divination or prophecy is not found in Greek literature.

There is, however, evidence that his formal threefold classification of the sources of dreams, corresponding to the implied threefold classification of sources we have found in his discussion of prophecy, is directly based upon a Greek text, but that still, while the formal classification is based upon a Greek text, his entire treatment of the subject of dreams is again a combination of scriptural and Greek texts.

In Scripture not only prophecy but also dreams are said to come from God, and the prophet and the dreamer of dreams are both considered as receiving divine communications.[5] In Scripture, furthermore, are recorded many true dreams. As a close student of Scripture Philo must have observed that with regard to these dreams, sometimes it is God himself who is said to appear to men in dreams, as in the case of the dream of Abimelech,[6] in the dream of Laban,[7] and in the dream of Solomon;[8] sometimes it is an angel who is said to appear in dreams, as in the case of the dreams of Jacob;[9] but sometimes men are said to dream without any mention of God or angels, as in the case of the dreams of Joseph,[10] Pharaoh's chief baker and chief butler in prison[11] and Pharaoh himself,[12] of the dream overheard by Gideon,[13]

---

[4] Cf. above, p. 34.
[5] Num. 12: 6; Deut. 13: 2, 4; I Sam. 28: 6, 15; Jer. 23: 25; 27: 9; 29: 8.
[6] Gen. 20: 3.
[7] Gen. 31: 24.
[8] I Kings 3: 5.
[9] Gen. 28: 12, 13; cf. below, p. 58; Gen. 31: 11.
[10] Gen. 37: 5, 9.
[11] Gen. 40: 8, 9, 16.
[12] Gen. 41: 1, 5.
[13] Judges 7: 13.

and of the dream of Nebuchadnezzar.[14] Similarly in Greek philosophy frenzy and dreams are considered as two natural modes of divination, approved of by both Peripatetics and Stoics, and are contrasted with those artificial modes of divination, which, like the various forms of witchery in Scripture,[15] were disapproved of by the Peripatetics.[16] Moreover, corresponding to the three kinds of dreams recorded in Scripture, there is the view of Posidonius that "there are three ways in which men dream as the result of divine impulse: first, the soul is clairvoyant of itself because of its kinship with the gods; second, the air is full of immortal souls (i.e., demons), already clearly stamped, as it were, with the marks of truth; and third, the gods in person converse with men when they are asleep."[17] Following his general method of casting scriptural material in a philosophic framework, Philo combines the various classes of dreams recorded in Scripture with the classification of dreams as found in Posidonius. This he does in his work "On Dreams, That They Are God-Sent," of which only two of the original three or five parts are now extant.[18]

The part of the work which is not extant is said by Philo to have dealt with dreams in which "the Deity of His own motion sends to us the visions which are presented to us in sleep"[19] and in which the dreams are clear and distinct after the nature of plain oracles.[20] In this lost part of the

[14] Dan. 2: 1 ff.   [15] Deut. 18: 10–11.

[16] Cicero, *De Divinatione* I, 3, 5; I, 6, 11–12; I, 33, 72. See Pease's notes in his edition.

[17] *Ibid.* I, 30, 64. Cf. Colson, V, 593, §§ 1–2; *Philos Werke*, VI, 173, n. 2.

[18] Cf. L. Massebieau, "Le Classement des Oeuvres de Philon," *Bibliothèque de l'École des Hautes Études ... Sciences Religieuses*, I (1889), 30; L. Cohn, "Einteilung und Chronologie der Schriften Philo's," *Philologus*, Supplementband VII, iii (1899), 402; M. Adler, "Das philonische Fragment *De Deo*," *Monatsschrift für Geschichte und Wissenschaft des Judenthums* 80 (1936), 168.

[19] *Somn.* I, 1, 1; cf. II, 1, 2.   [20] *Ibid.* II, 1, 3.

work, Philo, who confines himself in this book to the Pentateuch, must have undoubtedly dealt with the dreams of Abimelech [21] and Laban,[22] for in both these dreams God speaks in His own person and His message is clear and distinct.

The first extant part of the work deals with the two dreams of Jacob, (1) the dream of the ladder at Bethel [23] and (2) the dream of the flock with varied markings.[24] Now in the second of these two dreams it is explicitly said that it was an angel who spoke to Jacob. But in the first dream, while angels are said to have appeared to Jacob, it is the Lord who is said to have spoken to him. But in Philo's interpretation, the term Lord stands there' not for God himself but for the archangel (ἀρχάγγελος),[25] the eldest Logos (πρεσβύτατος λόγος),[26] the one who appeared "in the place of God," that is, as a substitute of God, "with a view to the profit of him who was not yet capable of seeing the true God." [27] Consequently, in describing this class of dreams in his own words and by the use of scriptural vocabulary, he says: "You see that the sacred Scripture proclaims as dreams sent from God not only those which appear before the mind under the direct action of the Highest of Causes, but those also which are revealed through the agency of His interpreters and attendant angels who have been held meet to receive from the Father to whom they owe their being a divine and happy portion." [28] But the angels, as we have seen, are to Philo powers of God immanent in the world,

[21] Gen. 20: 3–7.
[22] Gen. 31: 24.
[23] Gen. 28: 12–15.
[24] Gen. 31: 11–13.
[25] *Somn.* I, 25, 157.
[26] *Ibid.* I, 39, 230.
[27] *Ibid.* I, 41, 238; cf. I, 33, 189–190; I, 39, 229. This is Philo's interpretation of the Septuagint rendering of the verse "I am the God of Beth-el" (Gen. 31: 13) by "I am the God who appeared to thee in the place of God."
[28] *Ibid.* I, 33, 190.

analogous not only to the demons inherited by Greek philosophy from popular religion but also to those immanent powers or souls or minds in the world which in the Stoic philosophic vocabulary are considered fragments of that active power in the primary fire of the world which they call the mind of the universe. Consequently, in trying to describe this type of dream in strictly philosophical terms of the Stoics, he says that it is "that in which our mind, moving out of itself together with the mind of the universe, seems to be possessed and God-inspired, and so capable of receiving some foretaste and foreknowledge of things to come." [29]

The second extant part of the work deals with the dreams of Joseph,[30] the dreams of Pharaoh's chief baker and chief butler,[31] and the dreams of Pharaoh.[32] In none of these dreams does either God or an angel make his appearance. Consequently, in describing this class of dreams, Philo says that they arise "whenever the soul in sleep, setting itself in motion and agitation of its own accord, becomes frenzied, and with the prescient power due to such inspiration foretells the future." [33]

V. CONCLUSION, INFLUENCE, ANTICIPATION

In the mind of Philo, we assume, the various classifications of the types of knowledge in Plato's writings shaped themselves into a threefold classification: (1) sensation and opinion; (2) knowledge of scientific concepts formed by the mind on the basis of data ultimately furnished by sensation; (3) knowledge of the incorporeal ideas attained through recollection. Now the knowledge of the incorporeal ideas

---

[29] *Ibid.* I, 1, 2; cf. II, 1, 2.
[30] Gen. 37: 5, 9.
[31] Gen. 40: 8, 9, 16.
[32] Gen 41: 1, 5.
[33] *Somn.* II, 1, 1.

attained through recollection is called by Plato philosophic frenzy, which is the highest among the four kinds of frenzy enumerated by him, the lower three kinds being (1) the frenzy of divination, called prophecy, (2) the frenzy of priests, and (3) the frenzy of legislators and poets, which is inspired by the Muses. But in the Greek translation of the Hebrew Scripture the term prophecy is used as a description not only of the power of divination but also of the power to see things incorporeal which are not perceived by the senses, thus corresponding to Plato's philosophic frenzy. Accordingly, Philo, in his threefold classification of the types of knowledge, substitutes for Plato's third type, that of recollection or of philosophic frenzy, the scriptural term prophecy. Moreover, in Scripture the term prophecy is used to include also powers corresponding to the remaining two kinds of frenzy enumerated by Plato. Consequently with Philo the term prophecy comes to be used in the sense of all the four kinds of frenzy enumerated by Plato, and all of them, because they are an immediate sort of knowledge inspired by God, become with him the highest kind of knowledge. The prophet to Philo, therefore, is not only a diviner but he is also one who, like a priest, expiates the sins of the people, like a philosopher, has a direct vision of things incorporeal, and especially, like a legislator, through divine revelation, becomes the author of laws.

Prophecy in this its fourfold function comes from God. But it may come from God in three different ways. First, it may come through the divine spirit. Now the term divine spirit in one sense means the incorporeal rational soul in man, through which, out of data of sensation, man forms scientific concepts, which is the second of Philo's threefold division of knowledge. But the divine spirit which is the instrument of prophecy means an incorporeal rational being or soul which is not in man; its contact with man is only through man's rational soul, which, on freeing itself of the rational concepts formed out of the data of sensation, becomes filled with a new knowledge communicated to it by that divine prophetic spirit. Second, prophecy may come through angels. Angels, too, like the divine prophetic spirit, are incorporeal beings, but, unlike the divine prophetic spirit, there are many of them; and, again, unlike the divine prophetic spirit, they perform other tasks besides inspiring men with prophecy. Third, prophecy may come by the voice of God. This voice of God, like the divine prophetic spirit or angels, is an incorporeal rational being. But, unlike the divine prophetic spirit or angels, which are permanent, though created, beings through which prophecy is communicated, the voice of God is created especially for each occasion of prophetic revelation. Then also, unlike the divine prophetic spirit and angels, which do not communicate directly the words of God, the voice of God communicates directly God's very words. Consequently prophecy by the voice of God is described as a form of direct communication in which God speaks "in His own person." All these three types of prophecy come by divine grace, but there is the following difference between them. Prophecy through an angel may come even to a non-Jew and even to one who had neither moral nor intellectual distinction. Prophecy through the divine spirit may also come to a non-Jew, but the recipient must have certain moral and intellectual qualifications. Prophecy by the voice of God is that by which laws are revealed and it comes only to Jews. Such prophecies by the voice of God were received by the entire people of Israel at the revelation on Mount Sinai and by Moses in the revelation of all the other laws to him, except those laws which were communicated to him in answer to certain questions addressed by him to God. This latter group of laws was communicated to him by a combination of the divine spirit and the voice of God. The predictive prophecies of Moses, however, were communicated to him by the divine spirit. But unlike most of the other prophets, who are visited by the divine spirit only periodically, Moses was permanently under the influence of the divine spirit. Besides prophecy, there are also prophetic dreams, and such prophetic dreams, like prophecy, come either through the divine spirit or through an angel or directly from God.

From now on, in the history of philosophy, whether Christian, Moslem, or Jewish, revelation or prophecy is considered as a source of knowledge by the side of the other sources of knowledge derived from philosophic writings. Clement of Alexandria [1] and St. Augustine,[2] to mention but two outstanding examples, consider faith as a source of knowledge, and faith is assent to the revealed knowledge of Scripture. St. Thomas discusses the question "whether prophecy pertains to knowledge" [3] and his answer is that it "pertains to a knowledge that is above natural reason." [4] In Arabic philosophy, the Ikhwān al-Safā, in their formal classification of the sources of knowledge, mention also "prophecy" (al-wahy) and "divine inspiration" (al-ilhām)[5] as sources of knowledge. Alfarabi places prophecy at the top of the various stages of knowledge to which man may attain.[6] In Arabic Jewish philosophy, Saadia includes among the sources of knowledge which he enumerates also "true tradi-

---

[1] *Stromata* VII, 16 (PG, 9, 532 c).
[2] *In Joannis Evangelium*, Tractatus CX, Caput XVII, § 4 (PL, 35, 1922).
[3] *Sum. Theol.* II, II, 171, 1.
[4] *Ibid.*, 2 c.
[5] F. Dieterici, Arabic, *Die Abhandlungen der Ichwâin Es-Safâ in Auswahl*, p. 521, l. 5; German, *Die Lehre von der Weltseele*, p. 99.
[6] *Al-Siyâsât al-Madaniyyah*, Hyderabad, 1346 A. H., p. 49, l. 15–p. 50, l. 2.

tion," [7] by which he means knowledge based upon revelation as recorded in Scripture, and both Judah ha-Levi and Abraham Ibn Daud explain the Aristotelian immediately known primary premises as coming by divine inspiration.[8]

Prophecy in both Christianity and Islam, as in Philo's analysis of the prophecy of the Pentateuch, means more than mere divination. In both the New Testament and the Koran, while prophecy means also prediction, it means primarily the revelation of certain knowledge for the guidance of men both in their intellectual and moral life. In Christian philosophy, St. Thomas raises the question "whether prophecy is only about future contingencies," that is to say, whether prophecy is only divination as among the Greeks and Romans, and his answer is that by prophetic knowledge it is also possible to know "all things both divine and human, both spiritual and corporeal" and that "it also contains matters relating to human conduct."[9] In Moslem philosophy, prophecy is considered as the source of religious legislation [10] and also as the source of man's knowledge of intelligible things or concepts.[11] Ibn Khaldun states that the function of prophecy is to "make known to men what is most advantageous for them" and that it is also "the power to predict the occurrence of events which are hidden from mankind."[12]

---

[7] *Emunot we-De'ot, Hakdamah*, ed. Josefov, § 4, p. 44 (Arabic, p. 14, ll. 2 ff.).

[8] *Cuzari* V, 12 (Arabic, p. 314, l. 28); *Emunah Ramah* II, iv, 1, p. 58.

[9] *Sum. Theol.* II, II, 171, 3 c.

[10] Avicenna, *Najāt*, ed. Cairo, 1331 A. H., p. 499, ll. 5 ff.; Latin, N. Carame, *Avicennae Metaphysices Compendium*, 1926, p. 254.

[11] Alfarabi, *Fuṣūṣ al-Ḥikam*, § 40, ed. F. Dieterici, in *Alfārābī's philosophische Abhandlungen*, 1890, p. 75; German, 1892, p. 123.

[12] *Muqaddimah* I, i, 6. Arabic text in *Prolégomènes d'Eben-Khaldoun*, ed. M. Quatremère, Paris, 1858, I, p. 165, ll. 8 and 10–11. M. de Slane's French translation, Paris, 1863, I, 184; cf. D. B. Macdonald, *The Religious Attitude and Life in Islam*, 1909, p. 43.

In the New Testament two modes of prophecy are mentioned, that by the Holy Spirit,[13] corresponding to Philo's divine spirit, and that by angels.[14] But, as in Philo, on the basis of the statements in the Old Testament, the ten commandments are taken in Christianity to be direct prophetic revelation from God, that is, what Scripture describes as being by the voice of God or what Philo describes as having been given by God "in His own person." [15] Thus St. Thomas who, unlike Philo, maintains that the Mosaic Law, because of its imperfection, was given through angels,[16] still admits, with regard to the ten commandments, that "God himself is said to have given the precepts of the ten commandments to the people" and that the knowledge of them "man has from God himself." [17] In the Koran, too, only two modes of prophecy are mentioned, one by the Holy Spirit and the other by the angel Gabriel. These two, moreover, are identified by the commentators on the Koran,[18] as well as by Moslem philosophers.[19] But later Moslem tradition holds that "at the time of the Mi'rāj, or night ascent into heaven, God spoke to the prophet without the intervention of an angel," [20] thus corresponding to the manner of the revelation of God to the entire people on Mount Sinai or to Moses also on other occasions, which kind of prophecy is described by Philo as having been communicated by God "in His own person." Sometimes it is said that not only to Mohammed on the night of the ascension to heaven but

---

[13] I Cor. 12: 10–11; Eph. 3: 5.

[14] Matt. 1: 20; Luke 1: 11, 13; Acts 10: 3 ff.; 27: 23; Rev. 1: 1.

[15] *Decal.* 33, 175; cf. above, p. 36.

[16] *Sum. Theol.* I, II, 98, 3 c.

[17] *Ibid.,* 100, 3 c.

[18] See notes on Surah 2:81 and 17:87, in Rodwell's translation of the Koran.

[19] Cf. Alfarabi, *Fuṣūṣ al-Ḥikam,* § 28; Avicenna, *Najāt,* p. 500, ll. 4 and 9.

[20] E. Sell, *The Faith of Islam,* 3d ed., 1907, p. 60, referring to the *Mudarij al-Nabūwah*; cf. also F. A. Klein, *The Religion of Islam,* 1906, p. 6, referring to Suyūtī.

also to Moses God spoke directly without an intermediary.[21]
In mediaeval Jewish philosophy, Judah ha-Levi mentions
the voice of God and the Holy Spirit and angels as descriptions of various modes of prophecy [22] and so does also
Maimonides.[23]

As to what in these three groups of religious philosophies
was meant by angels, it differed according to the different
conceptions of angels maintained by the individual philosophers in each of these three groups of philosophy.[24] As for
the Holy Spirit, in Christianity it is generally taken to be a
real incorporeal being; in Islam, with its identification with
Angel Gabriel, it is part of the problem of angels; in Judaism,
there is a difference of opinion about it. Judah ha-Levi, for
instance, considers it as a real incorporeal being;[25] Maimonides, on the other hand, seems to take it either as a description of the gift of prophecy in general [26] or as a description of
the first two of his eleven stages of prophecy.[27] Directly
under the influence of Philo, through a condensed Arabic
translation of his *De Decalogo*, is the explanation in Arabic
Jewish philosophy of the voice of God which was heard at
the revelation on Mount Sinai as a voice created by God in
some miraculous way, called the created voice or sound (*al-
saut al-makhluq*).[28] An echo of this conception of the voice,
though it is a question whether it was eternal or created, is
to be found in Arabic philosophy when that kind of prophecy (*al-wahy*) which is said to come directly from the angel
without any intermediary (*wāsiṭah*) is described as being in

[21] Cf. E. Sell, *op. cit.*, p. 187, quoting Muhammad al-Birkawī.
[22] *Cuzari*, II, 4; IV, 3; I, 89.
[23] *Moreh Nebukim* I, 65; II, 33, 34, 45 (1) and (11).
[24] Cf. above, I, 418–419.
[25] *Cuzari* II, 4.
[26] *Moreh Nebukim* I, 40.
[27] *Ibid.* II, 45 (1 and 2).
[28] *Moreh Nebukim* I, 65; II, 33; cf. *Cuzari* I, 89.

the strict sense of the term "word" or "speech" (*kalām*) and this "word" or "speech" is described as being conceived by the prophet as "audible voices or sounds" (*aswāt masmū'ah*).[29]

As in Philo, so also in Christian, Moslem, and Jewish philosophy there is mention of certain qualifications which are required for prophecy. Whether natural and intellectual perfection is required is a matter of controversy, but it is generally agreed that moral conduct is a required condition. In Christianity, the question is formally raised by St. Thomas "whether a good life is requisite for prophecy" and, while he does not consider a disposition to goodness as a necessary requisite, he maintains that an evil life and the practice of evil are an obstacle to prophecy.[30] In Islam, Ibn Khaldun says that "even before inspiration prophets have a good and pure disposition and turn away from blameworthy things and uncleanness generally." [31] In Judaism, Maimonides insists upon moral perfection as one of the requirements of prophecy.[32] But whatever requirements are set up for prophecy, it is generally assumed, as in Philo, that prophecy ultimately comes to man as a divine gift. In the New Testament, prophecy is enumerated among the gifts (χαρίσματα) of the Spirit,[33] and St. Thomas argues to prove that "prophecy strictly so called cannot be from nature, but only from divine revelation" [34] or "through the gift (*ex dono*) of the Holy Spirit." [35] In Islam, the Ikhwān al-Ṣafā speak of prophecy and inspiration as "a gift (*muhabah*) from God" [36]

---

[29] Alfarabi, *Fuṣūṣ al-Ḥikam*, § 46.
[30] *Sum. Theol.* II, II, 172, 4.
[31] *Muqaddimah, l.c.*, Arabic, p. 146, ll. 14–16; French, p. 186; Macdonald, *op. cit.*, p. 47.
[32] *Moreh Nebukim* II, 32 (3).   [34] *Sum. Theol.* II, II, 172, 1 c.
[33] I Cor. 12: 4 and 10.   [35] *Ibid., Contra.*
[36] Cf. Dieterici, *op. cit.*, Arabic, p. 521, l. 6; German, p. 99.

and Ibn Khaldun says of prophecy that "God has chosen (*istafa*) from mankind certain individuals whom He has favored with the privilege (*faddalahum*) of conversing with Him." [37] In Jewish philosophy, Maimonides insists that prophecy depends on the "divine will." [38] The question whether prophecy is confined to Jews, concerning which, as we have seen, Philo believed that some types of prophecy are open to non-Jews and one type, that of the revelation of the Law, is open only to Jews, is answered in Christian, Moslem, and Jewish philosophy in different ways. Among the Church Fathers, Justin Martyr takes prophecy to have been confined to Jews and then transferred to Christians. [39] St. Augustine, however, maintains that before Christian times there had been also non-Jewish prophets. [40] In Islam, among the names of the twenty-eight prophets which are said to occur in the Koran some are those of non-Jews. [41] In mediaeval Jewish philosophy, Maimonides refers to Scripture and tradition as to the existence of prophets before Moses, mentioning "Shem, Eber, Noah, Methuselah, and Enoch," though he qualifies the function of these prophets by the statement that "of these none said to any portion of mankind that God sent him to them and commanded him to convey to them a certain message or to prohibit or to command a certain thing." [42] In another place he mentions other non-Jewish prophets, such as Job and Balaam, [43] though, again, he places them, together with some Jewish

[37] *Muqaddimah, l.c.*, Arabic, p. 165, ll. 6–7; French, p. 184; Macdonald, *op. cit.*, p. 47.

[38] *Moreh Nebukim* II, 32 (3).

[39] *Dialogus cum Tryphone*, 82.

[40] *De Civitate Dei* XVIII, 47.

[41] Such as Jethro, Job, Balaam or Aesop, and Alexander the Great. Cf. T. P. Hughes, *A Dictionary of Islam*, under "Prophet."

[42] *Moreh Nebukim* II, 39.

[43] *Ibid.* II, 45.

prophets, in the second of his eleven stages of prophecy. Even Judah ha-Levi, who is generally taken to confine prophecy to Jews, may mean, according to our interpretation, as does Philo, that only a certain special higher type of prophecy is confined to Jews, whereas other types of prophecy are open also to non-Jews.[44]

In his grand assault upon traditional philosophy Spinoza, in disagreement with all religious philosophers in the past ever since Philo, denies that the prophets of the Old Testament attained a knowledge of what were usually called intellectual virtues. "Thus," he says, "he who supposes to gain wisdom and a knowledge of natural and spiritual things from the prophetic books completely mistakes his way," [45] for the Bible "has nothing in common with philosophy." [46] The prophets, according to him, taught only what used to be called moral and practical virtues, for "the mind of the prophet was disposed only to what was right and good." [47]

Like all his predecessors ever since Philo, he finds in Scripture three modes of prophecy: (1) by the "words" (verba)[48] or the "voice" (vox) of God; [49] (2) through "images" (imagines) or "angel" (angelus); [50] (3) by the "spirit of God" (spiritus Dei).[51] Of these three terms, the first and second are taken by him, as they were by his predecessors, to have sometimes meant in Scripture a "voice" and an

---

[44] This question as well as the question of the meaning of the Holy Spirit, angels and the voice of God and also the question of the qualifications for prophecy are discussed by the present writer in "Hallevi and Maimonides on Prophecy," *Jewish Quarterly Review*, N.S., 32 (1942), 345–370; 33 (1942), 49–82,

[45] *Tractatus Theologico-Politicus*, ch. 2 (*Opera*, ed. Gebhardt), p. 29, ll. 29–31.

[46] *Ibid.*, *Praefatio* (p. 10, l. 17).

[47] *Ibid.*, ch. 2 (p. 31, ll. 30–31).

[48] *Ibid.*, ch. 1 (p. 17, l. 10).

[49] *Ibid.* (p. 17, l. 16); cf. p. 21, l. 9: *vox Dei*.

[50] *Ibid.* (p. 19, ll. 24–25); cf. p. 17, l. 11: *figura = imago*.

[51] *Ibid.* (p. 21, ll. 27–28).

"angel," or rather "words" and "appearances," which were "real (*verae*) to the imagination of the prophet who heard or saw them." [52] The third of these terms, however, the spirit of God, is taken by him, as it is by Maimonides, never to have meant anything real.[53] Again, unlike Philo and the other religious philosophers, and especially Maimonides, who considered prophecy by the voice of God, which was peculiar to the prophecy of Moses, as an immediate form of communication from God, he considers that form of communication also as being through an intermediary, and hence, according to him, even Moses had no immediate communication with God.[54]

In opposition to those of his predecessors, especially Maimonides,[55] who required intellectual perfection as a condition of prophecy, he maintains that "in order to prophesy there is no need of a peculiarly perfect mind but rather of a peculiarly vivid imagination." [56] This, on the whole, is a restatement in his own terms, with some essential modifications, of the view of Maimonides.[57] But unlike Maimonides, who says that in the case of Moses "he did not receive prophetic inspiration through the medium of the imaginative faculty, but directly through the intellect,[58] he maintains that even the prophecy of Moses was not without the aid of the imagination.[59] While admitting that the prophets "could indisputably perceive much that is beyond the boundary of the intellect, for many more ideas can be constructed from words and images than from the principles and

---

[52] *Ibid.* (p. 17, ll. 12–13).
[53] *Ibid.* (p. 27, ll. 24–27).
[54] *Ibid.* (p. 20, l. 12–p. 21, l. 12).
[55] *Moreh Nebukim* II, 32 (3).
[56] *Tractatus Theologico-Politicus*, ch. 1 (p. 21, ll. 25–26).
[57] *Moreh Nebukim* II, 36.
[58] *Ibid.*   [59] *Tractatus Theologico-Politicus*, ch. 1 (p. 21, ll. 23–24).

notions on which the whole fabric of reasoned knowledge is
reared," [60] still he maintains, in opposition to all the religious
philosophers who preceded him, that "prophetic knowledge
is inferior (*cedit*) to natural knowledge." [61] This is in direct
opposition to the statement of St. Thomas that "prophecy
pertains to a knowledge that is above (*supra . . . existit*)
natural reason." [62] Reflecting the view of Maimonides that
all the other prophets differed from Moses in that they
prophesied only periodically,[63] which in its turn is analogous
to a view expressed by Philo,[64] he says of all the prophets,
including Moses, that "inasmuch as imagination is fleeting
and inconstant, we find that the power of prophecy did not
remain with a prophet for long." [65]

The question whether prophecy was confined to Jews or
was open also to non-Jews, on which religious philosophers
ever since Philo expressed an opinion, is discussed also by
Spinoza in its wider aspect as part of the problem of the
"vocation of the Hebrews." [66] Trying to show that the
doctrine of the selection of Israel has no basis in Scripture, he
argues, evidently with an eye to the passage quoted above
from Maimonides,[67] that "although from the sacred histories
of the Old Testament it is not evident that . . . any gentile
prophet was expressly sent by God to the nations . . . it
suffices . . . that we find in the Old Testament gentiles, and
uncircumcised, as Noah, Enoch, Abimelech, Balaam, etc.,

[60] *Ibid.* (p. 28, ll. 22–25).
[61] *Ibid.*, ch. 2 (p. 30, ll. 32–33).
[62] *Sum. Theol.* II, II, 171, 2 c.
[63] *Mishneh Torah: Yesode ha-Torah* VII, 6; Introduction to Commentary on *Mishnah, Sanhedrin* X, Principle 7.
[64] *Spec.* IV, 8, 49; *Gig.* 7, 28; cf. 5, 19; *Immut.* 1, 2; *Gig.* 11, 47–49; cf. above, p. 33.
[65] *Tractatus Theologico-Politicus*, ch. 1 (p. 29, ll. 2–4).
[66] *Ibid.*, ch. 3.
[67] *Moreh Nebukim* II, 39; cf. above, p. 67.

exercising prophetic gifts." [68] But as against this, Spinoza says, "that the Pharisees, however, vehemently contend for the contrary view, maintaining that the divine gift was peculiar to their nation" and that "the principal passage in Scripture which they cite, by way of conforming their theory with authority, is Exodus 33: 16, where Moses says, 'For wherein now shall it be known that I have found grace in Thy sight, I and Thy people? is it not in that Thou goest with us, so that we are distinguished, I and Thy people, from all the people that are upon the face of the earth?' from which verse they would infer that Moses asked God that He should be present to the Jews and should reveal himself to them prophetically; further, that He should grant this favor to no other nation." [69] The "Pharisees" to whom he contributes this interpretation of the verse is Johanan bar Nappaha, a Palestinian Amora of the third century after the Christian era, who reports it in the name of Jose [ben Zimra], another Palestinian Amora of the second century.[70] This homily, however, does not deny prophecy to gentiles; it merely states that Moses prayed for the withdrawal of prophecy from gentiles. Elsewhere the withdrawal of prophecy is assumed by the rabbis, but it is explained by them to have been caused by the evil conduct of the greatest of the gentile prophets, Balaam.[71] This particular homily which attributes the withdrawal of prophecy from gentiles to a prayer of Moses may have originated as a polemic against Christians who at the time of the author of this homily still claimed the gift of prophecy for themselves, and even for those who were of gentile birth.

[68] *Tractatus Theologico-Politicus*, ch. 2 (p. 50, l. 35–p. 51, l. 6).

[69] *Ibid.*, ch. 3 (p. 53, ll. 9–22).

[70] *Berakot* 7a.

[71] *Numbers Rabbah*, 20, 1; *Tanḥuma*, *Balaḳ*, § 1; cf. L. Ginzberg, *The Legends of the Jews*, III, 355; VI, 124, n. 726.

The fundamental departure of Spinoza from traditional philosophy is his denial of the view held ever since Philo that the prophecy of the Old Testament was of divine origin. "All natural knowledge," he says, "may be called prophecy." [72] Prophecy indeed may be called "divine," but only in the same sense that any natural phenomenon can be called divine. [73] But prophets have no "superhuman minds" and their "sensations and consciousness" are not different from ours. [74] Indeed, he admits that the prophets of the past may have, with their vivid imagination, perceived "much that is beyond the boundary of the intellect" [75] and he confesses that he does not know how to explain that by "laws of nature," [76] but he is quite certain that prophecy does not come in a miraculous way from God. Inasmuch, therefore, as he considers prophetic knowledge as being knowledge based upon imagination, in his classification of the sources of knowledge [77] he would not put it as the highest kind of knowledge but rather as the lowest, though in restating what he believed to be the genuine New Testament teaching, [78] he maintains that the prophecy of Jesus, unlike that of Moses, was without the aid of the imagination; it was a revelation "truly and adequately" and "immediately" perceived, [79] thus corresponding to what Spinoza himself calls the third class of knowledge, or intuitive knowledge.

[72] *Tractatus Theologico-Politicus*, ch. 1 (p. 15, ll. 18–19).
[73] *Ibid.* (p. 15, ll. 25–31).
[74] *Ibid.* (p. 16, ll. 2–5).
[75] *Ibid.* (p. 28, l. 22); cf. above, p. 69.
[76] *Ibid.* (p. 28, ll. 7–8).
[77] *Ethics* II, Prop. 40, Schol. 2; *Short Treatise* II, 1; II, 4, § 9; *Tractatus de Intellectus Emendatione*, § 19.
[78] *Tractatus Theologico-Politicus*, ch. 1 (p. 21, ll. 15–16).
[79] *Ibid.*, ch. 1 (p. 21, ll. 23–24), ch. 4 (pp. 64, l. 16–65, l. 2).

CHAPTER X

PROOFS OF THE EXISTENCE OF GOD

IN OUR SEARCH for God, says Philo, two principal questions arise, "one is whether the Deity exists . . . the other is what the Deity is in essence," and while the second question, he says, is "perhaps impossible to solve," "to answer the first question does not need much labor."[1] Why not much labor is required to establish the existence of God is explained by Philo himself in the words which he makes Moses say to God: "That Thou art and dost subsist, of this the world has been my teacher and guide."[2] Elsewhere, however, Philo qualifies this statement by saying that God in so far as His existence is taught by the world is "more easily conceived by the mind than made known by verbal demonstration."[3] This probably reflects Plato's statement that "the Maker and Father of this all it is a hard task to find and, having found Him, it is impossible to declare Him to all men,"[4] which statement Philo evidently takes to refer to the existence of God rather than to His essence,[5] and, in opposition to it, maintains that to declare the existence of God to others by verbal demonstration is not impossible but only less easy a task than merely to find it for oneself, that is, merely to conceive it in one's own mind. But still, while to prove the existence of God to the satisfaction of others by verbal demonstration is less easy a task than one would like it to be, Philo does not shrink from undertaking that task. The manner in which the existence of God may be demonstrated from the con-

---

[1] *Spec.* I, 6, 32.
[2] *Ibid.* I, 8, 41.
[3] *Post.* 48, 167.
[4] *Timaeus* 28 c.
[5] Cf. below, p. 113, for various interpretations of this passage by Church Fathers, who take it to refer to the essence of God.

templation of the world is either fully stated or briefly alluded
to by Philo in several places in his writings. Four such arguments are advanced by him, three cosmological and one
teleological. To these, as we shall see, he adds also what may
be called a nascent ontological argument.

One of Philo's arguments is based upon the premise that
the world came into being, supplemented by the principle
that nothing comes into being without a cause. It is modeled
after Plato's argument in the *Timaeus*, which reads: "All
that comes to be must needs be brought into being by some
cause, for without a cause it is impossible for anything to
come to be." [6] As restated by Philo, this argument reads
that "the world has come into being and assuredly it has
derived its existence from some cause." [7] The principle of
causality upon which this Platonic argument is based is
alluded to by Philo in his explanation that the scriptural
description of the "earth," by which is meant the "world of
our senses," as God's "footstool" in the verse "the heaven
is my throne and the earth is my footstool" [8] is "to show
that not in that which comes into existence is to be found
the cause which brought it into existence." [9] The implication
of this statement is that if anything has come into existence
there must be a cause that has brought it into existence
and that that cause must be distinct from its effect.

A second argument for the existence of God is alluded to
by him in his refutation of Aristotle's view that the world
is eternal and that God is only the cause of the motion of
the world. In that refutation of Aristotle, Philo says that
Moses, because he "had been divinely instructed in the
greater and most essential things of nature, could not fail to
recognize that in existing things there must be an active

[6] *Timaeus* 28 A.
[7] *Fug.* 2, 12.
[8] Isa. 66: 1.
[9] *Conf.* 21, 98.

cause and a passive object and that the active cause is the thoroughly unmixed and thoroughly unadulterated mind of the universe." [10] In our discussion of this passage in the chapter on Philo's theory of the creation of the world, we have shown that it contains an argument from Aristotle's own proof for the existence of God from the eternity of motion against his view that God is only the cause of the motion of the world and not of its existence.[11] The inference to be drawn from this passage then is that even on the Aristotelian assumption of the eternity of the world there is proof for the existence of a god who as the immovable mover of the world is also the cause of its existence. Allusions to the Aristotelian proof from motion are also to be found in his description of God as the "moving cause" ($\kappa\iota\nuοῦν\ αἴτιον$)[12] and more especially as the immovable mover, which is expressed by him in such statements as that God "who moves and turns all else is himself immovable and unalterable," [13] or that "the strangest thing of all is that, whereas the stars as they go past moving objects are themselves in motion, God who outstrips them all, remains standing still" [14] or that God "moves the whole composition of the world, not by means of his legs, for He is not of the form of a man, but by showing His unalterable and unchangeable nature." [15]

A third argument, described by him as an argument "from the world and its constituent parts and the powers subsisting in these" and ascribed by him to "those whose philosophy is reputed the best" [16] is what came to be known as the teleological argument. By the time of Philo this argu-

---

[10] *Opif.* 2, 8.
[11] Cf. above, I, 295–297.
[12] *Fug.* 2, 8.
[13] *Post.* 9, 28.
[14] *Ibid.* 6, 19.
[15] *Mut.* 7, 54. Cf. discussion of reading of text in Wendland and in Colson *ad loc.* But whatever the reading, the meaning is quite clear that God is an immovable mover.
[16] *Leg. All.* III, 32, 97.

ment already had a long tradition dating back to Plato, the
early writings of Aristotle, and the Stoics. In Plato this
argument is described as an argument from "the earth
and the sun and the stars and the universe and the fair
order of the seasons and the division of them into years and
months." [17] Aristotle is reported to have said in one of his
early writings that men derived their conception of God
"from celestial phenomena also, for when they beheld the
sun circling round in the day-time, and by night the orderly
motions of the other stars, they supposed some God to be
the cause of such motion and orderliness." [18] Among the
Stoics, Cleanthes is reported to have said that one of the
causes which led men to the idea of God is "the uniformity of
motion, the revolutions of the heavens, the grouping of the
sun, and moon, and all the stars, their serviceableness,
beauty and order, the mere appearance of which things would
be sufficient indication that they were not the result of
chance." [19] This argument, like the Platonic argument from
creation, is also based upon the principle of causality, the
contention being that without a cause such an order could
not have come to be. In support of this contention, the
analogy of the products of human art is introduced. "Just
as a man going into a house, or gymnasium, or market-
place, would find it impossible, when he saw the plan, and
scale, and arrangements of everything, to suppose that those
things came into being uncaused," so in the case of the
world "it is much more inevitable that he should conclude
that such great operations of nature are directed by some
intelligence." [20] In Philo's restatements of this argument, the

[17] *Laws* X, 886 A; cf. XII, 966 E.
[18] Fragment of his *De Philosophia* (Bekker, 1476a, 5–9) from Sextus, *Adversus Physicos* I, 22; cf. also 1476a, 34–b, 11, from Cicero's *De Natura Deorum* II, 37, 95.
[19] Cicero, *De Natura Deorum* II, 5, 15 (Arnim, I, 528).
[20] *Ibid.*

description of the orderly processes of nature, in which one is to find evidence for the existence of God, refers similarly to the spheres and planets and stars, but also to the elements and animal beings and plants underneath the spheres.[21] Like the Stoics he brings into his argument the analogy of artificial things: "Should a man see a house carefully constructed with a gateway, colonnades, men's quarters, women's quarters, and the other buildings, he will get the idea of the artificer, for he will be of the opinion that the house never reached that completeness without the skill of the craftsman; and in like manner in the case of a city and a ship and every smaller or greater construction." [22]

Of these three arguments, the second, the Aristotelian argument, as we have seen, is used by Philo to prove not only the existence of a God but the existence of a God of a special kind. Like Aristotle, he finds that argument to prove that God is "the thoroughly unmixed and thoroughly unadulterated mind of the universe," that is to say, He is a purely incorporeal being, but, unlike Aristotle, he finds it to prove that God is not only a cause of motion but also a cause of existence. Similarly the first argument, the Platonic, is used by him in its strictly Platonic sense as a proof for the existence of a creator who is incorporeal and exists outside the things created by him. This may be inferred from his restatement of the principle of causality upon which this argument is based, wherein he emphasizes that the

[21] *Leg. All.* III, 32, 99; *Spec.* I, 6, 34.

[22] *Leg. All.* III, 32, 98; *Spec.* I, 6, 33. Cf. *Genesis Rabbah* 39, 1: "It is like unto a man who was traveling from place to place when he saw a mansion all lighted up. He wondered: Is it conceivable that the mansion is without a caretaker? Thereupon the master of the mansion looked out and said to him: I am the master of the mansion and its caretaker. Similarly, because Abraham our father wondered: Is it conceivable that the world is without a caretaker? Thereupon the Holy One, blessed be He, looked at him and said: I am the master of the universe and its caretaker."

cause which brings a thing into existence is not to be found in that which comes into existence.[23] But as for the third argument, the teleological, in the restatement of which, as we have seen, Philo follows Stoic sources, there is nothing to show that he does not use it in its original Stoic limited sense to prove the existence of a God against those who denied His existence, irrespective of the problem whether that God is immanent in the world, as is maintained by the Stoics, or not, as is maintained by Philo himself.

But then Philo has a fourth argument, which, according to his own statement, is directed against those whom he describes as Chaldeans and who are presented by him as believing that the physical universe "either is itself God or contains God in itself as the soul of the whole." [24] This, as we have seen, is a restatement of the Stoic conception of God in its two common versions.[25] But this argument which by his own statement is directed against the Stoics is made up, as we shall try to show, of two Stoic arguments which, combined by him so as to form two parts of one argument, were turned by him into an argument against the Stoics themselves.

In the first part, Philo begins with an appeal to the so-called Chaldeans not to look for evidence for the existence of God in the order of the heaven nor even in the order of things underneath heaven, such as earth and sea and rivers and plants and animals, but to explore themselves and their own nature. By observing conditions prevailing in their own nature, he says, they will discover that within the body there is a mind which is distinguished from the latter as master from subject, as the animate from the inanimate, as the rational from the irrational, as the immortal from the mortal and as the better from the worse. From this, he

---

[23] Cf. above, n. 9.　　　[24] *Migr.* 32, 179.　　　[25] Cf. above, I, 176 f.

argues, they will gain a knowledge of God and His works, for reason will show that as there is a mind in man so is there in the universe and that as man's mind governs the body so the universal mind or God governs the universe.[26] Now this first part of the argument is nothing but a vague restatement of a Stoic argument for the existence of God in the world from the existence of mind in man. This argument from the mind occurs in a variety of forms, all but one of them based upon the principle of causality, contending that there could be no mind in man unless there was a mind in the world to cause its coming into existence.[27] Three characteristic forms of this argument, one based upon mere analogy and two upon causality and all of them attributed to Zeno, may be quoted here. They read as follows: (1) "The rational is better than the non-rational . . . the intelligent is better than the non-intelligent and the animate than the non-animate. But nothing is better than the universe. Therefore the universe is intelligent and animate." [28] (2) "Nothing that is inanimate and without reason can generate from itself a being that is animate and possessed of reason. The universe generates beings that are animate and possessed of reason. Therefore the universe is animate and possessed of reason." [29] (3) "No part can be sentient where the whole is not sentient. But parts of the universe are sentient. Therefore the universe is sentient." [30] In Philo's reproduction of this argument here the expressions "the animate and the inanimate, the rational and the irrational, . . . the bet-

---

[26] *Migr.* 33, 185–186.

[27] Sextus, *Adversus Physicos* I, 77, 85, 95–104; Cicero, *De Natura Deorum* II, 6, 18; 8, 21–22; 9, 23–30; 12, 32; 14, 37.

[28] Sextus, *Adversus Physicos* I, 104; cf. Cicero, *De Natura Deorum*, II, 8, 21; III, 9, 22–23 (Arnim, I, 111); refutation of this argument in III, 8, 21 (cf. J. B. Mayor's note in his edition on II, 8, 21).

[29] Cicero, *op. cit.*, II, 8, 22; Sextus, *Adversus Physicos* I, 101 (Arnim, I, 113).

[30] Cicero, *loc. cit.*; Sextus, *Adversus Physicos* I, 85 (Arnim, I, 114).

ter and the worse" [31] would seem to reflect the first of the
three versions of Zeno's argument we have reproduced, the
argument based upon analogy. But when in the conclusion
of his argument he says that "your reason will show you
that, as there is mind in you, so is there in the universe," [32]
his statement does not make it clear whether the inference
is to be based upon analogy or upon the principle of causality. But however that may be, there is nothing in Philo's
reproduction of this Stoic argument to prove the existence
of a God who, unlike the Stoic God, is not to be immanent
in the world. The argument so far merely proves, as is con-
tended by the Stoics, that as there is a mind within man so
there must be a mind within the world.

Philo was evidently aware of this limitation of the Stoic
argument which he has so far reproduced, and therefore he
does not stop with it. After he has shown, on the basis of
the Stoic argument, that there must be a mind in the universe, he proceeds to show, in opposition to the Stoics, but,
again, as we shall show, on the basis of another Stoic argument, that that mind of the universe, unlike the mind of
man, is not immanent in the body of the universe. This new
supplementary argument reasons again from the mind of
man, and is based upon two kinds of experience of the human
mind: first, that of divination respecting future events which
may take place in dreams, and, second, that of philosophic
inspiration which may take place in waking hours. [33] Now
the experience of divination, whether in dreams or in waking
hours, is used both in the early writings of Aristotle [34] and
by the Stoic Cleanthes [35] either as an explanation of how

[31] *Migr.* 33, 185.
[32] *Ibid.*, 186.
[33] *Migr.* 34, 190–191.
[34] Sextus, *Adversus Physicos* I, 20–21.   The reference is to Aristotle's *De Philosophia* (Bekker, 1475b, 37).   [35] Cicero, *De Natura Deorum* II, 5, 13.

men arrived at a belief in the existence of God or as a proof for the existence of God. Similarly the experience of philosophic inspiration is used by Plato as a description of the state of mind during which man becomes aware of the existence of the ideas.[36] Combining these two kinds of experience, Philo uses them as an argument against the Stoics to prove that the mind of the universe, whose existence has already been established from the existence of a mind in man must, unlike the mind of man, abide always outside the body of the universe.

This argument, which forms the second part of Philo's fourth argument, is based upon the contention that even the human mind occasionally exists apart from the human body and consequently, it concludes, whatever is true of the human body occasionally must be true of God all the time. The argument may be restated as follows.

In the case of divination experienced in dreams, argues Philo, "the mind quits its place and, withdrawing from the perceptions and all other bodily faculties,[37] begins to turn itself about and to consider the object of its thought (νοή-ματα) clearly by itself, then, looking into the liver as into a mirror, it sees clearly every one of the intelligible objects (νοητῶν) . . . and, being content with all its visions, it prophesies future events by dreams." [38] Similarly in the case of philosophic possession, "when the mind, possessed by some philosophic speculation, is drawn by it, then it follows this, and necessarily forgets all other things which concern its corporeal abode . . . so that no object of sense-perception may bedim the eye of the soul, to which God has given the power to see things intelligible (νοητά)." [39] By the intelligible things (νοητά) in both these passages, I take it,

---

[36] *Phaedrus* 249 b–d.
[37] *Migr.* 34, 190.

[38] *Spec.* I, 39, 219. Cf. Arnim, II, 1196–1206.
[39] *Migr.* 34, 191. Cf. *Phaedrus* 249 b–d.

Philo means not merely concepts of thought but rather real incorporeal beings, the ideas or, as he calls them also, powers. Thus the human mind in our experiences of true dreams and philosophic inspiration divests itself from our body and from sense-perception and, divorced from these, sees the intelligible beings in their nakedness [40] as they exist apart from matter.[41] Now, concludes Philo in his argument, if our mind can on certain occasions have an existence apart from our body, how much more so is it reasonable to assume that God, who is the mind of the universe, dwells outside of all material nature, that He contains everything and is not contained by anything, and that He goes forth beyond things not only by His thought alone, as man does, but also by His essential nature, as befits God.[42] Thus by the analogy of the human mind Philo has established, in opposition to the Stoics, that God is immaterial and is not immanent in the world. But this analogy, he wants to show, is not perfect. The mind is only on certain extraordinary occasions divested of the body; in its normal state it exists within the body; but God is always outside the world; He penetrates the world only through His powers.[43]   To point out this difference, and to give a reason for it, he adds the following statement. "For our mind has not created the body, but is the workmanship of Another, and it is therefore contained in the body as in a vessel; but the Mind of the universe has brought the universe into existence, and the maker of a thing is superior to the thing made, so that it could not be included in its inferior; nor indeed would it be fitting that a father should be contained in a son, but rather that a son should attain full growth under the father's care." [44]   In this last statement, then, with the help of an analogy of artificial

[40] Following the reading γυμνά as in Colson.   [41] *Migr.* 35, 192.
[42] *Ibid.*, 193.   [43] Cf. above, I, 326 ff.   [44] *Migr.* 35, 193.

craftsmanship and natural procreation, he turns the Platonic argument for the existence of God from creation into an argument against the Stoics, showing that the latter are wrong in assuming that God is immanent in the world.

All these four arguments are arguments from causality intermingled with analogies of artificial things. The arguments from creation and from the perfection of the universe are expressly described by him as being based upon the principle of causality. The Aristotelian argument, we know, is in its original form based upon the principle of causality. As for the argument from the mind, we have shown, it is based either upon the analogy of the universe to man or upon the principle of causality, in the latter case arguing that there could be no mind in man unless there was a mind in the world conceived as the cause of the mind in man. All these arguments, therefore, are derived from things in the world, reasoning from effect to cause or from analogy.

As distinguished from this method of proving the existence of God from the world, Philo mentions another method. This other method as well as its difference from the first method is described by him in a passage which immediately follows his description of the teleological argument. In that passage he distinguishes between two types of mind: first, a mind which gains its knowledge of God "from created things, as one may learn the substance from the shadow," and second, a mind which, "having risen above and beyond creation, obtains a clear vision (ἔμφασιν ἐναργῆ) of the uncreated One, so as from Him to apprehend himself and also His shadow, that is to say, to apprehend also the Logos and this world." [45] As exponents of these two types of mind

[45] *Leg. All.* III, 33, 100. The term "shadow," it will be noticed, is used in the first part of this passage as referring to this world and in the latter part as referring both to this world and the Logos. Previously (31, § 96) Philo uses it only with reference to the Logos.

he takes Moses and Bezalel. "The former," he says, "receives the clear vision of God directly from the first cause himself, whereas the latter discerns the Artificer, as it were from a shadow, from created things, by virtue of a process of reasoning" [46] and, again, "Moses has God for instructor . . . but Bezalel is instructed by Moses." [47] The scriptural proof-text in the case of Moses is the verse which in Hebrew reads "Make known to me Thy way, that I may know Thee" but which in the Septuagint reads "Reveal thyself to me, that I may see Thee with knowledge." [48] Quoting this verse from the Septuagint, Philo paraphrases it as follows: "For I would not that Thou shouldst be manifested to me by means of heaven or earth or water or air or any created thing at all, nor would I find Thy way (ἰδέαν) [49] reflected in aught else than in Thee who art God, for the reflections in created things are dissolved, but those in the Uncreated will continue abiding and sure and eternal." [50] This gift of having a clear vision of God is, however, not confined to Moses; it is open to all Israel. The name "Israel," according to Philo, means "seeing God" [51] and the people of Israel are described by him as "those who are members of that race endowed with vision (ὁρατικόν)" [52] or as those to whose lot it has fallen "to see the best, that is the Truly Existing." [53] And not only Israel but all virtuous men may be seeing God. "What among all the blessings which the virtues give can be more perfect than the sight (ἰδεῖν) of the Absolutely Existing?" [54] And "What

[46] *Ibid.*, 102.
[47] *Ibid.* [48] Exod. 33: 13.
[49] I take the term ἰδέα here as a translation of the original Hebrew word "thy way."
[50] *Leg. All.* III, 33, 101.
[51] *Fug.* 38, 208; *Conf.* 20, 92; *Heres* 15, 78; *Mut.* 12, 82; *Somn.* II, 26, 173; *Abr.* 12, 57.
[52] *Immut.* 30, 144.
[53] *Congr.* 10, 51. [54] *Ebr.* 20, 83.

garland more fitting for its purpose or of richer flowers could be woven for the victorious soul than the power which will enable him to behold the Existent with clear vision (ὀξυδερκῶς)?"[55]

On the whole, this distinction between the two methods of knowing God and with God also the Logos reflects the distinction made by Philo himself between the two kinds of knowledge of the mind, one that is indirectly derived from sense-perception and another which is directly derived from God by revelation and prophecy. These two kinds of knowledge, as we have shown, correspond to two similar kinds of knowledge of mind which is found in Plato, with the only difference that, in the case of the direct kind of knowledge, Philo substitutes prophecy for Plato's dialectic and recollection.[56] The vocabulary in which this distinction between these two kinds of knowledge is couched here by Philo reflects the vocabulary used by Plato in his parable of the cave. His statement that one type of mind arrives at a knowledge of God "as one may learn the abiding thing (τὸ μένον) from the shadow (σκιᾶς)"[57] reflects Plato's view that the indirect kind of knowledge of the mind, by which one may develop the arts and sciences, ultimately rests upon the shadows (σκιαί) which one may perceive by the senses while yet in the cave.[58] His description of the other type of mind as that which "rising above creation obtains a clear vision of the uncreated one"[59] reflects Plato's description of direct cognition or *nous* as a power in the soul which enables it, in its ascent (ἐπάνοδος) above the subterranean cave, to rise to the vision (θέαν) of the ideas.[60]

The verse from which, in the passage quoted, Philo infers

---

[55] *Mut.* 12, 82.
[56] Cf. above, pp. 7–11.
[57] *Leg. All.* III, 33, 100.
[58] *Republic* VII, 514 A ff.; 532 B; cf. above, p. 7.
[59] *Leg. All.* III, 33, 100.
[60] *Republic* VII, 532 A–C.

that Moses' knowledge of God was direct and not from the
world, is verse 13 in Exodus, Chapter 33, which, as quoted
by him from the Septuagint, reads, as we have seen, " Reveal
thyself to me, that I may see Thee with knowledge." Sup-
plementing this prayer, Moses says: "If Thou thyself goest
not with me, lead me not up hence." [61] This supplementary
statement is interpreted by Philo to mean that "Moses prays
that he may have God himself as guide to the road which
leads to Him." [62] This prayer of Moses is granted by God in
His answer to Moses, "Thou hast found grace in My sight,"[63]
which is interpreted by Philo to mean that "by His own
agency alone does the Existent think the exceeding wisdom
which is found in Moses to be worthy of grace." [64] In all
these three passages, both in his discussion of the prayer of
Moses and in his discussion of God's answer to Moses'
prayer, Philo tries to show that what Moses prayed for was
that God should reveal himself to him directly and not
through the created beings in the world, so that God himself would be "the guide to the road which leads to Him,"
and similarly that God's answer to him was that Moses was
worthy of grace by the direct agency of God himself. But
as to what kind of knowledge of God did Moses pray for,
whether it was for a knowledge of God's existence or for a
knowledge of God's essence, Philo does not specify it in any
of these passages.

But then in verse 18 of the same chapter, according to one
reading of the Septuagint text, the same prayer of verse 13,
" Reveal thyself to me," occurs again, but without the words
"that I may see Thee with knowledge." God's answer to

[61] Exod. 33: 15.

[62] *Migr.* 31, 171.

[63] Exod. 33: 17, quoted by Philo as "Thou hast found grace with me" (*Immut.*
24, 109).

[64] *Immut.* 24, 110.

that second prayer, in verses 19 — 23, is discussed by Philo in several places in his works. In all of them he says that Moses prayed for a knowledge of God's essence and that God answered him that only His existence could be known, and it could be known only from the world, but that His essence could not be known by any created being.[65]

Thus, according to Philo, Moses made two successive prayers, one in verse 13 and the other in verse 18. The first prayer was for a direct knowledge of God, without specifying whether that was a prayer for a direct knowledge of God's existence or for a direct knowledge of God's essence. God granted this prayer of Moses for a direct knowledge of Him, again without specifying whether that knowledge was to be of His existence or of His essence. The second prayer was for a knowledge of God's essence. This prayer was refused by God. From this refusal of a knowledge of the essence of God it may be inferred that the granting of the first prayer, namely, that of having a direct knowledge of God, refers to a direct knowledge of God's existence and not of His essence. Hence, it may be further inferred that, according to Philo, there are two modes of arriving at a knowledge of God's existence, a direct and indirect one, and that Moses was granted the distinction of having a direct knowledge of God's existence.

But here a question may arise. What does it mean to have

---

[65] *Post.* 5, 15; 48, 169; *Fug.* 29, 165; *Mut.* 2, 9; *Spec.* I, 8, 41–44. Consequently when Philo quotes the words "Reveal thyself to me" (*Post.* 5, 16, cf. 4, 13; *Spec.* I, 8, 41) and takes them to be a prayer for the knowledge of God's essence, the quotation is not from v. 13 of Exod. 33, as is given in Cohn-Wendland's and Colson's editions, but rather from v. 18. The quotation "Reveal thyself to me, that I may know Thee with knowledge," in *Mut.* 2, 8, is, as it stands, from v. 13. But inasmuch as it is explained to be a prayer for a knowledge of God's essence, it must undoubtedly be a quotation from v. 18, and the words "that I may know Thee by knowledge" are undoubtedly a careless addition either by Philo himself or by some copyist.

a direct knowledge of God's existence, and how does such a
knowledge differ from the indirect kind of knowledge?

An answer to this question, we shall now try to show, is
furnished by Philo in two passages.

First, in one passage Philo tries to explain how Moses has
arrived at a knowledge of the existence of an active cause
or God by two methods, "[1] because he had early attained
the very summit of philosophy and [2] because he had been
instructed by divine revelation in the most numerous and
most important things of nature." [66] In this passage, it is
quite evident, as it is in that passage in which he distinguishes between two types of mind, that Philo enumerates two
ways by which Moses has arrived at the existence of God:
first, in his early life, in Egypt, before God revealed himself
to him, through philosophy, and then, later, after God revealed himself to him, through prophecy. The latter way is
described by him as that in which "he had been instructed
(ἀναδιδαχθείς) by divine revelation," [67] which corresponds
exactly to his description of the direct knowledge of God in
the other passage as that in which "Moses has God for instructor (ὑφηγητῇ)." [68] The difference then in this passage
between Moses' earlier knowledge of God's existence and
his later knowledge is that the former was indirect and the
latter was direct. Now the later direct knowledge is described by Philo as that in which Moses "had been divinely
instructed in the greater and most essential part of nature's
lore," [69] from which it may be inferred that the direct knowledge of the existence of God is a knowledge derived from a
knowledge of nature imparted in him by divine revelation.
The conclusion to be drawn from this passage, therefore, is
that both methods by which Moses arrived at a knowledge

[66] *Opif.* 2, 8.   [68] *Leg. All.* III, 33, 102.
[67] *Ibid.*   [69] *Opif.* 2, 8.

of the existence of God, the indirect and the direct, were based upon a knowledge of the world, but that in the indirect method the knowledge of the world was attained by philosophy, whereas in the direct method it was attained by prophecy.

The implication of this passage is that the knowledge of the existence of God is always based upon the contemplation of the world but that such a knowledge, though based upon the contemplation of the world, may still be either indirect or direct. It is indirect when the knowledge of the world is gained by observation and the proof for the existence of God is derived therefrom by reasoning; it is direct when the knowledge of the world as well as the proof for the existence of God derived therefrom come to man by prophecy or revelation. In the former case, the knowledge of nature is gathered slowly and painstakingly by observation and experience, and the proof for the existence of God is derived, again, slowly, syllogistically, from premise through premise to conclusion. In the latter case, however, the knowledge of nature is showered upon a person suddenly by divine revelation, and similarly the proof of the existence of God derived therefrom is flashed upon a person's mind suddenly, again by divine revelation. In the former case, it is what in Philo's classification of knowledge would be called reason, which is ultimately based upon sensation; in the latter case, it is what would be called prophecy, which is independent of sensation: it is a direct knowledge of God's existence manifesting itself in the world when that knowledge of the world is revealed to man by God.

Then, in another passage, which deals with the second prayer of Moses, Philo makes Moses say, in explanation of this second prayer, and evidently with reference to God's answer to his first prayer that He himself would lead him to

a knowledge of His existence, that with regard to the existence of God, "the world has been my teacher," but that
what he wished to pray for is to understand "what Thou art
in Thy essence," [70] In His answer, God tells him that His
essence cannot be known to any created being.[71] But then
God adds: "But I readily and with right good will will admit you to a share of what is attainable. That means that
I bid you come and contemplate the world and its contents." [72] From the wording of this statement it is quite evident that it is meant to be an answer to Philo's own statement: "That Thou art and dost exist, of this the world has
been my teacher and guide, instructing me as a son might of
his father and a work of its contriver." [73] God seems to say to
Moses: Indeed, like all other men, you can arrive at a knowledge of my existence, indirectly, by means of reason, and
after a long and laborious process of the study of the world.
But in your case, because you are deserving of special grace,
I will myself lead you directly to a knowledge of my existence, by revealing to you a knowledge of the most numerous
and the most important things of nature and by causing you
to see by means of your prophetic insight clear evidence and
a clear vision of my existence everywhere in the world.

It is in this sense, then, that in the passage quoted Philo
distinguishes between the direct and indirect knowledge of
the existence of God, the former of which is described by him
as a "clear vision (ἔμφασις ἐναργής) of the uncreated One." [74]
This "clear vision" of God means, as we have tried to show,
a direct perception of the evidence in nature for the existence
of God which one may acquire with the help of God by
means of prophecy and revelation.

---

[70] *Spec.* I, 8, 41.
[71] *Ibid.*, 44 and 49.
[72] *Ibid.*, 49.

[73] *Ibid.*, 41.
[74] *Leg. All.* III, 33, 100; cf. above, p. 83.

It is in this sense also that the expression "to see God" or "the vision of God" is used by him in other passages. In one place he says that "it well befits those who have entered into comradeship of knowledge to see (ἰδεῖν) the Existent if they may, but, if they cannot, to see at any rate His image, the most holy Logos, and next to that, the most perfect work of all that our senses know, namely, the world. For to philosophize is nothing else but to desire to see things exactly as they are." [75] In another place, he says that "the central Being with each of His powers as His body-guard presents to the mind which has vision (ὁρατικῇ) the vision (φαντασίαν) sometimes of one, sometimes of three." [76] Then, speaking of the Therapeutae, he says that because they are "a people always taught from the first to use their sight," they "may well desire the vision (θέας) of the Existent and soar above the sun of our senses and never leave their place in this company which carries them on to perfect happiness . . . until they see (ἴδωσι) the object of their yearning." [77] Then, also, the name "Israel," whether referring to an individual or to the nation, is interpreted by him to mean "seeing God." [78] Students of Philo usually take all those passages which speak of the vision of God as referring to a knowledge of God's essence and hence they find these passages contradictory to Philo's explicit statements, in his interpretation of God's answer to the second prayer of Moses, that God's essence cannot be known.[79] But, as we have been trying to show, in none of these passages does the seeing of God mean having a knowledge of God's essence, and hence they are not contradictory to those passages in which a knowledge of the essence of God is said by him to be un-

[75] *Conf.* 20, 97.
[76] *Abr.* 24, 122.   [78] *Post.* 18, 63; *Immut.* 30, 144.
[77] *Cont.* 2, 11–12.   [79] Cf. Gfrörer, I, 136–137; Zeller, III, 2⁴, 463–464.

attainable. Still less is a knowledge of the essence of God implied in the passage in which he says concerning the mind that "amid its longing to see (ἰδεῖν) Him, pure and untempered rays of concentrated light stream forth like a torrent, so that by its gleams the eye of the understanding is dazzled." [80] This quite evidently refers to an indirect knowledge of God's existence.

The distinction between a direct and indirect knowledge of the existence of God is not new with Philo. Before him the Stoics speak of the innateness of the idea of God as a direct· method of knowing the existence of God as distinguished from all the other methods which are based upon arguments reasoning from effects to cause. [81] The direct method of knowing God may still further be traced, as we have already suggested, to Plato's theory of the recollection of the ideas. [82] But the new element introduced by Philo into his discussion of the proofs of the existence of God, no less than into his discussion of the sources of knowledge, is his substitution, under the influence of Scripture, of divine revelation or prophecy for Plato's theory of the recollection of ideas or for the Stoic theory of the innateness of the idea of God.

The arguments for the existence of God used by Philo, as we have seen, are not new, though one of them, that from divination, has been given by him a new turn. The only new element introduced by him into these arguments is his substitution of revelation for Plato's recollection of the ideas and the Stoics' innateness of the idea of God. From now on, revelation as a proof of the existence of God is continued to be used by all religious philosophers, whether Christian, Moslem, or Jewish, even when, under the influence of Stoic

[80] *Opif.* 23, 71.
[81] Cicero, *De Natura Deorum* I, 17, 44; II, 4, 12.   [82] Cf. above, p. 85.

writings, the innateness of the idea of God is reinstated as another direct proof. Thus John of Damascus, summarizing the views of the Greek Church Fathers, divides all the proofs of the existence of God into three types: " [1] The knowledge that there is a God has been implanted by Him as something innate in all men. [2] Then also the creation itself, as well as the conservation and government thereof, proclaims the majesty of the divine nature. [3] Finally, at first through the Law and prophets and then through His only begotten Son, our Lord and God and Saviour, Jesus Christ, He revealed the knowledge of himself to us in accordance with our power of comprehension." [83] Of these three types of proof, the first and third may be considered as direct proofs of the existence of God, the first being the Stoic proof in its original form, except for the attribution of the innateness of the idea of God in us to an act of God himself, and the third being the Philonic version of the direct proof of the existence of God. Out of these direct proofs there developed, in Christian philosophy, what came to be known as the ontological proof. It is this ontological proof, based upon the premise that God can be directly and immediately known, that is used by Spinoza in a variety of forms as proof for the existence of God. But the immediate knowledge of God, which constitutes the basis of that proof, whatever it may mean in the case of Spinoza, is with him not a knowledge based upon revelation.[84]

[83] *De Fide Orthodoxa* I, 1 (PG, 94, 789 B–792 A); cf. I, 3 (793 B–797 A).
[84] Cf. H. A. Wolfson, *The Philosophy of Spinoza*, chapter on "Proofs of the Existence of God."

CHAPTER XI

THE UNKNOWABILITY OF GOD AND DIVINE PREDICATES

I. Unity, Incorporeality, Simplicity

AMONG the scriptural presuppositions with which he started his philosophy Philo mentions explicitly the existence and unity of God. He does not include among them the incorporeality of God. Still throughout his writings the incorporeality of God is assumed. He directly describes God as incorporeal (ἀσώματος).[1] He criticizes those who assign to God a "space" (χώρα),[2] that is to say, those who consider God as a corporeal being. He includes among his scriptural presuppositions the belief in the existence of "incorporeal ideas" (ἀσώματοι ἰδέαι),[3] with the implication that the God who created the ideas is likewise incorporeal.

This difference in Philo's treatment of the principles of the unity and incorporeality of God reflects a similar difference in the treatment of these two principles in Scripture. The principle of the unity of God is explicitly stated in Scripture in a variety of passages, ranging from the assertion that no other god is like God [4] to the assertion that there is none else beside the Lord who is God [5] or that all other acclaimed deities are no gods or vanities.[6] Whatever difference in the conception of the unity of God may be indicated by these two types of assertion, there can be no doubt that by the time of Philo, in both Palestinian and Hellenistic Judaism, the conception of the absolute unity of God was already

---

[1] *Spec.* II, 30, 176.
[2] *Somn.* I, 32, 184; cf. above, I, 176.
[3] *Spec.* I, 60, 327.
[4] Deut. 3: 24, *et passim.*
[5] Deut. 4: 35; I Kings 8: 60.
[6] Deut. 32: 21.

firmly established.[7] Philo dwells on it in his explanation of
the first two of the ten commandments [8] and when he once
happens to quote from Scripture the expression "the most
high God" (θεὸς ὕψιστος),[9] which expression is used in Greek
with the implication of polytheism,[10] he hastens to quote the
verse "there is none beside Him," [11] in order to show that in
Scripture that expression does not mean that "there is any
other God not most high." [12] In Palestine this belief in the
unity of God constituted a principle of faith which was twice
daily confessed by the recitation of the verse "Hear, O
Israel; the Lord our God, the Lord is one." [13] Undoubtedly
the same confession of the belief in the unity of God was also
followed twice daily by Hellenistic Jews. It is probably because this principle was so commonly well known among
those of his contemporaries to whom he addressed himself
in his works that Philo never directly quotes in support of it
that classical scriptural proof-text. The principle of the
incorporeality of God, however, with its implication of a
distinction between things corporeal and things incorporeal
does not directly occur in Scripture. It is doubtful whether in
Scripture there is any conception of a distinction between
corporeality and incorporeality with all its philosophic implications of a distinction between matter and form, po-
tentiality and actuality, divisibility and simplicity, and mutability and immutability. Indeed there is in Scripture an
indication of some contrast between flesh and spirit [14] or between flesh and soul,[15] but there is no indication that by
spirit and soul were meant any such principles as form or
immateriality.

[7] Cf. above, I, 9 f., 13 f.
[8] *Decal.* 12, 52–16, 81; *Spec.* I, 3, 12–5, 31.
[9] Gen. 14: 18.
[10] Cf. above, I, 12, 40.
[11] Deut. 4: 39.

[12] *Leg. All.* III, 26, 82.
[13] Deut. 6: 4.
[14] Isa. 31: 3.
[15] Ps. 84: 3; Job 14: 22.

Still that which later came to be known as the principle of
the incorporeality of God is a fundamental scriptural belief.
"Incorporeality" is merely the expression in philosophic
terminology of what is implied in the scriptural doctrine of
the unlikeness of God to other beings. This doctrine is repeatedly stated in Scripture in a variety of ways. It is to be
found in the reminder of the historical fact that "ye saw no
manner of form on the day that the Lord spoke unto you in
Horeb out of the midst of the fire"; [16] it is similarly to be
found in the legal injunction not to represent God by "a
graven image, even any manner of likeness, of anything that
is in heaven above, or that is in the earth beneath, or that
is in the water under the earth"; [17] and it is also to be found
in the rhetorical question "To whom will ye liken Me, and
make Me equal, and compare Me, that we may be like." [18]
One can readily see the great philosophical potentialities contained in this scriptural doctrine of the unlikeness of God.
All that was necessary for its transformation into the philosophic principle of the incorporeality of God was an acquaintance with philosophical speculations about the world
and its constituent parts. Once one had learned that the
world consists of elements and that elements consist of
matter and form at once the doctrine of the unlikeness of
God to other beings could come to mean exactly what Plato
and Aristotle meant when they speak of the ideas or of God
as being incorporeal.

Philo had learned that the world and all things therein
consist of elements and of matter and form, and in the light
of this new knowledge which he had learned from Greek

[16] Deut. 4: 15.
[17] Deut. 4: 15; Exod. 20: 4.
[18] Isa. 46: 5; cf. 40: 18; 40: 25. In Greek philosophy the unlikeness of God to
other beings is asserted by Xenophanes (cf. above, I, 17) and by Antisthenes (cf.
below, p. 125).

philosophy he raised the scriptural principle of the unlikeness of God to the philosophic principle of the incorporeality of God.

As a scriptural proof-text for the principle of the unlikeness of God Philo quotes the verse which in the Septuagint reads "God is not like a man," [19] and, though Scripture elsewhere compares God to man,[20] it is the former statement which he declares to be "leading to the truth," [21] or to be "confirmed by the most certain truth," [22] or to be the one which "pertains to the truth, for, in reality, God is not as man, nor again, as the sun, nor as the heaven, nor as the perceptible universe, but as God, if it is justifiable to assert that also." [23] Retaining the original scriptural vocabulary he restates this principle in his statements that God "will not admit of similitude (ὁμοιότητα) or comparison (σύγκρισιν) or analogy (παραβολήν)." [24] But as one trained in philosophy he saw that the underlying reason for the unlikeness of God to other beings is the incorporeality of His nature and thus restating that scriptural principle in philosophic language he says that "the friends of the soul" or "the companions of the soul, who can hold converse with intelligible incorporeal natures, do not compare the Existent to any form of created things." [25] The expression "friends of the soul" (ψυχῆς φίλοι) reflects Plato's expression "friends of ideas" (εἰδῶν φίλοι)[26] as a description of those philosophers who believe in the existence of incorporeal natures, and what Philo therefore means to say here is that the scriptural doctrine of the unlikeness of God rests upon the philosophic doctrine of the incorporeality of God. "Unlikeness" thus with

---

[19] Num. 23: 19.
[20] Deut. 1: 31.
[21] *Somn.* I, 40, 237.
[22] *Immut.* 11, 54.
[23] *Qu. in Gen.* II, 54 (Harris, *Fragments*, p. 24).
[24] *Ibid.*
[25] *Immut.* 11, 55.
[26] *Sophist* 248 A.

him becomes "incorporeality" and the denial of the likeness
of God to any other being comes to mean with him the exclusion from God's nature of anything that may, however
indirectly, imply corporeality, so that God, he says, not only
has no body or bodily organs or sense-perception [27] but also
no such human emotions as jealousy, wrath, and anger.[28]
Moreover, since the philosophic principle of incorporeality
implies also simplicity and uncompoundedness, the scriptural doctrine of the unlikeness of God comes also to mean
with him that God is simple and uncompounded. He thus
says, by implication, of those friends of the soul who do not
compare God to any form of created things that they believe also that He is a simple nature (ἁπλῆ φύσις) and unmixed (ἀμιγῆ) and that He is also ἀσύγκριτον, a term which
means both "incomparable" and "not compounded." [29]
The scriptural principle of the unlikeness of God is thus
raised to the philosophic principle of the incorporeality and
hence also simplicity of God.

Having thus raised scriptural "unlikeness" to philosophic
"incorporeality" and hence "simplicity," Philo then undertakes to raise also scriptural "unity" to its philosophic implication of "simplicity," thus ultimately making the
principles of "unity," "incorporeality," and "simplicity"
mutually implicative.

In Scripture, the term one, when applied to God, means
only numerical unity. It is merely a denial of external plural-
ity: in this case a denial of polytheism. There are not many
gods; there is only one God. In the Aristotelian philosophic
vocabulary by the time of Philo, this kind of unity of God
would be described by the term one (τὸ ἕν) as distinguished
from the term simple (τὸ ἁπλοῦν). As stated by Aristotle,

[27] *Immut.* 12, 57–13, 60.
[28] *Ibid.*, 60.　　　[29] *Ibid.* 11, 56.

"one means a measure" and it may apply to things which
in themselves are constituted of many parts, whereas "simple means that the thing itself has a certain nature," that
is to say, it is indivisible and without parts.[30] But in the
philosophy of Aristotle, owing to the principle of the incorporeality of God, God is not only one but He is also
simple,[31] for He is indivisible and without parts.[32] Moreover, while the one and the simple are different, still the term
one is, according to Aristotle, always relative to the term
indivisible, for, as he says, "in general those things that do
not admit of division are one in so far as they do not admit
of it," [33] and "that which is one is indivisible, either absolutely or *qua* one," [34] so that the more indivisible a thing is
the more one it is. The term one, according to Aristotle,
therefore, has two meanings. On the one hand, in so far as
it may apply also to things which are divisible, it is to be
distinguished from the term simple; but, on the other hand,
in so far as, in its application to those things divisible, it
applies to them only with reference to that aspect of them
which does not admit of division, it is to be understood as
having the same meaning as the term simple. Since God is
absolutely indivisible, the term one applied to Him must
include, according to Aristotle, also His simplicity.

Evidently with all this in the back of his mind Philo tries
to show that the scriptural conception of the unity of God
means not only numerical unity but also indivisibility and
hence simplicity. The numerical unity of God has already
been established in his mind by the first two of the ten commandments [35] and also by the verse "the Lord thy God is

---

[30] *Metaph.* XII, 7, 1072a, 32-34; cf. *Phys.* VIII, 10, 267b, 25-26.
[31] *Metaph.* XII, 7, 1072a, 32-33.
[32] *Phys.* VIII, 10, 267b, 25-26.
[33] *Metaph.* V, 6, 1016b, 3-5.
[34] *Ibid.* X, 1, 1053b, 7-8.   [35] *Decal.* 12, 52-16, 81; *Spec.* I, 3, 13-5, 31.

alone God, in heaven above and on earth beneath, and there is none beside Him." [36] Taking now the verse "It is not good that man should be alone (μόνον)," [37] he tries to show, by playing upon the word "alone" — μόνον — that this verse contains, as we have shown above,[38] three other meanings of the principle of the unity of God: first, the uniqueness of God; second, the self-sufficiency of God; third, the simplicity of God. The third of these meanings, which is characterized by him as a "better" interpretation of the verse, is stated as follows: "God is alone and one alone; not composite; a simple (ἁπλῆ) nature," that is to say, not composite as we are "of soul and body," nor composite as soul is "of a rational part and an irrational part"; nor, again, composite as body is of different contrarieties, such as "hot — cold, heavy — light, dry — moist." [39]

Of these three examples of composition which he excludes from God's nature, the first one, that of body and soul, is a general philosophic commonplace; the last one, that of "warm — cold, heavy — light, dry — moist," reflects Aristotle's description of the four elements out of which all bodies are composed as the contrarieties of "hot — cold, dry — moist, heavy — light"; [40] but, with regard to the second one, that of "a rational part and irrational part" in the soul, it is to be assumed that he refers to Plato's and his own conception of the rational and irrational parts of the soul as constituting real parts, differing from each other in their essential nature, one being material and the other immaterial.[41] In itself this statement probably does not exclude

[36] Deut. 4: 39; *Leg. All.* III, 26, 82: cf. above, I, 171.
[37] Gen. 2: 18.
[38] Cf. above, I, 171–173.
[39] *Leg. All.* II, 1, 2.
[40] *De Gen. et Corr.* II, 2, 329b, 18–19.
[41] Cf. above, I, 385 ff., 389 ff.

from God a purely logical distinction such as Aristotle con-
ceives between the rational and irrational parts of the soul.
In all these statements, therefore, the exclusion of divisibility from God's nature refers only to such divisibility as is
incompatible with His incorporeality.

II. "Without Quality" — ἄποιος

But in a number of passages in Philo there occurs the
statement that God is "without quality" (ἄποιος). This
statement has been taken to mean that God "does not belong to a class, but is *sui generis*," for the term "quality" is
said to be used by Philo in "its proper logical meaning" as
"that the possession of which makes you a member of a
class; and when any quality is ascribed to you, you are to
that extent placed on a level with a number of other individuals." [1] By this interpretation it is meant that the term
"quality" is used by Philo in the sense of "genus" or
"species" or "specific difference," and therefore whenever
he says of God that He is "without quality" he means
thereby that God has no genus and no species and no specific
difference.

True though it is, as we shall see later, that God to Philo
cannot be described by genus and species and specific difference, it is still doubtful whether the denial of this manner
of describing God may be derived directly from his statements that God is without quality. For the term quality,
by the time of Philo, had three distinct meanings, though not
altogether unrelated to each other. In the first place, it
meant, in Aristotle, one of his ten categories, and as such it
was used by him in the sense of an accident inherent in a

---

[1] Drummond, II, 24. It is also in this sense that the term ἄποιος is usually
translated in Colson.

corporeal object.[2] In the second place, it meant, again in Aristotle, "genus" or "species" [3] or "differentia," [4] the last of which is also described by him as "the differentia of the substance" [5] or a "differentia according to substance." [6] In the third place, it meant, among the Stoics, one of their own four categories, in which sense it was the equivalent of the Aristotelian "form" as contrasted with "matter." [7] When, therefore, Philo repeatedly says that God is "without quality," we must make a thorough examination of all the passages in which he uses the term quality, as well as of all the passages in which he says that God is without quality, before we can decide with certainty in which of these three senses he uses the terms quality and without quality.

An examination of all such passages will prove that nowhere does Philo definitely use the term quality or without quality in the second of its Aristotelian senses, namely, as that of genus or species or specific difference.

With regard to passages in which the term "quality" occurs, it can be determined from its various contexts that, with the exception of only one passage, in all of them the term is used by Philo in its first Aristotelian sense, namely, as that which expresses an accident in some corporeal object. He thus speaks of the stars shining with their own true quality,[8] the sweet quality of water,[9] the qualities of body and soul,[10] the created man partaking of qualities,[11] virtues as qualities,[12] the material out of which God created every

---

[2] *Categ.* c. 8, 8b, 25 ff.

[3] *Ibid.*, 5, 3b, 19–21. In this sense, on the whole, is the term quality also used by Plato.   [4] *Topica* IV, 6, 128a, 26–27.

[5] *Metaph.* V, 14, 1020a, 33.   [6] *Ibid.*, 35–36.

[7] Cf. A. Trendelenburg, *Geschichte der Kategorienlehre*, p. 222.

[8] *Opif.* 18, 57.   [10] *Ibid.* 49, 141.

[9] *Ibid.* 45, 131.   [11] *Ibid.* 46, 134.

[12] *Leg. All.* I, 26, 79; cf. Aristotle's use of quality as an accident in the sense of virtue and vice and good and evil in general (*Metaph.* V, 14, 1020b, 18–25).

particular quality,[13] the quality of a brazen serpent,[14] the heaven and the world are forms endowed with qualities perceptible by the senses,[15] the qualities of things,[16] the qualities as the handiwork of passion,[17] qualities as distinguished from properties and hence in the sense of accidents,[18] qualities of colors and figures,[19] passion and vice as a substance devoid of form and quality,[20] the qualities of mixtures,[21] the qualities of the elements,[22] the quality of living creatures,[23] the qualities of material substances,[24] the quality of scents,[25] bodily qualities,[26] quality as one of the ten Aristotelian categories and hence in the sense of accident,[27] qualities in sculpture and painting,[28] qualities in things patterned after the ideas,[29] qualities of bodily things perceived by the senses,[30] the loss of quality in anything crushed,[31] qualities created by God in things,[32] virtues judged not by quantity but by quality,[33] matter as the substratum for every kind of shape and quality,[34] and the quality of the physical world.[35]

The one exception which we have referred to is to be found in a passage in which Philo seems to use the term quality in the sense of specific difference. In that passage he speaks of the right-angled triangle as "the starting-point

[13] Ibid. II, 7, 19.
[14] Ibid. II, 20, 80.
[15] Immut. 13, 62.
[16] Deter. 6, 15.
[17] Ibid. 6, 16; cf. above, n. 12.
[18] Agr. 3, 13; cf. below, p. 132.
[19] Plant. 32, 133.
[20] Conf. 18, 85.
[21] Ibid. 37, 185, 186, 187.
[22] Heres 50, 247.
[23] Fug. 2, 13.
[24] Somn. I, 5, 27.
[25] Jos. 23, 142.
[26] Mos. I, 27, 97.
[27] Decal. 8, 31. In the statement here "I have quality in so far as I am a man," the term "quality," we take it refers to the accident quality, as in the statement that the created man partakes of quality (Opif. 46, 134). Drummond (II, 24), however, takes the term "quality" in the sense of species.
[28] Spec. I, 5, 29.
[29] Ibid., 8, 47; 60, 327, 329.
[30] Ibid., 16, 90.
[31] Ibid., 60, 328.
[32] Ibid. IV, 35, 187.
[33] Praem. 19, 112; cf. above, n. 12.
[34] Cont. 1, 4.
[35] Aet. 16, 79, 81.

of all qualities (ποιοτήτων)" or as "the source of every figure
(σχήματος) and every quality (ποιότητος)." [36] By this he
undoubtedly means that the different "species" of figures
are to be known as the different "qualities" of the generic
"figure," and consequently the right-angled triangle, which
is the generic figure, is the starting-point or the source of all
those different qualities, or different species, of that generic
figure. Thus also Aristotle, wishing to illustrate his use of
the term "quality" in the sense of "specific difference," says
that "a circle is a figure of a particular quality because it is
without angles," [37] that is to say, "figure" is the genus and
"without angles" is its quality or specific difference.

Similarly with regard to passages in which Philo says that
God is "without quality," it can also be determined from
the various contexts that, with the exception of only three
passages, in all of them the quality denied of God is quality
in the sense of an accident existing in a body, and the denial
of such a quality of God is either said or assumed by Philo
to follow from the incorporeality of God or from His being
unlike any corporeal creature. Thus in one passage he asks:
"For why, O mind, dost thou hoard and treasure in thyself
those wrong opinions, that God is as graven images are, of
this or that quality (ποιός), God the being that is without
quality (ἄποιος), and that He, the incorruptible, is, as molten
images are, corruptible." [38] From the context of this passage
it is quite evident that just as by the qualities of graven
images he means accidents in a corporeal object, so also by
the qualities which he denies of God he means accidental
qualities. Similarly in another passage he says that "God
is without quality (ἄποιος) and not only without the shape
of man (ἀνθρωπόμορφος)." [39] In this passage the contrast be-

[36] *Opif.* 32, 97.
[37] *Metaph.* V, 14, 1020a, 35.
[38] *Leg. All.* III, 11, 36.
[39] *Ibid.* I, 13, 36.

tween "shape of man" and "quality" probably has reference to Aristotle's enumeration of four kinds of "quality"
($\pi o\iota \acute{o}\tau \eta s$), one of which he calls "shape" ($\mu o\rho \phi \acute{\eta}$),[40] and the
meaning of this statement therefore is that God is not only
without the quality of "shape" but also without any of the
other three kinds of "quality." Anyhow, there is no con-
clusive evidence that the term "without quality" here is
used in the sense of without genus and species. Still less
reason have we to assume that Philo denies genus and species
of God in the passage in which he says that "the companions
of the soul, who can converse with intelligible incorporeal
natures, do not compare the Existent to any form ($\iota \delta \acute{e}a$) of
created things, but dissociate Him from every quality
($\pi o\iota \acute{o}\tau \eta \tau o s$)," apprehending God as "bare existence ($\H{u}\pi a\rho \xi \iota \nu$)
without any figure ($\chi a\rho a\kappa \tau \^{\eta} \rho o s$)" and admitting to their
minds "the conception of existence ($\tau \grave{o}$ $\epsilon \^{\iota} \nu a\iota$) only, without
investing it with any shape ($\mu o\rho \phi \acute{\omega} \sigma a\nu \tau \epsilon s$)," in contrast to
those who "are unable to cast off from them the garment of
flesh and to descry a nature which is alone, self-sufficient,
simple, unmixed, and uncompounded." [41] In this passage,
it will be noticed, the term "quality" is contrasted with the
"form" and "shape" of "created things" and also with
"the garment of flesh." From this it may be inferred that
it is used in the sense of accidental quality. This is quite
evidently also the meaning of the denial of qualities of God
in his statement that Laban, as his name which means
"white," implies, relied on "qualities" ($\pi o\iota o\tau \acute{\eta} \tau \omega \nu$), whereas
Jacob discerned "the nature which is without quality
($\H{a}\pi o\iota o\nu$)," [42] for the association of the term "qualities" with
"white" quite evidently implies that the term "qualities"
here is used in the sense of accidental qualities. Finally this
meaning of the denial of qualities of God is quite obviously

[40] *Categ.* c. 8, 10a, 12. [41] *Immut.* 11, 55–56. [42] *Cher.* 21, 67.

also implied in his passage wherein from the verse "Ye shall
not make together with Me gods of silver, and gods of gold
ye shall not make to yourselves"[43] he derives the principle
that God is "without quality (ἄποιον) and one [and un-
originate] and incorruptible and unchangeable."[44]

The three exceptions which we have referred to are to be
found in three passages in which the qualities denied of
God refer, as we shall try to show, to qualities in the Stoic
sense of the term. In one of these passages, after stating that
God has shown his "nature" (φύσιν) to no human being but
has rendered it "invisible" (ἀόρατον) to our whole race, he
exclaims: "Who can assert of the First Cause either that
it is without body or that it is a body, that it is with quality
(ποιόν) or that it is without quality (ἄποιον)? In a word who
can make any positive assertion concerning His substance
(οὐσίας) or quality (ποιότητος) or state (σχέσεως) or motion
(κινήσεως)?"[45] In this passage, it will be noticed, Philo
uses four terms, namely, substance, quality, state, and motion. These four terms, it can be shown, represent three of
the four Stoic categories. The Stoic categories are usually
given as (1) substratum (ὑποκείμενον) or substance (οὐσία),
(2) quality (ποιόν), (3) changing states (πὼς ἔχον), (4) varied
relations (πρός τί πως ἔχον).[46] Now, of the four terms used
by Philo, the first two, substance and quality, are exactly the
terms used by the Stoics for the first two of their four categories. As for the other two terms used by Philo, the term
"state" (σχέσις) is used by the Stoics themselves as synonymous with their third category "changing states"[47] and
the term "motion" is included by them under the same

[43] Exod. 22: 23.
[44] Leg. All. I, 15, 51.
[45] Ibid. III, 73, 206.
[46] Cf. Arnim, II, 369–375.
[47] Cf. Arnim, II, 376, p. 126, ll. 14–15.

third category "changing states." [48] Thus the four terms used in the passage quoted from Philo represent three of the four categories of the Stoics. That by the terms "substance" and "quality" in the passage quoted Philo means the two Stoic categories may be inferred also from the fact that by the term substance here, as may be judged from his previous use of the term body in the same passage, he means body or matter, which corresponds exactly to the Stoic use of the term substance. As in this passage it is quite evident that the terms substance and quality are used by Philo in the sense of the Stoic categories, we may infer further that it is in the same sense that he also uses these two terms in two other passages. Thus when he says, in one passage, that "to inquire about substance ($oὐσίας$) or quality ($ποιότητος$) in God is a folly fit for the world's childhood" [49] or when he asks, in another passage, "Who the Creator is as to His substance or quality," [50] the terms substance and quality are used in the Stoic sense. Inasmuch, however, as the Stoic "substance" and "quality" correspond to the Aristotelian "matter" and "form," [51] the statements in all these three passages to the effect that God has no qualities merely mean that in God there is no distinction of "matter" and "form."

From all this, then, we may gather that as a corollary of the principles of the incorporeality, simplicity, and indivisibility of God Philo excluded from God any composition (a) of body and soul, or (b) of the four elements, or (c) of substance and accidental quality, or (d) of matter and form.

[48] Cf. Arnim, II, 399–400, where $τὸ πὼς ἔχον$ is said to include "time," "place," and "number," and hence also by inference "motion," for "time," according to the Stoic definition, reproduced also by Philo, "is the interval of the motion of the world" (cf. above, I, 319).

[49] *Post.* 48, 168.   [50] *Abr.* 31, 163.

[51] Cf. Trendelenburg, *op. cit.*, p. 222.

But so far we have not yet found any definite evidence that he excluded from God also any distinction of genus and species.

Still, logically, it can be shown, Philo's statement in the three passages quoted above that in God there is no distinction of what the Stoics call "substance" and "quality" may imply also that, according to him, there is in God no distinction of genus and species. For with regard to the Stoic "substance" and "quality," while on the one hand they correspond to Aristotle's "matter" and "form," on the other hand they also correspond to "genus".and "species."[52] In fact, in Aristotle himself, the distinction between genus and species is often conceived after the analogy of the distinction between matter and form.[53] In those passages, therefore, in which Philo states that there is no distinction of substance and quality in God, while he undoubtedly, as we have shown, draws upon the vocabulary of the Stoic enumeration of the four categories, he may also use these terms in the sense of genus and species, meaning thereby also that there is no distinction of genus and species in God, for logically, it may be maintained, that which does not consist of matter and form has no genus and species.

Having once established that logically Philo would be justified in denying that in God there is any distinction of genus and species, we may now discern the implication of such a denial in several places in his writings.

In one place, after explaining that the essence of God cannot be apprehended by any direct or immediate approach, he adds that by such a mode of approach, had it been possible, "His quality (οἷος) would have been made known." [54] Here quite evidently the relative pronominal adjective οἷος is

---

[52] *Ibid.*
[53] Cf. *Metaph.* V, 28, 1024b, 8–9; VII, 12, 1038a, 6–8.   [54] *Post.* 48, 169.

used by him in the sense of genus and species or genus and specific difference. By the same token, we have reason to believe, the indefinite pronominal adjective ποιός could also be used by him in the same sense. Consequently, his many statements quoted above about God being "without quality" (ἄποιος), which in themselves, as we have shown from their context, mean only that God is without accidental quality, may now be taken to imply also indirectly that He is without genus and species.

In another place he says that "the contemplation of God by the soul alone without speech . . . is based on the indivisible unity (κατὰ τὴν ἀδιαίρετον μονάδα)." [55] It is quite evident that what he means here is that God cannot be described by spoken words because He is in His essence an indivisible unity. Now the indivisible unity of His essence means not only that He is not composed of matter and form but also that in Him there is no distinction of genus and species, for it is the absence of the latter that makes it impossible for us to describe Him in words.

In still another place he says that God is "the most generic" (τὸ γενικώτατον). [56] In a previous discussion of this statement we have already explained the general meaning of this designation of God. [57] But in its present connection we want to show that it has an additional meaning. It means that God, being the highest genus, has within Him no distinction of genus and species, for only that which is between the highest genus and the ultimate species has within it the distinction of genus and species, being the genus of that which is below it and the species of that which is above it. But since God is the highest genus He has no distinction of genus and species, that is, He belongs to no

[55] *Gig.* 11, 52.
[56] *Leg. All.* II, 21, 86.   [57] Cf. above, I, 251–252.

class and hence we do not know what He is. That this is the meaning of his description of God as "the most generic" may be inferred from the proof-text upon which he bases his view and from his discussion of that proof-text. The proof-text is the verse in which it is said that when the children of Israel saw the manna, "they said to one another, what is this (τί ἐστι τοῦτο)? — for they knew not what it was." [58] Drawing upon this explanation, he says that manna is "the most generic (τὸ γενικώτατον)," for the manna is called "what (τί), and that suggests the primary genus of all things." [59] Elsewhere the term manna is more fully explained by him as meaning "what is this (τί ἐστι τοῦτο)." [60] Undoubtedly this statement reflects the Stoic teaching that "the something" (τὸ τι) is "the most generic (τὸ γενικώτατον) of all," [61] the interrogative and the indefinite pronouns meaning to him the same, both of them implying that it is something which belongs to no class. What he therefore means to say is that God is a highest genus because one may ask of Him, as one does of the manna, what is this (τί ἐστι τοῦτο)? — that is to say, we do not know its τί ἐστι, its essence, its whatness. Now to say of God that we do not know His essence means that He has no genus and species.

III. THE UNNAMABILITY AND UNKNOWABILITY OF GOD

Philo's denial of a distinction of genus and species in God must have led him to a denial of the possibility of defining God, for a definition, as may be gathered from Philo's definition of man as being either a "rational mortal animal" or a "hopeful animal," [1] consists, according to him, as it does

---

[58] Exod. 16: 15.
[59] *Leg. All.* II, 21, 86.
[60] *Leg. All.* III, 49, 169.
[61] Sextus, *Pyrrhoniae Hypotyposes* II, 86.

[1] *Deter.* 38, 139.

according to Aristotle, of the combination of genus and species. And since God cannot be defined, no concept can be formed of His essence, for the concept of the essence of a thing is formed by its definition.[2] Philo therefore maintains that "it is wholly impossible that God according to His essence should be known (κατανοηθῆναι) by any creature," [3] for God is "incomprehensible." [4] Together with the incomprehensibility of God he speaks also of the unnamability and ineffability of God, for God, he says, "is unnamable (ἀκατονομάστου) and ineffable (ἀρρήτου) and in every way incomprehensible (ἀκαταλήπτου)." [5] By "incomprehensible" he does not mean that God is not comprehended by the senses but rather, as he explicitly says elsewhere, that "He is not comprehended by the mind." [6]

Now neither Plato nor Aristotle definitely says that God according to His essence cannot be known or is incomprehensible or cannot be envisaged even in mind. In Plato indeed the ideas are like the God of Philo "incorporeal," [7] "invisible and imperceptible by the sense," [8] "immovable" [9] and "immutable" [10] and similarly of God, whether He is the idea of the good or something distinct from the ideas, he says that He is simple (ἁπλοῦν) and is unchangeable,[11] and still the ideas as well as God are considered by him as knowable. With regard to the ideas he says that "being" (οὐσία), that is, the totality of the ideas, is known by the intelligence (γνῶσις) and that after proper preparation we can ultimately arrive at a knowledge of "what the essence of beauty is" (ὅ ἐστι καλόν),[12] and with regard to that which is

---

[2] *Topica* I, 5, 101b, 39; *Anal. Post.* II, 10, 93b, 29.
[3] *Post.* 48, 167.
[4] *Ibid.* 169.
[5] *Somn.* I, 11, 67.
[6] *Immut.* 13, 62.
[7] *Sophist* 246 B.
[8] *Timaeus* 52 A.
[9] *Ibid.* 38 A.
[10] *Phaedo* 78 D.
[11] *Republic* II, 382 E.
[12] *Symposium* 211 C.

"ever unchangeably real," evidently including both God and the ideas, he says that it is "comprehensible (περιληπτόν) by the mind with the aid of reason." [13] He admits, of course, that "we do not sufficiently know the good" [14] and that "in the world of knowledge the idea of the good appears last of all and is seen only with an effort," [15] but this does not mean that it is unknowable.

Similarly in Aristotle, God is described as one and incorporeal and simple and indivisible. [16] If that simplicity and indivisibility excluded the distinction of genus and species in God, then, of course, God could not be defined and hence God could not be known. But Aristotle never says explicitly that the simplicity of God excludes the distinction of genus and species and that God cannot be defined and cannot be known. Quite to the contrary, on the basis of an analysis of his own statements, it can be shown that, according to him, God's simplicity does not exclude from His essence the distinction of genus and species.

And just as Plato and Aristotle do not definitely say that God is unknowable so do they not definitely say that God cannot be named or spoken of. Indeed Plato says that "the Maker and Father of this All it is a hard task to find and having found Him it is impossible to declare Him to all men." [17] The meaning of this passage, however, is not that God cannot be *declared*, that is, described, but rather that He cannot be declared to *all men*, because, according to Plato, it requires certain specific preparations to arrive at a knowledge of the ideas, [18] and by the same token also at a

[13] *Timaeus* 28 A.
[14] *Republic* VI, 505 A.
[15] *Ibid.* VII, 517 B.
[16] *Phys.* VIII, 10, 267b, 25–26; *Metaph.* XII, 7, 1072a, 32–33.
[17] *Timaeus* 28 C.
[18] *Phaedrus* 249 B f.

knowledge of God, which preparations are not common to all men. It was not until later, on their becoming acquainted with Philo's view of the unknowability and ineffability of God, that the Church Fathers raised the question whether Plato meant by his statement that God was ineffable or not. Clement of Alexandria takes this passage as meaning that God is ineffable, "for," he asks, "how can that be effable (ῥητόν) which is neither genus, nor difference, nor species, nor individual, nor number?"[19] So was also the interpretation of this passage of Plato by Celsus.[20] In opposition to Celsus, however, Origen argues that from the wording of Plato's statement it is to be inferred that "he does not speak of God as ineffable (ἄρρητον) and unnamable (ἀκατονόμαστον); on the contrary, he implies that He is effable and that there are a few to whom he may be declared."[21]

Nor is the conception of the ineffability or unnamability of God found in any other Greek philosopher before Philo. The statement that the view "that God has no name was likewise known to the Greeks"[22] is ill-founded. The sources quoted in corroboration of this statement are the pseudo-Aristotelian *De Mundo*,[23] Dio Chrysostom,[24] Seneca,[25] Maxi-

---

[19] *Stromata* V, 12 (PG, 9, 121 A); cf. quotation from Plato on p. 116 B.

[20] Origen, *Contra Celsum* VII, 42 (PG, 11, 1481 C–1484 A). So also Numenius is of the belief that the Gnostic doctrine of an "unknowable God" is based upon Plato. Cf. Eusebius, *Praeparatio Evangelica* XI, 18, 539b–c.

[21] *Ibid.* VII, 43 (PG, 11, 1481 C). Cf. H. A. Wolfson, "The Knowability and Describability of God in Plato and Aristotle," *Harvard Studies in Classical Philology*, LVI–LVII (1945–46), pp. 233–249.

[22] J. Geffcken, *Zwei griechische Apologeten* (1907), p. 38, followed by A. Marmorstein, *The Old Rabbinic Doctrine of God*, I (Oxford University Press, 1927), p. 17. On the basis of this statement, Marmorstein (p. 18) says of the magic tablet of the Necropolis of Adrumetum that its reference to "the sacred name which is not to be uttered . . . was very old and reflects the conditions on which the LXX is based." This magic tablet belongs to the second and third centuries A.D. (cf. G. A. Deissmann, *Bible Studies*, p. 279

[23] *De Mundo*, c. 7, 401a, 12 ff.

[24] *Orationes*, XII, 75–78.   [25] *Naturales Quaestiones*, II, 45.

mus of Tyre,[26] Celsus,[27] and Hermes Trismegistus.[28] Now, with the exception of Seneca, who was a contemporary of Philo, all these sources are later than Philo. Besides, not all these sources state that God is unnamable. The pseudo-Aristotelian *De Mundo* and Seneca only state that God has many names, which is only a repetition of the Stoic view that God is called by many names.[29] This is quite different from saying that God has no name. Nor does Dio Chrysostom say that God has no name. All he says is that either Zeus is called by certain names (ἐπονομάζεται) or his attributes are represented without the help of words in art, concluding that, with regard to the latter, "I have presented them as far as it was possible to do so, since I was not able to name them."[30] This does not mean that Zeus is unnamable. Indeed, among the Greeks, the appellation "the God" was used at Delphi for Apollo and at Eleusis for Pluto, and also the appellation "the Goddess" was used at Athens for Athena and at Eleusis for Persephone, but this does not mean that the proper names of these deities were not allowed to be uttered; it only means that their proper names were so well known that there was no need to mention them.[31] Nor is evidence for the conception of the ineffability of God among the Greeks prior to Philo to be derived from Stobaeus' attribution to the Neopythagorean pseudo-Archytas the view that the principle which is above mind, namely, God, "pertains to an unutterable (ἄλογον) and in-

---

[26] *Dissertationes*, VIII, 10.

[27] Origen, *Contra Celsum* I, 24.

[28] *Hermetica* (ed. W. Scott) V, 1a; V, 10. Reference to *Hermetica* as the source of Philo's conception of the ineffability of God is given also by Azariah dei Rossi, *Me'or 'Enayim: Imre Binah*, ch. 4, ed. Wilnah, 1866, p. 111.

[29] Diogenes, VII, 147; cf. VII, 135.

[30] *Op. cit.*, XII, 78.

[31] Cf. M P. Nilsson, *Greek Popular Religion* (Columbia University Press, 1940), p. 47.

effable (ἄρρητον) nature," [32] for it is not impossible that this view as reported and phrased by Stobaeus was formed under the influence of Philo.[33] From a period long before Philo, quite to the contrary, we have the explicit statement of the Stoic poet Aratus that Zeus is he "whom we human beings never allow to remain ineffable (ἄρρητον.)" [34]

The conclusion we have reached with regard to the absence of any evidence that in Greek philosophy before Philo there existed a conception of God as a being unknowable in His essence and unnamable and ineffable cannot be refuted by the findings of Norden in his study on the *agnostos theos*.[35] Norden proceeds in his study as follows. He starts out with the verse in Acts 17:23, in which Paul says to the people of Athens: "For as I passed by, and beheld your devotions, I found an altar with this inscription, 'To the unknown God' ('Αγνώστῳ θεῷ)." Usually the expression "the unknown God" here is taken by students of the New Testament to mean a God whose name happened to have been unknown to those who had set up the altar. Norden, however, takes it in the sense of an "unknowable God," that is to say, a God that by His nature cannot be known. He then

---

[32] Stobaeus, *Eclogae* I, p. 281, ll. 1–2.

[33] Cf. O. F. Gruppe, *Ueber die Fragmente des Archytas und der alteren Pythagoreer*, 1840, pp. 125 ff.; Zeller, III, 2⁴, p. 123, n. 5, with regard to the general question as to the dependence of the Neopythagoreans upon Hellenistic Judaism.

[34] *Phaenomena*, ll. 1–2.

[35] Cf. E. Norden, *Agnostos Theos*, 1913, pp. 1–124.
Nor is our conclusion to be refuted by the occurrence of the expression *agnostos theos* in other sources. In the Egyptian papyrus published by E. Kornemann in *Klio*, 7 (1907), 278, the expression οὐκ ἄγνωστος Φοῖβος θεός, does not mean "not unknowable God Phoebus" but rather "not unfamiliar God Phoebus" (cf. R. Reitzenstein, "Die Areopagrede des Paulus," *Neue Jahrbücher für das klassische Altertum*, 31 (1913), 415, n. 2). So also is undoubtedly the meaning of the expression θεοῖς ἀγν[ώστοις, assuming that this is how the expression is to be completed, in the Pergamum inscription published by H. Hepding in *Athenische Mitteilungen*, 35 (1910), 455. Cf. A. Wikenhauser, *Die Apostelgeschichte und ihr Geschichtswert*, 1921, pp. 371, 387–390.

goes on to show that Paul's reference to such an unknowable
God reflects a widely spread Greek philosophic view, and in
support of this he quotes passages (pages 24–30) in which
God is spoken of as "invisible" (ἀόρατος, ἀθεώρητος, ἀφανής)
and "incomprehensible" (ἀκατάληπτος). The term *agnostos*
used by Paul, he admits, is not found in the passages quoted
by him, but, as for that, he finds it in the Gnostic literature
(pages 65–73). The Gnostic literature, again he admits,
comes from a later period, but, as for that, he refers to the
view of certain scholars that there must have been a Gnosticism even before the Christian era (pages 65 and 70), and
this pre-Christian Gnosticism, he tries to show, had derived its conception of the unknowable God from Greek
philosophy (page 83). In support of his view, however, he
admits that he can produce only one passage — a passage in
which Heraclitus is reported to have said that "they pray
to these images, as if one were to talk with a man's house,
knowing not what gods or heroes are," taking the last phrase
to have the technical meaning of "knowing not the essence
of either gods or heroes" (pages 87–89).

Thus, apart from the conjectural assumption that the
Gnostic conception of the "unknowable God" dates from
pre-Christian times, Norden advances only two arguments
in support of the Greek origin of such a conception of God:
first, the passages in which God is spoken of as "invisible"
and "incomprehensible"; second, the fragment of Heraclitus. Now, with regard to the first, all the terms for the in-
visibility and the incomprehensibility of God in the passages
quoted, as may be judged from the contexts, deny only that
God can be seen or comprehended by the senses; they do
not say that God's essence cannot be comprehended by the ·
mind. With regard to the second, there is no definite proof
that in the vague words of Heraclitus there is anything be-

yond the mere assertion that those who worship the images of gods and heroes know nothing about those gods and heroes except what they have heard about them from hearsay, inasmuch as they have never seen them with their own eyes. In Philo, as we have seen, there is a formal distinction between the knowability of God's existence and the unknowability of His essence, and, in connection with the latter, expressing himself in terms not used by others before him about God, he says of God that He is "unnamable" and "ineffable" and "not comprehended by the mind."

In view of all this, when Philo derives from the principle of the simplicity of God the principle of the unknowability and unnamability of God, he has given expression to a view which must have been meant by him to be either a new interpretation of Plato and Aristotle or in opposition to them. Indirectly, from the fact that Plato's statement with regard to the difficulty of finding God and the impossibility of declaring Him to others is taken by Philo, as we have shown, to refer to the existence of God,[36] it may perhaps be inferred that he believed Plato to have held that as for the essence of God it is even impossible to find it and not merely to declare it to others. But, as against this, there is the passage in which he tries to show how "all Greeks and barbarians," that is, all Greek and barbarian philosophers, acknowledge the existence of a God "whose nature is not only invisible by the eye but also hard to guess by the mind." [37] It will be noticed that with reference to the eye he says here that God's nature is "invisible" (ἀόρατος) and not merely "hard to see" (δυσόρατος), whereas with reference to the mind he says that it is only "hard to guess" (δυστόπαστος) but not "unguessable" (ἀτόπαστος) or "incomprehensible" (ἀκατά-

---

[36] Cf. above, p. 73.
[37] *Spec.* II, 29, 165.

$\lambda\eta\pi\tau\sigma s$).[38] Is it not possible that his choice of words here
was deliberate, because, to him, while philosophers have
indeed the conception of a God whose nature is "invisible"
and "hard to guess," they have no conception of a God whose
nature is absolutely "incomprehensible"? But, however
that may be, Philo was either giving new emphasis to a view
which he considered as being implicit in the views of philosophers or else he was giving utterance to an entirely new
view. In either case, we must probe for the reason of his
new view, or of his new emphasis upon a view of which he
thought to have found corroboration in the teachings of the
philosophers.

The explanation, we shall now try to show, is suggested
by Philo himself in two passages.

In one of these passages Philo shows how, starting with
the philosophic principle of the incorporeality of God,
which to him was also a scriptural principle, he arrives by
the aid of scriptural verses at the principles of the unknowability and unnamability of God. The passage is a homily
on the verse "And the Lord was seen by Abraham and said
to him, 'I am thy God.'"[39] Commenting upon this verse,
he first tries to disabuse the reader of the thought that God
was seen by Abraham in the literal sense of the term. "Do
not suppose," he says, "that the vision was presented to the
eyes of the body, for they see only the objects of sense and
those are composite, brimful of corruptibility, while the
divine is uncompounded and incorruptible."[40] The vision
of God here means, he argues, a mental vision, for "it is
natural that an intelligible object can be apprehended only

[38] Philo sometimes applies to God the terms δυστόπαστος καὶ δυσκατάληπτος
(*Spec.* I, 6, 32) and also the terms δυσόρατος καὶ δυστόπαστος (*Praem.* 6, 38). But,
strictly speaking, God is to him both ἀόρατος and ἀκατάληπτος.

[39] Gen. 17: 1.

[40] *Mut.* 1, 3.

by the mind.[41] Up to this point, it will be noticed, his interpretation of the verses contains nothing which is not in complete harmony with philosophic reasoning. For given a God who is incorporeal and uncompounded, He cannot be perceived by the senses. Whatever conception one forms of Him must be only in the mind. Plato and Aristotle and others have said that much.

But then Philo goes further and maintains that God cannot be apprehended by any man, not only as an object of sense but even as an object of intelligence, "for we have in us no organ by which we can envisage it, neither in sense, for it is not perceptible by sense, nor yet in mind." [42] This is quite evidently going beyond what is warranted by purely logical reasoning from the philosophic principle of the incorporeality of God. No philosopher, as we have seen, ever said so explicitly. Philo himself seems to have been conscious of the fact that he was going here beyond philosophy or, at least, beyond the explicit statements of philosophers, and so he hastens to support his view by scriptural verses. The scriptural verses which he quotes are "Moses went into the thick darkness, where God was" [43] and "Thou shalt see what is behind Me, but My face thou shalt not see." [44] From these verses he infers that God "by His very nature cannot be seen," [45] by which he means that God cannot be comprehended by the mind. Once he has established the incomprehensibility of God by these verses, he derives therefrom the impossibility of naming God, for "it is a logical consequence that no proper name even can be appropriately assigned to the truly existent," [46] and in proof of

[41] *Ibid.*, 6.
[42] *Ibid.* 2, 7.
[43] Exod. 20: 21; *Mut.* 2, 7; cf. *Post.* 5, 14.
[44] Exod. 33: 23; *Mut.* 2, 9; cf. *Spec.* I, 8, 41–49; *Post.* 5, 16.
[45] *Mut.* 2, 9.   [46] *Ibid.* 2, 11.

this he says: "Note that when the prophet desires to know what he must answer to those who ask about His name He says 'I am He that is,' [47] which is equivalent to 'My nature is to be, not to be spoken.'" [48] Another proof-text quoted by him is the verse "I appeared to Abraham, Isaac and Jacob as their God, but my name Lord I did not reveal to them." [49] And once he has established the unnamability of God by these verses, he derives therefrom the incomprehensibility of God, arguing that "indeed, if He is unnamable, He is also inconceivable and incomprehensible." [50] One may perhaps find a sort of circle in his reasoning here. Starting first with scriptural verses which he interprets to mean that God is incomprehensible, he derives therefrom that God is also unnamable. Then, supporting his logical conclusion that God is unnamable by a verse which explicitly says that the name of God was not revealed to those to whom He appeared, he derives therefrom that God is also incomprehensible. Probably what Philo means to say is that the incomprehensibility and the unnamability of God are logically implied in one another and that both of them rest primarily upon scriptural verses. As for these scriptural verses, it will be noticed, the ones which serve him as a proof-text for the unnamability of God are more explicit than the one which serves him as a proof-text for the incomprehensibility of God, and, consequently, even though the latter verse is quoted by him first, it is the former verse, that about the unnamability of God, which may be considered as the primary basis of his view about the incomprehensibility of God.

The verse "but my name Lord I did not reveal to them" is thus the basis of Philo's view that God is unnamable,

[47] Exod. 3: 14.   [49] Exod. 6: 3; *Mut.* 2, 13.
[48] *Mut.* 2, 11.   [50] *Mut.* 3, 15.

whence also his view, stated more generally, that God is incomprehensible and ineffable.

But besides this verse, which is quoted by him for that purpose, Philo must have found support for his view in several legal prohibitions in the Pentateuch.

First, there is the law which is described by Philo as a prohibition against naming (τὸ ὀνομάζειν) God.[51] The law, as it reads in Hebrew, is usually translated: "And he that blasphemeth the name of the Lord, he shall surely be put to death." [52] Now the Hebrew word *nakab* which is translated here "blaspheme" means both "to name" and "to curse." While in the Mishnah it is taken in the sense of "to curse," [53] in the Aramaic version, called Targum Onkelos, it is taken in the sense of "to name." In the Septuagint, just as in Targum Onkelos, the law reads: "Whoever names the name of the Lord shall die." Drawing upon this translation of the verse,[54] Philo interprets the law to apply to those "who out of volubility of tongue have spoken unseasonably and being too free of words have repeated carelessly the most holy and divine name of God." [55] By "the most holy and divine name of God" he means the name YHVH, commonly pronounced Jehovah, which in Jewish traditional literature is described as the quadriliteral name [56] or the proper name [57] or the distinctive name.[58] Philo similarly refers to that name as the quadriliteral (τετραγράμματον) name [59] or the proper name (κύριον ὄνομα),[60] dis-

---

[51] *Mos.* II, 37, 204.   [52] Lev. 24: 16.

[53] *M. Sanhedrin* VII, 5; *Targum pseudo-Jonathan*, Lev. 24: 16.

[54] *Mos.* II, 37, 203.   [55] *Ibid.*, 208.

[56] *Kiddushin* 71a: *shem ben arba' otiyyot.*

[57] *Sanhedrin* 60a: *shem ha-meyuḥad.*

[58] *Sifre Num.* § 39, F, p. 12a; H, p. 43: *shem ha-meforash.*

[59] *Mos.* II, 23, 115; 26, 132.

[60] *Mut.* 2, 11, 13, 14; *Somn.* I, 39, 230; but in *Abr.* 24, 121, the name "He that is" (ὁ ὤν) of Exod. 3: 14 is described by him as the κύριον ὄνομα of God, probably mean-

tinguishing it from the many other forms of the name
(πολυώνυμον ὄνομα) of God.⁶¹ Following again Jewish tradition, according to which this quadriliteral name was not to
be pronounced except by the high priest in the temple,⁶²
Philo also refers to that name as that "which only those
whose ears and tongues are purified may hear or speak in the
holy place, and no other person, nor in any other place at
all." ⁶³

Second, any name of God, which, as distinguished from
the proper name of God, is described by Philo as a title
(κλῆσις),⁶⁴ cannot, according to him, be taken in vain, when
there is no need for it, as, for instance, in the case of an oath
which, though true, is superfluous. Philo derives this from
the third of the ten commandments, "Thou shalt not take
the name of the Lord thy God in vain," ⁶⁵ which, as a purely
legal prohibition, is taken by him to refer to the taking of the
name of God in a false oath.⁶⁶ The·same disapproval of the
purposeless use of the name of God is reflected also among
the Talmudic rabbis, when on the basis of the third commandment they prohibit the purposeless pronouncement of
benedictions which contain the name of God.⁶⁷

Third, there is the law against blasphemy,⁶⁸ which, ac-

ing thereby that that name is to be taken as though it were God's proper name (cf.
Mut. 2, 12). I do not think Siegfried (p. 203) is right in inferring from this passage
that Philo takes the name Jehovah to mean the same as the name "He that is."
On the contrary, he always distinguishes between these two names.

⁶¹ *Decal.* 19, 94.
⁶² *Sifre Num.* § 39, F, p. 12a; H, p. 43; M. *Soṭah* VII, 6; M. *Tamid* VII, 2.
⁶³ *Mos.* II, 23, 114; *Decal.* 19, 93–94.
⁵⁴ *Decal.* 17, 83.
⁶⁵ Exod. 20: 7; Deut. 5: 11; cf. *Decal.* 19, 92–93.
⁶⁶ *Decal.* 17, 82–18, 91; cf. Belkin, *Philo and the Oral Law* (Cambridge: Harvard
University Press, 1940), pp. 140 ff.
⁶⁷ *Berakot 33a; Jer. Berakot* VI, 1, 10a. Among post-Talmudic authorities the
question was raised whether this prohibition is meant to be Biblical or only rabbini-
cal (cf. *Magen Abraham* on *Shulḥan 'Aruk Oraḥ Ḥayyim*, § 215).
⁶⁸ Lev. 24: 15; Exod. 33: 27.

cording to Philo, is a law prohibiting the cursing or reviling even of the deities of other nations.[69] This law against blasphemy means, according to him, as may be gathered from his discussion of the subject, not only that one is not to curse and revile a god or other gods, but also, at least morally, that one is not "to treat lightly or disregardfully (ἀλογεῖν) the name 'god' in general"[70] or to apply to God descriptions which other nations are in the habit of applying to their gods.[71]

From all this Philo must have gathered that it was highly difficult, and well-nigh impossible, to speak of God or to describe Him in words. To describe Him by His proper name is not allowed outside the temple. To describe Him by any of the other of His generally accepted titles is not allowed except in the case of some special occasion, when it serves some useful purpose. To describe Him by any other terms may always raise the question whether thereby one does not treat the name of God lightly and disregardfully and hence, morally at least, commit the sin of blasphemy. To Philo, with his belief in the absolute incorporeality and simplicity and unlikeness of God, the description of God in terms by which one does usually describe corporeal and compound beings would mean, at least in a moral sense, the treatment of the name of God lightly, disregardfully, and blasphemously. It is exactly this kind of reasoning that is employed later by Maimonides in rejecting the application to God of any predicates which are inappropriate descriptions of His nature. The application of such predicates to God, he says, "is not an ordinary sin, but the sin of reviling and blaspheming committed unwittingly."[72]

It is thus the restrictions as to the naming of God, ex-

[69] Mos. II, 38, 205; Spec. I, 9, 53.
[70] Mos. II, 38, 205.
[71] Spec. I, 9, 53.
[72] Moreh Nebukim I, 59

pressed in Scripture in a variety of ways, that was taken by Philo to imply that God is incomprehensible. But once he has found the implication of the principle of the incomprehensibility of God in the scriptural restrictions as to the naming of God, he comes to find the same implication also in the scriptural teaching as to the unlikeness of God, though in its primary sense, as we have seen, it implies only that God is incorporeal. Thus, commenting upon the verse "How dreadful is this place," [73] he says that the verse refers to the question of the whereabouts of God, and he mentions two views on the subject. "Some say that everything that subsists occupies some space, and of these one allots to the Existent One this space, another that, whether inside the world or a space outside it in the interval between worlds. Others maintain that the Uncreated resembles nothing among created things, but so completely transcends them that even the swiftest understanding falls far short of apprehending Him and acknowledges its failure." [74] Here then the principle of the unlikeness of God, which is a scriptural principle, is taken as the basis of the principle of the incomprehensibility of God. But there is more than that to this passage. The exponents of the first view which he mentions are the Stoics and Epicureans.[75] Consequently the exponents of the view which he opposes to that of the Stoics and Epicureans must also be some Greek philosophers. Now, as we have seen, no Greek philosopher before Philo has ever said explicitly that God is incomprehensible. But it is possible, as we have suggested,[76] that Philo has read into those philosophers, such as Plato and Aristotle, who believed in the incorporeality and simplicity of God, his own belief, derived by him from Scripture, as to the unlikeness

[73] Gen. 28: 17.
[74] *Somn.* I, 32, 184.
[75] Cf. above, I, 176.
[76] Cf. above, p. 118.

and the incomprehensibility of God. Or, it is possible that in his reference here to philosophers who maintain that "The Uncreated is like nothing among created things" Philo had in mind specifically the statement reported in the name of Antisthenes to the effect that "God does not become known from an image, nor is He seen with eyes; He is like no one. Wherefore no man can come to the knowledge of Him from an image." [77] But it will be noticed that this statement of Antisthenes by itself does not say that, because of His unlikeness to anything corporeal, God cannot be comprehended even by the mind. All he says is that "no man can come to the knowledge of Him from an image," which may merely mean that God cannot be adequately described in terms borrowed from corporeal objects. Philo's additional inference, in the statement quoted, that, because of His unlikeness to any created being, God is incomprehensible even to the mind is a view at which he has arrived, as we have been trying to show, by reasoning from his own combination of the scriptural principle of the unlikeness of God with the scriptural restrictions on the naming of God.

In the light of all that we have said, we can reconstruct the mental processes by which Philo must have arrived at the view of the unnamability and unknowability of God. From philosophic sources he derived the belief that God is incorporeal and hence indivisible and simple. With this philosophic belief he identified the scriptural teaching of the unlikeness of God. Now this principle of incorporeality would on purely philosophic grounds explicitly exclude only such compositions in the divine nature as what philosophers would call (a) body and soul, (b) the four elements, (c) substance and accident, and (d) matter and form. It would not of itself exclude the distinction of genus and

<hr>

[77] F. W. A. Mullach, *Fragmenta Philosophorum Graecorum* II, p. 277, no. 24.

species, and hence it would not exclude definition and hence
also it would not of itself lead to the indescribability and
unknowability of God. But in Scripture Philo has found
(a) statements to the effect that God has not revealed His
name to those to whom He appeared and also (b) laws prohibiting (1) to mention the proper name of God, (2) to take
in vain any other name of God and (3) to treat lightly the
word "God" in general. Scripture thus teaches the doctrine
of the unnamability of God. This scriptural doctrine of the
unnamability of God logically led him to the doctrine of the
indefinability of God and the indefinability of God logically
led him to the doctrine of the incomprehensibility of God,
and once he arrived at the incomprehensibility of God, he
found corroboration for it, by means of interpretation, in
the verse "Moses went into the thick darkness, where God
was." Then, having arrived at the doctrine of the incomprehensibility of God, he is led to extend the meaning of the
scriptural doctrine of the unlikeness of God to include also
His incomprehensibility; but, inasmuch as the scriptural
doctrine of unlikeness has already been identified by him
with the philosophic principle of incorporeality and simplicity, he is thus also led to ascribe the principle of the
incomprehensibility of God to all those Greek philosophers
who believed in God's incorporeality and simplicity.

IV. DIVINE PROPERTIES

The principles of the unnamability and the unlikeness of
God would inevitably lead to the conclusion that God could
be described only by terms which state directly His unlikeness to other beings, such, for instance, as unborn (ἀγένητος),[1]
unbribable (ἀδέκαστος),[2] incomprehensible (ἀκατάληπτος),[3]

---

[1] *Mos.* II, 32, 171.
[2] *Cher.* 5, 17.   [3] *Deter.* 24, 89.

unnamable (ἀκατονόμαστος),[4] invisible (ἀόρατος),[5] uncir-
cumscribable (ἀπερίγραφος),[6] ineffable (ἄρρητος),[7] and incomparable (ἀσύγκριτος),[8] all of which are used by Philo himself.
In Scripture, however, and following Scripture also in Philo,
God is described also by many positive terms, such as good
and great and merciful and their like, each of which by the
very nature of language names God and affirms something
about God and thereby implies a likeness between God and
other beings. Philo himself refers to all these terms applied
to God as the "multiform name of God" (τοῦ θεοῦ πολυώνυμον ὄνομα).[9] What then is the meaning of all these terms
or names by which God is described? In other words what
is the meaning of the anthropomorphisms in Scripture?

The problem of anthropomorphisms was not new with
Philo. It appeared in Greek religion prior to Philo and in
Palestinian Judaism prior to, and also independently of,
Philo. The origin of the problem, however, differed in each
of these religions. In Greek religion the rise of the problem
of anthropomorphisms was due to the impact of philosophy
upon popular conceptions of the gods; there was nothing in
the teachings of popular religion itself which would impel its
adherents to raise any objections to the use of anthropomorphic descriptions of the gods. In Judaism, however, the
rise of the problem was not due to the impact of any external system of thought; it arose out of an inner contradiction which native Jewish speculation could not help
noticing in Scripture between its doctrine of the unlikeness
of God on the one hand and its use of anthropomorphic
descriptions of God on the other. An echo of the dilemma
confronted by those who first began to speculate about the

---

[4] *Somn.* I, 11, 67.
[5] *Cher.* 30, 101.
[6] *Sacr.* 15, 59.

[7] *Somn.* I, 11, 67.
[8] *Fug.* 25, 141.
[9] *Decal.* 19, 94.

tenets of Judaism is resounded by later rabbis who on meeting in the Book of Ezekiel [10] with an anthropomorphic expression exclaimed: "Great is the boldness of the prophets who describe God by the likeness of the creature." [11] The boldness which they found in the use of anthropomorphism was that it seemed to infringe upon the prohibition to liken God to any other being. Then, again, in Greek religion, the objections to anthropomorphisms on philosophic grounds led either to a rejection of the popular deities altogether or to a transformation, by the allegorical method, of the popular deities into philosophic entities or concepts. In native Judaism, the objection to anthropomorphisms on the ground of the scriptural doctrine of the unlikeness of God merely led to the general explanation that anthropomorphic expressions are not to be taken literally, and that they are used in Scripture only as a practical pedagogical device to instruct the people in the knowledge of the ways of God in the world. "We describe God by terms borrowed from His creations in order to cause them to sink into the ear." [12] More particularly, the various anthropomorphic descriptions of God are said to have as their purpose the teaching of moral lessons to men. [13]

Philo, on the whole, starts out on the problem of the predications of God, as in native Jewish tradition, with a discussion of its relation to the principle of the unlikeness of God and, again, as in native Jewish tradition, he justifies the use of anthropomorphic descriptions of God on the ground of their pedagogical value.

Throughout Scripture, says Philo, two conflicting tend-

[10] Ezek. 1: 26.
[11] *Genesis Rabbah* 27, 1; cf. above, I, 135.
[12] *Mekilta, Baḥodesh*, 4, F, p. 65a; W, p. 73b; HR, p. 215; L, II, 221; cf. above, I, 135.
[13] Cf. above, I, 272.

encies are to be discerned. One of these insists upon the unlikeness of God to anything else, the chief expression of
which Philo finds in the statement that "God is not man" [14]
which in the Septuagint version from which Philo quotes
reads: "God is not as man." The other assumes a likeness
between God and other beings, which is evidenced by the
numerous anthropomorphic terms predicated of God in
Scripture and of which the chief example quoted by Philo
is the statement, which reads: "The Lord thy God bore thee,
as a man doth bear his son." [15] Of these two statements, he
says, the former "is warranted by grounds of surest truth,
whereas the latter is introduced for the instruction of the
many," for all such anthropomorphical expressions are said
"for the sake of instruction and admonition, and not because God is really such by nature." [16]

Thus on purely scriptural grounds the problem of the
divine predicates presents itself to Philo merely as a problem of the apparent contradiction between a God who is
said to be unlike any of His creatures and descriptions of
that God which liken Him to His creatures. By declaring
that these predicates are not meant to be taken literally and
that they are used only for the purpose of instruction, the
problem, in its scriptural aspect, is solved for him. But
Philo is also a philosopher, and as a philosopher he has
already presented all the teachings of Scripture concerning
God and the world and man in the language of philosophy.
Now in dealing with the terms which Scripture predicates
of God he is also going to present the matter in the language
of philosophy. In this new presentation of the problem he
will aim to establish two things. To begin with, the terms
predicated of God are to be interpreted in such a way as not

[14] *Num.* 23:19.
[15] *Deut.* 1:31.
[16] *Immut.* 11, 53–54; cf. *Sacr.* 30, 101.

to infringe upon the scriptural doctrine of the unlikeness of God, with all the philosophic implications he has read into it — the implications of incorporeality and simplicity and unknowability. Then, also, however these terms may be interpreted, their new interpretation must not deny of God any of those elements of knowledge, freedom, and power by which his conception of God is distinguished from the God of the philosophers with whom, in a general way, he is willing to identify the God of Scripture.

In dealing with the problem of anthropomorphisms philosophically, Philo will start with the assumption that all the terms which are predicated of God must be regarded in their relation to God after the manner of what philosophers at his time, following Aristotle, regarded as relations which are to obtain between the predicate and the subject in a logical proposition. The problem of the divine predicates, as it presents itself to him as a philosopher, is therefore a problem of the relation of the terms applied to God as predicables to God who is their subject. Now in Aristotle predicables in their relation to the subject may be one of the following four: property or definition or genus or accident.[17] While Philo does not formally investigate the question whether any of the terms predicated of God can be any of these four Aristotelian predicables, he has said enough on this subject to indicate that the problem was in his mind. That they cannot be accidents is quite clear from his denial of the corporeality of God and from his assertion that God is without human shape and without human passions.[18] Human shape and human passions are what Aristotle would classify under accidents.[19] That they are not genera or species is also quite clear from his denial that God can be

---

[17] *Topica* I, 4, 101b, 25.
[18] Cf. above, pp. 98, 104–106.   [19] *Categ.* 8, 9b, 33–10a, 16.

described by generic or specific terms.[20]   By the process of elimination, then, the predicates of God logically can be nothing but what Aristotle calls property. And so we find that Philo repeatedly uses the term property (ἴδιον) as a description of the terms predicated of God in their relation to their subject.[21]

With the aid of what we know about the philosophic implications of the term property we may now try to reconstruct what was in the mind of Philo when he spoke of the terms predicated of God as properties of God.

The term "property," in the fixed Aristotelian terminology which was already known to Philo, was used in contrast to such universal terms as genus, specific difference, and definition. A term predicated of a thing as a "property," says Aristotle, "belongs to that thing alone," [22] for "no one calls anything a property which may possibly belong to something else." [23] A property is therefore also said by Aristotle to distinguish the thing of which it is predicated from everything else.[24] Hence he maintains that when the predicate is a property it must not contain "any such term as is a universal attribute (ὄνομα ὃ πᾶσιν ὑπάρχει)." [25] Consequently Aristotle lays down the rule that a property is not a definition inasmuch as definition shows the essence of a thing (τὸ τί ἦν εἶναι σημαίνων),[26] but "the property of a thing ought not to show its essence" (οὐ δεῖ δηλοῦν τὸ τί ἦν εἶναι).[27] Nor can a property be a differentia (διαφορά), for a differentia is predicated of a thing according to participation (κατὰ μέθεξιν), that is to say, the subject is conceived as partaking of that predicate, and that "which is predicated of a sub-

---

[20] Cf. above, pp. 108–110.
[21] Leg. All. II, 9, 33; Cher. 24, 77.
[22] Topica I, 5, 102a, 18–19.
[23] Ibid., 22–23.

[24] Ibid. V, 1, 128b, 35.
[25] Ibid. V, 2, 130b, 11-12.
[26] Ibid. I, 5, 101b, 39.
[27] Ibid. V, 3, 131b, 38–132a, 1.

ject according to participation is a constituent part of its
essence," [28] but a property is predicated of a subject
neither according to participation nor as showing the essence. [29] Reflecting all this, Philo says that the properties
(ἰδιότητα) of a thing are distinguished from its qualities
(ποιοτήτων), inasmuch as qualities are shared by it in common with others, [30] whereas properties, by implication, are
not shared by it with others. When Philo therefore speaks
of the terms predicated of God as properties of God he
means to emphasize that they are not universal terms —
genus or difference or definition.

In its relation to accident, though property is sometimes
described by Aristotle as a sort of accident, it differs from
accident in that it belongs to the subject in virtue of its
own self (καθ' αὐτό). [31] This belonging to the subject in
virtue of its own self, however, does not make property
a definition, for the latter not only belongs to the subject in
virtue of its own self but also is in its essence (ἐν τῇ οὐσίᾳ). [32]
Thus, for instance, it is a property of a triangle that its
angles are equal to two right angles, but this equation is
not included in the definition of a triangle. [33] Again, unlike
accident, which can never be eternal, property can be eternal, provided the subject to which it belongs is eternal. [34] As
an illustration of an eternal property Aristotle mentions the
terms "immortal living being" in their application to God. [35]
When Philo therefore speaks of the terms predicated of God
as properties of God he means, again, to emphasize that
they are not accidents.

This is exactly what Philo means when he says that in
philosophic terminology all the predicates of God are

28 *Ibid.* V, 4, 132b, 36–133a, 1.   32 *Ibid.*, 31–32.
29 *Ibid.*, 133a, 5–6.   33 *Ibid.*, 32.
30 *Agr.* 3, 13.   34 *Ibid.*, 32–33; cf. *Topica* V, 1, 128b, 16–17.
31 *Metaph.* V, 30, 1025a, 30–34.   35 *Topica* V, 1, 128b, 19–20.

properties. They are properties in the sense that, while they must necessarily be assumed to belong to the essence of God, they do not tell us anything about the essence of God, for this, according to him, must remain unknown. They are properties also in the sense that they are not accidents, for these God, as an incorporeal being, cannot possess. For the conception of divine predicates as properties Philo may have found for himself support in Aristotle's statement that "life also belongs (ὑπάρχει) to God; for the actuality of thought is life, and God is that actuality; for the actuality of God in virtue of itself (καθ' αὐτὴν) is most good and eternal." [36] The expression "in virtue of itself," as we have seen, is used by Aristotle as a designation of property.[37] But another question must have arisen in the mind of Philo. The essence of God is one and simple and consequently whatever belongs to it as a property must be one and simple, for, if you assume that He has many properties, then you will have to say either that His essence is not one or simple or that some of these properties do not belong to Him in virtue of His essence; in the latter case they would be not properties but accidents. How could one therefore explain the multiplicity of properties which Scripture predicates of God? In answer to this Philo reduces all the properties predicated of God to only a single property, that of acting. Whatever property Scripture predicates of God it is only a different phase of one single property, and that one single property is the property of God to act. For action is in the true sense of the term a property only of God, no other being possesses such a property. "It is the property of God to act (τὸ ποιεῖν)," he says, "which property," he adds, "we do not ascribe to any created being, for the

[36] *Metaph.* XII, 7, 1072b, 26–28.
[37] Cf. above, n. 31.

property of the created is to suffer action (τὸ πάσχειν)." [38]
To act is thus a property of God in the sense that it is not a
universal, inasmuch as nothing shares with Him in it.
Moreover it is a property of God also in the sense that it is
not an accident, for "God never pauses in His activity," [39]
but He is "ever active," [40] and an accident, as we have seen,
as distinguished from a property, cannot last forever.[41] The
ever-activity of God is also expressed by him in his statement that "unchangeableness is the property of God." [42]

As a further description of this property of God to act
Philo says of it that it is the source of all action in the
world. "Even as it is the property of fire to burn and of
snow to chill, so it is the property of God to act; nay more
by far, inasmuch as He is to all besides the source of action."[43]
Now, in Aristotle, to be the source of movement or change
in another thing is described by the term "power" (δύναμις),
for "power," he says, "means a source of movement or
change which is in another thing than the thing moved." [44]
What Aristotle says of the source of movement or change in
another thing, Philo could reasonably argue, would also be
true of the source of action in another thing and consequently since the property of God to act is the source of
action in other things that property to act may be called
power. Plato, too, as we have seen, uses the term power as
a description of the causative aspect of the ideas.[45] Philo
accordingly calls the properties of God, which are His properties to act and to be the source of action in others, by the
term "powers." "It is impious and false," he says, to conceive of God as being in a state of "complete inactivity,"
when "we ought on the contrary to be astounded at His

[38] *Cher.* 24, 77.   [42] *Leg. All.* II, 9, 33.
[39] *Leg. All.* I, 3, 5.   [43] *Leg. All.* I, 3, 5.
[40] *Gig.* 10, 42.   [44] *Metaph.* V, 12, 1019a, 15–16.
[41] Cf. above, n. 34.   [45] Cf. above, I, 217.

powers (δυνάμεις) as Maker and Father." [46] These powers of God, as they manifest themselves in certain actions in the world, are many, and Philo, on several occasions, attempts to enumerate them and to classify them. Sometimes he divides them into four: (1) creative, (2) regal, (3) propitious, and (4) legislative, subdividing the last one into preceptive and prohibitive, [47] sometimes he reduces these four powers to two, either goodness and authority,[48] or beneficent and regal,[49] or beneficent and punitive; [50] but in all these classifications all the powers are reduced to one, which he calls the power of God, or the property of God, to act with goodness as well as with authority, with beneficence as well as with regality, with graciousness as well as with punition.

The properties of God are thus the powers of God, and the names by which God is called are nothing but designations of these properties or powers of God. Thus in one place, taking the term "peace" in the expression the "vision of peace," by which he translates the word "Jerusalem," as referring to God, he says that the "vision of peace" means the same as the "vision of God," for peace is the chief of the "many-named powers" (πολυωνύμων δυνάμεων) of God.[51] A similar use of the terms "powers," "names," and "properties" is to be found also in the Stoics. The God of the Stoics, who is the primary fire which is immanent in the world and pervades all the parts thereof, is said by them to be called by "many names (πολλαῖς προσηγορίαις) according to his various powers (δυνάμεις)," which names are given to him by men with reference to some of his "peculiar prop-

[46] Opif. 2, 7.
[47] Fug. 18, 94–95.
[48] Cher. 9, 27–28; Sacr. 15, 59.
[49] Abr. 25, 124–125; Qu. in Exod. II, 68 (Harris, Fragments, p. 67).
[50] Heres 34, 166; cf. above, I, 224–225.
[51] Somn. II, 38, 254.

erties" (οἰκειότητος).[52] Here then we have all the three
characteristic terms used by Philo, "names," "powers,"
"property."[53] More directly is the term power applied by
Philo to the names of God, and hence to the properties of
God, in his discussion of the two names by which God is
called in the Septuagint, namely, *Theos*, God, corresponding
to the Hebrew Elohim, and *Kyrios*, Lord, corresponding to
the Hebrew Jehovah. The term *Theos* is taken by him as
a designation of the "creative power" (ποιητικὴ δύναμις), so
that "'I am thy God' is equivalent to 'I am thy maker and
creator.'"[54] This etymologizing on the Greek term θεός reflects Herodotus,[55] who derives it from τίθημι, *to put, to
make*. Plato derives it from θέω, *to run*.[56] But inasmuch as
God's creative power is identified with His goodness, he also
says that "God is the name of goodness."[57] The term
Kyrios, on the other hand, which in the Septuagint translates
the Hebrew Adonai, the spoken substitute for the Tetra-
grammaton Jehovah, is taken by him to indicate "authority" (ἐξουσία)[58] or the royal power (δύναμις βασιλική).[59] This
on the whole represents a Jewish tradition on these two
names of God, and especially one version, the older one, of
that tradition. According to this tradition, in its old version, the name Elohim means the measure of goodness and
the name Jehovah means the measure of punishment.[60] But
as in native Jewish tradition, where the name Jehovah, despite its being taken as designating a divine "measure" or
property, is also taken as the distinctive, ineffable name of
God, so also in Philo, despite its being taken, in its translated

---

[52] Diogenes, VII, 147.   [53] οἰκειότης = ἰδιότης.
[54] *Mut.* 4, 29; *Abr.* 24, 121; cf. *Conf.* 27, 137.
[55] Herodotus, II, 52; cf. J. Cohn, *Philos Werke* I, 122, n. 1, on *Abr.* 24, 121.
[56] *Cratylus* 397 D.
[57] *Leg. All.* III, 23, 73.   [59] *Abr.* 24, 121.
[58] *Ibid.*   [60] Cf. above, I, 224.

Greek form, as designating the divine property of authority, it is also taken by him, in its original Hebrew form, as we have seen above,[61] in the sense of the proper ineffable name of God.[62]

The view arrived at by Philo that all the terms predicated of God are properties and that they are properties which express the one and all-comprehensive property of God, that of His power to act, removes from them the stigma of their being generic terms or accidental terms, or of their implying a multiplicity in God. But another question arises. Every action of an agent upon a patient establishes a relation between them, a relation which in Aristotle is designated as the relation between active and passive [63] or of active to passive.[64] Every such relation, however, according to Aristotle, establishes also a reciprocal dependence between the correlatives, for relative terms of this kind are, according to him, called relative "because each derives that which it is from reference to another," [65] so that "the servant is said to be servant of the master, and the master, master of the servant." [66] Consequently, in predicating of God terms which establish a relation between Him as active and other objects as passive, it would mean that God's activity is dependent upon something else. But this is contradictory to the principle of the self-sufficiency of God, "for the Existent considered as existent is not relative; He is full of himself and He is sufficient for himself. It was so before the creation of the world, and is equally so after the creation of all that is. He cannot

[61] Cf. above, pp. 121–122.

[62] There is no ground for Siegfried's inference (p. 203) that Philo had no knowledge of the fact that the Hebrew Jehovah, of which he speaks as the proper name of God, is the same as the Greek "Lord" which he takes to be a "power" of God. The same two uses of the term, as we have seen, are to be found also in rabbinic literature.

[63] *Phys.* III, 1, 200b, 30.

[64] *Metaph*, V, 15, 1020b, 28–30.

[65] *Ibid.*, 1021a, 26–28.

[66] *Categ.* 7, 6b, 28–30.

change nor alter and needs nothing else at all, so that all
things are His but He himself in the proper sense belongs to
none." [67] In answer to this difficulty Philo maintains that
all those properties which indicate action, while they establish a relation, the relation is not to be understood to be a
reciprocal relation: the suffering action by the patient indeed
depends upon the agent, but the activity of the agent does
not depend upon the patient. In the strictly logical sense,
therefore, such a non-reciprocal relation is not a true relation; Philo consequently describes it as a *quasi*-relation
(ὡσανεὶ πρός τι).[68] It is called a relation only because in
ordinary speech the activity of an agent upon a patient,
analogous to that of God, who is the "Father" (πατήρ),
"Maker" (ποιητής), and "Artificer" (δημιουργός)[69] of the
world, upon the world, is called relation and such a relation
is reciprocal in the same way as "a king is king of someone
and a benefactor is the benefactor of someone." [70] In reality,
however, the activity of God is not dependent upon anything
outside of God. Like the essence of God it is self-sufficient;
it is an activity which is absolute and in the real sense not
relative; it is an activity peculiar to God, a property of God
in which nothing else shares.

V. The Essence of the Created Powers

The powers of God in the sense of the property of God to
act, as we have seen, are not distinct from the essence of
God, and if the essence of God, as it is assumed by Philo, is
unknowable, then the powers of God are also unknowable
in their essence. They are known to us only through the

[67] *Mut.* 4, 27–28; cf. above, I, 172.
[68] *Mut.* 4, 28. Cf. Drummond, II, 48–49; Colson, *ad loc.*
[69] *Mut.* 4, 29.
[70] *Ibid.*, 28.

effect which they produce in the world, for the world itself in its totality came into being as a result of God's power or property to act. But, according to Philo, when God, by the determination of His will, decided to create the world, He created prior to it an intelligible world consisting of intelligible beings called ideas. These ideas have been endowed by God with some part of that power to act which had existed in Him as a property from eternity. The ideas are therefore called also powers; they are, however, only created powers and, unlike the powers in the sense of eternal properties, they are distinct from God.[1] Of these created powers there are, according to Philo, two kinds: first, incorporeal powers or ideas, and, second, powers immanent in the physical world.[2] The question may therefore arise, with regard to these created powers, whether, like God, they are unknown in their essence or, unlike God, they are known in their essence.

The question is dealt with by Philo in his homily on the second prayer of Moses. In that second prayer, as will be recalled, Moses asks God, according to the Septuagint version used by Philo, "Reveal thyself (σεαυτόν) to me."[3] To this God answers, "Thou shalt see what are behind Me, but My face shall not be beheld by thee."[4] The meaning of these verses is discussed by Philo in five places in his writings. We shall examine them one by one.

In one passage, he starts with the statement that God, to whom he refers as "He who exists in truth" (τὸ πρὸς ἀλήθειαν ὄν), is perceived and known "with the eyes of the understanding, from the cosmic powers and from the constant and ceaseless motion of His innumerable works."[5] Then, quot-

---

[1] Cf. above, I, 220–222.
[2] Cf. above, I, 327, 343–345.
[3] Exod. 33:18.
[4] Exod. 33:23.
[5] *Post.* 48, 167.

ing the verse "See, see that I am," [6] he argues from the fact
that God did not say "See Me" that God's statement means
"Behold My existence, for it is quite enough for a man's
reasoning faculty to advance as far as to learn that the cause
of the universe is and exists." [7] Then, also, quoting God's
answer to Moses' second prayer, he says: "This meant, that
all that follows in the wake of God is within the good man's
apprehension, while He himself alone is incomprehensible —
but He may become perceived and known [8] by the powers
that follow and attend Him, for these make evident not
His essence but His existence from the things which He accomplishes." [9] Here in this passage he quite clearly distinguishes between God who is incomprehensible and the
powers who are comprehensible, from which it may be inferred that the powers, unlike God, are comprehensible in
their essence.

In a second passage, in the same treatise, Philo mentions the powers but says nothing about the question of the
comprehensibility of their essence. In that passage the
second prayer of Moses is explained as meaning that "he
implored Him to reveal clearly His own nature," [10] and God's
answer is explained as meaning that "when therefore the
God-loving soul probes the question of the essence ($\tau\grave{o}$ $\tau\acute{\iota}$
$\acute{\epsilon}\sigma\tau\iota$) of the Existent Being, he enters on an obscure and dark
subject of investigation from which the greatest benefit that
accrues to him is to comprehend that God, as to His es-
sence ($\tau\grave{o}$ $\epsilon\tilde{\iota}\nu\alpha\iota$), is utterly incomprehensible to any being." [11]

[6] Deut. 32: 39 (LXX).
[7] Post. 48, 168.
[8] Wendland, followed by Colson, adds here the word $\kappa\alpha\tau\alpha\lambda\eta\pi\tau\acute{o}s$. But if the
word $\acute{\alpha}\kappa\alpha\tau\acute{\alpha}\lambda\eta\pi\tau os$ used previously by Philo refers to essence, then the word to be supplied here should be one that refers to existence and not to essence. Such a word
should be a participle of $\kappa\alpha\tau\alpha\nuο\epsilon\tilde{\iota}\sigma\theta\alpha\iota$ or $\gamma\nu\omega\rho\acute{\iota}\zeta\epsilon\sigma\theta\alpha\iota$ mentioned previously in § 167.
[9] Post. 48, 169, or "they accomplish," if the reading is $\alpha\grave{\upsilon}\tauο\tilde{\iota}s$ instead of $\alpha\grave{\upsilon}\tau\tilde{\omega}$.
[10] Ibid. 4, 13.   [11] Ibid. 5, 15.

But with regard to the powers, he merely says that "though He is superior to that which He has created and external to it, none the less He filled the universe with himself, for He has caused His powers to extend themselves throughout the universe to its utmost bounds." [12] He does not say, however, whether they are known or unknown as to their essence.

In a third passage, God's answer to the second prayer of Moses is explained by Philo as follows: "He did not succeed in finding anything by search respecting the essence of Him that is," for God told him that "it amply suffices the wise man to come to a knowledge of all the things that attend upon God, follow Him and are behind Him, but he who wishes to see the Supreme Essence, will be blinded by the rays that beam forth all around Him before he sees Him." [13] In this passage, too, there is a contrast between a knowledge of the essence of God and a knowledge of "all the things that attend upon God, follow Him and are behind Him," that is, His powers, with the implication that the powers are known in their essence.

The same implication is to be found in a fourth discussion of God's answer to the second prayer of Moses. It is interpreted by him there to mean that "all below the Existent, things corporeal and incorporeal alike, are available to the apprehension, even if they are not actually apprehended as yet, but He alone by His very nature cannot be seen." [14] Here again there is a contrast with regard to the comprehensibility of their essence between God and "things corporeal and incorporeal," that is, the immanent powers in the visible world and the incorporeal powers in the intelligible world, with the implication that the powers of either kind can be apprehended in their essence, "even if they are

[12] Ibid., 14; cf. above, I, 344.
[13] Fug. 29, 165.   [14] Mut. 2, 9.

not actually apprehended as yet." It is because the powers are as yet not actually apprehended that later in the same passage he says that "not even the powers who serve Him tell us their proper name." [15] Not to tell us their proper name means not to reveal to us their essence, and this refusal to reveal to us their essence is to be taken not as implying that their essence cannot be known but rather as implying that the knowledge of their essence is to be acquired by us only through study and research.

As against at least three of these four passages there is a fifth passage in which he definitely says that the powers, like God, are unknown in their essence. In that passage, he starts with the verse "Reveal thyself to me." From the words quoted here by Philo from the Septuagint it is not clear whether they are from verse 13 of chapter 33 in Exodus or from verse 18, but we take them to be a quotation from verse 18, in which the Hebrew reads, "Show me Thy glory," and not from verse 13, in which the Hebrew reads, "Show me Thy ways," that is to say, they are from the second prayer of Moses and not from the first.[16] Commenting upon these words, Philo says: "In these words we may almost hear plainly the inspired cry 'That Thou art and dost exist, of this the world has been my teacher and guide. . . . But what Thou art in Thy essence I desire to understand, yet find in no part of the All any to guide me to this knowledge.'" [17] In view of the fact that God's answer to Moses' first prayer is interpreted by Philo to mean that God has offered Moses to be himself his guide to a knowledge of His

---

[15] *Ibid.*, 14.

[16] Colson (note on *Spec.* I, 8, 41) takes this to be a quotation of the first prayer of Moses contained in verse 13, but, as he himself has noted, the answer of God to this prayer as paraphrased by Philo is based upon verses 19–23, which follow the second prayer in verse 18. Cf. our analysis of Philo's treatment of these two prayers of Moses above, pp. 86–87.   [17] *Spec.* I, 8, 41.

existence,[18] Philo's interpretation here of Moses' second prayer makes Moses reject God's offer, causing him to say to God that, as for a knowledge of His existence, he has already learned it by himself from the world, but that what he would like to have the direct help of God for is to attain to a knowledge of His essence. To this God's answer, given by Philo without proof-text, is that "the apprehension of Me is something more than human nature, yea even the whole heaven and universe, will be able to contain." [19] The proof-text for this is, of course, the verse quoted in the other passages, "My face shall not be beheld by thee" [20] or the verse, "Thou canst not see My face." [21] Then Philo makes Moses say: But I beseech Thee that I may at least see the glory (δόξα) that surrounds Thee, and by Thy glory I understand the powers that keep guard around Thee." [22] No proof-text is quoted here by Philo. God's answer to this is given by Philo again without proof-text. It contains the following statements: (1) "The powers which thou seekest to know are discerned not by sight but by mind even as I, whose they are, am discerned by mind and not by sight." [23] (2) "When I say 'they are discerned by mind' I speak not of those which are now actually apprehended by mind but mean that if these other powers could be apprehended it would not be by sense but by mind at its purest." [24] (3) "Do not, then, hope to be ever able to apprehend Me or any of My powers in our essence." [25] (4) "But while in their essence they are beyond your apprehension, they nevertheless present to your sight a sort of impress and copy of their active working." [26] Here, then, Philo definitely states that the powers, like God, are not comprehensible in their essence.

[18] Cf. above, p. 86.
[19] *Spec.* I, 8, 44.
[20] Exod. 33:23.
[21] Exod. 33:20.
[22] *Spec.* I, 8, 45.
[23] *Ibid.*, 46.
[24] *Ibid.*
[25] *Ibid.*, 49.
[26] *Ibid.*, 47.

There is thus a change of view between at least three of the first four passages and the fifth passage. In the former, the powers are said to be knowable in their essence; in the latter, they are said to be unknowable in their essence. Without attempting to reconcile passages which obviously indicate a change of view,[27] we shall try to find out what was it that has brought about that change of view. This change of view must have undoubtedly come about as a result of a change in his interpretation of God's answer to the second prayer of Moses. But what is it that has caused that change of interpretation?

Let us first examine the text of this second prayer. In the original Hebrew it reads: "Show us Thy glory." Now the expression "glory of God" or "glory of the Lord" in Scripture may mean two things. It may mean God himself and it may also mean something produced by God and distinct from Him.[28] These two meanings of the term glory in the verse in question are to be found in the two Greek translations of that verse. One translation of this verse reads "Reveal thyself to me." It is this verse and in this translation that Philo, as we have tried to show, always quotes when he interprets it to be a prayer for God's essence. The other translation of the verse reads, literally, as in the Hebrew, "show me Thy glory."[29]

Let us now assume that in those three of the first four passages in which the powers are explicitly said by him to be knowable in their essence, Philo took the second prayer of Moses to read "Reveal thyself to me." When therefore God in His answer said to him, again according to the Greek

[27] *Post.*, *Fug.* and *Mut.* were all written before *Spec.*, according to Cohn, or after *Spec.*, according to Massebieau and Bréhier (cf. references above, I, 87, n. 1).
[28] Cf. G. B. Gray, "Glory," *Dictionary of the Bible*, II, pp. 184–186.
[29] See critical apparatus to Septuagint.

reading, "I will go before thee with My glory and I will call by My name the Lord before thee, and I will have mercy upon whom I please to have mercy . . . but, said He, thou canst not see My face . . . and when My glory is passing by, I will place thee in a cleft of the rock and cover thee with My hand over thee, until I pass by, then I will withdraw My hand and then thou shalt see what are behind Me but My face cannot be seen by thee," [30] he took this answer to mean that while My "face," that is, my essence, cannot be known, My "glory" and "what are behind Me," that is, My powers, can be known in their essence.

Then let us assume that in the fifth passage, where the powers are said to be unknown in their essence, Philo had before him the two Greek readings of this second prayer of Moses, one "Reveal thyself to me" and the other "show me Thy glory." Let us also assume that he knew that these two Greek translations represented the two possible meanings of the underlying Hebrew word "glory." Assuming all this, we can readily see how Philo, having before him a verse which in the original Hebrew lends itself to two interpretations, interpreted the verse actually to contain two distinct prayers, one for a knowledge of God's essence and the other for a knowledge of God's glory, that is, His powers. This is an exegetical method which is quite common in traditional Jewish interpretation of Scripture.[31] Since, therefore, Philo took the second prayer of Moses in verse 18 to contain two distinct prayers, God's answer to this double prayer was also taken by him to contain two distinct answers to the two prayers. The answer to the first prayer was taken by him to be contained in the verses "I will go before

[30] Exod. 33: 19–23.
[31] As, for instance, the exegetical uses made in many places of the differences between the ḳere and the ketib or of the al tiḳre; cf., e.g., Baba Ḳamma 10b.

thee with My glory and I will call by My name the Lord
before thee, and I will have mercy upon whom I please to
have mercy . . . but, said He, thou canst not see My face." [32]
This part of the answer was interpreted by Philo to mean:
"To him that is worthy of My grace [33] I extend all the boons
which he is capable of receiving; but the apprehension of Me
is something more than human nature, yea even the whole
heaven and universe, will be able to contain." [34] The
answer to the second prayer was taken by him to be contained in the verses, "When My glory is passing by, I will
place thee in a cleft of the rock and cover thee with My hand
over thee, until I pass by, then I will withdraw My hand and
then thou shalt see what are behind Me but My face cannot
be seen by thee." [35] This part of the answer was interpreted
by Philo to mean: "The powers which thou seekest to know
are discerned not by sight but by mind even as I . . . but
while in their essence they are beyond your comprehension,
they nevertheless present to your sight a sort of impress and
copy of their active working." [36] According to this interpretation, the expression "thou shalt see what are behind
Me but My face cannot be seen by thee" is taken by Philo
to mean that the powers themselves cannot be known; only
their copies can be known.

   The double meaning of the term glory of God in Scripture
is reflected also in Philo's interpretation of the verse "And
the glory of God descended on Mount Sinai." [37] Comment-
ing upon this verse, he says that the term glory ($\delta \acute{o} \xi a$), has
two meanings: (1) "the presence of His powers ($\pi a \rho o \upsilon \sigma \acute{\iota} a \nu$
. . . $\tau \hat{\omega} \nu \delta \upsilon \nu \acute{a} \mu \epsilon \omega \nu$), since the power of an army is spoken of

---

[32] Exod. 33: 19–20.
[33] The term $\chi \acute{a} \rho \iota s$ used here by Philo and the term $\grave{\epsilon} \lambda \epsilon \acute{\eta} \sigma \omega$ used in the Septuagint
are translations of the same Hebrew word.
[34] *Spec.* I, 8, 43–44.   [36] *Spec.* I, 8, 45–46.
[35] Exod. 33: 21–23.   [37] Exod. 24: 16.

as the glory of a king"; (2) "a mental image (δόκησις) of Him alone and a notion (ὑπόληψις) of His divine glory," [38] that is to say, the term glory refers to God himself, of which the people thought to have caught a glimpse. In this passage he quite obviously plays upon the two meanings of the Greek term δόξα, that of "glory" and that of "notion." But undoubtedly behind this discussion there is the knowledge of the double meaning of the expression glory of God in Scripture, which must have been known to every intelligent reader of the Septuagint no less than to that of the original Hebrew text.

The view that the powers are unknown in their essence is also stated by Philo in his comment on the verse in which Jacob exclaimed: "This is none other but the house of God, and this is the gate of heaven." [39] What is meant by "house" and "gate" and "heaven"? Philo asks, and in answer to this question he says that by "house" and "gate" is meant this visible world of ours, and by "heaven" is meant the intelligible world of the ideas or the powers. He then proceeds to say that the intelligible world, and hence also the powers or ideas of which it consists, "cannot be apprehended otherwise than by passing on to it from this world which we see and perceive by our senses, for neither indeed is it possible to get an idea of any other incorporeal thing among existences except by making material objects our starting-point." [40] The implication of this statement is quite evident: purely incorporeal beings, which include the powers, cannot be known in their essence; only their existence can be known, seeing that nothing can be known of them except through the corporeal world.

Thus, according to the fifth passage in Philo, Moses made

[38] *Qu. in Exod.* II, 45 (Harris, *Fragments*, p. 60).
[39] Gen. 28:17.   [40] *Somn.* I, 32, 185–187.

three prayers. First, in verse 13, he prayed for a direct knowledge of God. In verses 14 to 17, God granted him a direct knowledge of His existence.[41] Second, in verse 18, in accordance with that Greek version which translated the Hebrew term "glory" by "thyself," he prayed for a knowledge of God's essence. This is refused by God in verses 19 and 20. Third, again in verse 18, in accordance with that Greek version which translated the Hebrew term "glory" literally, he prayed for a knowledge of the essence of the powers. This is also refused by God in verses 21 to 23.

But though God, and, according to one of Philo's statements, also the powers, cannot be known in their essence, that lack of knowledge is not of the same degree. Some people may have a greater knowledge of the essence of God than others, for the more one knows of God's works in the world the more one knows of God's existence, and the more one knows of His existence the more may also one know of His essence, even though no complete knowledge of the divine essence is possible. When therefore God denied Moses to have a knowledge of His own essence, and of the essence also of His powers, and allowed him only to have a knowledge of the existence of both Himself and His powers, as much as could be gained through a knowledge of the world, He advised him to continue to have "a constant and profound longing for wisdom, which fills its scholars and disciples with glorious and most beautiful doctrines."[42] The implication of this advice is that though the knowledge of the essence of God, and of the essence also of His powers, can never be fully attained, by a continuous desire for that kind of knowledge one will continuously learn more about the world, whereby one will grow in the knowledge of the existence of God and thereby also in the knowledge of His

---

[41] Cf. above, p. 86.   [42] *Spec.* I, 8, 50.

essence. Consequently, according to Philo, "when Moses heard this, he did not cease from his desire but still kept the yearning for the invisible things aflame in his heart," [43] for although a complete knowledge of their essence was unattainable, it was still possible for him to grow in the knowledge thereof. When therefore in several places Philo speaks of a desire to have a vision of God he only means to have a desire for a direct and greater knowledge of the existence of God, which may lead to a greater knowledge of the essence of God, even though never to a complete knowledge of it. [44]

VI. CONCLUSION, INFLUENCE, ANTICIPATION

Philo starts on his discussion of the nature of God with two fundamental scriptural principles: first, the unlikeness of God to other beings; second, the unity of God. Under the influence of philosophy, the scriptural principle of unlikeness comes to mean with him incorporeality, and incorporeality implies simplicity. Similarly, under the influence of philosophy, the scriptural principle of unity also comes to mean with him simplicity. The simplicity of God thus becomes with him the outstanding characteristic of God's nature. Now, on purely philosophic grounds, simplicity would exclude from God's nature only such composition as

[43] *Ibid.*

[44] Zeller (III, 2⁴, 463–464) takes Philo's references to a desire for a vision of God to mean a desire to have a knowledge of God's essence, which desire may also be fulfilled, and consequently he finds Philo to contradict himself. Cf. above, p. 91. The other passages to which Zeller refers as evidence of Philo's belief in the possibility of a vision of God's essence (p. 463, n. 2) do not prove his point. They merely state that "in the understanding of those who have been purified to the utmost the Ruler of the universe walks noiselessly, alone, invisibly" (*Somn.* I, 23, 148), or that, when man has arrived at full knowledge, he will follow God himself as his leader (*Migr.* 31, 175), or that "they who live in knowledge of the One are rightly called 'sons of God'" (*Conf.* 28, 145). All these statements might mean almost anything; they do not necessarily mean that man can have a knowledge of God's essence.

is inconsistent with His incorporeality, namely, body and soul, substance and accident, the four elements, and matter and form. No philosopher before Philo is known to have stated that God, in His essence, is unknowable and indescribable. But Scripture teaches also that God is not to be named, and this scriptural principle of the unnamability of God, again under the influence of philosophic reasoning, comes to mean with Philo that God cannot be described by any accidental predicates nor can He be defined in terms of genus and species or difference. Being indescribable and indefinable, God thus becomes with Philo unknowable in His essence, which is a new principle introduced by him into the history of philosophy.

All this has led Philo to raise the question as to what is meant by all those terms which in Scripture are predicated of God. To this he offers two answers. On purely Jewish traditional grounds, his answer is that all these terms are not to be taken literally and that they are used in Scripture only for the purpose of instruction. But, on philosophic grounds, he tries to find some meaning for all these terms, by explaining that they are what philosophers call properties. Having once suggested that explanation, he then tries to show how properties differ from genus and specific difference and accident, how all these properties are in reality one property, how that one property is a property of action, and how that property of action, when predicated of God, does not vitiate His self-sufficiency. This God's property of action is furthermore also called by Philo the power of God; but, inasmuch as any property or power of God must be identical with His essence, the power of God must of necessity be unknowable in the same way as God's essence is unknowable. But the term powers, besides its sense as God's property to act, which is identical with His essence, means to Philo also the ideas created by God both as incorporeal beings and as immanent in the world. The question therefore arises whether these latter two kinds of power, which are creations of God and are distinct from His essence, are knowable or unknowable. In his answer to this question, Philo sometimes says that they are knowable and sometimes he says that they are unknowable. The questions with regard to the knowability of the essence of God as well as that of His powers is found by Philo to be the subject of Moses' prayer to God and God's answer to that prayer.

From now on in the history of philosophy, whether Christian, Moslem, or Jewish, all the philosophers, in their discussion of the nature of God, will take up those problems raised by Philo and will proceed in their solution after the manner of Philo.

Like Philo, the Christian Church Fathers feel that the principle of the incorporeality of God is not explicitly stated in Scripture and it has to be indirectly derived therefrom. Origen gives utterance to this view in his statement that "the term ἀσώματον, that is, incorporeal, is unused and unknown, not only in many other writings, but also in our own Scriptures," [1] but "we shall inquire, however, whether the thing which Greek philosophers call ἀσώματον, or incorporeal, is found in holy Scripture under another name." [2] Origen himself finds it implied in such verses of the New Testament as "No man hath seen God at any time," [3] "The image of the invisible God," [4] and "God is a Spirit." [5] But Clement of Alexandria derives it also from the Old Testament principle of the unlikeness of God, quoting as proof-text the verses

[1] *De Principiis* I, *Praefatio*, 8.
[2] *Ibid.*, 9.
[3] John 1: 18.
[4] Col. 1: 15.
[5] John 4: 24; cf. *Contra Celsum* VII, 27; *De Principiis* I, 1, §§ 1–4.

"To whom have you likened me?" [6] and "To whom have you likened the Lord? or to what likeness have you likened Him?" [7]

In the Koran, as in the Hebrew Bible, there is no explicit statement of the incorporeality of God, but there are these statements denying any likeness between God and other beings: "Nought is there like Him" [8] and "And there is none like Him." [9] The unlikeness of God becomes in Arabic Moslem philosophy the basis for the rejection of the corporeality and also of the attributes of God. One of the earliest recorded Moslem philosophers who rejected divine attributes, Jahm Ibn Ṣafwān, is reported to have said: "It is not permissible that the creator should be described by terms by which His creatures are described, for this would lead to likeness." [10] So also the extreme attributists or anthropomorphists are said to have lapsed into likeness (tashbīh). [11] Similarly in Arabic Jewish philosophy, the doctrine of the unlikeness of God as taught in the Hebrew Scripture is made the basis of the rejection of the corporeality as well as the anthropomorphisms of God. This is clearly brought out in the writings of such philosophers as Saadia, [12] Baḥya, [13] Joseph Ibn Ṣaddiḳ, [14] Abraham Ibn Daud, [15] and Maimonides. [16]

As in Philo, with whom the principle of the unity of God

[6] Isa. 40: 25; cf. *Stromata* V, 14 (PG, 9, 164 B).
[7] Isa. 40: 18; cf. *ibid.* (PG, 9, 176 A).
[8] Surah 42: 9.
[9] Surah 112: 4.
[10] Shahrastani, ed. Cureton, p. 60, ll. 8–9.
[11] *Ibid.*, p. 64, ll. 9–10; 19–20.
[12] *Emunot we-Deʿot* II, 1 (Arabic, p. 79, ll. 13–14; p. 80, ll. 5–6).
[13] *Ḥobot ha-Lebabot* I, 10 (Arabic, pp. 76, l. 16–77, l. 6).
[14] *ʿOlam Ḳaṭan* III, ed. S. Horovitz, p. 51, ll. 17 ff.
[15] *Emunah Ramah* II, iii, p. 57.
[16] *Moreh Nebukim* I, 55.

came to mean not only external unity but also internal unity, or rather simplicity, so also in the subsequent history of philosophy, whether Christian, Moslem, or Jewish, the unity of God is formally said to include also His simplicity. Among the Church Fathers the simplicity of God is the main premise which made it necessary to look for an explanation for the doctrine of the Trinity [17] as well as for the use of divine predicates.[18] In Arabic Moslem philosophy, the term one is formally divided into external unity and simplicity, and God is said to be simple and indivisible.[19] In Arabic Jewish philosophy, the discussion of the unity of God always tries to show that God is not only numerically one but that He is also simple and indivisible. This formal statement is to be found in Baḥya,[20] Joseph Ibn Ṣaddiḳ,[21] Judah ha-Levi,[22] and Abraham Ibn Daud.[23] In mediaeval Latin philosophy, to take but one outstanding example, St. Thomas similarly says that the unity of God means both numerical unity and simplicity.[24]

Then, as in Philo, the simplicity of God is said to exclude not only the composition of matter and form, or of the four elements, or of substance and accident, but also the composition of genus and species and, as a result of that, God is said to be incomprehensible ($\dot{\alpha}\kappa\alpha\tau\dot{\alpha}\lambda\eta\pi\tau\sigma s$), unnamable ($\dot{\alpha}\kappa\alpha\tau\sigma\nu\dot{\sigma}\mu\alpha\sigma\tau\sigma s$), and ineffable ($\ddot{\alpha}\rho\rho\eta\tau\sigma s$). These views appear from now on throughout the history of philosophy,

---

[17] Cf. John of Damascus, *De Fide Orthodoxa* I, 8.

[18] *Ibid.*, I, 12.

[19] Cf. Alfarabi, *Al-Siyāsāt al-Madaniyyah*, Hyderabad, 1346 A. H., pp. 13, l. 20-14, l. 20; Avicenna, *Najāt*, Cairo, 1331 A. H., pp. 375-383; Algazali, *Maqāṣid al-Falāsifah* II, Cairo, no date, pp. 114-118.

[20] *Ḥobot ha-Lebabot* I, 8.

[21] *'Olam Ḳaṭan* III, pp. 49-51.

[22] *Cuzari* II, 2.

[23] *Emunah Ramah* II, ii, 1.

[24] *Sum. Theol.* I, 11, 3; 3, 1-8.

whether Christian, Moslem, or Jewish, and, also perhaps
through the influence of Philo, in pagan Greek philosophy.
All these Philonic terms, incomprehensible, unnamable, and
ineffable, appear in the writings of almost all the Church
Fathers. In Origen this incomprehensibility of God is said
to be derived directly from His incorporeality. "Having
refuted, then," he says, "as well as we could, every notion
which might suggest that we were to think of God as in any
degree corporeal, we go on to say that, according to strict
truth, God is incomprehensible." [25] We have already shown
that on purely philosophic grounds the mere incorporeality
of God did not lead philosophers before Philo to say that
God is incomprehensible. It must have been also as an inference from Philo's statements that God is "without
quality" [26] and that He is the "highest genus" [27] that Clement of Alexandria came to say that God is "neither genus,
nor difference, nor species, nor individual, nor number." [28]
John of Damascus, summarizing what was commonly believed by Church Fathers about God, mentions among
other things also that He is indescribable (ἀπερίγραπτον) and
indefinable (ἀπεριόριστον). [29] In Arabic Moslem as well as in
Arabic Jewish philosophy, the statements constantly occur
that God has no name (ism) and no description (ṣifah) and
that He cannot be defined or that He has no genus and
species or difference. [30] In mediaeval Latin philosophy, to
take again but one outstanding example, St. Thomas argues
from the simplicity of God that in Him there is not only no

---

[25] De Principiis I, 1, 5.
[26] Cf. above, p. 104.
[27] Cf. above, p. 109.
[28] Stromata V, 12 (PG, 9, 121 A); cf. above, p. 113.
[29] De Fide Orthodoxa I, 8.
[30] Baghdadi, p. 93, l. 16 — p. 94, l. 1; Avicenna, Najāt III, p. 381; Algazali,
Maqāṣid al-Falāsifah II, p. 145; Moreh Nebukim I, 52.

composition of matter and form [31] or of subject and accident [32] but also no composition of genus and difference,[33]
and hence that God cannot be defined.[34] Like Philo, he also
maintains that "it is impossible for any created intellect to
comprehend (comprehendere) God," inasmuch as God is "infinite" and is "infinitely knowable" and "no created intellect
can know God infinitely," [35] though he maintains that it is
possible for souls of the blessed after death to see the essence
of God [36] through a strengthening of their intellect [37] by the
grace of God.[38]

Furthermore, as in Philo, who finds the problem of the
unknowability discussed in the prayer of Moses to God and
in God's answer to that prayer, so also in Christian and Jewish philosophy the prayer of Moses is similarly interpreted.
Clement of Alexandria, probably under the direct influence
of Philo, though not verbally following him, says: "Whence
Moses, persuaded that God is not to be known by human
wisdom, said 'Show me thyself'; and into the thick darkness where God's voice was, pressed to enter — that is, into
the inaccessible and invisible ideas respecting the Existent." [39] Again: "Therefore also Moses says, 'Show thyself to me' — intimating most clearly that God is not capable
of being taught by man, or expressed in speech, but to be
known only by His own power." [40] Similarly St. Augustine,
from the prayers of Moses, which he quotes as "Show me
now thyself plainly" [41] and "Show me Thy glory," [42] infers

[31] Sum. Theol. I, 3, 2c; Cont. Gent. I, 17 and 27.
[32] Sum. Theol. I, 3, 6c; Cont. Gent. I, 23.
[33] Sum Theol. I, 3, 5c; Cont. Gent. I, 24–25.
[34] Cont. Gent. I, 25.
[35] Sum. Theol. I, 12, 7c; cf. IV Sent., 49, 2, 3c.   [37] Ibid., 2c.
[36] Sum. Theol. I, 12, 1c.   [38] Ibid., 4c.
[39] Stromata II, 2 (PG, 8, 936 B–937 A).   [40] Ibid., V, 11 (PG, 9, 109 B).
[41] Exod. 33: 13, following the Septuagint reading.
[42] Exod. 33: 18, following the Hebrew reading.

that what Moses prayed for was: "Show me Thy substance"
and that "this was not granted to him." [43] In another place
he similarly infers from the prayer "Show me Thy glory"
that Moses "desired what he saw not." [44] And Maimonides,
independently of Philo but like him, explains that the prayer
of Moses contains two petitions. One of them, exactly as
in Philo, is a petition for the knowledge of God's essence, to
which God's answer was that His true essence could not be
known.[45] The other, analogous to what Philo takes to be a
petition for a knowledge of the essence of God's created
powers,[46] is a petition for the knowledge of God's "attributes," to which God's answer was that "He would let him
know all His attributes, and that these were nothing but
His actions." [47] In mediaeval Latin philosophy, St. Thomas
quotes the verse "Man shall not see me and live" [48] in God's
answer to the prayer of Moses to prove that "God cannot be
seen in His essence by a mere human being, except he be
separated from this mortal life," [49] though he adds that by
his power to work miracles God may "raise the minds of
some, who live in flesh but make no use of the senses of the
flesh, even up to the vision of His own essence." [50] Elsewhere,[51] however, he says of Moses that "he saw God's very
essence, even as Paul in his rapture did according to Augustine,[52] and to prove this he quotes Scripture to the effect

[43] *De Trinitate* II, 16, 27.
[44] *Super Genesim ad Litteram* XII, 27, 55 (PL, 34, 477). Cf. *Sum. Theol.* I, II,
98, 3, ad 2.
[45] *Moreh Nebukim* I, 54.   [46] Cf. above, p. 143.
[47] *Moreh Nebukim* I, 54.
[48] Exod. 33: 20; *Sum. Theol.* I, 12, 11 contra; *Cont. Gent.* III, 47; *De Veritate* X,
11, Obj. 2.
[49] *Sum. Theol.* I, 12, 11 c.
[50] *Ibid.*, ad 2.
[51] *Ibid.*, II, II, 174, 4 c.
[52] *Super Genesim ad Litteram* XII, 27, 55 (PL, 34, 477), 28, 56 (PL, 34, 478); cf.
Sum. Theol. II, II, 175, 3 c.

that "Moses beheld God 'manifestly and not in dark speeches.'"[53]

The answers given in the subsequent history of philosophy to the problem of divine predicates started by Philo went far beyond Philo's answer. New solutions will make their appearance in pagan, Christian, Moslem, and Jewish philosophy, solutions of which the complexity of history and meaning will be discussed by us in great detail in the subsequent volumes of this series of studies. But the solution offered by Philo to the problem by declaring that all predicates of God are descriptions of His property or power of action continues to be one of the standard solutions of the problem in Christian, Moslem, and Jewish philosophy. John of Damascus, speaking for the Church Fathers, declares that some of the predicates of God indicate an action ($\dot{\epsilon}\nu\dot{\epsilon}\rho\gamma\epsilon\iota\alpha$).[54] The explanation of divine predicates as actions is to be found also, either under the guise of the term relation, that is, the relation of the agent to the patient,[55] or directly under the term action, in Arabic Moslem and Arabic Jewish philosophers, such as Alfarabi,[56] Avicenna,[57] Algazali,[58] Baḥya Ibn Pakuda,[59] Joseph Ibn Ṣaddik,[60] Judah ha-Levi,[61] Abraham Ibn Daud,[62] and Maimonides,[63] though, in the case of Maimonides, according to our interpretation of his view, the explanation of predicates as actions has an entirely new meaning.[64]

---

[53] Literally the verse in question reads: "With him do I speak . . . manifestly, and not in dark speeches; and the similitude of the Lord doth he behold" (Num. 12:8).

[54] *De Fide Orthodoxa* I, 9 (PG, 94, 836 A).

[55] Cf. above, p. 137.

[56] *Al-Siyāsāt al-Madaniyyah*, p. 20, ll. 2-3.

[57] *Najāt*, pp. 410–411.

[58] *Maqāṣid al-Falāsifah* II, p. 150, ll. 8–9.

[59] *Ḥobot ha-Lebabot* I, 9.

[60] *'Olam Ḳaṭan* III, p. 48.

[61] *Cuzari* II, 2.

[62] *Emunah Ramah* II, iii, p. 54.

[63] *Moreh Nebukim* I, 52.

[64] Cf. H. A. Wolfson, "The Aristotelian Predicables and Maimonides' Division of Attributes," *Essays and Studies in Memory of Linda R. Miller*, 1938, pp. 220–232.

If we were right in our reasoning from the absence in the extant writing of pre-Philonic Greek philosophers of any definite statement to the effect that God is "unnamable" or "ineffable" or "incomprehensible" that such descriptions of God were not used by Greek philosophers before Philo, then when we do find these terms used by pagan Greek philosophers after Philo we have reason to assume that they have come into use under the influence of Philo or, when chronology permits, under the influence of the Church Fathers who have used Philo. Of course I am aware of the opinion prevailing among some scholars today that no pagan authors of that time read the works of Philo.[65] But neither the absence of any mention of his name nor the absence of any direct quotation from his writings definitely proves that he was not read, or that those who had read him were not influenced by some of his ideas. In fact, Eusebius, who lived at a time when pagan philosophy was still flourishing, testifies that Philo was a man of great note not only among Christians but also among pagans.[66] We shall mention here two pagan Greek authors, after the time of Philo, in whose writings we find some of the views of Philo, discussed in this chapter, which we have tried to show were new with Philo.

First, there is Albinus. "God," he says, "is ineffable ($\ddot{a}\rho\rho\eta\tau\sigma$) and is comprehended ($\lambda\eta\pi\tau\delta\varsigma$) only by the mind ($\nu\tilde{\omega}$)." [67] The first part of the statement is definitely like Philo's many assertions as to the ineffability of God, using the same term $\ddot{a}\rho\rho\eta\tau\sigma\varsigma$.[68] The second part of the statement,

[65] Cf. Goodenough, *The Politics of Philo Judaeus with a General Bibliography of Philo* (Yale University Press, 1938), p. 250, n. 1; *idem, An Introduction to Philo Judaeus* (Yale University Press, 1940), p. 125. Cf. also A. D. Nock, "The Loeb Philo," *The Classical Review*, 75 (1943), pp. 77–78.

[66] *Historia Ecclesiastica* II, 4, 2; cf. above, I, 100, n. 64.

[67] *Didaskalikos* X, in C. F. Hermann, *Platonis Dialoghi*, VI, 165, ll. 4–5.

[68] Cf. above, p. 111.

that God is "comprehended only by the mind," would at first sight seem to be in contradiction to Philo's repeated statement that God is incomprehensible (ἀκατάληπτος)[69] and more so to his statement that "He is not comprehended by the mind" (οὐδὲ τῷ νῷ καταληπτός).[70] But Philo himself, despite his assertions of the incomprehensibility of God, says of God that He "can be comprehended (καταλαμβάνεσθαι) only by the mind (νοήσει)," [71] and from the context of that statement it is quite evident that by this positive statement that "God can be comprehended only by the mind" he merely means to deny that "God was seen by man," that is to say, in its positive form it is merely an assertion that God's existence can be comprehended only by the mind but cannot be seen by the eye; [72] it does not mean that God's essence can be comprehended by the mind. That similarly here Albinus means by his positive statement only that God cannot be perceived by the senses, without implying that His essence can be comprehended by the mind, is evident from another statement of his in which he says that God is incomprehensible (ἄληπτος).[73] He furthermore says of God that "He is not a genus (γένος) nor a species (εἶδος) nor a difference (διαφορά)." [74] This is exactly, as we have seen, the implication of Philo's statements that God is "the highest genus." [75] Finally, after asserting the ineffability and incomprehensibility of God, he argues that while on the one

[69] Cf. above, p. 111.
[70] *Immut.* 13, 62.
[71] *Mut.* 1, 6.
[72] Cf. above, p. 118.
[73] *Didaskalikos* IV, 154, l. 19. Cf. comment on these apparently contradictory statements in Albinus himself and between Albinus and Philo in J. Freudenthal, "Der Platoniker Albinos und der falsche Alkinoos" in his *Hellenistische Studien*, Heft 3, p. 284, n. **.
[74] *Didaskalikos* X, 165, ll. 5–6.
[75] Cf. above, p. 109.

hand we cannot say that God is of a certain quality (ποιόν), on the other, we cannot say of Him that He is without quality (ἄποιον).[76] This last part of the statement is quite evidently a criticism of Philo's repeated statement that God is without quality.[77]

Second, there is Plotinus. In many places he repeats the statement that God is ineffable (ἄρρητος),[78] that "He has no name" [79] or that to Him "no name is really suitable," [80] and that "He cannot be grasped by thought," [81] or that "we have of Him neither knowledge nor thought." [82] All these views about God, as we have seen, do not occur in Greek philosophy before Philo.

Spinoza, in his grand assault on traditional philosophy, discusses also all these traditional problems. He accepts what he can; what he cannot he rejects. He is willing to accept the traditional principle of the unity of God and to treat that principle of unity after its traditional manner as meaning both numerical unity and simplicity.[83] He is willing to say that his God, like the God of tradition, is one both in a numerical sense and in the sense of being simple and indivisible. He is willing also to describe his God by many of the predicates which traditional philosophy applied to its own God, including such predicates as omniscient, almighty, the highest good, of infinite compassion,[84] intelligent, endowed with will, living.[85] He is also willing to follow the tradition

[76] *Didaskalikos* X, 165, ll. 8–10.
[77] Cf. above, pp. 101 ff.
[78] *Enneads* V, 3, 13; cf. VI, 9, 4.
[79] *Ibid.* 3, 13.
[80] *Ibid.* VI, 9, 5.
[81] *Ibid.* V, 3, 13 end.
[82] *Ibid.* V, 3, 14 beginning.
[83] Cf. H. A. Wolfson, *The Philosophy of Spinoza*, I, chapter on "Simplicity of Substance," I.
[84] *Short Treatise* I, 7, § 2.
[85] *Cogitata Metaphysica* II, 11 end.

established by Philo by calling these predicates properties
(*propria*)[86] and to define property, after Aristotle, as that
which "may belong to an object and yet never explain what
the object is," [87] that is to say, it does not explain the "essence" of a thing,[88] though it necessarily follows from the
definition of a thing.[89] Moreover, following also the tradition
established by Philo, he is willing to describe these properties of God as having "reference to His activity" [90] or as
explaining God's "active essence." [91] But, in opposition to
this traditional philosophy, he is unwilling to derive from
the simplicity and indivisibility of God that he must also
be incorporeal, contending that corporeal substance, if
properly understood, can be simple and indivisible.[92] God
is thus not only what traditional philosophy used to call pure
form; He is also pure corporeality. Using for the term pure
corporeality the term extension and for the term pure form
the term thought, he now says that we can predicate of
God both extension and thought. But these two predicates,
unlike all the other predicates, are not properties of God, for
by property, as we have seen, is meant something which belongs to a substance but does not explain its essence, whereas
extension and thought explain the essence of God. These
two predicates, in order to distinguish them from all the
other predicates, he calls by the mediaeval term "attributes."
Having called these two predicates, extension and thought,
by the mediaeval term attributes, he follows the mediaeval

[86] *Short Treatise* I, 7, § 6.

[87] *Ibid.*

[88] *Ethics* III, *Affectuum Definitiones*, VI, Expl.

[89] *Ibid.* I, Prop. 16, Dem. Cf. Aristotle, *Topica* I, 5, 102a, 18–19; 101b, 39; V, 3, 131b, 38–132a, 1; *Metaph.* V, 30, 1025a, 30–34; cf. above, p. 132.

[90] *Short Treatise* I, 2, § 29.

[91] *Cogitata Metaphysica* II, 11 end. Cf. *The Philosophy of Spinoza*, I, chapter on "Extension and Thought," II.

[92] Cf. *The Philosophy of Spinoza*, I, chapter on "Infinity of Extension."

method in his explanation why the attribution of extension and thought to God does not vitiate the simplicity of His nature. His explanation is that extension and thought are not real beings which either constitute the essence of God or are appended to the essence of God. They are the way in which the essence of God manifests itself to us; or, to quote his own words, "By attribute I understand that which the intellect perceives of substance, as if constituting its essence," [93] and on this point he is opposed even to the general tradition of Plato and Aristotle.

Then he is also unwilling to accept without reservation the traditional view that God is indefinable and hence incomprehensible. It all depends, he says, on what you mean by definition. If you mean by it definition in the Aristotelian sense as that which consists of genus and species, then, of course, God being the highest genus cannot be defined and hence cannot be known [94] and in this sense he says that "of God's essence we can form no general idea." [95] But this conception of definition, argues Spinoza, must be rejected. [96] According to him, there are two kinds of definition, one phrased in terms of the cause of the thing to be defined and the other phrased in terms of its attributes. If the thing to be defined is, like all things in the world, dependent upon a cause for its existence, then its definition must "comprehend its proximate cause"; [97] and, if the thing defined is self-existent and has no cause, such as God is, then, since it has no cause to be comprehended in its definition, its definition must comprehend its attributes, the knowledge of which

---

[93] *Ethics* I, Def. 4.
[94] *Short Treatise* I, 7, §§ 3 ff.
[95] Epistola 50 (*Opera*, ed. Gebhardt, IV, 240, ll. 2–3); cf. *The Philosophy of Spinoza*, I, 142.
[96] *Short Treatise* I, 7, § 9.
[97] *Tractatus de Intellectus Emendatione*, § 96 (*Opera*, II, 35, ll. 15–16).

THE UNKNOWABILITY OF GOD 163

leads to a knowledge of its essence.[98] In his own way, then, God is defined as "substance consisting of infinite attributes," and inasmuch as two of these attributes, extension and thought, are known, to that extent God's essence is known, for these attributes are the manifestations of God's essence to our intellect, and these attributes and essence of God, moreover, are known to us immediately by that third kind of knowledge which Spinoza calls intuitive knowledge. The essence of God is thus, we may conclude for Spinoza, both definable and knowable, according to his own conception of definition and according to his own use of the term knowledge.

Finally, he is unwilling to accept the tradition established by Philo that Scripture, in the prayer of Moses and in other passages, teaches the unknowability of God's essence. Indeed he admits that "Scripture nowhere gives an express definition of God" [99] or "an intellectual knowledge of God, which takes cognizance of His nature in so far as it actually is " [100] nor does it teach anything "special about the divine attributes," [101] that is, about those attributes which express the essence of God. But this does not mean that God's essence cannot be known; it only means that the authors of Scripture "held quite ordinary notions about God, and to these notions their revelations were adapted " [102] and therefore they teach only what he calls properties or actions of God, namely, "that God is supremely just, and supremely merciful — in other words, the one single pattern of the true life." [103] Taking up the prayer of Moses, which ever since Philo was taken to be a philosophic petition for a knowledge of God's es-

[98] *Ethics* II, Prop. 40, Schol. 2 (*Opera*, II, 122, ll. 16–19). Cf. *The Philosophy of Spinoza*, I, 383–385; II, 37–38; 142–144.
[99] *Tractatus Theologico-Politicus*, ch. 13 (*Opera*, III, 171, ll. 22–23).
[100] *Ibid.* (ll. 25–26).
[101] *Ibid.*, ch. 2 (p. 37, ll. 12–13).
[102] *Ibid.* (ll. 13–14).   [103] *Ibid.*, ch. 13 (p. 171, ll. 21–22).

sence, he maintains that Moses was no philosopher, that his conception of God was rather primitive and that what he prayed for was actually to see (*videre*) God,[104] for "Moses believed that God is visible, that is, on the part of the divine nature the visibility of God involves no contradiction."[105] Then, he takes up the verse, "I appeared unto Abraham, unto Isaac, and unto Jacob, as God Almighty, but by my name the Lord I made me not known to them,"[106] from which Philo, as we have seen, infers that according to Scripture God is unnamable[107] and hence unknowable in his essence. Here, again, Spinoza tries to show that, while indeed the meaning of the verse is, as maintained by Jewish interpreters, that the Patriarchs "were not cognizant of any attribute of God which expresses His absolute essence, but only of His deeds and promises, that is, of His power, as manifested in visible things,"[108] it does not mean that the divine essence, as well as the attributes which express it, is unknowable; it merely means that, as simple-minded believers, the Patriarchs "possessed no extraordinary knowledge of God."[109]

[104] *Ibid.*, ch. 2 (p. 40, l. 7).
[105] *Ibid.* (ll. 15–16).
[106] Exod. 6:3.
[107] *Mut.* 2, 13.
[108] *Tractatus Theologico-Politicus*, ch. 13 (*Opera*, III, p. 169, ll. 22–24).
[109] *Ibid.* (ll. 26–27).

CHAPTER XII

ETHICAL THEORY

I. "Under the Law" and "In Accordance with Nature"

His conception of the Pentateuch as a divinely revealed document which contains the true knowledge of things divine and human[1] has led Philo to a revision of the ethical theories of Greek philosophy analogous to his revision of its metaphysical theories. Making use again of common philosophic concepts and terms, he modifies them in conformity with certain presuppositions derived from Scripture.

Philosophic ethics, as developed by Socrates, Plato, Aristotle, and the Stoics, begins, in Aristotle's formulation of it, with the statement that "the good is that which all things aim at (ἐφίεται)"[2] or aspire to (ὀρέγεται).[3] That good is generally agreed upon, as Aristotle says, by both the multitude and the refined few, to be happiness (εὐδαιμονία).[4] But as to what happiness consists in there is no agreement. Some people identify it with pleasure (ἡδονή) or wealth (πλοῦτος) or honor (τιμή),[5] or what both Plato and Aristotle call external goods.[6] But Aristotle, and before him Plato, did not agree with this conception of happiness. Nor is happiness, according to them, what they call the goods of the body,[7] or the virtue of the body,[8] such, for example, as

---

[1] Cf. above, I, 149.
[2] *Eth. Nic.* I, 1, 1094a, 2.
[3] *Ibid.* I, 4, 1095a, 15; (cf. *Sympos.* 205 A).
[4] *Ibid.*, 18–19.
[5] *Ibid.*, 23.
[6] *Laws* V, 743 E, *Philebus* 48 E; *Euthydemus* 279 A–B; *Eth. Nic.* I, 8, 1098b, 12–14.
[7] *Eth. Nic.* I, 8, 1098b, 13–14; *Laws* III, 697 B.
[8] *Eth. Nic.* I, 13, 1102a, 16; *Gorg.* 479 B.

health. It is rather the virtue of the soul.⁹ Moreover, inasmuch as the virtue of the soul may be either intellectual
(διανοητική) or moral (ἠθική),¹⁰ happiness consists in both these
kinds of virtue.¹¹ This is how the problem of ethics is formulated by Aristotle. This formulation of the problem is repeated in a variety of ways in the Stoic literature, wherein
happiness is defined in terms of the good,¹² the good is divided
into three kinds, two of which are external goods and goods
of the soul,¹³ and happiness is identified with the good of the
soul or rather the virtue of the soul.¹⁴

    Philo starts his discussion of ethics with a similar formula-
tion of the problem. He begins with the statement that hope
(ἐλπίς) is "the fountainhead of the lives which we lead." ¹⁵
This is evidently a paraphrase of Aristotle's statement that
"the good is that which all things aim at" or "aspire to."
The substitution of the term "hope" for the term "the good"
may be explained by Plato's statements that "hope is an expectation of good" ¹⁶ and that "we are always filled with
hopes all our lives" ¹⁷ and Philo's own statement elsewhere
that "the beginning of the enjoyment of good things is
hope." ¹⁸ Then like Aristotle he proceeds to enumerate the
various kinds of good things that men hope for. Though
in this connection he mentions only two of the three objects
of desire enumerated by Aristotle, namely, the hope of
gain (κέρδος) and the hope of glory (δόξα),¹⁹ elsewhere he

⁹ *Eth. Nic.* I, 8, 1098b, 14–15; *Laws* III, 697 B.
¹⁰ *Eth. Nic.* I, 13, 1103a, 4–7.
¹¹ *Ibid.* II, 1, 1103a, 15–18.
¹² Cf. Arnim, III, 73.
¹³ *Idem*, III, 96, 97, 97a.
¹⁴ *Idem*, III, 57.
¹⁵ *Praem.* 2, 11.
¹⁶ *Definitiones* 416 A; cf. Xenophon, *Cyropaedia*, I, 6, 19.
¹⁷ *Philebus* 39 E.
¹⁸ *Abr.* 2, 7.   ¹⁹ *Praem.* 2, 11.

mentions all the three, wealth (πλοῦτος), glory (δόξα), and pleasure (ἡδονή).[20] Finally he mentions "the hope of happiness" of which he says that "it incites the devotees of virtue to study philosophy, believing that thus they will be able to discern the nature of all that exists and to do what is agreeable to the perfecting of the best forms of life, the contemplative and the practical, on the attainment of which one is forthwith happy." [21] This is quite evidently a restatement of Aristotle's view that the highest good is happiness and that happiness is an activity according to both the intellectual and the moral virtues. In another place happiness is said by Philo to consist of wisdom (σοφία) and prudence (φρόνησις),[22] wisdom referring here to intellectual virtue and prudence to moral virtue.[23]

Now when philosophers have arrived at the conclusion that happiness is based on virtue, both the moral and the intellectual kinds of virtue, they raise the question as to what is to guide man to a life based upon intellectual and moral virtues. To this Aristotle, speaking for all the philosophers, answers in his statement that "intellectual virtue in the main owes both its birth and its growth to teaching," whereas "moral virtue comes about as a result of habit," [24] so that we acquire intellectual virtues only after "experience and time"[25] and we acquire moral virtues only "by first having actually practiced them." [26] To be taught in the knowledge of the truth of things and to be trained in practices which develop character are thus the essential conditions in the attainment of the intellectual and moral virtues. Accordingly both Plato and Aristotle consider it as the duty of the state to educate

---

[20] *Sobr.* 12, 61; cf. 11, 56; *Decal.* 28, 153.
[21] *Praem.* 2, 11.
[22] *Praem.* 14, 81.
[23] Cf. above, I, 147; but cf. below, p. 211.
[24] *Eth. Nic.* II, 1, 1103a, 14–17.
[25] *Ibid.*, 16–17.
[26] *Ibid.*, 31.

its citizens in both moral and intellectual virtues,[27] and to
enact laws with a view to making the citizens acquire the
habits of right action. These laws, the obedience to which
is to train men in the habits of moral virtues, are called by
Aristotle practical virtues (πρακτικαὶ ἀρεταί),[28] or virtuous
actions (κατ' ἀρετὴν πράξεις),[29] or virtuous activities (κατ'
ἀρετὴν ἐνέργειαι),[30] and by the Stoics they are called befitting
acts or duties (καθήκοντα).[31]

But what are the right opinions and the right laws which
are to teach men intellectual virtues and train them in
moral virtues? The Greek philosophers, when they began to
speculate on these matters, had before them a set of intellectual virtues consisting of the popular beliefs about the
deities and also a set of practical virtues consisting of the
laws which prevailed in various Greek cities, and which were
believed to have come from certain deities. But Greek
philosophy on the whole was hostile to the beliefs about the
deities and critical of the traditional laws. Even philosophers
who endowed the popular deities with some philosophic
meaning and advocated their worship did not allow their
philosophy to be affected by the popular conception of the
deities. In Plato, and even in the Stoics, despite their use of
popular religious terms in the description of what they called
God, their philosophic God remained a strictly philosophic
concept unchanged by any view imported from religion.
There was no harmonization of philosophic and religious beliefs among Greek philosophers; there was only a pragmatic
union established between two systems of thought.

Nor did the Greek philosophers accept the popular belief

---

[27] *Statesman* 309 C–D; *Euthydemus* 292 B; *Politica* VIII, 1, 1337a, 21 ff.; cf. Zeller,
II, 1⁴, p. 896, nn. 3 and 4 (*Plato*, p. 465, nn. 14 and 15); II, 2³, p. 732, n. 3 (*Aristotle*,
II, p. 264, n. 1).

[28] *Eth. Nic.* X, 7, 1177b, 6.   [30] *Ibid.* I, 10, 1100b, 10.
[29] *Ibid.* IV, 1, 1120a, 23.   [31] Diogenes, VII, 108.

about the divine origin of established laws, with the implication of the belief in the perfection of these laws. Obedient
to the established law indeed they were and obedience to it
they also advocated, but they had no belief in their perfection and immutability and divine origin. Socrates, even
though the charges for which he was condemned were
groundless, did not consider the Athenian constitution as
perfect and was opposed to traditional morality based on
the existent laws and customs.[32] Plato did not believe that
any of the laws existing in Greece at his time was perfect
or of divine origin,[33] though in the *Laws* [34] and in *Minos* [35]
he makes reference to the popular belief in the divine origin
of the Cretan laws and in the *Laws* he makes an additional
reference to the divine origin of the laws of Lacedaemon.[36]
Still less did Aristotle believe that these laws of Crete and
Lacedaemon were of divine origin and perfect.[37] The Stoic
view is reëchoed in Cicero's statements that none of the
existent laws in any of the states is divine; they are all man-
made.[38]

With their disbelief in the divine origin and hence perfection of any of the existent constitutions and any of the
existent systems of law and with their disbelief also that
what they called God in their philosophies could reveal constitutions and laws to men, various Greek philosophers took
it upon themselves to devise ideal constitutions and laws, or
at least constitutions and laws approaching the ideal.[39]

[32] Cf. Zeller, II, 1⁴, pp. 221–224 (*Socrates*, pp. 189–193).
[33] Cf. *idem*, p. 894, n. 4 (*Plato*, p. 463, n. 8).
[34] *Laws* I, 624 A.
[35] *Minos* 320 B.
[36] *Laws* I, 624 A. Cf. similar reference to these popular beliefs among the
Greeks in Josephus, *Apion.* II, 16, 161–162.
[37] *Politica* II, 10, 1271b, 31–32; VII, 2, 1324b, 5–9.
[38] Cicero, *De Re Publica* III, 11, 18 ff.; *De Legibus* II, 4, 11.
[39] Cf. below, pp. 375 ff.

Hippodamus is said by Aristotle to be the first person not a statesman, but a philosopher, who devised plans for an ideal state governed by laws drawn up according to philosophic principles.[40] Plato did the same in his *Republic* and *Laws*. Zeno and Chrysippus did it in their lost treatises, of which only the titles are preserved,[41] and Cicero did it in his *Republic* and *Laws*. They devised laws which they considered ideal and hoped for the best.

These ideal laws enacted by philosophers for the guidance of men are described by them as being "in accordance with reason" or "in accordance with virtue." But whether enacted law can also be described as being "in accordance with nature" is a matter of discussion among them.

As reported by Plato, the Sophists maintain that "nature" is the opposite of "law." The term nature, when used in the sense of human nature, means to them the impulse to domination. As such it is regarded by them as the opposite of any law enacted by men. "A true life in accordance with nature (κατὰ τὴν φύσιν ὀρθὸν βίον)" is in their opinion the opposite of a life in accordance with any kind of law enacted by men, for a true life in accordance with nature, they maintain, means "to live in real dominion over others and not in legal (κατὰ νόμον) subjection to them."[42] A similar view, but with a notable qualification, is also to be found in a work falsely ascribed to Hippocrates. According to this work, "law and nature . . . do not agree, though sometimes they do agree, for law was given by men, without their knowing why they gave it; but the nature of all things was ordered by the gods."[43] The implication of this statement quite

[40] *Politica* II, 8, 1267b, 29 ff.
[41] Diogenes, VII, 4, 33, 131; Plutarch, *De Alexandri Magni Fortuna aut Virtute* I, 6.
[42] *Laws* X, 890 A.
[43] *De Victu* I, 11 (*Oeuvres d'Hippocrate*, VI, 486, ed. É. Littré). Cf. Zeller,

evidently is that not all laws are in opposition to nature; only those laws are in opposition to nature which were enacted by men without their knowing why they enacted them, that is, laws enacted without reason, but laws enacted on the basis of reason are in accordance with nature.

Plato himself seems to think that certain enacted laws can be in accordance with nature. The term nature, however, is used by him in two senses.

In one sense, like the Sophists, he takes the term nature to mean impulse. But the impulse to him is not one to domination but rather one to "reverence" or "friendship," as, for instance, when he says that "every right-minded man fears and respects the prayers of parents, knowing that many times and in many cases they have proved effective" and that these things are determined "by nature" (φύσει); [44] or when he says that "those philosophers who debate and write about *nature* and the universe" tell us that "like must needs be always friend to like." [45] Now a mode of conduct based upon the principle that "like is friend to like" is described by him as being "dear to God and following in His steps," [46] that is to say, it follows the law of reason, for by the term God here, as is obvious from the context, he means that which he has previously described as "the immortal element within us," [47] that is, reason (νοῦς), and law (νόμος), furthermore, is explained by him etymologically to mean the "ordering of reason" (νοῦ διανομή). [48] Accordingly, it may be inferred that laws enacted by wise legislators to further reverence or friendship would be described by Plato as

---

"Über Begriff und Begründung der sittlichen Gesetze," *Abhandlungen der Berliner Akademie der Wissenschaften, Philos.-histor. Klasse*, 1882, Abh. II, p. 5.

[44] *Laws* XI, 931 E.
[45] *Lysis* 214 B.
[46] *Laws* IV, 716 B–C.
[47] *Ibid.*, 714 A.   [48] *Ibid.*

being both "in accordance with reason" and "in accordance with nature."

In another sense, the term nature is taken by him to mean
the capacities with which human beings were endowed by
nature and therefore laws enacted in accordance with the
natural capacities of those who are to be governed by those
laws are described by him as laws in accordance with
nature. Thus in his discussion of the law of the equality of
men and women with regard to the holding of office in his
ideal republic, he says that "the law which we have established is neither impossible nor a mere aspiration, since we
have established it in accordance with nature (κατὰ φύσιν)," [49]
for "the gifts of nature (αἱ φύσεις) are alike diffused in both,
and woman by nature (κατὰ φύσιν) shares in all the pursuits
the same as man, though in all cases the woman is weaker
than the man." [50] Thus, in this sense, law in accordance
with nature means with Plato rational laws enacted by wise
legislators to secure for each individual the enjoyment of
those rights to which he is entitled by his natural gifts and
capacities.

That laws enacted by legislators may be in accordance with
nature seems to be also the view of Plato's followers in the
Old Academy, especially Polemo. [51] The term "nature" by
itself is used by them in the sense of "the primary endow-
ments of nature" (*prima, data natura*, τὰ πρῶτα κατὰ φύσιν)
by which "they mean soundness of body and mind." [52]
When therefore they say that the highest good or happiness
is "to live in accordance with nature" one would expect
them to mean thereby that happiness consists in the enjoyment of a sound body and a sound mind. However, they

---

[49] *Republic* V, 456 c.
[50] *Ibid.*, 455 D–E.   [51] Cf. below, n. 55.
[52] Cicero, *De Finibus* II, 11, 34; *Academica Posteriora* I, 5, 19–20.

do not mean that. Happiness, according to them, does not consist in mere physical and mental well-being. To this must be added, they maintain, virtuous activity, which means an activity based upon reason. When they, therefore, happen to say that "the end of good is to live in accordance with nature," they immediately add, "that is to say, to enjoy the primary gifts of nature's bestowal with the accompaniment of virtue"[53] or "to live honorably, enjoying those things which nature makes most dear to man."[54] The implication, therefore, is that life in accordance with nature which is to constitute happiness is not opposed to enacted law; on the contrary, it is to include enacted law, provided only that the enacted law is a rational law and is based on virtue.[55]

The two senses of the expression "in accordance with nature," one as the opposite of enacted law and the other as a description of law enacted on the basis of reason, are to be found also in Aristotle. The first of these two senses is used by him directly; the second sense is implied in some of his statements.

In his direct discussion of the subject, he uses the term law in accordance with nature (κατὰ φύσιν)[56] as the opposite of law enacted by legislators as a result of convention (συνθήκῃ).[57] By natural law he means, as he himself explains,

---

[53] Idem, De Finibus II, 11, 34.

[54] Idem, Academica Priora II, 42, 131. Cf. Zeller, II, 1⁴, p. 1029, n. 2; p. 1045, n. 3, p. 1046, n. 1 (Plato, p. 600, n. 66; p. 617, n. 63; p. 618, n. 64).

[55] J. S. Reid, in a note to his edition of the Academica, l.c. (l. 19), and W. M. L. Hutchinson, in the Introduction, 26 (3), to his edition of the De Finibus are inclined to think that originally, in Polemo, the expression "life in accordance with nature" meant to be the opposite of life in accordance with convention (θέσις) or law (νόμος), the element of virtue having been added later by Antiochus who glossed it with Stoic phrases. Zeller, however, takes the element of virtue to have been added to this statement by Polemo himself (II, 1⁴, pp. 1045–1046; Plato, pp. 617–618).

[56] Rhet. I, 13, 1373b, 7.

[57] Eth. Nic. V, 7, 1134b, 32; Rhet. I, 13, 1373b, 8–9.

a law arrived at by all men, without any communication or agreement between them, but by the mere fact that they all possess by nature a common idea of just and unjust.[58] As the equivalent of "law in accordance with nature" he therefore also uses the term "general law" (νόμος κοινός)[59] and, by implication, also the term moral (ἠθικός) law.[60] In contrast with this, conventional law is also called by him "particular law" (νόμος ἴδιος),[61] and human (ἀνθρώπινος) law.[62] By "particular law," he says, he means that law "in accordance with which a state is administered"[63] or "which each community lays down and applies to its own members."[64] Natural law and conventional law are also described by him respectively as "unwritten (ἄγραφος) law" and "written (γεγραμμένος) law,"[65] though sometimes the term "unwritten law" is also used by him as a description of a subdivision of conventional law.[66] As illustrations of what he means by natural law he quotes Sophocles to the effect that the burial of the dead is "just by nature,"[67] he also quotes Empedocles to the effect that not to kill any living creature is an "all-embracing law,"[68] and he finally quotes Alcidamus probably to the effect that "nature has made no man a slave."[69] As illustrations of particular or

---

[58] *Rhet.* I, 13, 1373b, 7–9.

[59] *Ibid.*, 4.

[60] *Eth. Nic.* VIII, 13, 1162b, 21–23: φιλία ἠθική and νομική are compared by him with τὸ δίκαιον ἄγραφον (= κατὰ φύσιν) and κατὰ νόμον respectively.

[61] *Rhet.* I, 13, 1373b, 6.

[62] *Eth. Nic.* V, 7, 1135a, 4, where he contrasts δίκαια φυσικά and ἀνθρώπινα.

[63] *Rhet.* I, 10, 1368b, 7–8.

[64] *Ibid.*, 13, 1373b, 4–5.

[65] *Ibid.* I, 10, 1368b, 7–9; 15, 1375a, 27–33, *Eth. Nic.* VIII, 13, 1162b, 22.

[66] *Rhet.* I, 13, 1373b, 4–6; cf. R. Hirzel, Ἄγραφος νόμος, *Abhandlungen der sachsischen Gesellschaft der Wissenschaften, philol-histor. Klasse,* 20 (1903), pp. 3–13.

[67] *Rhet.* I, 13, 1373b, 10–11.

[68] *Ibid.*, 14–16.

[69] *Ibid.*, 18; cf. commentaries *ad loc.*

conventional law he mentions such laws as "that a prisoner's ransom should be a mina, or that a goat and not two sheep shall be sacrificed, and again all the laws that are passed for particular cases, for example, that sacrifice shall be made in honor of Brasidas." [70] The significant thing about these illustrations of conventional law is that they contain examples of what may be called ceremonial or religious laws. What that human nature is that prompts all men without communication and agreement between them to evolve universal laws or universal conceptions of just and unjust common to all of them Aristotle does not say. Probably it is that nature in man with reference to which he says that "man is by nature a political animal" [71] and that "a social impulse (ὁρμή) is implanted in all men by nature," [72] so that men "desire to live together." [73] These natural laws which arise from that social impulse or instinct are quite obviously not considered by Aristotle as the result of what he calls demonstrative reasoning or conclusions from premises. They are rather what he calls primary premises which according to his characterization of them are self-evident.[74]

But indirectly it may be inferred that also enacted law, man-made law, if it is based upon reason, that is, upon demonstrative reasoning, is considered by Aristotle as being, in a certain sense, in accordance with nature. Happiness, he says, is an "activity in accordance with virtue," [75] by which he explains is meant "the highest virtue," [76] the virtue of "the best thing in us" [77] and the best thing within us is the contemplative activity of reason,[78] and consequently

---

[70] *Eth. Nic.* V, 7, 1134b, 21–24.
[71] *Politica* I, 2, 1253a, 2–3.
[72] *Ibid.*, 29–30.
[73] *Ibid.* III, 6, 1278b, 21.
[74] *Anal. Post.* I, 2, 71b, 21, and I, 9, 76a, 16–17.
[75] *Eth. Nic.* X, 7, 1177a, 12.

[76] *Ibid.*, 13.
[77] *Ibid.*
[78] *Ibid.*, 17–18.

in the expressions "life in accordance with virtue" and "life in accordance with reason," the term virtue means intellectual virtue and the term reason means contemplative reason. But in a secondary degree, Aristotle maintains, happiness also means life in accordance with virtue which is not intellectual virtue but rather moral virtue.[79] Now moral virtue involves prudence (φρόνησις),[80] or practical reason, and is defined as being a state of character "in accordance with the right rule (ὀρθὸν λόγον)."[81] Furthermore, moral virtue, according to him, requires also good laws, for, as he says, "legislators ought to stimulate men to virtue"[82] and "the man who is to be good must be well trained and habituated." But this training and habituation can be secured only "if men live in accordance with a sort of reason, and by a right system, invested with adequate force," and it is law which provides that force and that reason and that right system for "the law has compulsive power, while it is at the same time a rule proceeding from a sort of practical wisdom and reason."[83]

Thus, according to Aristotle, life in accordance with virtue, which means the same as life in accordance with reason, may have two meanings. It may mean life in accordance with contemplative reason, which has nothing to do with law, or it may mean life in accordance with practical reason, in which case it means the same as life in accordance with law enacted by wise legislators. Now of contemplative reason Aristotle says that it is thought "to rule and lead us in accordance with nature (κατὰ φύσιν) and to have cognizance of what is noble and divine,"[84] for "the life in accordance with reason" is that which is proper "to the

[79] Ibid., 8,1178a, 9 ff.
[80] Ibid., 16–17.
[81] Ibid. VI, 13, 1144b, 23.
[82] Ibid. X, 9, 1180a, 6–7.
[83] Ibid., 1180a, 14–22.
[84] Ibid., 7, 1177a, 13–15.

nature (τῇ φύσει)" of man.[85] By the same token, of practical reason, or law based upon practical reason, Aristotle could logically also say that, in a secondary sense, it, too, is to rule and lead us "in accordance with nature" and that life in accordance with practical reason, or in accordance with law based upon practical reason, is proper "to the nature" of man. Law enacted by wise legislators, therefore, though it is not exactly "in accordance with nature" in the strictly technical sense of the term, for it often thwarts certain natural impulses of men, still, proceeding as it does "from a sort of practical wisdom and reason," it may be described as being "in accordance with nature," inasmuch as reason is that which is "to rule and lead us by nature and to have cognizance of what is noble and divine." For, as he himself seems to say, in man there are certain natural impulses which are good and rational, so that while, as a rule, "people hate men who oppose their impulses (ὁρμαῖς), even if they oppose them rightly, the law in its ordaining of what is good is not an object of hatred." [86]

The conception of life in accordance with nature as a rational and virtuous life, and not a mere instinctive life, is to be found also in the Stoics. To them the purely instinctive life is life in its endeavor toward self-preservation. "An animal's first impulse (ὁρμήν), say the Stoics, is self-preservation, because nature from the outset endears it to itself." [87] For brute animals, therefore, whom nature has endowed with an impulse to self-preservation, and nothing more than that impulse, "that which is in accordance with nature means to be regulated by that which is in accordance with impulse." [88] For men, however, whom nature has endowed with reason in addition to impulse, to live in accord-

[85] *Ibid.*, 1178a, 5–7.
[86] *Ibid.*, 9, 1180a, 22–24

[87] Diogenes, VII, 85; cf. Arnim, III, §§ 178 ff.
[88] Diogenes, VII, 86.

ance with nature means to live in accordance with reason, for "when reason (λόγου) by way of a more perfect leadership has been bestowed on the beings we call rational, for them life in accordance with reason rightly becomes life in accordance with nature, for reason supervenes to shape impulse scientifically." [89] Or, as this last statement is phrased elsewhere, for the purpose of self-preservation "the sciences too have been invented, to bring aid to nature, and the chief among them is reckoned to be the science of conduct, which helps the creature to maintain whatever nature has bestowed, and to obtain that which is lacking." [90] The old formula that the highest good is "to live in accordance with nature" is therefore explained by the Stoics as meaning "to live with an understanding of the natural course of events, selecting things that are in accordance with nature and rejecting the opposite." [91] All this merely means that life in accordance with nature is life in accordance with reason, which reason invents the arts and sciences as well as the laws and rules of human conduct. With reference to law, the Stoics, therefore, like Aristotle, while distinguishing between natural law and enacted law, or between universal law and particular law, or between unwritten law and written law, still admit,[92] again like Aristotle, that enacted law, if based upon reason and virtue, is a law in accordance with nature. "Law is the distinction between things just and unjust, made in agreement with that primal and most ancient of all things, nature; and in conformity to nature's standards are framed those human laws which inflict punishment upon the wicked but defend and protect the good." [93]

The main point in our analysis of the concept of natural

---

[89] *Ibid.*
[90] Cicero, *De Finibus* IV, 7, 16.
[91] *Ibid.*, II, 11, 34; cf. IV, 6, 14.
[92] Cicero, *De Legibus* II, 4, 8–5, 11.
[93] *Ibid.* II, 5, 13.

law in Greek philosophy was to show that, according to Plato, Polemo, Aristotle, and the Stoics, enacted laws, if they are enacted by wise legislators on the basis of reason, are in a certain sense also laws in accordance with nature. To Plato they are in accordance with nature in the sense that they secure for each individual the enjoyment of those rights to which he is entitled by his natural capacities, or in the sense that they are in accordance with the natural instincts of reverence and friendship. To Polemo they are in accordance with nature in the sense that they enable each individual to enjoy the primary gifts of nature "honorably" and "with the accompaniment of virtue." To Aristotle they are in accordance with nature because they are the work of reason and reason is that which is "to rule and guide us by nature" and because also life in accordance with reason is proper "to the nature" of men. To the Stoics they are in accordance with nature because it is nature which has implanted reason in man to aid him in his striving for self-preservation.

But still despite all this, these enacted laws, even when based on reason, are the work of men and not the work of nature and they differ from the work of nature in that they are not universal, they are not eternal, and they are not immutable. Plato gives expression to this view in his statement that "law could never, by determining exactly what is noblest and most just for one and all, enjoin upon them that which is best; for the differences of men and of actions and the fact that nothing, I may say, in human life is ever at rest, forbid any science whatsoever to promulgate any simple rule for everything and for all time." [94] Aristotle repeats the same sentiment in many passages in which he maintains that written or enacted laws "ought not always to remain unaltered" and this because, as has already been

[94] *Statesman* 294 B.

said by Plato, in law, as in other sciences, it is impossible
that the law "should have been written down aright in all
its details, for it must of necessity be couched in general
terms, but our actions deal with particular things." [95] Indeed the Stoics express a desire that enacted laws which are
based on reason and are in accordance with nature should
never be abrogated, but knowing that they are only man-
made laws they make this unabrogability of the laws dependent upon their acceptability to those who are to be
ruled by them.[96]

It is at this point that Philo steps in with his contention
that, if it is law in accordance with nature that is sought
after, then philosophers might as well give up their effort to
devise such a law by their own reason. Only a law which
was revealed by God, who is the creator of nature, can be in
accordance with nature in the true sense of the term, for
such a law, being the work of God, is like nature itself, and
like nature it is universal and eternal and immutable. In the
passages in which Philo tries to make this point we shall
find him restate the general conception of Greek philosophers
of (1) what is meant by natural law; we shall find him also
restate the view generally accepted among Greek philosophers that (2) the prevailing laws of the cities are not always
in accordance with nature; and, finally, we shall find him try
to show (3) how the Mosaic Law is in the true sense of the
term a law in accordance with nature.

With regard to the term natural law, Philo uses it in the
strictly Aristotelian sense as "general" law or "unwritten"
law, as opposed to "particular" law and "written" law.
Referring to the laws of Moses as "particular" (ἐπὶ μέρους)
laws and to the laws which existed prior to the revelation of

<hr>

[95] *Politica* II, 8, 1269a, 8–12; cf. III, 11, 1282b, 4–6.
[96] Cicero, *De Legibus* II, 5, 14.

the laws of Moses as "more universal" (καθολικωτέρους) laws,[97] he says that "the first generations, before any at all of the particular (ἐν μέρει) statutes was set in writing (ἀναγρα-φῆναι), followed the unwritten (ἀγράφῳ) law with perfect ease — for they were not scholars or pupils of others, nor did they learn from teachers what was right to say or do: they listened to no voice or instruction but their own: they gladly accepted conformity with nature, holding that nature itself was, as indeed it is, the most venerable of statutes, and thus their whole life was one of happy obedience to law." [98] In another passage, he says of Enos that he has acquired the virtue of hope "by an unwritten, self-taught law, which nature has laid down." [99] In still another place, he describes Abraham as being "not taught by written law, but by unwritten nature, seeing that he was anxious to follow wholesome and untainted impulses (ὁρμαῖς)." [100] In all these passages the term natural law is used exactly, as in Aristotle, in the sense of general and unwritten law. But, as in Aristotle, too, he sometimes uses the terms "written" and "unwritten" law as subdivisions of "particular" law, or, as Philo himself says, of "the laws of cities." [101] The term "unwritten law," we may add in passing, is also used by Philo in the sense of the Jewish "oral law." [102] Moreover, the "written" or Mosaic Law, which in contrast to the "un-written" or pre-Mosaic laws, is described by him in these passages as the "particular" Law, is elsewhere said by him to contain the ten commandments which he describes as "general heads" (γενικὰ κεφάλαια), that is, general laws, in

[97] *Abr.* 1, 3.
[98] *Ibid.*, 5–6; cf. also 3, 16; 46, 276.
[99] *Ibid.* 3, 16.
[100] *Ibid.* 46, 275.
[101] *Heres* 59, 295; cf. Hirzel, *op. cit.*, p. 17.
[102] Cf. above, I, 188–194.

contradistinction to all the other laws which he describes as particular (κατὰ μέρος; ἐν μέρει) laws.[103]

But in his use of the term natural law we may notice three new elements which are not based upon Greek philosophy. First, the natural laws to him are not laws which exist by the side of the enacted laws, but they rather mark a stage in the history of the development of the enacted laws. They existed prior to the laws revealed by God through Moses, wherein they were later incorporated. Second, these natural laws are associated by him with certain scriptural personages of the pre-Mosaic age. Of these personages he mentions two groups of three, namely, (1) Enos, Enoch, and Noah; (2) Abraham, Isaac, and Jacob.[104] Of these two trios, Noah and Abraham are the chief personages with whose names he connects the pre-Mosaic laws. Of Noah he says that unlike Enos and Enoch who had each acquired only one virtue, namely, hope and repentance respectively, "he acquired not one virtue but all, and having acquired them continued to exercise each as opportunities allowed." [105] With regard to Abraham he quotes the verse that Abraham kept "my laws" (τὰ νόμιμά μου),[106] which in his paraphrase becomes "all my law" (πάντα τὸν νόμον μου) and to which he adds that by law is meant the enjoining what we ought to do and the forbidding what we should not do.[107] Third, while the term "nature" in the various forms of the expression "law of nature" is used by him in its original Greek sense of natural instinct or impulse, as when he says that the natural law was learned by the pre-Mosaic generations from "no voice or instruction but their own" [108] or from their "wholesome and untainted impulses," [109] it is also used by him in a new

---

[103] Congr. 21, 120; Decal. 5, 19; cf. below, p. 189.
[104] Abr. 1, 4 ff.; Praem. 2, 14 ff.　　　　[107] Migr. 23, 130.
[105] Ibid. 6, 34.　　　　　　　　　　　　[108] Cf. above, n. 98.
[106] Gen. 26: 5.　　　　　　　　　　　　[109] Cf. above, n. 100.

sense, as a law for men which is modeled after the law which
exists for nature. The Patriarchs, he says, "gladly accepted
conformity with nature, holding that nature itself was, as
indeed it is, the most venerable of statutes."[110] By "nature"
here he does not mean the natural instinct or impulse or
reason in man; he means thereby the law implanted in the
universe as a whole. We may recall that to him there had
been prior to the creation of the world an incorporeal Logos
created by God [111] and that upon the creation of the world
it was implanted by God in it to act as its Law.[112] When he
says here, therefore, that the Patriarchs "gladly accepted
conformity with nature, holding that nature itself was, as
indeed it is, the most venerable of statutes," he means that
the laws followed by the Patriarchs were modeled after those
laws which they discovered in nature. Now these three new
elements which appear in Philo's presentation of natural
law are based, as we shall try to show, upon Jewish tradition.

According to Jewish tradition, certain laws which are
found in the Law of Moses were observed by certain scriptural personages prior to Moses. These personages are
Adam, Noah, and Abraham,[113] but particularly Noah, after
whose name these pre-Mosaic laws are known as the Noachian laws, of which a list of seven is generally given.[114] Of
these seven Noachian laws only two, that of not eating of
the flesh cut from a living animal and that of not murder-
ing, are mentioned as direct revelations of God to Noah.[115]
As for the others, no scriptural proof-text is to be found,
though later rabbis try to derive them, by the usual homiletical method, from the verse "And the Lord God commanded
the man, saying, of every tree of the garden thou mayest

---

[110] Cf. above, n. 98.   [111] Cf. above, I, 229 ff.   [112] Cf. above, I, 326 ff.
[113] *The Book of Jubilees* 7: 39; 21: 10; cf. below nn. 115, 116, 122.
[114] Cf. below, p. 185.   [115] Gen. 9: 4, 6.

freely eat." [116] But from certain statements by the rabbis
with regard to these Noachian laws, and especially with regard to Abraham, we may gather that these pre-Mosaic
laws were considered by them as having been discovered by
what we may call "reason" or "nature." Concerning these
Noachian laws, with the exception only of the law prohibiting the eating of the flesh cut from a living animal, it is said
that "if they were not written in the Law [as divine revela-
tions], they would have to be written in it [on rational
grounds]." [117] Concerning two of these Noachian laws, those
prohibiting robbery and adultery, it is said that, if they were
not revealed by God, man would have discovered them by
a study of the behavior of the ant and the dove.[118] Especially
emphatic are the statements in describing how Abraham arrived at a knowledge of the existence of God and a knowledge of the Law without divine revelation. As for his knowledge of the existence of God, Abraham is said to have "of
himself recognized the existence of the Holy One, blessed
be He; there was no man who taught him how to recognize
the existence of God; he recognized it by himself," [119] and
he obtained that knowledge, according to other statements,
by a study of nature, the sun, the moon, the stars, and the
elements.[120] As for his knowledge of the Law, one rabbi
states that "Abraham learned it from himself, for it is said
'and a good man shall be satisfied from himself.' [121] " [122] Another rabbi raises the question: "No father instructed him,

[116] Gen. 2: 16; *Sanhedrin* 56b. Cf. Maimonides, *Mishneh Torah, Melakim* IX, 1.
[117] *Sifra, Aḥre, Pereḳ* 13, p. 86a.
[118] *'Erubin* 100b.
[119] *Numbers Rabbah* 14, 2; cf. *Pesiḳta Rabbati*, 33, p. 150.
[120] Apocalypse of Abraham 1–7; *Midrash ha-Gadol* on Gen. 11: 28 (ed. Schechter,
pp. 189–190). Cf. Ginzberg, *Legends of the Jews*, I, 189, 212–213; V, 210, n. 16;
217, n. 49.
[121] Prov. 14: 14.
[122] *Genesis Rabbah* 95, 3; *Tanḥuma, Wayyiggash*, § 11. Cf. Ibn Ezra on Exod. 20: 2.

nor had he a teacher, whence, then, did he learn the Law?"
and, in answer to this question, he says: "The Holy One,
blessed be He, made his two kidneys serve like two teachers
for him, and these welled forth and taught him wisdom." [123]
By this is meant that Abraham, with the help of God, discovered the Law by his own conscience and reason, for "kidneys" are conceived in the Bible and Talmud as the seat
of moral conscience as well as of intellectual deliberation.[124]
In these traditional utterances we find, then, the three new
elements in Philo's discussion of natural law: (1) its existence prior to the revealed Law; (2) its association with certain scriptural personages; (3) the use of the term "natural"
not only in the sense of conformity to a natural impulse in
man but also in the sense of being modeled after laws implanted by God in nature.

A similarly striking analogy between the Noachian laws
and Philo's natural laws is to be found in their respective
enumerations of such laws. The Noachian laws are generally said to contain the following seven: (1) To establish
courts of justice, (2) not to worship idols, (3) not to blaspheme the name of God, (4) not to commit adultery, (5) not
to murder, (6) not to rob, (7) not to eat of the flesh cut from
a living animal.[125] Now it is interesting to note that four out
of this list of Noachian laws are described by Philo as natural
laws. First, the belief that "the place of the created in all
things is lower than that of the creator" and that "there
must be a providence" is described by him as a law of
nature.[126] This, of course, corresponds to the Noachian law

---

[123] *Genesis Rabbah* 61, 1, and parallels. Cf. above, nn. 108, 109.

[124] For Bible, see Jer. 11: 20; 12: 2; 17: 10; 20: 12; Ps. 7: 10; 16: 7; 26: 2; 51: 8;
Job 38: 36, and cf. F. Delitzsch, *System der Biblischen Psychologie*, Leipzig, 1861,
p. 269. For Talmud, see *Berakot* 61a.

[125] *Tos. 'Abodah Zarah* VIII (IX), 4–6.

[126] *Plant.* 32, 132; *Praem.* 7, 42.

186   PHILO

prohibiting the worship of idols, for in another place he
describes the sin of idolatry as consisting in the payment of
the same tribute "to the creatures as to their Creator." [127]
Second, courts of justice, both divine and human, are described by him as existing "in nature," [128] which is only
another way of saying that the establishment of courts of
justice is a law of nature. Third, murder is described by
him as a subversion of the laws of nature. [129] Fourth, adultery
is similarly described by him as a violation of the laws of
nature. [130] Still more interesting is the fact that the junction
of heterogeneous animals by hybridization [131] is described by
him as "upsetting a law of nature." [132] Now in a rabbinic
tradition this prohibition is also included by one authority
among the Noachian laws. [133] In Greek literature, to be sure,
some of these things mentioned by Philo are also spoken of
as natural laws, such, for instance, as worshiping the gods [134]
and not killing that which has life. [135] But in Philo, the
natural law does not command to worship the "gods," but
it rather prohibits the worship of idols, that is, the "gods."
Then also there is a similarity in the use of the term "courts
of justice" in Philo's statement that "courts of justice"
(δικαστήρια), the divine and the human, are both "in nature," [136] and the rabbinic statement that the establishment
of "courts of justice" (batte dinin)[137] in cities is one of the

[127] Decal. 13, 61. Cf. also his statement (Somn. II, 43, 283) that the denial of the
existence of God is "against nature" (κατὰ φύσεως).
[128] Ibid. 23, 111.
[129] Ibid. 25, 132.
[130] Abr. 26, 135.
[131] Lev. 19: 19.
[132] Spec. IV, 39, 204.
[133] Sanhedrin 56b.
[134] Xenophon, Memorabilia IV, 4, 19.
[135] Aristotle, Rhet. I, 13, 1373b, 14–16; cf. above, p. 174.
[136] Decal. 23, 111.
[137] Cf. Tos. 'Abodah Zarah VIII (IX), 4.

Noachian laws. His inclusion of the prohibition of adultery among the natural laws also reflects Scripture and Jewish tradition. In Greek philosophy, Hippias, who argues for the existence of unwritten or universal laws, that is, natural laws, explicitly states that incest is not to be included among these laws.[138] Finally, his description of hybridization as "upsetting a law of nature" quite obviously reflects Scripture and the rabbinic tradition.[139]

So much for Philo's treatment of natural law, which, as we have tried to show, reflects both Greek conceptions of natural law and traditional Jewish conceptions of the Noachian laws.

As distinguished from these natural or general laws are those particular laws which he describes as "the laws of cities."[140] These laws are man-made laws; they are neither the product of nature nor the work of God; they are "the ordinances of the legislators of the different cities."[141] Philo's

[138] Xenophon, *Memorabilia* IV, 4, 20; *Cyropaedia* V, 1, 10.

[139] An allusion to the law of not eating the flesh of a living animal as being what the rabbis call a Noachian law is also to be found in Philo. This law is based upon Gen. 9: 4, which reads: "Only flesh with the life thereof, which is the blood thereof, shall ye not eat." Preceding this law, there is another law, in 9: 3, which reads: "Every moving thing that liveth shall be for food for you; as the green herb have I given you all." In rabbinic literature, just as verse 9: 4 is taken as a Noachian law, i.e., directed to all mankind, prohibiting the eating of the flesh of a living animal, so also verse 9: 3 is taken as a Noachian law permitting all mankind the eating of the flesh of dead animals (*Sanhedrin* 59b). Now Philo, commenting upon verse 9: 3, quotes "some persons" (*nonnulli*) who say that "by this expression, 'as the green herb have I given you all,' the eating of flesh was permitted," and subsequently adds that "the power of this command is not adapted to one nation alone [i.e., the Jews] . . . but to all mankind, who cannot possibly be universally prohibited from eating flesh" (*Qu. in Gen.* II, 58). The interpretation of verse 9: 3 quoted by him in the name of "some people" is the same as the rabbinic interpretation. His own comment that this law applies to all mankind again corresponds to the rabbinic interpretation. We may therefore reasonably assume that the law in verse 9: 4 prohibiting the eating of the flesh of a living animal is similarly taken by Philo as applying to all mankind, i.e., as being a Noachian law. In *Qu. in Gen.* II, 95, where Philo discusses verse 9: 4, he assumes that the verse contains a prohibition.

[140] *Heres* 59, 295.   [141] *Mos.* I, 1, 2; cf. *Abr.* 3, 16; *Spec.* IV, 10, 61; 23, 120.

Hellenization never went so far as to accept the beliefs of popular Greek religion about the divine origin of certain Greek laws. In fact, it is not impossible that the environment in which he lived has made him doubt whether the Greeks themselves took these myths about the divine origin of some of their laws as truths, for he speaks of the Jews as being unique in "looking upon their laws as oracles given to them by God." [142] Of Greek lawgivers he says that some of them "have nakedly and without embellishment drawn up a code of the things they considered to be right," while others "have sought to bewilder the people, by burying the truth under a heap of mythical inventions." [143] None of the Greek laws were thus, according to Philo, divine revelations. They were all inventions of lawgivers, and, if some lawgivers claimed for them a divine origin, their claims were only mythical inventions. In a general sense, indeed, he admits that "laws and customs," including evidently also Greek laws and customs, just like all the "arts and professions," are from God,[144] as he also says that philosophy was showered down from heaven,[145] but by this he only means that, like all other human achievements, the achievement of law and philosophy was made possible only by an act of divine providence,[146] for, as he says, that God himself "is the lawgiver and the fountain of laws, and on Him depend all particular lawgivers." [147] But while these laws, in so far as they contain rational elements, may be regarded as the work of divine providence, they are far from being ideal laws in accordance with reason and in accordance with nature. Reechoing the common complaint of all the Greek philosophers against the existent constitutions and laws, he says that

[142] *Legat.* 31, 210.
[143] *Opif.* 1, 1.
[144] *Leg. All.* III, 9, 30.

[145] *Spec.* III, 34, 185; cf. above, I, 142.
[146] Cf. above, I, 143.
[147] *Sacr.* 39, 131.

"the polity as seen in various peoples is an addition to nature," [148] and "different peoples have different customs and regulations which are extra inventions and additions," [149] so that "the laws of the different states are additions to the right reason of nature." [150] The expression "an addition to nature" means here an excrescence upon nature, something adventitious to it and not in accordance with it.

In contradistinction to both these natural laws and the laws of the legislators of the different cities is the Law of Moses. Unlike natural law, which grows up spontaneously without a legislator, this law is described by him as "enacted laws" (τεθέντες νόμοι) or "enacted ordinances" (τεθειμένα διατάγματα). [151] Unlike natural laws, too, which are unwritten and general, this law is written [152] and also contains both general and particular laws. [153] But unlike the laws of the legislators of the different cities, who are human beings, [154] the legislator of this law is God himself, for legislator (νομοθέ- της) is one of the terms by which Philo describes God. [155] Indeed Moses, too, is called legislator, but he is called so only because he was the prophet of God and, according to Philo's conception of prophecy, one of the functions of prophecy is to act as a vehicle for divine legislation. [156] It is God, however, who is "the original and perfect lawgiver" [157] and who, by virtue of His being the creator of the world, is "in its truest sense also its lawgiver." [158] "The holy books of the Lord," he says, "are not monuments of knowledge or of vision, but are the divine command and the divine Logos." [159]

[148] Jos. 6, 28.
[149] Ibid., 29.
[150] Ibid., 31.
[151] Abr. 1, 5.
[152] Ibid.
[153] Ibid., 3; cf. above, n. 103.
[154] Cf. above, p. 187.
[155] Post. 43, 143; Fug. 13, 66; 18, 99; Mos. II, 8, 48.
[156] Cf. above, pp. 16 ff.
[157] Fug. 13, 66.
[158] Mos. II, 8, 48.
[159] Qu. in Gen. IV, 140. By "knowledge and vision" Philo means rational knowledge which ultimately rests upon sensation (cf. above, p. 6).

All these statements are not mere rhetorical phrases with
Philo. They are an expression of his philosophic belief.
According to him, before the creation of the world, God
created the Logos.[160] Upon the creation of the world, the
Logos was implanted in it by God to act as its law.[161] Then
later, when God revealed the Law to guide men in their
conduct in the world, that Law was the application to human
conduct of the same law which He had previously implanted
in the world for the regulation of the order of nature. God
is thus the true legislator of the laws for both nature and
men, and the laws of Moses, though enacted laws, are still
in the true sense of the term in accordance with nature, inasmuch as God who is their true legislator enacted them in
harmony with those laws of nature of which He is also the
legislator. No other enacted law is to Philo truly in accordance with nature, inasmuch as none of them was enacted by
God who is the author of the laws of nature. Thus, commenting on the verses "And Abraham gave all that he had
to Isaac, but unto the sons of the concubines, which Abraham had, Abraham gave gifts," [162] he says that the blessings
bequeathed by Abraham to Isaac "resemble natural (φύσει)
laws," whereas the blessings bequeathed by him to the sons
of the concubines resemble "enacted (θέσει) laws." [163]
When therefore he refers to the laws of the Pentateuch as
"laws of God-beloved (θεοφιλῶν) men," [164] he does not mean

---

[160] Cf. above, I, 229 ff.   [161] Cf. above, I, 326 ff.
[162] Gen. 25: 5–6.
[163] *Migr.* 16, 94; cf. above, p. 173. C. H. Dodd says: "In Hellenistic Judaism
the idea of law had already been influenced" by the Stoic idea of a "law of nature"
("Hellenism and Christianity" in *Harvard Tercentenary Publications: Independence,
Convergence, and Borrowing*, 1937, p. 113). The influence in our opinion was only
to the extent that Hellenistic Jewish philosophers argued against the Stoics and
other Greek philosophers that there was only one law which could be properly
described as a "law of nature" and that was the revealed Law of Moses.
[164] *Deter.* 5, 13.

that those laws were enacted by men whom God loves; he means thereby that those laws were revealed by God to men out of His love for them.[165]

Proof that "the laws were not the inventions of man but quite clearly the oracles of God" is found by Philo in the scriptural account of the revelation on Mount Sinai,[166] which he accepts as history.

Evidently having in mind the claims of divine origin for the laws of certain Greek states, he maintains that "Moses himself was the best of all lawgivers in all countries, better in fact than any that have ever arisen among either the Greeks or the barbarians, and that his laws are most excellent and truly come from God." [167] Evidently also counteracting the claim of a divine nature or origin for the laws of Minos on the ground, as restated by Plato, that they "have made Crete happy through the length of time, and Sparta happy also, since she began to use them," [168] he maintains, quite obviously with reference to what happened to both Sparta and Crete between the time of Plato and his own time, that the institutions of other peoples "have been unsettled by numberless causes — wars, tyrannies or other mishaps — which the revolutions of fortune have launched upon them," [169] whereas the laws of Moses alone "remain secure from the day when they were first enacted to now." [170] Evidently again having in mind the statements by Plato and Aristotle that laws cannot remain unaltered,[171] he expresses

[165] Cf. above, I, 123, n. 65, 143.
[166] *Decal.* 4, 15; cf. *Probus* 12, 80.
[167] *Mos.* II, 3, 12. Josephus, in claiming for the Mosaic laws a divine origin, compares him to "Minos and later legislators," of whom, he says, Minos attributed his laws to Zeus and Lycurgus attributed his to Apollo, adding, however, cautiously, "either believing this to be the fact, or hoping in this way to facilitate their acceptance" (*Apion.* II, 16, 161–162).
[168] *Minos* 320 B.   [170] *Ibid.*, 14.
[169] *Mos.* II, 3, 13.   [171] Cf. above, p. 179.

his hope, that is, his belief, that "they will remain for future ages as though immortal, so long as the sun and moon and the whole heaven and universe exist." [172] Finally, he tries to show that laws of Moses are more widespread and more universal than all the other systems of law at his time, mentioning especially the laws of the Athenians and the Lacedaemonians and the Egyptians and in general of the peoples of Asia and Europe.[173] "We may say," he concludes, "that mankind from east to west, every country and nation and state, show aversion to foreign institutions, and think they will enhance the respect for their own by showing disrespect for those of other countries. It is not so with ours. They attract and win the attention of all, of Barbarians, of Greeks, of dwellers on the mainland and islands, of nations of the east and west, of Europe and Asia, of the whole inhabited world from end to end." [174]

Then, with this conception of the divine origin of the Law of Moses, he tries to show how that Law is what philosophers would describe as being in accordance with nature. God, argues Philo, is the founder both of the laws of nature and the laws revealed through Moses and, since both these systems of law emanate from the same divine source, they are in harmony with each other, and consequently life in accordance with nature, which is recommended by philosophers, and life in accordance with the Law, which is enjoined by Scripture, mean one and the same thing. Why, asks Philo, did Moses preface his laws with the story of the creation of the world? It is to show, he answers, "that the world is in

[172] *Mos.* II, 3, 14.
[173] *Ibid.* II, 4, 19.
[174] *Ibid.*, 19–20. So also Josephus argues for the superiority of the Mosaic laws on the ground that for a longer time than any other laws "they have stood the test of our own use," i.e., they have remained unaltered, and have also "excited the emulation of the world at large" (*Apion.* II, 39, 280).

harmony with the Law, and the Law with the world, and that the man who observes the Law is constituted thereby a loyal citizen of the world regulating his doings by the purpose and will of nature, in accordance with which the entire world itself is administered." [175] In the historical part of the Pentateuch, he says again, Moses "wished to show two most essential things: first, that the Father and Maker of the world was in the truest sense also its Lawgiver; secondly, that he who would observe the laws will accept gladly the duty of following nature and live in accordance with the ordering of the universe." [176] In another place he identifies the scriptural reference to "all His commandments and ordinances and judgments which are written in the book of this Law" [177] with "the laws and statutes of nature." [178] And so when he happens to quote in the name of "the best philosophers," that the end which man is to strive after is "to live in accordance with nature," which is attained "whenever the mind having entered on the path of virtue, walks in the tracks of right reason and follows God" [179] — phrases and expressions borrowed from Plato, Aristotle, and the Stoics [180] — he hastens to add that by all these he means "remembering His commandments" [181] and as proof-text he quotes a Jewish traditional saying based upon a scriptural verse, to the effect that "Abraham did all thy Law," [182] adding "Law being evidently nothing else than the divine word, enjoining what we ought to do and forbidding what we should not do, as Moses testifies by saying 'he received

[175] *Opif.* 1, 3.
[176] *Mos.* II, 8, 48; *Opif.* 1, 3.
[177] *Deut.* 30: 10.
[178] *Somn.* II, 26, 174–175.
[179] *Migr.* 23, 128.
[180] Cf. above, pp. 171, 176, 178.
[181] *Migr.* 23, 128.
[182] The scriptural verse (Gen. 26: 5) reads: "Because Abraham thy father hearkened to my voice and kept My charge, My commandments, My statutes, and My laws." The Talmudic comment on this verse is: "Abraham our father had observed the entire Law even before it was given." (*Kiddushin* 82a.)

the law from His words.' [183] " [184] Similarly also when he happens to speak of "those who take pains to cultivate virtue," he adds immediately "and set the holy laws before them to guide them in all they do or say in their private or in their public capacity." [185] When philosophers speak of living in accordance with nature or reason or right reason, they mean thereby that man is to live in accordance with such principles discovered by human reason as would not bring him into conflict with his own nature or with the nature of the world around him. To Philo, however, it means to live in accordance with the revealed Law, for the Law revealed by God to man is in harmony with the law which God himself has implanted in man and in the universe.

He is especially eager to point out that while on the one hand there is a certain similarity between the *Laws* of Plato and the Law of Moses, on the other hand there exists an essential difference between them. The former is man-made and the latter is of divine origin. Evidently alluding to Plato's statement that all legislators before him have contented themselves with issuing only peremptory commands whereas he will preface his laws by preambles containing exhortations, [186] he tries to show how Moses, while in one respect uses the same method as Plato, in another respect differs from Plato. Like Plato, he prefixes his laws by preambles containing exhortations. [187] But unlike Plato, who began his laws with "the foundation of a man-made city" and hence with man-made laws, Moses began his laws "with the story of the creation of the Great City or the world" by God and hence also with the revelation of the Law by God. [188] When therefore in one place he quotes Plato that we ought "to become like God, as far as this is possible; and to become like

[183] Deut. 33: 4. [185] *Praem.* 20, 119. [187] *Mos.* II, 9, 49–51.
[184] *Migr.* 23, 130. [186] *Laws* IV, 722 B–E. [188] *Ibid.*, 51.

Him is to become holy, just and wise," [189] and when also in several other places he re-echoes Plato's statements to the effect that our true end is "likeness to God" and to be "following Him step by step in the highways cut out by virtues" [190] or that "the goal of happiness is to become like God," [191] or that good rulers should "imitate" God's actions "if they have any aspirations to become like God," [192] or that "a man should imitate God as much as may be and leave nothing undone that may promote such likeness as is possible" [193] — in all these he means, as similar statements in native Jewish tradition mean, to live according to the Law. One of these characteristic statements in native Jewish tradition, commenting upon the verse "after the Lord your God shall ye walk," [194] raises the rhetorical question, "Is it possible for a man to walk after the Shekinah?" and its answer is: "You cannot but say that it means to walk after the virtues or laws of the Holy One: as He clothed the naked (Gen. 3: 21), so do thou clothe the naked; as He visited the sick (Gen. 18: 1), so do thou visit the sick; as He comforted the mourners (Gen. 25: 11), so do thou comfort the mourners; as He buried the dead (Deut. 34: 6), so do thou bury the dead." [195]

Other texts from which native Jewish tradition derives the principle of the imitation of God and the assimilation to Him are the verses "But ye that cleave unto the Lord thy God" [196] and "For as a girdle cleaveth to the loins of a man, so have I caused to cleave unto me the whole house of

---

[189] *Fug.* 12, 63; cf. *Theaetetus* 176 B; *Laws* IV, 716 c f.

[190] *Opif.* 50, 144.

[191] *Decal.* 15, 73.

[192] *Spec.* IV, 36, 188.

[193] *Virt.* 31, 168.

[194] Deut. 13: 5 (4).

[195] *Soṭah* 14a. On the principle of *imitatio Dei* in Judaism, see S. Schechter, *Some Aspects of Rabbinic Theology*, pp. 199 ff.; G. F. Moore, *Judaism*, I, 441; II, 110 f., 172 f.

[196] Deut. 4: 4.

Israel," [197] which verses are used as an explanation of the
verse " Ye shall be holy, for I the Lord Thy God am holy." [198]
Similarly Philo infers the same principle from the use of the
word "cleave" in the verse "Thou shalt fear the Lord Thy
God, and Him thou shalt serve and to Him shalt thou
cleave." [199] "What then is the cementing substance?" he
asks rhetorically, and his answer is: "Do you ask, what?
Pity, surely, and faith: for these virtues adjust and unite
the intent of the heart to the incorruptible Being: as Abraham when he believed is said to 'come near to God.' [200] " [201]

With his conception of the Pentateuch as a revealed system of law which aims to regulate life in accordance with
virtue and hence leads to happiness, Philo tries to answer
the question discussed by Socrates, Plato, and Aristotle as to
the acquisition of happiness or virtue. As stated by Aristotle,
the "question is asked, whether happiness is to be acquired
by learning (μαθητὸν) or by habit (ἐθιστὸν) or some other sort
of practice (ἀσκητόν), or comes in the way of some divine
dispensation (τινα θείαν μοῖραν)." [202] Or, as the same question is stated by him with reference to virtue, "some think
that we are made good by nature (φύσει), others by habit
(ἔθει), others by teaching (διδαχῇ)," and explains that by the
term "by nature" is meant that it comes as a result of some
divine causes (τινας θείας αἰτίας). [203] By "some divine
causes" he means what he himself in the other passage calls,
in the language of Plato, "divine dispensation." His own

[197] Jer. 13: 11.
[198] Lev. 19: 2. Cf. *Yalkuṭ Shim'oni* I, 604, quoting *Tanḥuma*; cf. *Tanḥuma* ed.
Buber *Ḳedoshim*, § 5.
[199] Deut. 10: 20.
[200] Gen. 18: 23.
[201] *Migr.* 24, 132. The same verse, Deut. 10: 20, is quoted also as proof-text for
the same principle by a medieval rabbi, Eliezer of.Metz, in *Sefer Yere'im*, § 3.
[202] *Eth. Nic.* I, 9, 1099b, 9–10.
[203] *Ibid.* X, 9, 1179b, 20–23.

view is that virtue does not depend upon "nature" or "some divine dispensation" or "some divine causes"; it is acquired through learning (μάθησις) or teaching (διδασκαλία) and through practice (ἄσκησις) or habit (ἔθος).[204] The Stoics, on the other hand, maintain that virtue comes to us only through knowledge [205] and learning,[206] denying therefore by implication that it can come through nature or through practice.[207]

This is how the problem stood at the time of Philo. With neither of these views, however, does he agree. To him virtue and happiness are acquired by all these three methods, nature, practice, and learning, and all these three methods ultimately come as a result of a divine dispensation or a divine cause. He thus attributes to Moses the view that "virtue is gained either by nature (φύσει) or by practice (ἀσκήσει) or by learning (μαθήσει)," [208] qualifying, however, this statement elsewhere by adding that these three methods of acquiring virtue depend upon each other, for "teaching cannot be consummated without nature or practice, nor is nature capable of reaching its zenith without learning and practice, nor practice either unless the foundation of nature and teaching has first been laid." [209] These three sources of virtue are repeatedly mentioned by him in many other passages.[210] On the whole, by the term "nature" he means, as it was explained by Aristotle, "some divine dispensation" [211] or "some divine causes," except that with him it

---

[204] Ibid. I, 9, 1099b, 15–16; cf. II, 1, 1103a, 14–18.
[205] Diogenes, VII, 93.   [206] Idem., VII, 91.
[207] Cf. Zeller, III, 1⁴, p. 240 (Stoics, Epicureans and Sceptics², p. 255).
[208] Somn. I, 27, 167.
[209] Abr. 11, 53.
[210] As, e.g., Mut. 14, 88; Abr. 11, 53; Praem. 11, 64–65; cf. Leisegang, Indices, under ἄσκησις, ἀσκητικός.
[211] The term θεία μοῖρα occurs frequently in his writings; cf. Leisegang, Indices, under μοῖρα.

has assumed a more definite meaning, due to the fact that a dispensation which is divine or a cause which is divine means to him something different, not something which brings about a result by necessity but rather something which brings about a result by the free will of God. When Philo says, therefore, that virtue may be acquired "by nature," he means thereby that certain persons, by the special grace of God, have been endowed from birth with a predisposition for virtue.[212] Similarly with regard to the terms "practice" and "learning," they have acquired with him some special meaning. It is not every kind of practice and every kind of learning through which one acquires virtue and hence also happiness; it is the practice and the learning of the laws revealed by God by His "graciousness and beneficence."[213] Ultimately, therefore, it is God who is the source of virtue and the source of happiness. In accordance with this view, God is described by him as "sowing for the race of mortals the seed of happiness in good and virgin soil"[214] and the service of God is said by him to be the source ($\pi\eta\gamma\dot{\eta}$)[215] and the beginning ($\dot{\alpha}\rho\chi\dot{\eta}$)[216] of happiness. Again, the divine powers are said by him to descend, at the bidding of their Father, with laws and ordinances from heaven and sow in virtue-loving souls the nature of happiness.[217]

His special emphasis upon God as the source of nature and the source of the laws of virtue and the source of happiness is to be discerned in passages in which he gives his own version of certain philosophic sentiments. In one place he reproduces the common Stoic view that "the hope of happiness incites also the devotees of virtue to study wisdom, believing that thus they will be able to discern the nature of

[212] Cf. above, I, 450.
[213] Mos. II, 35, 189; cf. above, pp. 51-52.
[214] Cher. 14, 49.

[215] Post. 54, 185.
[216] Spec. II, 9, 38.
[217] Cher. 31, 106.

all that exists and to act in accordance with nature." [218] But immediately after that he restates the same view with a new emphasis upon the need of setting one's hope on God who is above nature and is the source of nature. "He alone is worthy of my approval," he says, "who sets his hope on God both as the source to which his coming into existence itself is due and as the sole power which can keep him free from harm and destruction." [219] Not merely "to discern the nature of all that exists" is the highest intellectual virtue but to know that God is "the source" of the existence of all things, not merely "to act in accordance to nature" is the highest practical and moral virtue but to act in accordance with the knowledge that God rewards and punishes each man in accordance with his deeds. In other places he says that "no man should be thought a man at all who does not set his hope on God" [220] and only he who sets his hope on God is of the race of men which is "truly rational" ($\lambda o \gamma \iota \kappa \acute{o} \nu$).[221] This is evidently his own revision of Aristotle's statement that "it is characteristic of the good man to work out the good, and he does so for his own sake, for he does it for the sake of the intellectual element ($\delta \iota a \nu o \eta \tau \iota \kappa o \hat{\upsilon}$) in him, which is thought to be the man himself." [222]

This conception of revelation was a logical consequence of his conception of God as a free agent who created the world by His own free-will and established within it laws which can be upset by His own free-will. Creation, miracles, and revelation are three fundamental concepts which are connected in Philo's mind with the concept of the free-will of God. If asked for proof for the possibility of miracles, Philo refers to the act of creation which is to him the greatest of all mira-

[218] *Praem.* 2, 11.
[219] *Ibid.*, 13.
[220] *Ibid.*, 14.
[221] *Abr.* 2, 9.
[222] *Eth. Nic. IX*, 4, 1166a, 16–17.

cles.²²³ And if asked for proof for the possibility of revelation, he refers to miracles. In describing the revelation of
the Law on Mount Sinai, he says: "I should suppose that
God wrought on this occasion a miracle of a truly holy kind
by bidding an invisible sound to be created in the air." ²²⁴
Revelation, to him, is a miracle; given a God who can perform miracles, He can also reveal a law.

II. COMMANDMENTS AND VIRTUES

(a) Classification of Commandments and Virtues

With his identification of the Law of Moses with that ideal
law in accordance with nature sought after by philosophers,
Philo undertakes to show that the commandments which
constitute the laws of Moses are identical with the virtues
upon which the ideal philosophic law is to be based. As
preliminary to this identification he tries to classify the
Mosaic commandments as well as the philosophic virtues.

In his attempt to classify the commandments, he makes
use of three methods of classification which were current in
native Jewish tradition. First, he divides the laws into
"commands (προστάξεις) and prohibitions (ἀπαγορεύσεις)." ¹
This corresponds to the traditional Jewish division of the
laws into positive and negative commandments,² though he
expresses himself in language borrowed from the Stoics.³
Then, he divides the laws into two groups, one of them containing "duties to God" and the other "duties to men." ⁴
This again corresponds to the traditional Jewish division of
the laws into those between man and God and those be-

²²³ Mos. II, 48, 267; cf. above, I, 354.   ²²⁴ Decal. 9, 33.

¹ Spec. I, 55, 299; cf. Migr. 23, 130; Jos. 6, 29; Mos. II, 1, 4; Praem. 9, 55.
² Makkot 23b.
³ Arnim, II, 1003; III, 314, 613, 614. Cf. Cohn, Philos Werke, and Colson, on
Praem. 9, 55.
⁴ Heres 35, 168; Decal. 22, 106.

ETHICAL THEORY 201

tween man and man.[5] Then also the laws contained in the
Pentateuch are regarded by him as special laws under the
heading of the ten commandments, the latter of which he
describes as heads (κεφάλαια),[6] general heads (γενικὰ κεφάλαια), roots (ῥίζαι), sources (ἀρχαί), and fountains (πηγαί).[7]
In rabbinic literature, it is similarly said that the ten commandments contain all the laws of the Torah.[8] This last
method of classification is adopted by Philo in his direct discussion of the laws of Moses. First, in his *De Decalogo*, he
enumerates and discusses the ten commandments. Then,
in his *De Specialibus Legibus*, he discusses the special laws
which he arranges under the ten commandments.

To these three methods of the classification of the laws,
all of which are of traditional origin, he adds two other
methods, one based upon Scripture, to be discussed later
under "*Deeds, Words, Intentions*," and another, a new
method of his own, based upon his own conception that the
Law of Moses is that ideal law looked for by philosophers
which is to guide men in what philosophers call life in accordance with virtue. As that looked-for ideal code of law,
the ten commandments of Moses as well as the special laws
included under them are "the virtues of universal value," in-
citing and exhorting us to "wisdom and justice and godliness and the rest of the company of virtues," [9] they all
"inculcate the highest standard of virtue," [10] and "those who
take pains to cultivate virtue" are those who "set the holy
laws before them to guide them in all they do or say," [11] so
that those who conform to these laws "must be exempt from
every unreasoning passion and every vice in a higher degree

[5] *M. Yoma* VIII, 9.
[6] *Decal.* 5, 19.
[7] *Congr.* 21, 120.
[8] *Canticles Rabbah* to Cant. 5: 14. Cf. Bentwich, *Philo-Judaeus of Alexandria*,
p. 117.

[9] *Spec.* IV, 25, 134.
[10] *Ibid.*, 34, 179.
[11] *Praem.* 20, 119.

than those who are governed by other laws."[12] Consequently the laws can be classified, according to him, under
the headings of the various virtues which they are meant to
implant in men. And so within his general scheme of classifying the laws under the headings of the ten commandments
there is another scheme, that of classifying them under the
headings of cardinal virtues. Now the conception that laws
are to implant virtues is Platonic. In his criticism of the
laws of Crete and Lacedaemon Plato contends that their
purpose was to implant only one virtue, that of courage,
which was necessary for war.[13] In his own ideal laws, he
makes their purpose the implantation of all the virtues.[14]
Philo's contention is that the laws of Moses are the ideal
laws which do actually implant all the virtues. With this
in view, he tries to classify the virtues, and in accordance
with this classification of the virtues he classifies also the
laws.

There is no single formal classification of the virtues in
Philo. But throughout his writings he throws out certain
hints at their classification. Examining all his statements
on this subject and combining them together, we get the
following general picture of his classification of virtues.

To begin with, in conformity with his acceptance of the
Platonic theory of ideas, he believes there is an idea of
virtue corresponding to every particular virtue in the visible
world. This distinction between the idea and the copy of
virtue is designated by him by the terms "heavenly virtue"
and "earthly virtue."[15] This is a new classification of his
own.

Then the virtues are divided by him into two classes.
First, there are "virtues of the soul," such as "prudence,

[12] *Spec.* IV, 9, 55.   [14] *Ibid.* III, 688 A f.
[13] *Laws* I, 630 D f.   [15] *Leg. All.* I, 14, 45. Cf. above, I, 233, 261.

temperance and each of the others." Second, there are
"virtues of the body," such as "health, efficiency of the
senses, dexterity of limb and strength of muscle." Third, in
contradistinction to virtues, there are "external advantages," such as "wealth" and "glory" and "pleasures." [16]
In another place he describes all these "virtues" and "external advantages" as the "three goods" (*triplicia bona*),
and refers to "Aristotle with the Peripatetics." [17] The reference is to that passage in Aristotle, where the latter,
referring to Plato,[18] says that "goods (ἀγαθά) have been
divided into three classes, and some are described as external, others as relating to soul or to body." [19] In still another
place he describes bodily goods as being more nearly connected with us (οἰκειότερα) than external goods.[20] Now in our
first quotation from Philo, it will be noticed that under
"virtues of the soul" he mentions only what Aristotle calls
moral virtues. In Aristotle, however, the term "virtues of
the soul" is used to include both intellectual and moral
virtues.[21] Again, in the same quotation from Philo it will
also be noticed that bodily goods are called "virtues of the
body." In Aristotle and Plato, however, the term virtue,
in its strict and technical sense, refers only to the goods of
the soul,[22] and the Stoics, in their reproduction of this threefold classification of goods, say definitely that the virtues,
according to the "Academics and the Peripatetics," belong

---

[16] *Sobr.* 12, 61. A similar threefold division is implied in *Abr.* 38, 219 (cf J.
Cohn in *Philos Werke, ad loc.*).

[17] *Qu. in Gen.* III, 16.

[18] *Euthydemus* 279 A–B; *Philebus* 48 D–E; *Laws* V, 743 E.

[19] *Eth. Nic.* I, 8, 1098b, 12–14.

[20] *Praem.* 20, 118.

[21] *Eth. Nic.* VI, 1, 1138b, 35–1139a, 1.

[22] Cf. Aristotle, *op. cit.*, I, 8, 1098b, 14–15: "We call those that relate to the soul
most properly and truly goods." Similarly Plato, *Philebus* 48 E, after enumerating
the three goods, applies the term virtue only to those of the soul.

only to the soul.[23] But Philo's application of the term virtue to bodily goods may be justified on the ground that the description of "health," and also of other bodily goods, as a "virtue of the body" occurs in Plato [24] and Aristotle.[25]

Another division of the virtues in Philo is that into divine (θεῖαι) and human (ἀνθρώπιναι). These two terms are used by him in two senses. First, he uses the term "divine virtues" in the sense of "virtues of the soul" and the term "human virtues" in the sense of "virtues of the body," referring to them respectively as "real" and "reputed" virtues.[26] In a somewhat similar sense, these two terms are also used by Plato in his division of "good things" into divine and human.[27] Second, the terms "divine virtue" and "human virtue" [28] are used by him respectively in the sense of Aristotle's purely scientific type of both "intellectual virtue" and "moral virtue." Intellectual virtue of this purely scientific kind is described by Aristotle as that which has for its object that which exists "of necessity" and is "eternal" in the sense of being "ungenerated and imperishable." [29] Such an object would undoubtedly include what he calls God. So also the description of "divine virtue" in Philo is that which has God for its object.[30] "Human virtue" is described

[23] Sextus, *Adversus Ethicos*, 45; cf. Diogenes, VII, 102.

[24] *Gorgias* 479 B; 504 C.

[25] *Rhet.* I, 5, 1361b, 3; I, 6, 1362b, 15.

[26] *Migr.* 29, 158–160. In 158, he speaks of "virtues human and divine," characterizing them respectively as "the real and reputed virtues." In 160, he refers to these two classes of virtues as "the concerns of the soul" and "the concerns of the body" respectively.

[27] *Laws* I, 631 B–C. Under "human" goods Plato includes both bodily goods and external advantages, the latter of which is illustrated by him by the term "wealth."

[28] *Somn.* II, 42, 277.

[29] *Eth. Nic.* VI, 3, 1139b, 22–24.

[30] *Somn.* II, 43, 283, where those who oppose "divine virtue" are described as those who deny the existence of God as an incorporeal being who created the world and is its guardian and protector.

by Philo as that kind of virtue which is rejected by "the company of those devoted to their passions (φιλοπαθοῦς)." [31] This kind of virtue quite obviously refers to moral virtue. Similarly Aristotle describes moral virtue as "human virtue." [32]

In Aristotle a distinction is made between the possession (κτῆσις) of virtue and its use (χρῆσις), or between a state of mind or character (ἕξις) and an activity (ἐνέργεια). [33] This distinction is intimated by Philo when in contrast to "virtues" he speaks of (1) "activities in accordance with virtues" (κατ' ἀρετὰς ἐνέργειαι), (2) "right actions" (κατορθώματα) and (3) "what philosophers call duties (καθήκοντα)." [34] As the equivalent of "activities in accordance with virtues" he uses also the expression "actions (πράξεις) in accordance with virtues." [35] In another place, in addition to "duties" and "right actions," which are mentioned together with "virtue existing among men" (κατ' ἀνθρώπους ἀρετή), that is, human or moral virtue, [36] he mentions also (4) "acts in accordance with laws laid down by legislators" (νόμιμα θέσει). [37] In still another place he says: "Let that which seems good to virtue be law for each one of us." [38] We have thus in Philo four kinds of activities which are to be distinguished from virtue as a mere state of mind or character, namely, (1) "activities in accordance with virtue," (2) "right actions," (3) "duties," and (4) "acts in accordance with enacted laws." We shall comment upon the history and meaning of these four activities as well as upon the terms and expressions by which they are designated.

[31] *Ibid.* 42, 277.
[32] *Eth. Nic.* II, 6, 1106a, 22–24; cf. I, 13, 1102a, 14.
[33] *Ibid.* I, 8, 1098b, 31–33.
[34] *Leg. All.* I, 17, 56; cf. *Sacr.* 20, 73, where the term "duties" is omitted.
[35] *Abr.* 6, 31.
[36] Cf. above, n. 32.
[37] *Leg. All.* III, 43, 126.
[38] *Ibid.*, 87, 245.

The expression "activity in accordance with virtue" is of Aristotelian origin,[39] and, in Aristotle, it applies to an activity which is either in accordance with intellectual virtue or in accordance with moral virtue.[40] The term "right action" (κατόρθωμα) occurs in Aristotle,[41] but it was made popular by the Stoics, who invested it with a special technical meaning.[42] Philo seems to use it in the same sense as "activity in accordance with virtue" or "action in accordance with virtue," though he sometimes uses it in the same list together with either one of these two expressions.[43] He once says that "right action proceeds from virtue," [44] which means the same as "action or activity in accordance with virtue."

The term "duties" in the passage quoted is introduced by the statement "what philosophers call duties." The reference is, of course, to the Stoic use of the term.[45] Within duties we find that he distinguishes between two kinds of duties. First, he speaks of duties which he describes as sufficient in themselves (αὐτάρκη).[46] This seems to reflect a combination of (1) that class of "preferred things" (προη-γμένα) which the Stoics describe as being preferred "for their own sake" (δι' αὐτά)[47] and that class of duties which they describe as being unconditional (ἄνευ περιστάσεως),[48] always (ἀεί) incumbent[49] and perfect (τέλεια).[50] With this

---

[39] *Eth. Nic.* I, 10, 1100b, 10; X, 6, 1177a, 10; X, 8, 1178a, 9–10.

[40] Cf. *loc. cit.*

[41] *Magna Moralia* II, 3, 1199a, 13.

[42] See Arnim, Index, s.v.; cf. Zeller, III, 1⁴, p. 250, nn. 4 and 5 (*Stoics, Epicureans and Sceptics*², p. 265, nn. 1 and 2).

[43] Cf. *Leg. All.* I, 17, 56; *Sacr.* 20, 73.

[44] *Probus* 9, 60.

[45] Cf. Diogenes, VII, 108; Arnim, Index, sub καθῆκον; Zeller, III, 1⁴, pp. 271–274 (*Stoics, Epicureans and Sceptics*², pp. 287–290).

[46] *Leg. All.* III, 57, 165.

[47] Diogenes, VII, 107.

[48] *Ibid.*, VII, 109.

[49] *Ibid.*

[50] Stobaeus, *Eclogae* II, p. 85, l. 19.

kind of duty the Stoics also identify right action (κατόρ-θωμα).[51] Second, he speaks of intermediate (μέσα) duties.[52] In one place, without mentioning the word duty, he speaks of "indifferent" (ἀδιάφορα) actions as distinguished from "right actions proceeding from virtue." [53] Both these terms are used by the Stoics synonymously as a description of a certain type of duty.[54]

His inclusion of acts performed in accordance with established law among virtuous acts reflects Aristotle's statement that "all lawful acts (νόμιμα) are in a sense just acts, for acts laid down by the legislative art are lawful, and each of these, we say, is just." [55]

Another division of the virtues found in Philo is that into contemplative (θεωρητική) virtue and practical (πρακτική) virtue.[56] This division in its verbal form is taken from the Stoic Panaetius,[57] with whom it probably means the same as Aristotle's division of the virtues into intellectual and moral, for, according to Aristotle, the activity of intellectual virtue is "contemplative" [58] and the activity of moral virtue is an "activity of practical virtue." [59] But with Philo the term "contemplative" seems to include both intellectual and moral virtues, as distinguished from "practical" which similarly includes actions corresponding to both intellectual and moral virtues. We may gather this from his statement in which he explains that virtue is contemplative on the ground that "it clearly involves contemplation, since philosophy, the road that leads to it, involves contemplation

[51] Ibid., l. 20.
[52] Sacr. 10, 43; Plant. 22, 94; 23, 100.
[53] Probus 9, 60; cf. Leg. All, I, 30, 93.
[54] Stobaeus, Eclogae II, p. 86, ll. 10–16; f. Arnim, Index, sub ἀδιάφορον, καθῆκον, μέσον.
[55] Eth. Nic. V, 1, 1129b, 12–14.
[56] Leg. All. I, 17, 57.
[57] Diogenes, VII, 92.
[58] Eth. Nic. X, 7, 1177b, 19–20.
[59] Ibid., 6.

through its three parts, logic, ethics, physics." [60] In this statement, as will be noticed, contemplative virtue is said to involve ethical philosophy, which means that it involves the philosophy of moral virtue. On the whole, Philo's distinction here between "contemplation" and "practical" virtues, with his use of the term "contemplative" to include both "intellectual" and "moral" virtues, may correspond to the Aristotelian distinction, already quoted above, between the "possession" of virtue and the "use" thereof,[61] the former meaning only a state of mind or character, the latter meaning certain actions in conformity with that state of mind or character.

The result of our analysis of Philo's texts bearing upon the classification of the virtues is that on the whole he divides virtue into three classes, (1) intellectual, (2) moral, and (3) practical, calling both "intellectual" and "moral" virtues by the general term "contemplative" and using the term "practical" as a designation of the actions corresponding either to the intellectual or to the moral virtues. It is according to this threefold classification of the philosophic virtues that he undertakes to classify the laws of Moses, treating them, when they involve no actions, as virtues — contemplative, intellectual, or moral — and, when they involve actions, as actions corresponding to virtues or, as he himself calls them, practical virtues.

(b) Intellectual Virtues and Actions

Intellectual virtues, which in the language of Philo are called divine virtues, have God as their object. They include right opinions not only of God in His own nature but also of God as creator and of His creations in so far as they were

[60] *Leg. All.* I, 17, 57.   [61] Cf. above, p. 205.

created by Him. These right opinions have been enumerated in our discussion in a previous chapter of the eight fundamental principles which to him constitute the religious teachings of Scripture: (1) that God exists, (2) that He is one, (3) that He exercises providence, (4) that He created the world, (5) that the world which He created is one, (6) that He created incorporeal ideas, (7) that He revealed a Law, and (8) that the Law which He revealed is eternal.[62] All these principles are taught, according to him, in the various verses which he quotes as proof-texts. But they are also taught, he maintains, indirectly in the historical framework of the Pentateuch which forms the setting of the laws. For the Pentateuch, which in native Jewish tradition as well as in Philo is considered primarily as a book of Law, is in its framework a history, beginning with the story of the creation of the world, passing on to the history of mankind, and tapering off to a history of the Jewish people. The question why a book which is primarily intended to be a code of law should begin with the creation of the world must have occurred to many a mind. A rabbi gave utterance to this question in the statement that "the Torah should have started with the verse 'This month shall be unto you the beginning of months,'"[63] which is the first legal injunction delivered to the people of Israel as a whole, and his answer to this question is that the story of creation as well as the subsequent historical part is for the purpose of "making known the power of His might, as it is said 'He hath declared to His people the power of His works, that He may give them the heritage of the nations.'[64]"[65] Philo similarly says: "We must give the reason why he began his law book with the history, and put the commands and prohibitions in the sec-

---

[62] Cf. above, I, 164 ff.
[63] Exod. 12: 2.
[64] Ps. 111:6.
[65] *Tanḥuma* ed. Buber, *Bereshit*, § 11, p. 4a.

ond place." [66] His answer is that this history, unlike the history of other writers, is not written for the purpose of entertainment; it is meant "to show two most essential things." [67] The story of the creation of the world is meant to show that, since God is the creator of the world and the founder of the laws of nature, the Law for human guidance which was subsequently revealed by him is in harmony with these laws of nature. The story of mankind is meant to show that all human beings are rewarded and punished according to their conduct and hence it is the duty of man to live in accordance with the Law revealed by God. [68] In other words, the narrative part of the Pentateuch contains proofs for the existence of God and divine providence.

Thus Scripture contains certain teachings of intellectual virtues, or right opinions about God and the things created by God. Now in Aristotle, "intellectual virtue" is said to owe "its origin and development, for the most part, to teaching . . . whereas moral virtue comes about as a result of habit." [69] The qualifying expression "for the most part" is significant, for it means that even the intellectual virtues may receive some help in their rise and development from habit. [70] Then also, according to Aristotle, habits are formed "by first having actually practiced them" [71] and it is in order to habituate people in the practice of good actions that laws are enacted by legislators. [72] With these views in the back of his mind, Philo tries to show that many of the laws of Moses have for their purpose the inculcation of intellectual virtues.

[66] *Mos.* II, 8, 47.
[67] *Ibid.*, 48.
[68] *Mos.* II, 8, 48; *Praem.* 1, 1–2; *Opif.* 1, 1–3.
[69] *Eth. Nic.* II, 1, 1103a, 15–17.
[70] Cf. J. A. Stewart's note in his edition.
[71] *Eth. Nic.* II, 1, 1103a, 31.
[72] *Ibid.*, 1103b, 2–6.

The laws of this class are thus identified by him with those practical virtues which correspond to the contemplative virtues of the intellectual type. To this class of laws belong, in the first place, the first four of the ten commandments, dealing with polytheism, the worship of images, the taking God's name in vain, and the sacred seventh day,[73] and, in the second place, the particular laws which fall under these four commandments, namely, the laws about the temple service, oaths and vows, festivals and the sabbatical year.[74] In all of these laws he finds that their purpose is to train those who practice them in the attainment of the intellectual virtues.

These intellectual virtues as well as the laws which promote them are described by Philo in their totality as the virtue of "wisdom." Let us study the origin and meaning of this virtue.

The term wisdom ($\sigma o\phi la$), in the history of the enumeration of virtues in Greek philosophy, has undergone several changes of meaning. In Plato it is used as synonymous with the term prudence ($\phi\rho\delta\nu\eta\sigma\iota\varsigma$) and in his various enumerations of the cardinal virtues these two terms are used by him interchangeably.[75] In Aristotle a distinction is made between wisdom and prudence, the former dealing with things divine[76] and the latter with things human,[77] but still both of them are classified by him as intellectual virtues in contradistinction to moral virtues.[78] The Stoics widen still further the difference between these two terms. The term prudence is used

[73] Decal. 12, 52–21, 105.
[74] Spec. I–II, 36, 222.
[75] Cf., e.g., Laws I, 631 c, where $\phi\rho\delta\nu\eta\sigma\iota\varsigma$ is used and Republic IV, 428 B, where $\sigma o\phi la$ is used.
[76] Metaph. I, 2, 983a, 6–7; cf. above, I, 147.
[77] Eth. Nic. VI, 5, 1140a, 24–1140b, 30; cf. above, I, 148.
[78] Ibid. I, 13, 1103a, 5–6; cf. VI, 5, 7, 12.

by them as one of the four cardinal virtues.[79] As for the term wisdom, they contrast it with the term philosophy, the former being mere knowledge and the latter being practice; but, as a designation of mere knowledge, the term "wisdom" is used by them, as distinguished from its use by Aristotle, both with reference to things divine and with reference to things human. They thus say that "philosophy is the practice (ἐπιτήδευσιν) of wisdom, and wisdom is the knowledge (ἐπιστήμην) of things divine and human." [80] Now as for Philo, while on the one hand he differs from all the philosophers in the use of the term wisdom, on the other he follows both Aristotle and the Stoics. Differing from all the philosophers, he uses the term wisdom as a designation of the teachings contained in the revealed Law.[81] But within that revealed Law, sometimes, like the Stoics, he defines wisdom as "the knowledge of things divine and human," [82] and sometimes, like Aristotle, he distinguishes between wisdom which is "the service of God" and prudence which is "the regulation of human life." [83] Like the Stoics, however, he uses the term prudence in his various enumerations of the cardinal virtues.[84] Thus wisdom becomes with Philo a designation of the intellectual or divine virtues together with the actions corresponding to them. In other words, the term wisdom is used by him as a designation of both the revealed doctrines and the revealed laws contained in the Pentateuch.[85]

But in the same sense as the virtue of wisdom, which he defines as "the service of God," he uses also four other

[79] Arnim, III, 262 ff.
[80] Sextus, *Adversus Physicos* I, 13 (Arnim, II, 36); Zeller, III, 1⁴, p. 243, n. 5 (*Stoics, Epicureans and Sceptics*,² p. 258); cf. above, I, 148.
[81] Cf. above, I, 148–149.
[82] *Congr.* 14, 79; cf. above, I, 148.
[83] *Praem.* 14, 81; cf. above, I, 147.
[84] *Post.* 37, 128; for other references see Leisegang, *Indices*, under ἀρετή, 7.
[85] Cf. above, I, 149.

virtues, namely, piety (εὐσέβεια), godliness (θεοσέβεια), holiness (ὁσιότης), and faith (πίστις). Let us see how the grouping of these four virtues together with wisdom has come
about.

The first three of these four virtues which Philo uses in the
same sense as wisdom are to be found in Greek philosophic
literature. Piety is defined as being "either a part of justice
or an accompaniment of it" [86] and as having among its four
meanings also that of an act of justice "towards the gods." [87]
It is defined as "the knowledge of how to serve God" [88] or
the "science of the service to the gods," [89] and the "service
of God" is placed together with the "contemplation of
God" as a characterization of the virtuous life.[90] And just
as "piety" is defined as "the knowledge of how to serve
God," so also "the godly" or rather literally "those who fear
God" (θεοσεβεῖς) are described as "having acquaintance
with the rites of the gods." [91] In Plato, man is described as
"the most God-fearing (or godly) of all living creatures." [92]
Similarly, "holiness" is in some of Plato's dialogues reckoned as a fifth cardinal virtue [93] and together with piety it
is defined by him as being that part of justice which has to
do with service to the gods,[94] or it is intimated by him as being connected with justice.[95] Among the Stoics it is similarly
defined as a "kind of God-ward justice." [96] It is in accordance with Greek philosophic usage, then, that Philo uses the

[86] *De Virtutibus et Vitiis*, 5, 1250b, 22–23.
[87] *Ibid.*, 19–20. Cf. also Plato, *Definitiones* 412 E; Diogenes, III, 83.
[88] Diogenes, VII, 119.
[89] Sextus, *Adversus Physicos* I, 123 (Arnim, II, 1017).
[90] *Eth. Eud.*, 15, 1249b, 20.
[91] Diogenes, VII, 119.
[92] *Timaeus* 41 E; *Laws* X, 902 B.
[93] *Protagoras* 330 B; *Laches* 119 D.
[94] *Euthyphro* 12 E.
[95] *Protagoras* 329 C, 349 D.
[96] Sextus, *Adversus Physicos* I, 124.

3214214362146214

terms "piety," "godliness," and "holiness" as the equivalent of "wisdom" in the sense of the "service of God." It is also in accordance with Greek philosophic usage that he considers these three virtues as a special kind of justice, for in several places where he enumerates various virtues he puts immediately after justice either piety [97] or godliness [98] or holiness.[99] In one place he gives a more direct indication that these virtues are a sort of justice towards God in his statement that "the same person will also exhibit both qualities, holiness to God and justice to men." [100] Previous to this, in the same passage, for "holiness" he uses the term "piety." "Piety and holiness" are also used by him as a description of studies about God or theology, in contradistinction to "natural philosophy," "meteorology," and "moral philosophy." [101]

But in connection with two of these three virtues Philo makes a statement which calls for special comment. Piety and holiness are each described by him as queen (βασιλίς) or leader (ἡγεμονίς)[102] among the virtues. Now in Plato and among the Stoics there are statements to the effect that prudence or wisdom is the leader (ἡγεμών, *princeps*) among the virtues,[103] and Philo himself re-echoes these statements in his attempt to explain why prudence (φρόνησις) should be the first (πρώτη) among the four cardinal virtues.[104] Neither of them, however, has said that piety and holiness are the leaders among the virtues.

---

[97] *Cher.* 28, 96; *Deter*, 21, 73.

[98] *Spec.* IV, 25, 134; 33, 170.

[99] *Ibid.* I, 56, 304; II, 3, 12; *Virt.* 8, 47; *Praem.* 11, 66.

[100] *Abr.* 37, 208.   [101] *Ebr.* 22, 91.

[102] *Spec.* IV, 27, 147, and *Praem.* 9, 53 (piety); *Spec.* IV, 25, 135, and *Decal.* 23, 119 (piety, holiness); *Virt.* 18, 95 (piety, philanthropy, cf. below, p. 220); *Abr.* 46, 270 (faith).

[103] Plato, *Laws* III, 688 B (φρόνησις); Cicero, *De Officiis* I, 43, 153 (σοφία).

[104] *Leg. All.* I, 22, 70–71.

In Aristotle, however, there are the statements that "justice is often thought to be the greatest (κρατίστη) of virtues"[105] and that "piety" is "either part of justice or an accompaniment of it."[106] By such statements as these Philo could have justified his own statements that "piety," and with "piety" also "holiness," is the "queen" or "leader" among the virtues. But more likely his assignment of leadership to the virtue of "piety" was inspired by Scripture. It happens that the Greek term for piety (εὐσέβεια), composed of the two words "well" and "fear," is used in the Septuagint as the equivalent of the Hebrew word "fear" in connection with God, in the verse which in the Septuagint reads: "The fear of the Lord (φόβος Κυρίου is the beginning (ἀρχή) of wisdom ... and piety towards God (εὐσέβεια εἰς θεόν) is the beginning of discernment."[107] That it is this scriptural verse that is responsible for Philo's assignment of leadership to the virtue of "piety" may be gathered from his use of the scriptural term "beginning" in his statement elsewhere that "piety is the beginning (ἀρχή) of the virtues."[108] So also the Letter of Aristeas, with evident reference to this scriptural verse, in one place says: "Our Lawgiver first of all (πρῶτον) laid down the principles of piety and justice,"[109] and in another place says: "If you take the fear of God as your starting-point (καταρχὴν), you will never miss the goal."[110]

The fourth virtue, namely, faith (πίστις) in God or simply faith, which, together with piety, the fear of God and holiness, is used by Philo as connected with wisdom in the sense

---

[105] *Eth. Nic.* V, 1, 1129b, 27–28.
[106] Cf. above, n. 86.
[107] Prov. 1: 7.
[108] *Decal.* 12, 52 (the term ἀρχή here is to be supplied from the context).
[109] Aristeas, 131; cf. 229.
[110] *Ibid.*, 189; cf. 200, 235.

of the "service of God," is not found in Greek philosophy as a virtue. It is used indeed in Greek philosophy as an epistemological term and as such it is defined by Plato as an opinion (δόξα) about real things,[111] by Aristotle as a vehement assumption (ὑπόληψις σφοδρά),[112] and by the Stoics as a strong assumption (ὑπόληψις ἰσχυρά).[113] This definition is also used by Philo in his comment on the verse "And Abraham believed (ἐπίστευσεν) in God"[114] that "he had an unswerving and firm assumption (ἀκλινῆ καὶ βεβαίαν ὑπόληψιν)."[115] But in Greek philosophy prior to Philo neither faith in general nor faith in God in particular is spoken of as a virtue on a par with piety, the fear of God and holiness. Philo's treatment of it as a virtue is based, as may be gathered from his many texts, on the verse just quoted, where it is said concerning Abraham's belief in God that "it was counted to him for justice (δικαιοσύνην)." On the basis of this verse Philo therefore describes faith in God ·by the adjective just (δίκαιος)[116] and considers it as a species of the virtue of justice, that is, justice towards God, in the same way, as we have seen, piety, the fear of God and holiness are considered in Greek philosophy as justice towards the gods. Accordingly, just as piety and holiness were said by Philo, on the basis of the verse that the "fear of God" or "piety" is the beginning of wisdom, that they are the queens or leaders or the beginning of virtues, so also with regard to faith he says that it is the queen (βασιλίς) of virtues[117] or the most perfect (τελειοτάτη) of virtues[118] or the most certain (βεβαιοτάτη) of

[111] Cf. *Republic* VII, 534 A; cf. VI, 511 E.
[112] *Topica* IV, 5, 126b, 18.
[113] Stobaeus, *Eclogae* II, p. 112, l. 12; Arnim, III, 548, p. 147, l. 11. Wachsmuth's change of ὑπόληψις to κατάληψις, adopted also by Arnim on the basis of the statement in Aristotle, does not seem necessary.
[114] Gen. 15:6.
[115] *Virt.* 39, 216. Cf. above, I, 152.
[116] *Heres* 19, 94–95.

[117] *Abr.* 46, 270.
[118] *Heres* 18, 91.

the virtues [119] or "a perfect good" (ἀγαθὸν τέλειον).[120] As the queen and most perfect of virtues faith in God is contrasted by him with faith in "high offices or fame or honors or abundance of wealth and noble birth or health and efficacy of the senses or strength and beauty of body." [121] All these, as will be recalled, constitute what is called "external goods" or "external advantages," and some of them "virtues of the body," all of which are contrasted with true virtue, the virtue of the soul.[122] As defined by him, faith in God means to believe (1) that "there is one cause above all," [123] that is, "to believe in God alone and join no other with Him," [124] and (2) that God "provides for the world and all that there is therein." [125] Belief in the existence of one God who exercises His providence over the world is thus that which, according to Philo, constitutes the virtue of faith.[126]

But this faith in God is contrasted by him not only with the allurement of external goods but also with the allurement of reason, for in one passage, in a comment on the verse quoted above about Abraham's faith in God and on the verse "Not so my servant Moses; he is faithful (πιστός) in all my house," [127] he says: "So then it is best to have faith in God and not in our dim reasonings (λογισμοῖς) and insecure conjectures (εἰκασίαις)," for "if we repose our faith in our own reasonings, we shall construct and build up the city of mind that corrupts the truth." [128] Thus faith, or faith in God, means to him belief in the revealed truths of Scripture, in contrast to opinions which are discovered by reason. But then faith, or faith in God, means to him also belief in the fulfillment of the promises made by God

[119] *Virt.* 39, 216.
[120] *Migr.* 9, 44.
[121] *Abr.* 45, 263.
[122] Cf. above, p. 203.
[123] *Virt.* 39, 216.

[124] *Heres* 19, 92.
[125] *Virt.* 39, 216.
[126] Cf. also above, I, 151–152.
[127] *Num.* 12: 7.
[128] *Leg. All.* III, 81, 228.

as recorded in Scripture, for, again, commenting upon the apparent inconsistency between the verse "and Abraham believed in God" and the verse in which Abraham asks "O Lord God, whereby shall I know that I shall inherit it," [129] he says: "He has believed that he will be the inheritor of wisdom, but he merely asks how this shall come to pass; that it will come to pass is a fact that he has completely and firmly grasped in accordance with the divine promises." [130] It is in its first sense that the term faith is taken by St. Augustine in his interpretation of the verse "and Abraham believed in God." [131] Hence the term faith means with Philo two things: (1) belief in the unity and providence of God as well as in all the truths revealed directly by God, (2) trust in God. Both these meanings are logically interrelated, and it is faith in both these meanings that he has in mind when he says that "faith in God is one sure and infallible good" [132] or when he describes "faith in the Existent" as "the queen of virtues." [133]

(c) Moral Virtues and Actions

The cardinal virtues of the intellectual type are thus piety, godliness, holiness, and faith, all of which are included under wisdom, by which is meant the service of God. As for the cardinal virtues of the moral type, they are prudence, courage, temperance, and justice,[134] which list by the time of Philo was already a philosophic commonplace. There is much of the preacher's eloquence in his discussions of these cardinal virtues, but they are not of any philosophic significance, except in so far as they deal with the problem of the mean, which will be discussed later.[135] With the virtue of justice he often couples the virtue of humanity (φιλανθρω-

---

[129] Gen. 15:8.
[130] Heres 21, 100–101.
[131] De Spiritu et Littera XXXI, 54 (PL, 44, 235).
[132] Abr. 46, 268.
[133] Ibid., 270.
[134] Mos. II, 39, 216; Leg. All. II, 6, 18.
[135] Cf. below, pp. 268 ff.

πία),¹³⁶ and both justice and humanity in their relation to
actions corresponding to the moral virtues are compared by
him to piety and holiness in their relation to actions corresponding to the intellectual virtues, for both these two sets
of virtues are the "two mainheads" of all the "particular
lessons and doctrines," the former two constituting the
rules regulating one's conduct towards men and the latter
two constituting the rules regulating one's conduct towards
God.¹³⁷ The term humanity (φιλανθρωπία), is used by him
in the sense of giving help to those who are in need of it,¹³⁸
and he describes it as "the virtue closest akin to piety, its
sister and its twin," for it is a "high road leading to holiness" ¹³⁹ and "the nature which is pious is also humane, and
the same person will exhibit both qualities, holiness to God
and justice to men." ¹⁴⁰ Then, also, with the virtue of humanity he connects the virtues of fellowship (κοινωνία),
concord (ὁμόνοια), equality (ἰσότης),¹⁴¹ grace (χάρις),¹⁴² and
mercy (ἔλεος).¹⁴³

All these, on the whole, reflect such statements in Greek
philosophy as that in which "equality" (ἰσότης) and "kindness of heart" (εὐγνωμοσύνη) are said to be connected with
justice.¹⁴⁴ But the term *philanthropia*, for which we have
been using the English "humanity," judging from a passage
in which it is discussed, does not seem to rank in Greek
philosophy among the virtues,¹⁴⁵ though in later Latin
philosophy the term *humanitas* does occur as a virtue under

---

¹³⁶ *Mut.* 40, 225; *Mos.* II, 2, 9; *Decal.* 30, 164.

¹³⁷ *Spec.* II, 15, 63.   ¹⁴¹ *Spec.* I, 53, 295.
¹³⁸ *Virt.* 13, 80 ff.   ¹⁴² *Mos.* II, 43, 242.
¹³⁹ *Virt.* 9, 51.   ¹⁴³ *Somn.* I, 23, 147.
¹⁴⁰ *Abr.* 37, 208.

¹⁴⁴ Diogenes, VII, 126; cf. also "caritas, amicitia, iustitia, reliquae virtutes" in
Cicero, *Academica Priora* II, 46, 140.

¹⁴⁵ Diogenes, III, 98; cf. Colson, VIII, General Introduction, p. xi, n.b. Cf. also
R. Reitzenstein, *Werden und Wesen der Humanität im Altertum*, 1907.

220   PHILO

the virtue of justice.¹⁴⁶ Then, again, as of piety and holiness,
so also of justice he says that it is the "leader" and "ruler"
among the virtues,¹⁴⁷ and similarly of humanity he says that
it is one of the two "leaders of the virtues," ¹⁴⁸ the other being piety. Now his statement with regard to justice may
reflect Aristotle's statement quoted above that "justice is
often thought to be the greatest of virtues," ¹⁴⁹ and one can
readily see how Philo, having coupled humanity with
justice, should consider also humanity as the greatest of
virtues. But there may be another reason for his elevation
of humanity or philanthropy to the leadership of the virtues,
and that is the influence of Jewish tradition, which we have
already found to be the direct reason for his treatment of
piety and holiness as leaders among the virtues. In the
Septuagint the Greek word for justice (δικαιοσύνη) translates
the Hebrew word ṣedaḳah,¹⁵⁰ and the same term ṣedaḳah is
also translated there by the Greek term for "mercy" or
"alms" (ἐλεημοσύνη),¹⁵¹ which, as we have seen, is treated by
Philo as a virtue akin to the virtue of humanity.¹⁵² Thus the
Hebrew term ṣedaḳah means both justice and philanthropy
or humanity, the latter in the sense of giving help to those
who are in need of it. Now in native Judaism the view has
been expressed that "the commandment of ṣedaḳah is bal-
anced against all the commandments together." ¹⁵³ Philo's
statement that justice and humanity are the leaders among
the virtues is probably only another way of expressing the
same traditional view. So also in the Letter of Aristeas

¹⁴⁶ Cf. Macrobius, *Commentarius ex Cicerone in Somnium Scipionis* I, 8 (M. Nis-
ard, *Collections des Auteurs Latins*, p. 33, col. 1).
¹⁴⁷ Plant. 28, 122 (ἔξαρχος, ἡγεμονίς); cf. *Abr.* 5, 27 (ἡγεμονίς).
¹⁴⁸ *Virt.* 18, 95.
¹⁴⁹ Cf. above, p. 215.
¹⁵⁰ Gen. 18: 19.   ¹⁵² Cf. above, n. 138.
¹⁵¹ Deut. 6: 25; 24: 13; Isa. 1: 27; Dan. 4: 24.   ¹⁵³ *Baba Batra* 9a.

justice (δικαιοσύνη) is said to be one of the two principles which "our Lawgiver first of all (πρῶτον) laid down," [154] the other being "piety." [155]

Connected with the four cardinal virtues, of which in this particular passage he happens to mention only temperance and justice, is also nobility, for "we must give the name of noble to the temperate and the just." [156] "Nobility," he re-echoes the common sentiment of the Stoics,[157] does not mean descent from "many generations of wealth and distinction," [158] but is rather "the peculiar portion of a mind purged of every spot." [159] He speaks of it therefore as "nobility of soul" (ψυχῆς εὐγένεια) and couples it with "greatness of spirit" (φρονήματος μέγεθος),[160] and asserts that the wise "alone is noble." [161] In Judaism, while importance is attached to nobility of descent, there was a similar tendency to lay greater importance upon nobility of learning, which is the equivalent of the Stoic nobility of virtue. The most characteristic expression on this point is that a learned bastard has precedence over an ignorant high priest.[162]

Following again Aristotle's statements that "moral virtue comes about as a result of habit," that habits are formed by practice, and that the practice of good actions is the purpose of laws,[163] Philo tries to show that the laws of Moses have for their purpose the inculcation of moral virtues. Such laws are in the first place the last five of the ten commandments and, in the second place, the many particular laws which fall

---

[154] Aristeas, 131.
[155] Cf. above, p. 214.
[156] *Virt.* 35, 189.
[157] Cf. Cohn, *Philos Werke*, II, p. 367, n. 2; Colson, VIII, p. 449, § 189; Arnim, Index, s.v.
[158] *Virt.* 35, 187.   [159] *Ibid.*, 189.
[160] *Mos.* I, 27, 149; cf. *Eth. Nic.* I, 10, 1100b, 32–33: γεννάδας καὶ μεγαλόψυχος.
[161] *Sobr.* 11, 56; cf. Arnim, III, 594, 597.
[162] Cf. *M. Horayot* III, 8.   [163] Cf. above, p. 210.

under them. These laws are each intended to promote a certain particular moral virtue. The laws concerning witnesses, judges, kings, and trade all tend to promote the virtue of justice;[164] those concerning the poor, the stranger, and the orphan — the virtues of humanity as well as of justice;[165] those concerning the waging of war — the virtue of courage;[166] and those concerning circumcision,[167] marriage,[168] and diet[169] — the virtue of temperance.[170] However, this classification of the laws according to virtues, we are warned by Philo, should not be taken too rigidly, for each of the ten commandments, as well as the particular laws which fall under it, "separately and all in common incite and exhort us to wisdom and justice and godliness and the rest of the company of virtues."[171] In native Jewish tradition the same view is expressed in the statement that the ten commandments "are all held fast to one another,"[172] that is to say, they are inseparable from one another, they are implied in one another. With regard to the fifth commandment, about honoring one's father and mother, he shows how it has both an intellectual and moral purpose,[173] for this commandment, he says, "stands on the border-line between the human and the divine,"[174] for "parents are to their children what God is to

[164] *Spec.* IV, 25, 132–52, 238.
[165] *Virt.* 9, 51–32, 174.
[166] *Ibid.* 1, 1–8, 50.
[167] *Migr.* 16, 92; *Spec.* I, 2, 8–11.
[168] *Spec.* III, 2, 7–14, 82.
[169] *Ibid.* IV, 14, 79–24, 131.
[170] In connection with circumcision Philo says that its purpose is "the excision of excessive and superfluous pleasure" (*Spec.* I, 2, 9; cf. *Migr.* 16, 92), which means temperance (cf. *Eth. Nic.* II, 7, 1107b, 4–6). In connection with the marriage laws and the dietary laws, he says that their purpose is "continence" (ἐγκράτεια) (*Spec.* III, 4, 22; IV, 16, 97), which term he constantly uses as synonymous with "temperance" (cf. Léisegang, *Indices*, s.v.), evidently following Aristotle's statement that by analogy "temperance" is called "continence" (*Eth. Nic.* VII, 10, 1151b, 32–1152a, 3); cf. below, p. 235.
[171] *Spec.* IV, 25, 134.
[172] *Mekilta de- Rabbi Simeon ben Yoḥai* on Exod. 20: 17, p. 112; *Pesikta Rabbati*, 21, p. 107a.
[173] *Spec.* II, 38, 224–43, 241.
[174] *Ibid.*, 38, 224; cf. *Decal.* 22, 106.

the world." [175] In native Jewish tradition the same view is expressed in the statement that "Scripture places the honoring of father and mother on a level with the honoring of God." [176]

The intellectual and moral virtues which the laws are meant to inculcate are called by Philo their underlying meaning (ὑπόνοια) as contrasted with the external observance which is their literal (ῥητή) or obvious (φανερά) meaning.[177] The underlying meaning is compared by him to the soul of the law and their external observance to the body.[178] It would seem that he considered all the laws of the Pentateuch as having some intellectual or moral purpose; there is no indication that some laws were considered by him as being arbitrary commands of God without any purpose. But the fact that the laws have an intellectual or moral purpose, a purpose which may perhaps be attained in some other way or by some other practices, does not mean that the external observance of the law can be neglected. These laws are God-given and therefore their mere observance has an intrinsic value. The laws of the Sabbath and of the festivals and of the Temple service have indeed an intellectual purpose, and so also indeed has the rite of circumcision a moral purpose, still the external observance of these laws and this rite as means of attaining that intellectual and moral purpose is of equal importance.[179] There is, however, one condition which is required in order to make the external observance of the law a meritorious act. The law must be performed, like any moral act, with intention, for "right

---

[175] *Ibid.*, 38, 225.
[176] *Mekilta, Baḥodesh*, 8, F, p. 70a; W, p. 78; HR, p. 321; L., II, p. 258; *Sifra, Ḳedoshim*, Proem, p. 86d; *Ḳiddushin* 30b. Cf. Heinemann, *Philos Werke*, II, p. 170, n. 2.
[177] Cf. above, I, 115.
[178] *Migr.* 16, 93; cf. above, I, 67; *Cont.* 10, 78.   [179] *Ibid.*, 89–93.

actions (κατορθώματα) that spring from forethought (ἐκ προνοίας) are of greater worth than those that are involuntary" [180] and "those who perform any other thing that they ought to do without the assent (ἀσυγκαταθέτῳ) of their mind or will, but by doing violence to their inclination, do not achieve righteousness." [181] The language used by Philo in these passages is Stoic. [182] But it also reflects the native Jewish sentiments with regard to the requirement of intention (kavvanah) and a feeling of joy (simḥah) in the performance of any commandment of the Law, expressed in the statement that "commandments require intention" [183] and in the frequent allusions to "the joy of the performance of a commandment." [184] The Hebrew "intention" and "joy" which must accompany the performance of a commandment are the equivalents of the Stoic "forethought" (πρόνοια) and "assent" (συγκατάθεσις) which must accompany right actions. The assent of the mind which according to Philo is to accompany the performance of any virtuous act is sometimes described by him as joy, as, for instance, in his statement that "the reward which is set aside for the victorious champion who gained his virtue through nature and without a struggle is joy (χαρά)," [185] or in his statement that "there is no sweeter delight (τέρψις) than that the soul should be charged through and through with justice," [186] or in his statement that only when a man "feels more joy at being the servant of God than if he had been king of all the human race" will he speak out freely to God, instead of

---

[180] Post. 3, 11. Cf. Aristotle's definition of virtue in Eth. Nic. II, 6, 1106b, 36.
[181] Immut. 22, 100.
[182] Cf. Arnim, III, 500 ff.; III, 177.
[183] Berakot 13a.
[184] Berakot 31a; Shabbat 30b; Pesaḥim 117a.
[185] Praem. 5, 31.
[186] Spec. IV, 26, 141.

being struck speechless out of fear of Him.[187] All these are nothing but what the rabbis, reflecting many scriptural passages,[188] refer to as the "joy" which is to be experienced in the performance of the commandments of the Law.

III. THE VIRTUE OF THE CONTROL OF DESIRE

In his discussion of the intellectual virtues, Philo has shown that the Pentateuch not only commands the performance of certain actions which symbolize such beliefs as the existence of God and His unity and His providence, but that it also teaches directly that man must believe in these principles and harbor them in his mind as an intellectual conviction. He now wants to show that similarly in the case of the moral virtues the Pentateuch demands not only what Aristotle calls the "use" of virtue but also what he calls the "possession" of it.[1] Not only must one act virtuously; one must also be of a virtuous state of character. Not only must one refrain from wronging others; one must also refrain from having wrong emotions. Had Philo chosen he could have quoted such direct commands as "Thou shalt not hate thy brother in thy heart . . . nor bear any grudge against the children of thy people, but thou shalt love thy neighbor as thyself."[2] He could have further shown how these commands not to hate and not to bear a grudge and to love all deal with what in philosophic language is called the emotion of desire, for "hatred" (μῖσος) and "grudge" (μῆνις) are ranged by the Stoics under the emotion of desire

[187] *Heres* 2, 7.
[188] As, for instance, Jer. 15: 16; Ps. 19: 9; 119: 162. Cf. S. Schechter, *Some Aspects of Rabbinic Theology*, pp. 148–169.

[1] *Eth. Nic.* I, 8, 1098b, 31–33; cf. above, p. 205.
[2] Lev. 19: 17–18. These verses are taken by Maimonides as examples of purely moral commandments dealing with emotions (*Sefer ha-Miṣwot, Shoresh* 9).

(ἐπιθυμία),[3] and "affection" (ἀγάπησις) is placed by them
under the good emotional state (εὐπάθεια) of wishing (βούλησις), which is the counterpart of desire (ἐπιθυμία).[4] Philo,
however, does not comment directly on these commandments not to hate and not to grudge but to love, though he
touches upon such vices of pure emotion as pride and arrogance.[5] But he comments directly upon the last of the ten
commandments, "Thou shalt not desire," and in his comments on it he points out the special character of this commandment as being one which does not deal with action but
rather with pure emotion.[6]

The special character of this commandment as dealing
with pure emotion rather than with action is already found
in native Jewish literature. Drawing upon the distinction between the two Hebrew terms *taḥmod*[7] and *tit'avveh*,[8] used
in the tenth commandment, which for the sake of convenience
we shall translate respectively by "covet" and "desire," [9]
a Tannaitic Midrash says that the prohibition "Thou shalt
not desire," as distinguished from the prohibition "Thou
shalt not covet," means that one is not to desire that which
belongs to another even though he has no intent to acquire
possession of the object desired. According to this interpretation, the tenth commandment contains two prohibitions,
one of them a prohibition against merely having a desire for
that which belongs to another and the transgression of this
prohibition, on purely legal grounds, is completed as soon
as the desire is conceived in the heart, and the other a pro-

[3] Diogenes, VII, 113.
[4] *Idem.*, VII, 116.
[5] *Virt.* 30, 161–163.
[6] *Decal.* 28, 142–153; *Spec.* IV, 14, 79–15, 94.
[7] Exod. 20: 14 (17); Deut. 5: 18 (21).
[8] Deut. 5: 18 (21).
[9] In the Authorized Version the terms "covet" and "desire" are used indiscriminately in the translation of this commandment.

hibition against coveting that which belongs to another and the transgression of this prohibition, again on purely legal grounds, is not completed until the object coveted is obtained possession of. The original text on this subject reads as follows: "To 'desire' is in the heart, as it is said, 'thou mayest eat flesh after all the desire of thy soul' [10]; to 'covet' is in action, as it is said, 'thou shalt not covet the silver and the gold that is on them and take it unto thee.'[11]"[12] The reason why the mere desiring of that which belongs to another is prohibited is explained as follows: "If a man desires that which others have, he will be led finally to covet [and to think of means to obtain] that which others have . . . if a man covets [and thinks of means to obtain] that which others have, he will be led finally to rob."[13] It is furthermore explained that the transgression of the commandment "thou shalt not covet or desire," as well as the transgression of any of the other commandments, will lead to the transgression of all the other commandments, for "all the commandments are held fast to one another, so that if a man has broken through one of them he will be led finally to break through all of them."[14]

The Septuagint, just as some of the later rabbis,[15] takes no cognizance of the difference between the two Hebrew terms used in the tenth commandment. Both these terms are translated by the same Greek word ἐπιθυμήσεις. Nor is such a distinction assumed by Philo in his discussion of this commandment. Like the Septuagint, he uses the term ἐπιθυμία

[10] Deut. 12: 20.
[11] Deut. 7: 25.
[12] *Mekilta de- Rabbi Simeon ben Yoḥai* on Exod. 20: 17 (14), p. 112.
[13] *Ibid.*
[14] *Ibid.*, p. 113; cf. *Pesikta Rabbati*, 21, p. 107a.
[15] *Rashi* on Deut. 5: 18; *Sefer Miṣwot Gadol*, Negative Commandment 158; *'Ammude Golah (Sefer Miṣwot Ḳaṭan)*, 19.

for both Hebrew words. From his discussion of this commandment it is quite evident that Philo takes the term ἐπιθυμία to mean the same as the term "desire" is taken in the Tannaitic Midrash in its distinction from the term "covet" and the commandment is accordingly interpreted by him as a prohibition of a mere desire, even though it is not accompanied by an intent to gain possession of the thing desired, so that the infraction of that commandment is completed as soon as such a desire is conceived. It is of course also to be assumed that the desire legally prohibited in this commandment is a desire for something which belongs to somebody else, for this is the obvious meaning of the commandment which reads "thou shalt not desire thy neighbor's house," or similar things which belong to one's neighbor. Though Philo speaks of desire in general, that is, of a desire for what we have not got,[16] and not of a desire for that which belongs to somebody else, still his discussion, in so far as it is a commentary upon the commandment, implies that the desire of which he speaks is that desire which the commandment explicitly describes as a desire for that which belongs to another person. When in his explanation why desire is prohibited he says, almost in the words of the rabbis quoted above, that "if the desire is directed to money, it makes men thieves and cut-purses and robbers and house-breakers," [17] the opening statement, to be sure, does not speak of a desire directed to the money which belongs to another person, still the subsequent statement that a desire for money leads to robbery and purse-cutting and house-breaking makes it quite evident that the desire for money spoken of was not a desire for money in general but rather for the money in the pocket or the purse or the house of one particular person, for

[16] This point is unduly stressed by Colson, VIII, General Introduction, p. x.
[17] *Spec.* IV, 15, 87.

however general the desire for money spoken of may be originally, it will certainly be transformed into a desire for the money of certain particular persons if it is to lead to stealing and robbery and house-breaking. It is exactly the latter kind of desire, the desire for that which belongs to somebody else, that the tenth commandment as a law, and not a mere moral maxim, legally prohibits, according to Philo, for the ten commandments, as Philo himself says, are not merely moral maxims but "laws or statutes in the true sense of the term." [18] Then, also, as the rabbis in their discussion of the commandment, so also Philo intimates that the breaking of the tenth commandment will ultimately lead to the breaking of all the other commandments. Speaking of the wrongdoings that desire might lead to he mentions "plunderings and robberies and repudiations of debts and false accusations, also seductions, adulteries, murders, and, in short, wrongful actions, whether private or public, whether in things sacred or in things profane." [19] This list of wrongdoings is almost a summary of the things prohibited in the ten commandments. Philo seems to say that the reason why the tenth commandment prohibits one from desiring a neighbor's house or wife or manservant or maidservant or ox or ass or anything that belongs to him, is that such a desire will lead to the breaking of the commandments against murder and adultery and stealing and bearing false witness against one's neighbor and also the first five commandments which deal with things sacred.

In his discussion of the legal prohibition not to desire that which belongs to one's neighbor, a prohibition, as we have said, of a mere desire for that which belongs to one's neighbor, even when not accompanied by an intent to get posses-

---

[18] *Decal.* 9, 32.
[19] *Spec. IV*, 15, 84; cf. *Decal.* 28, 151–153.

sion of the thing desired, Philo takes occasion to deliver himself of a homily on the evils of desire on purely moral grounds. Beginning with a diatribe against the evils of emotion in general,[20] describing it as "the vilest thing in itself and the cause of the vilest actions,"[21] he particularly denounces the emotion of desire as "a battery of destruction to the soul,"[22] characterizing it as "the fountain of all evil"[23] and urging that, in order to obtain perfection and happiness, desire "must be done away with or brought into obedience to the guidance of reason."[24] In native Judaism the same sentiments would be expressed in a diatribe against the evil *yeṣer* and the advice that "at all times let man stir up his good *yeṣer* against his evil *yeṣer*."[25] The evil *yeṣer* and good *yeṣer*, literally, the evil imagination and the good imagination, are the rabbinic equivalent of what Greek philosophers call emotion and reason, and sometimes the "evil *yeṣer*" is identified with "desire."[26] As we shall show later, Philo alludes to the terms evil and good *yeṣer* as meaning emotion and reason,[27] and his description here of emotion as "vilest thing" (αἴσχιστον)[28] also has its equivalent in the

---

[20] *Spec.* IV, 14, 79; *Decal.* 28, 142–146.
[21] *Spec.* IV, 16, 95.
[22] *Ibid.*; cf. *Decal.* 28, 142.
[23] *Spec.* IV, 15, 84.
[24] *Ibid.* IV, 16, 95; cf. *Decal.* 28, 150, where only the second remedy, that of checking desire by reason, is mentioned. Both these alternatives reflect the two definitions of virtue, the Stoic and the Aristotelian. The Stoic definition maintains that virtue is complete exemption from emotion (ἀπάθεια). Cf. Zeller, III, 1⁴, p. 240, nn. 1–2 (*Stoics, Epicureans and Sceptics,*² p. 254, nn. 4–5); Arnim. III, § 201. The Aristotelian definition means that the emotion is to be controlled by reason; cf. below, pp. 268 ff.
[25] *Berakot* 5a.
[26] Cf. *M. Abot* IV, 21: "Envy, desire and ambition take a man out of the world," in which the term "desire" evidently corresponds to the term "evil *yeṣer*" in *M. Abot* II, 11: "The evil eye, the evil *yeṣer* and hatred of his fellow-creatures put a man out of the world." Cf. *Tosefot Yom-Ṭob* on IV, 21.
[27] Cf. below, p. 288.   [28] *Spec.* IV, 16, 95; cf. above, n. 21.

rabbinic description of the evil *yeṣer* as the "vile thing" (*menuwwal*)[29] or the "unclean thing" (*ṭame*).[30] Sometimes instead of desire Philo makes pleasure the source of all sin and evil.[31] Sometimes the terms desire (*concupiscentia*) and pleasure (*voluptas*) are used by him interchangeably.[32] It is the Stoics, however, whom Philo follows here in the external formulation of his views. The particular teachings of the Stoics that are reflected in the passages quoted from Philo are those which are reported in their name to the effect that "the emotions of fear, grief, and lust (*libido*) are sins, even when no extraneous result ensues"[33] and that, while there is a difference between the various ailments of the soul, "in practice at any rate they are combined and their origin is found in lust (*libido*) and delight (*laetitia*),"[34] or that "the fountain of all disorders is intemperance, which is a revolt from all the guidance of mind and right reason."[35] He similarly follows the Stoics in his definition of emotion as an "inordinate and excessive impulse" and as an "irrational and unnatural movement of the soul."[36] Also of Stoic origin is his enumeration of the four primary emotions, namely, pleasure, pain, fear, and desire.[37]

But here as elsewhere he does not follow the Stoics blindly. Whenever forced by certain native Jewish presuppositions, he departs from the Stoics and follows some other philosopher or presents a new view of his own. In his discussion of desire in these passages he departs from the Stoics on one funda-

[29] *Kiddushin* 20b.
[30] *Sukkah* 52a.
[31] *Leg. All.* II, 18, 71–72; 19, 77–78; 26, 107; III, 21, 68; 35, 107; 36, 112; 37, 113.
[32] *Qu. in Gen.* I, 31.
[33] Cicero, *De Finibus* III, 9, 32.
[34] *Idem, Tusculanae Disputationes* IV, 11, 24.
[35] *Ibid.,* IV, 9, 22.
[36] *Spec.* IV, 14, 79; cf. Arnim, III, 377 ff.; I, 205 ff.
[37] *Decal.* 28, 143–149; cf. Arnim, I, 205 ff.; III, 377 ff.

mental point. In his attempt to explain why desire is worse
than all the other emotions and why it is singled out by
Moses for special condemnation, he says that "while each of
the others, coming from the outside (θύραθεν) and assaulting
from the outside (ἔξωθεν), seems to be involuntary, desire
alone derives its origin from ourselves and is voluntary." [38]
This distinction between desire and the other emotions is in
direct opposition to the view of the Stoics. According to the
Stoics, there is no such distinction between the emotion of
desire and the other emotions. To them all our emotions are
voluntary, for to them all the emotions are judgments
(κρίσεις) [39] and hence voluntary (voluntaria) [40] and within our
power (in nostra potestate). [41]

At first sight, this distinction drawn by Philo between the
emotion of desire and all the other emotions would seem to
be based upon Aristotle, for it contains two elements which
would seem to reflect two statements by Aristotle. To begin
with, his description of the contrast between involuntary and
voluntary as a contrast between that which comes from the
outside (θύραθεν, ἔξωθεν) and that which derives its origin
from ourselves corresponds exactly to Aristotle's description
of the contrast between involuntary and voluntary as a contrast between actions whose "origin is from the outside
(ἔξωθεν)" [42] and actions whose "origin lies in the agent." [43]
Then, also, his singling out of desire as the only emotion
which is voluntary would seem to reflect Aristotle's argument

[38] Decal. 28, 142.
[39] Diogenes, VII, 111.
[40] Cicero, Academica Posteriora I, 10, 39; cf. J. S. Reid's note in his edition.
[41] Idem, Tusculanae Disputationes IV, 7, 14; cf. Zeller, III, 1⁴, p. 234, nn. 1–3
(Stoics, Epicureans and Sceptics,² p. 248, nn. 1–3); A. Dyroff, "Die Ethik der Alten
Stoa," Berliner Studien für classische Philologie und Archaeologie, N. F. 2 (1897)
p. 155, n. 4.
[42] Eth. Nic. III, 1, 1110b, 15–17.
[43] Ibid., 3–6.

that, while on the whole emotions may be called involuntary, actions done from desire or from anger cannot be called involuntary.[44] "Anger," which in this passage is coupled by Aristotle with "desire," was, by the time of Philo, under the influence of the Stoic classification of the emotions, treated as a subdivision of desire.[45] Thus, according to Aristotle, desire is singled out from all the other emotions as not being involuntary. But as against these two similarities between Philo and Aristotle there is the following important difference. In Aristotle, all the emotions are said to have their origin in the agent himself and if some of the emotions, despite their being in the agent himself, are described by him as involuntary, it is only because, as he himself says, the agent is ignorant of the particular circumstances under which the emotions are experienced by him.[46] In Philo, on the other hand, all the emotions, with the exception of desire, are described as "coming from the outside and assaulting from the outside." [47] It is therefore not a preference of Aristotle that has led him to depart from the Stoics on this point. What has led him to depart here from the Stoics in declaring all the emotions, with the exception of desire, as being involuntary and to depart also from Aristotle in declaring all the emotions, with the exception of desire, as coming from without, must be something else.

That something else is his own particular use of the term voluntariness as distinguished from the use of that term by both Aristotle and the Stoics. The voluntariness which Philo attributes here to desire and denies of all the other emotions is unlike the voluntariness which the Stoics attribute to all

[44] *Ibid.*, 1111a, 22 ff.
[45] Stobaeus, *Eclogae* II, p. 91, ll. 10 ff.; Diogenes, VII, 113 (cf. Arnim, III, §§ 395–398).
[46] *Eth. Nic.* III, 1, 1110b, 18 ff.
[47] *Decal.* 28, 142; cf. above, n. 38.

the emotions and which Aristotle hesitates to deny altogether of the emotions of desire and anger. To both the
Stoics and Aristotle the voluntariness under consideration
is only a limited and determined voluntariness; it is not an
absolute voluntariness. With them, the question whether
the emotions, or any of the emotions, are to be considered as
voluntary is only a question of whether they take place (1)
without external compulsion and (2) with a knowledge of the
circumstances. To Philo, however, the voluntariness under
consideration is that undetermined free-will, the freedom to
do either good or evil, which is a gift of God to man.[48] Such
voluntariness and such freedom is attributed by Philo only
to desire. Free choice, Philo seems to argue, must imply free
desire (ἐπιθυμία), for free choice means the freedom to choose
between good and evil, and at the basis of such a choice,
according to the accepted Aristotelian psychology, there
is appetency (ὄρεξις),[49] and desire is nothing but "a species
of appetency," that kind of appetency which moves a
man "in opposition to reason." [50] Freedom or free choice
means both free will (βούλησις) and free desire (ἐπιθυμία):
the former, rational appetency, is freedom to do good ; the
latter, irrational appetency, is freedom to do evil.[51] But,
while on the ground of his belief in the absolute freedom of
the will Philo had to assume also the freedom of the emotion
of desire, there was no need for him to assume also on that
ground the freedom of all the other emotions. With regard to
all these other emotions, therefore, as far as he himself was
concerned, Philo could have left it to the Peripatetics and
the Stoics to fight it out among themselves whether, in the
limited sense in which they all use the term voluntary, they
are to be called voluntary or involuntary. For himself, to

48 Cf. above, I, 431.   50 *Ibid.*, 25–26.
49 *De Anima* III, 10, 433a, 13.   51 *Ibid.*, 23–26; cf. above, I, 431 ff.

whom voluntariness means absolute free will, all these other
emotions, though they are commonly spoken of as having
their origin within ourselves, really do not originate within
ourselves in the sense of their being the choice of our absolutely free will. In comparison with the absolute freedom of
desire and of will, they may be considered as coming from
the outside and as assaulting us from the outside, for they
are involuntary. His statement indeed literally reads, "while
each of the others, coming from the outside and assaulting
from the outside, *seems to be involuntary*," but in reality it
means that each of the other emotions *is involuntary*, for,
even though it is strictly speaking within us, *it seems as if it
were coming from the outside* and assaulting from the outside.
Desire, on the other hand, is voluntary in the absolute sense
of the term, for it "derives its origin from ourselves," inasmuch as its freedom has been implanted within us by God as a
special gift.

The negative tenth commandment is thus a command to
control one's desire. Now, the control of any emotion by
reason, if the control establishes a mean between two ex-
cesses, is to Aristotle, as well as to Philo, as we shall see,[52] a
virtue, and as most of the other virtues it can be expressed
by some positive term. What the positive term is by which
the control of excessive desire is to be described is supplied
by Aristotle. It is called by him the virtue of continence
(ἐγκράτεια),[53] for, "a man acts continently," he says, "whenever he acts against his desire in accordance with reason." [54]
"Continence" is also a virtue according to the Stoics, though,
with their definition of virtue as the extirpation of emotion rather than its control, they probably would con-

[52] Cf. below, p. 272.
[53] *Eth. Eud.* II, 7, 1223b, 11–12.
[54] *Ibid.* II, 7, 1223b, 12–14; cf. *De Anima* III, 9, 433a, 7–8.

sider continence as a virtue when its corresponding emotion is utterly extirpated.[55] "Continence" is thus defined by them as "a disposition which is never overcome in that which concerns right reason, or a habit which no pleasures can get the better of."[56] Following Aristotle in all this, Philo says that "the opposite of desire is continence"[57] and declares it to be "a pure and stainless virtue,"[58] or "the most profitable of virtues," which has "thriftiness (εὐτέλεια) and contentment (εὐκολία) and frugality (ὀλιγόδεια) for its bodyguards."[59] It is linked by him with "piety"[60] and "humanity"[61] and "godliness,"[62] and both "continence" and "contentment" (εὐκολία) are included by him among the virtues possessed by the Essenes.[63] It is the virtue of "continence," he says, that is taught by the tenth commandment[64] as well as by all those special laws of which the purpose, as seen by him, is to teach the control of desire.[65] In the Letter of Aristeas the same sentiment is expressed in the king's question "What is the highest form of government?" to which one of the elders answers: "To rule oneself and not to be carried away by impulses."[66] In native Jew-

---

[55] Cf. below, p. 269.

[56] Diogenes, VII, 93; cf. Sextus, *Adversus Physicos* I, 153. The connection of "continence" with pleasure is found in Aristotle's statement that both the "continent man" and the "temperate man" "do nothing contrary to rule for the sake of bodily pleasures" but that the continent man has "bad appetites" and feels pleasure but is not led by it (*Eth. Nic.* VII, 9, 1151b, 34–1152a, 3). Similarly Philo connects it with pleasure in his statement that "the lover of pleasure is barren of all the chief necessities, temperance, modesty and continence" (*Jos.* 26, 153) and also in his treatment of "the love of pleasure" and "continence" as opposites (*Abr.* 4, 24).

[57] *Spec.* I, 29, 149.   [60] *Ibid.* I, 35, 193; IV, 16, 97.
[58] *Ibid.* I, 29, 150.   [61] *Ibid.* IV, 16, 97.
[59] *Ibid.* I, 35, 173.   [62] *Mos.* I, 55, 303.
[63] *Probus* 12, 84. "Contentment" is also mentioned by him among the virtues of the Therapeutae (*Cont.* 9, 69).
[64] *Spec.* IV, 16, 96–97.
[65] *Ibid.*, 97 ff.; I, 29, 150; 35, 172–173; III, 4, 22.   [66] Aristeas, 222.

ish tradition, without the benefit of philosophic terminology, the praise of the virtue of the control of desire and of its kindred virtue of contentment is expressed in the following maxims: "Who is mighty? He that subdues his desire. Who is rich? He that is contented with his portion." [67]

IV. PRAYER, REPENTANCE, AND STUDY AS VIRTUES

In our study of Philo's lists of virtues so far we have come across two new virtues, faith [1] under intellectual virtues and humanity [2] under moral virtues. Three other new virtues mentioned by Philo are prayer, repentance, and study. These require special treatment.

(a) Prayer

Prayer is known in Greek literature by various terms,[3] and thanksgiving (εὐχαριστία or χαριστία) is mentioned in at least one source, as a virtue under the virtue of justice,[4] but prayer is not identified with the term "thanksgiving," and no Greek philosopher recommends it as a virtue. Philo, however, speaks of prayer, which, for reasons to be explained presently, he calls thanksgiving, as one of the virtues. "Each of the virtues (ἀρετῶν)," he says, "is a holy matter, but thanksgiving is preëminently so." [5] Again, "the mind that blesses (εὐλογῶν) God, and is ceaselessly engaged in conning hymns of thanksgiving to Him" is described by him as the mind of those who are "of a rational and virtuous

[67] M. Abot IV, 1.

---

[1] Cf. above, pp. 212 f.; 215 ff.
[2] Cf. above, pp. 218 ff.
[3] Cf. below, p. 239.
[4] Cf. Andronicus of Rhodes, De Affectibus: De Justitia (F. W. A. Mullach, Fragmenta Philosophorum Graecorum III, p. 577).
[5] Plant., 30, 126.

(σπουδαίας) nature." [6] This inclusion of prayer among the virtues is due to the fact that prayer is considered in Judaism as one of the commandments, and the commandments, as we have seen, are identified by Philo with what the philosophers call virtues. For him to speak of the virtue of prayer was the same as for a Palestinian Jew of his time to speak of the *miṣvah* or commandment of prayer.

In native Jewish tradition one of the pentateuchal sources for the commandment of prayer is found in the verses "Thou shalt fear the Lord thy God, Him thou shalt serve, and to Him thou shalt cleave, and by His name shalt thou swear. He is thy praise, and He is thy God." [7] Taking the expression "He is thy praise" to mean that God alone is to be praised, a Tannaitic source comments upon it that "prayer and praise mean the same thing." [8] There is an intimation in Philo that this verse was considered by him, too, as the pentateuchal source for the commandment of the virtue of prayer. It happens that the Hebrew expression which we have quoted as "He is thy praise" and is taken by the rabbis to mean that God alone is to be praised or prayed to, is translated in the Septuagint by "He is thy boast," meaning that God alone is that of which one is to be proud or to boast. [9] Philo, making use of this Septuagint translation, paraphrases it by "let God alone be thy boast (αὔχημα) and thy chief glory (κλέος)" [10] and explains it, exactly in the sense in which it is taken in the Septuagint, to mean that we are to pride ourselves only on God and not on wealth or

[6] *Ibid.* 33, 135.

[7] Deut. 10: 20–21.

[8] *Mishnat Rabbi Eliezer* XII, ed. Enelow, p. 228, ll. 15–16. For another pentateuchal source of prayer see below, n. 62.

[9] This is also the explanation of this expression given by the mediaeval Hebrew commentator Ibn Ezra, *ad loc.*

[10] *Spec.* I, 57, 311. The combination of the two terms αὔχημα and κλέος occurs also in Philo elsewhere (*Spec.* IV, 32, 164; *Virt.* 36, 197).

dominion or beauty or strength. But then he concludes: "Let us follow after the good that is stable, and unswerving and unchangeable, and let us cleave to our prayer (ἱκεσίας) to Him as suppliants and to our worship (θεραπείας) of Him."[11] This concluding statement makes it quite evident that, like the Tannaitic source, he takes the expression "He is thy boast" in connection with the expressions "Him thou shalt serve, and to Him thou shalt cleave" as having also the meaning of prayer and divine worship.

Not only is his description of prayer as a virtue based upon the institution of prayer in Judaism, but also of Jewish origin are the terms which he uses in connection with prayer as well as his fundamental conceptions of prayer.

In Greek, the principal terms for prayer are four. (1) εὔχεσθαι, referring primarily to a prayer of petition, (2) προσεύχεσθαι, normally meaning a prayer of thanksgiving, (3) ἐπεύχεσθαι, having also the meaning of praying a curse, and (4) λιτέσθαι, chiefly used in the sense of praying for forgiveness.[12] The first three of these terms, and many other Greek terms, are used in the Septuagint indiscriminately as translations of the various Hebrew words for prayer or for the various forms of prayer. In Philo, in addition to the terms used in the Septuagint, many other terms are used as designations of prayer or of the various kinds of prayer. As a rule, these terms are used indiscriminately. But occasionally we notice an attempt to individualize these terms, to define them and to classify them. The most general term for prayer, he suggests in one place, is the term "praise" (αἴνεσις),[13] which is used in the Septuagint most often as a translation of the Hebrew word *todah*. But inasmuch as

[11] *Spec.* I, 57, 311–312.
[12] Cf. A. W. Mair, "Prayer (Greek)," *Encyclopaedia of Religion and Ethics*, X, pp. 182–183, § 1.   [13] *Spec.* I, 41, 224.

this term in the original Hebrew means not only (1) praise, but also (2) thanksgiving and (3) confession of sin, the Septuagint is trying to convey all these meanings of the term by translating it besides by the term (1) αἴνεσις, also by the terms (2) δῶρον, χαρμοσύνη and (3) ἐξομολόγησις.[14] Philo similarly shows that he was aware of the three meanings of the Hebrew word *todah* when, in his attempt to explain the etymology of the Hebrew name Judah, he gives its meanings as (1) praised (αἰνετός) by God,[15] as (2) he "who blesses (εὐλογῶν) God and is ceaselessly engaged in conning hymns of thanksgiving (εὐχαρίστους) to Him," [16] and hence as the thanksgiver (εὐχάριστον)[17] and as (3) confession (ἐξομολόγη-σις) to the Lord,[18] that is, confession of thankfulness or praise to the Lord.[19] Evidently, therefore, when he says that the most general term for prayer is αἴνεσις, he uses this term as embracing all the meanings of its corresponding Hebrew term *todah*. Under this term αἴνεσις he therefore includes, as he says, all "expressions of thanksgiving (εὐχαριστίαις) as religion demands," of which he mentions in particular "hymns (ὕμνοις) and predications of happiness (εὐδαιμονισμοῖς) and prayers (εὐχαῖς) and sacrifices (θυσίαις)." [20] "Prayer" (εὐχή), however, which is here included under "thanksgiving" and "praise," he explains elsewhere in one place as "a petition (αἴτησις) for good things" [21] and in an-

---

[14] Cf. Hatch and Redpath, *A Concordance to the Septuagint*, s.v.

[15] *Plant.* 33, 135.

[16] *Ibid.*; cf. *Somn.* II, 5, 34.

[17] *Ibid.*, 136.

[18] *Ibid.*, 134; cf. *Leg. All.* I, 26, 80; II, 24, 96; III, 8, 26; 49, 146; *Mut.* 23, 136; *Somn.* I, 6, 37.

[19] There is no implication of confession of sin in his explanation of the meaning of the name Judah in any of the passages quoted in the preceding note, nor does Philo use the term ἐξομολόγησις in the sense of confession of sin. In the Septuagint it is used mostly in the sense of a confession of thankfulness but sometimes also in the sense of a confession of sin (cf. Josh. 7: 19; Dan. 9: 4).

[20] *Spec.* I, 41, 224.   [21] *Agr.* 22, 99.

other place as that which Moses "is accustomed to call benedictions (εὐλογίαις)," [22] that is, the Hebrew *berakot*.[23] Later we shall show that he also uses it in the sense of "confession of sin." [24] From all this we may gather that, while literally the Greek term εὐχαριστία is a translation of the Hebrew term *todah* in the sense of thanksgiving, the same Greek term is also used in the sense of (1) praise, αἴνεσις, (2) petition, εὐχή, (3) benediction, εὐλογία, (4) confession, ἐξομολόγησις. It is the term "thanksgiving" in this general sense of "praise," "petition," "benediction," and "confession" that Philo has in mind when he speaks of "thanksgiving" as a virtue, that is, a religious commandment. The use of the term "thanksgiving" by Philo in the general sense of prayer in all its forms is analogous to the use of the term *berakah*, benediction, in Hebrew in the same general sense of prayer.[25] It must be in this general sense that the term "thanksgiving" is also used in other Hellenistic Jewish writings.[26] From the New Testament we know that the terms εὐλογία and εὐχαριστία are used interchangeably,[27] and both of them undoubtedly as a translation of the Hebrew *berakah*.

Essentially Jewish is also Philo's conception of the relation of prayer to sacrifice.

Philo lived at a time when the temple in Jerusalem was still in existence and sacrifices were still in vogue. The Jews of the Diaspora, including those in Alexandria, participated

[22] *Praem.* 14, 79; cf. *Migr.* 20, 117.
[23] Deut. 28: 2.
[24] Cf. below, p. 245, nn. 47–48.
[25] Thus the "Eighteen Benedictions" contain "praises," "petitions" and "thanksgivings."
[26] Cf. Wisdom of Solomon 16: 28.
[27] Cf. Matt. 26: 26, and Mark 14: 22: εὐλογήσας; Luke 22: 17, and 1 Cor. 11: 24: εὐχαριστήσας, though it is possible that the latter term refers to Hallel which is recited on Passover Eve.

in these sacrificial rites, not only vicariously through their annual contribution of the temple tax, which was used for the purchase of the public sacrifice, but also personally through their pilgrimages to Jerusalem during the holidays. But by the side of the sacrificial worship in the temple there existed in Palestine and in the countries of the Diaspora another form of divine worship, that of organized prayer. Both these forms of worship were considered by Jews in Palestine as well as by those outside of Palestine as two acceptable modes of divine worship. Philo himself testifies to his belief in these two modes of divine worship in his statement in which he describes his pilgrimage to Jerusalem as "the time I was journeying to the Temple of my fathers to offer prayers and sacrifices." [28]

But the Jews at the time of Philo, who were brought up upon the prophets as well as the Pentateuch, while they accepted sacrifices as a prescribed form of divine worship, considered them acceptable to God only when combined with right conduct. The denunciation of sacrifices by the various prophets was taken by them not as a rejection of sacrificial worship but merely as an emphasis of the moral purpose that sacrifice ought to symbolize. This reconciliation of the Law and the prophets is already reflected in Sirach's statement to the effect that sacrifices are acceptable to God only when accompanied by the observance of the Law and the practice of righteousness.[29] It is in this sense also that one is to understand such statements in Hellenistic Jewish literature as that "to honor God" is to be done "not with gifts and sacrifices, but with purity of soul and holy conviction" [30]

[28] *Provid.* 2, 64 (Eusebius, *Praeparatio Evangelica* VIII, 14, 389b; Richter VI, 200; M. II, 646); Aucher, II, 107.

[29] Sirach 35: 1–11 (13).

[30] Aristeas, 234. That Aristeas does not completely eliminate sacrifices is evident from 170 and 172.

or that "when the Lord demands bread, or candles, or flesh, or any other sacrifice, then that is nothing; but God demands pure hearts." [31] Moreover, inasmuch as divine worship by sacrifices was inaccessible to the great numbers of Jews living outside of Palestine, there must have gradually arisen the view that prayer can serve as a substitute for sacrifices and that it is even better than sacrifices. In Palestine this conception of prayer as a substitute for sacrifices and as better than sacrifices found expression in many statements attributed to rabbis after the destruction of the temple.[32] All this is given utterance to by Philo in several passages.

In one passage, he begins with a statement that "God does not rejoice in sacrifices even if one offer hecatombs, for all things are His possessions and, because He possesses all things, He needs none of them." [33] The wording and sentiment of this statement quite evidently reflect such verses as "Will the Lord be pleased with thousand of rams?" [34] "For the world is mine and the fulness thereof: will I eat the flesh of bulls?" [35] That Philo does not mean by this the rejection of sacrifices as a proper means of divine worship is quite evident from his own account of his pilgrimage to Jerusalem for the purpose of offering sacrifices [36] and from his elaborate description of the sacrificial rites.[37] What he means by this statement is merely to emphasize, as did also Sirach, that the mere external performance of sacrifices, when not ac-

[31] The Book of the Secrets of Enoch 45: 3. That this does not mean the complete rejection of sacrifices, see 59: 1–2; 66: 2.

[32] *Berakot* 32b; *Tanḥuma, Ki Tabo,* § 1; cf. below, p. 245.

[33] *Spec.* I, 50, 271.   [34] Micah 6: 7.

[35] Ps. 50: 12–13. Cf. comment on this verse in *Sifre Numbers,* § 143, F, p. 54a; H, pp. 191–192: "There is no eating and drinking with reference to God. . . . But why did I tell you to bring sacrifices to me? It was only that you do my will." Cf. *Menahot* 110a.

[36] Cf. above, n. 28.   [37] Cf. *Spec.* I, 33, 162 ff.

companied by the observance of the Law and the practice of righteousness, is not acceptable to God. Philo then proceeds to say: "But He rejoices in the will to love Him and in men that practice holiness, and from these he accepts cakes of ground barley and things of least price, holding them most precious rather than those of highest cost." [38] This again reflects (1) such verses as "Hath the Lord as great delight in burnt-offerings and sacrifices as in hearkening to the voice of the Lord?" [39] (2) the law stating that meal offerings are to be prepared either (a) in the form of cakes or (b) in the form of flour,[40] and (3) such native Jewish sentiments as that expressed by the rabbis in their statement that "it does not matter whether a man brings a large offering or a small, provided he directs his heart to Heaven." [41] Finally he concludes: "And indeed, though the worshipers bring nothing else, in bringing themselves they offer the best sacrifices, the full and truly perfect oblation of noble living, honoring God, their Benefactor and Savior, with hymns and thanksgivings." [42] Here, too, the wording and the sentiment reflect such verses as "We will render for bullocks the offering of our lips"; [43] "Let my prayer be set forth before Thee

[38] *Spec.* I, 50, 271.

[39] I Sam. 15:22.

[40] I take it that Philo's ψαιστά and κριθάς here refer to the two kinds of meal-offering, namely, (a) cakes (Lev. 2: 4–8; 6: 13–14; 7: 9) and (b) flour (Lev. 2: 2; 5: 12; 6: 8). I do not accept Colson's translation here: "plain meal or barley" or "barley ground or unground." "Barley" is mentioned in the Pentateuch only in connection with the jealousy meal-offering (Num. 5: 15); in all other cases the term *solet* is used, which in the Septuagint is translated by σεμίδαλις, the finest wheaten flour. According to the Mishnah, all the meal-offerings are of wheat, except the jealousy meal-offering and the wave-offering, which are of barley (*M. Soṭa* II, 1). Philo himself elsewhere, in connection with the meal-offering of the sinner (Lev. 5: 11), explicitly says that it was of wheaten flour (λευκόπυροι) (*Mut.* 41. 235).

[41] *Menaḥot* 110a; *Sifra, Wayyiḳra, Pereḳ* 9, p. 9b. Cf. Heinemann, *Philos Werke*, II, p. 87, n. 1.

[42] *Spec.* I, 50, 272.

[43] Hosea 14: 3 (LXX: "We will render to Thee the fruit of our lips").

as incense." [44] In this last statement of Philo there is also an intimation of that view which among the rabbis, after the destruction of the temple, gave rise to the statements that for those who cannot worship God by means of sacrifice, prayer may serve as a substitute,[45] and that "prayer is greater than sacrifices." [46]

In another passage the condemnation, which in the preceding passage he utters against sacrifices when not connected with right conduct, is extended by him to prayer when it is similarly not connected with right conduct. "If the worshiper is without kindly feeling and justice, the sacrifices are no sacrifices, the consecrated oblation is desecrated, the prayers (εὐχαί) are words of ill omen with utter destruction waiting upon them. For, when to outward appearance they are offered, it is not a remission but a reminder of past sins which they effect. But, if he is holy and just, the sacrifice stands firm, though the flesh is consumed, or rather, even if no victim at all is brought to the altar. For the true oblation, what else can it be but the piety of a soul which loves God?" [47] In this passage, it will be noticed, he speaks of both sacrifices and prayer as if they took place simultaneously, and both of them are condemned when not offered in the right spirit and when not connected with right conduct. Prayer, furthermore, is assumed to be a part of sacrifice and connected with it. This undoubtedly refers to the prayer of confession of sin which, by Biblical law, was to accompany every expiatory sacrifice.[48] Rather than sacrifice as a mere

[44] Ps. 141: 2.
[45] *Tanḥuma, Korah*, § 12.
[46] *Berakot* 32b; cf. *Tanḥuma, Ki Tabo*, § 1.
[47] *Mos.* II, 22, 107–108.
[48] *Sifra, Wayyiḳra, Pereḳ* 17, on Lev. 5: 5, p. 24b; *Tos. Menaḥot* X, 12; *Yoma* 36a. By a post-Biblical enactment certain prayers were also recited in the Temple with the daily burnt-offering (*M. Tamid* V, 1). But from the context it would seem that the reference here is to the prayer of confession.

external ceremony and prayer as a mere confession with the lips, the true service of God, he says, is piety. All this is merely a paraphrase of the words of God in the prophecies of Isaiah, calling out to those whose hands "are full of blood": "To what purpose is the multitude of your sacrifices unto me? . . . It is an abomination to me. . . . And though you multiply prayer, I will not hearken to you. . . . Wash and become clean." [49] There is in it also an echo of the words of the Psalmist. "The sacrifices of God are a broken spirit." [50]

In a third passage he deals with the superiority of prayer to sacrifices. He says: "It is impossible genuinely to express our gratitude to God by means of buildings and oblations and sacrifices, as is the custom of most people, for even the whole world could not be a temple adequate to yield the honor due to Him; nay, it must be expressed by means of praise and hymns." [51] A statement as to the superiority of prayer, which needs only a devoted "soul," to sacrifices, which requires "buildings," is to be found also in another passage, in which he asks: "What house shall be prepared for God the King of kings? . . . Shall it be of stone or wooden material?" His answer is: "away with the thought, the very words are impious. . . . One worthy house there is — the soul that is fitted to receive Him." [52] The sentiment expressed in these passages must have been common, at the time of Philo, among the Jews living outside of Palestine, whose only direct mode of worship was that of prayer, just as it was later, with the destruction of the temple, to become common among the Jews in Palestine. But the wording of this passage is nothing but a paraphrase of two passages in Scripture. First, a passage in Isaiah, wherein, in order to show

[49] Isa. 1: 11–16.
[50] Ps. 51: 19.

[51] *Plant.* 30, 126.
[52] *Cher.* 29, 99–100.

that unrighteous sacrifices are like cutting off a dog's neck and unrighteous libations are like offering swine's blood, the prophet exclaims in the name of God: "The heaven is my throne, and the earth is my footstool: where is the house that ye may build unto me? and where is the place that may be my resting-place?"[53] Second, a passage in the prayer of King Solomon upon his completion of the building of the temple: "If the heaven and the heaven of heaven will not suffice thee, far less indeed this house which I have built for thy name. Yet thou, O Lord, the God of Israel, wilt look down on this supplication of mine to hearken to the prayer which thy servant this day in thy presence prayeth to thee."[54]

In all these passages we have noticed there is no indication that sacrifices are rejected by Philo as an improper means of divine worship; there is only an insistence that they must be inspired by a right motive and that they must be accompanied by righteous conduct. This is quite evident in his explanation of the Deuteronomic law of the centralization of sacrificial worship. "The highest, and in the truest sense the holy, temple of God," he says, "is, as we must believe, the whole universe, having for its sanctuary the most sacred part of all existence, even heaven, for its votive ornaments the stars, for its priests the angels."[55] Still despite all this he admits that there is need also for "the temple made by hands," except that there is to be "only one temple."[56]

It will have been further noticed that when improper sacrifices are condemned the substitute offered for them is always prayer. All this, as we have seen, reflects traditional Jewish views. It is quite possible that Philo was acquainted with some of the sayings of certain early Greek philosophers preserved by later authors to the effect that the gods are to

53 Isa: 66: 1.
54 I Kings 8: 27–28.
55 *Spec.* I, 12, 66.
56 *Ibid.*, 67.

be honored "not by luxurious display but rather by deeds of piety"[57] or that you must "consider that the noblest sacrifice and best divine worship is that you make yourself as good and as just as you possibly can."[58] If he was acquainted with such Greek sayings he must have found in them corroboration of some of the teachings which he has derived from the prophets, and perhaps, according to his own belief, he has considered them as having been inspired by the teachings of the prophets.[59] But there is not enough in the Greek sayings of this type to account for the language and the sentiment expressed by Philo in the passages quoted.[60]

Another recognizably Jewish feature in his conception of prayer is his discussion of the question as to the manner of praying. In native Jewish tradition there is a question as to whether prayer should be in silence or in a whisper or in an audible voice or in a loud voice. The origin of this discussion is evidently due to contradictory statements with regard to prayer that appeared to be found in Scripture. On the one

[57] Heinemann, *Bildung*, p. 66, n. 3; cf. also *Philos Werke* II, p. 86, n. 4.
[58] *Id.*, *Bildung*, p. 472. Cf. also above, I, 18.
[59] Cf. above, I, 141.
[60] According to Heinemann, Philo's chief contention in *Mos.* II, 22, 108, is that actual sacrifices are not necessary, for the true oblation is nothing but the piety of a God-loving soul. This he finds to be a Greek idea, altogether unknown to the rabbis (*Bildung*, pp. 66–67). But, as we have tried to show, in that passage Philo's contention is only that sacrifices, even when accompanied by external confession, are not acceptable, if not inspired by the right motives and accompanied by right conduct.

Again, says Heinemann, Philo betrays no knowledge of the rabbinic view that prayer and fasting and charity are substitutes for sacrifices (*ibid.*, p. 67). But, as we have suggested, at the time of Philo there was no need of stressing the importance of substitutes for sacrifices, and there is no evidence that it was stressed by the rabbis before the destruction of the temple. In so far as prayer was a substitute for sacrifices to the Jews in the diaspora, we have shown that there is an allusion to it in Philo. As for charity and fasting, they are included in his general statement to the effect that only the sacrifice of the holy and just and God-loving man is acceptable.

hand, the expression "to serve Him with all your heart" [61]
was taken to refer to prayer, whence prayer was described
as "the worship of God within the heart." [62] But on the other
hand, such verses as "I prayed therefore unto the Lord and
said," [63] "I prayed unto the Lord my God and made my
confession and said," [64] and "Give ear to my prayer, O God.
. . . Evening and morning and noon will I pray and cry
aloud, and He shall hear my voice" [65] would seem to indicate
that prayer was a matter of speech. The nature of the
speculation on this question is reflected in a few characteristic statements written in the form of interpretations of the
verse, "Now Hannah, she spoke in her heart; only her lips
moved, but her voice could not be heard." [66] One interpretation of this passage reads: "One might think that he who
prays should let his ears hear his voice, it is therefore explained in the case of Hannah that 'she spoke in her heart.'"[67]
Another interpretation reads: "One might think that he who
prays should raise his voice, it is therefore explained in the
case of Hannah that 'she spoke in her heart'; one might then
think that he who prays should only think his prayer in his
heart, the text therefore says 'only her lips moved.' How is
it then? He moves his lips." [68] A third interpretation reads:
"'Now Hannah, she spoke in her heart,' — from which we
infer that he who prays must direct his heart [to Heaven];
'only her lips moved,' — from which we infer that he who
prays must pronounce clearly with his lips; 'but her voice
could not be heard,' — from which we infer that it is not

[61] Deut. 11: 13.
[62] *Sifre Deut.*, § 41, F, p. 80a; HF, p. 88; *Ta'anit* 2a.
[63] Deut. 9: 26.
[64] Dan. 9: 4.
[65] Ps. 55: 2, 18.
[66] I Sam. 1: 13.
[67] *Tos. Berakot* III, 5; *Berakot* 31a; *Deuteronomy Rabbah* 2, 1.
[68] *Jer. Berakot* IV, 1, 7a.

allowed to raise one's voice in prayer." [69] Disapproval of prayer both in an audible voice and in a loud voice is expressed in the following statement: "He who lets his voice be heard in prayer is of those who are of little faith; he who raises his voice in prayer is of those who prophesy lies." [70] Another characteristic statement, which expresses common conceptions as to the manner in which one is to pray, is in the form of an interpretation of the verse, "Tremble, and sin not; commune with your heart upon your bed, and be still." [71] This verse is interpreted to mean that, if you cannot say your prayers, "think them in your heart." [72] Even with reference to the reading of the *shema'*, which reading must be audible to one's own ears,[73] there is a difference of opinion as to whether "thinking in the heart is as good as audible speech." [74] Of two Palestinian rabbis it is reported that "Rabbi Abba bar Zabda [when he prayed in the synagogue] prayed in a [n audible but not loud] voice; Rabbi Jonah, when he prayed in the synagogue, prayed in a whisper, but, when he prayed at home, he prayed in a [loud] voice, in order that the members of his household might learn the prayers." [75] In synagogues, however, there was a leader of public prayer who recited some of the prayers aloud, and

---

[69] *Berakot* 31a.

[70] *Ibid.* 24b; cf. Luke 12: 28, for the expression "of little faith," and Jer. 23: 26, for the expression "who prophesy lies."

[71] Ps. 4: 5.

[72] *Midrash Tehillim, ad loc.*, § 9, p. 23b; *Pesiḳta de-Rab Kahana, Shubah,* p. 158a.

[73] *M. Berakot* II, 3.

[74] *Berakot* 20b.

[75] *Jer. Berakot* IV, 1, 7a. See L. Ginzberg in his critical study of this passage in his *Perushim we-Ḥiddushim Birushalmi,* III, pp. 8–22, where he shows that the "voice" in which Rabbi Abba bar Zabda prayed in the synagogue was an "audible but not loud voice," whereas the "voice" in which Rabbi Jonah prayed at home was a "loud voice." Hence the bracketed additions in our translation of this passage.

it is reported that, "when Rabbi Jesa went up [from Babylonia] to Palestine, he saw the people bending down and whispering a prayer," while the leader of the congregation was reciting one of the Eighteen Benedictions, evidently in a loud voice.[76] There is evidence that also in the synagogue of Alexandria there was such a leader of the congregation.[77] The customary Jewish mode of praying in a whispering voice is contrasted by the rabbis with the heathen mode of praying in a loud voice. "The heathen," they say, "has his god in his own house and he cries aloud to him until he is dead, but his god does not hear him and does not save him from his distress. . . . A Jew enters a synagogue, takes a position behind the stand, prays in a whisper, and the Holy One, blessed be He, gives ear to his prayer." [78] While there is no complete agreement among these statements, they all maintain that prayer, with the exception of that of the leader in the synagogue, should not be in a loud voice; some of them approve of prayer in the heart; most of them require that he who prays should move his lips or pronounce his words clearly with his lips or utter his words in a whisper.

Reflecting all these various opinions and practices in Judaism with regard to spoken and silent prayer, Philo says of prayer that thereby the worshipers honor God "sometimes with the organs of speech, sometimes without tongue and mouth, when within the soul alone and appreciable only by the intellect they make their confessions and invocations, which one ear only can apprehend, the ear of God, for human hearing cannot reach to the perception of such." [79] In this passage, what Philo calls prayer "within the soul" quite obviously means silent prayer, corresponding to what the

[76] *Jer. Berakot* I, 8 (5), 3c.
[77] Cf. *Tos. Sukkah* IV, 6; *Jer. Sukkah* V, 1, 55a–b.
[78] *Jer. Berakot* IX, 1, p. 13a.   [79] *Spec.* I, 50, 272.

rabbis characterize as "the worship of God within the heart," and what he calls prayer "with the organs of speech" or with "tongue and mouth" is quite obviously to be taken as corresponding to what the rabbis describe as prayer in an "audible voice," or perhaps also to that kind of prayer concerning which they say that "he who prays must move his lips" or "pronounce clearly with his lips," the terms "tongue and mouth" used by Philo being thus the equivalent of the term "lips" used in Scripture and by the rabbis. No mention is made here by Philo of prayer in a loud voice, and we may assume that prayer in a loud voice on the part of the general public, as distinguished from the leader, would be discountenanced by him no less than by the rabbis. These Jewish modes of prayer, as described by both Philo and the rabbis, are in contrast to what is known of the modes of prayer among the Greeks. The latter are known to have been prejudiced against prayer in silence or in a low voice. Among the Pythagoreans there was a rule that all prayers should be uttered aloud. Only when there was some special reason for not praying aloud were prayers offered in silence or in a low voice.[80] In the Talmudic passage quoted above, the reference to the heathen crying aloud to his god thus reflects an actual acquaintance with the heathen method of praying.

(b) Repentance

It is also to scriptural teachings that we must go for the origin of Philo's view that repentance is a virtue. In Greek philosophy repentance is never held up as a virtue. Aristotle indeed describes the experience of regret or rather repentance (μεταμέλεια), observing that a man who has done wrong

[80] Cf. P. Gardner and F. B. Jevons, *A Manual of Greek Antiquities*, 2nd ed., 1898, p. 224; A. W. Mair, op. cit., p. 184, § 3.

out of ignorance and, on finding out what he has done, repents, is to be described as an involuntary agent (ἄκων)[81] and that "he who cannot repent cannot be cured." [82] But he does not urge repentance as a virtue. To him the penitent is a bad man; the good man is he who has nothing to repent of. This view is expressed by him in such statements as that "bad men are full of repentance" [83] but it is characteristic of good men that they do no wrong [84] and consequently a good man is "not given to repentance (ἀμεταμέλητος)," [85] nor, "like the penitent," does he find fault with his former actions.[86] The Stoics are reported to re-echo the same view in a statement which says of them that "they do not believe that the mind of the wise is able to repent, for repentance (μετάνοια) pertains to a false assent, as if one had previously gone utterly wrong." [87] According to these statements, then, never to have been wrong is a virtue; to have been wrong and repented is not in itself a virtue.

In Judaism, however, with the general belief that "there

[81] *Eth. Nic.* III, 1, 1110b, 22–23. [82] *Ibid.* VII, 7, 1150a, 22. Cf. Democritus, Fr. 43 in Diels: "Repentance for shameful deeds is lifesaving."

[83] *Ibid.* IX, 4, 1166b, 24–25: μεταμελείας οἱ φαῦλοι γέμουσι. Exactly the same statement, חרטות מלאים רשעים (read *ḥaraṭut* as an abstract noun and not *ḥaraṭot* as a plural), is ascribed by Elijah ben Solomon ha-Kohen (d. 1729) in his *Shebeṭ Musar*, ch. 25, to the sages of the Talmud. No such statement occurs in the Talmud (cf. A. Hyman, *Oṣar Dibre Ḥakamim u-Pitgamehem*, 1933, p. 514). The statement occurs verbatim in the Hebrew translation of Aristotle's *Ethica Nicomachea* (*Sefer ha-Middot* IX, 5) made from the Latin at the beginning of the 15th century. However, the author of the *Shebeṭ Musar* makes use of this Aristotelian statement as evidence that repentance is a virtue, seeing that even the wicked have a conscious-ness of sin and are full of repentance.

[84] *Ibid.* VIII, 8, 1159b, 6–7.

[85] *Ibid.* IX, 4, 1166a, 29.

[86] *Eth. Eud.* VII, 6, 1240b, 21–23.

[87] Stobaeus, *Eclogae* II, p. 113, ll. 5–7 (Arnim, III, 548, p. 147, ll. 21–23). Cf. E. F. Thompson, Μετανοέω and μεταμέλει in *Greek Literature until 100 A.D.*, in-cluding Discussion of their Cognates and their Hebrew Equivalents, 1908; E. Norden *Agnostos Theos*, 1913, pp. 134–140; W. W. Jaeger, "Norden, *Agnostos Theos*," *Göttingische gelehrte Anzeiger*, 175 (1913), pp. 589–592; A. H. Dirksen, *The New Testament Concept of Metanoia*, 1932, pp. 161–162, 165–196.

is not a righteous man upon earth, that doeth good, and sinneth not," [88] the conception of repentance as an act which is desired by God and towards which man was urged by Him runs throughout Scripture and is given the fullest expression in the verse: "Let the wicked forsake his way, and the unrighteous man his thoughts: and let him return unto the Lord, and He will have mercy upon him; and to our God, for He will abundantly pardon." [89] What is more significant, repentance, or rather confession of sin, which is the outward symbol of repentance, came to be regarded as a Mosaic commandment. In the Pentateuch, to be sure, confession is prescribed only in certain special instances — twice for lay individuals in connection with certain sacrifices which are to be offered in the case of the transgression of certain commandments, [90] once for the high priest, also in connection with a certain sacrifice, [91] and once for the people as a whole in connection with general apostacy. [92] According to a Tannaitic Midrash, however, confession is a prescribed duty in the case of the transgression of "all the other commandments," whether "negative commandments" or "positive commandments," including also commandments for the transgression of which there is "divine punishment" or "capital punishment," and furthermore this duty of confession devolves both upon individuals and upon congregations and is to be in force both at the time when sacrifices are being offered and at the time sacrifices are no longer offered and both in Palestine and outside of Palestine. [93] Repentance, with

[88] Eccl. 7: 20; 1 Kings 8: 46; 2 Chr. 6: 36.
[89] Isa. 55: 7.   [91] Lev. 16: 21.
[90] Lev. 5: 5; Num. 5: 7.   [92] Lev. 26: 40.
[93] *Sifre Zuṭa, Naso,* on Num. 5: 6. It is this Midrash which is quoted by Maimonides in his *Sefer ha-Miṣwot,* Positive Commandment 73, under the name of *Mekilta,* and upon which his statement in *Mishneh Torah, Teshubah* I, 1, is based. Cf. Commentary *Ambuha de-Sifre* on *Sifre Zuṭa, ad loc.,* by Jacob Ze'eb Joskowitz. Cf. also above, p. 245.

its outer symbol confession, as an act desired by God is also urged by Sirach.[94] In Hellenistic Jewish literature God is said to have made His sons "to be of good hope" because He gave "repentance when men have sinned"[95] and He is also said to overlook the sins of men "to the end that they may repent."[96]

It is in accordance with this conception of repentance as a Mosaic commandment, which in the language of Philo means that it is a practical virtue, that repentance is described by him as a virtue. His description of repentance as a virtue is to be found in his inclusion of his treatise on "repentance," together with his treatises on "courage," "piety," and "humanity" under the general title, "On the Virtues."[97] It is also implied in his statement that it is because "our most holy Moses" is "a lover of virtue and of goodness and especially of his fellow men" that "he offers to the repentant, as to conquerors, great rewards."[98] Almost in direct opposition to Aristotle and the Stoics, who consider it as a characteristic of the good or the wise man never to have occasion to repent[99] and that only the bad man is full of repentance,[100] he maintains that "the change from sin to a blameless life is characteristic of a wise man who has not been utterly ignorant of what is for his good."[101] In another place he similarly says that, in decreeing repentance, God is "not in any degree mocking or reproaching these men, who are believed to have offended."[102] The reason

[94] Sirach 18: 21; 4: 26; 17: 25–32.
[95] Wisdom of Solomon 12: 19; cf. 12: 10.
[96] Wisdom of Solomon 11: 23.
[97] The title "On the Virtues" for the group of treatises which includes that on "repentance" is found in Eusebius and in the oldest manuscript (cf. L. Cohn, *Philos Werke*, II, pp. 315–316). Hence it must have been used by Philo himself.
[98] *Virt.* 33, 175.
[99] Cf. above, p. 253.
[100] Cf. above, p. 253, n. 83.
[101] *Virt.* 33, 177.
[102] *Qu. in Gen.* I, 82.

why repentance is not unbecoming to a wise man is again the
Jewish principle as to the impossibility of sinlessness for the
ordinary run of man which, as restated by Philo, reads: "for
absolute sinlessness belongs to God alone, or possibly to a
divine man." [103] His conception of repentance as a virtue is
the logical consequence of his belief in the absolute freedom
of the will.

Not only is the general conception of repentance as a
virtue based upon Jewish tradition, but also the details of
his description of the virtue of repentance go back to the
same source.

In Judaism, repentance requires confession, and confession means an open acknowledgment of sin. In the language
of the rabbis this open acknowledgment of sin is called "confession of words" (*widduy debarim*).[104] One of the scriptural
sources for this expression is the verse: "Take with you words
and return to the Lord; say unto Him: Forgive all iniquity,
and accept that which is good, so we will render for bullocks
the offering of our lips." [105] But besides confession of words
or with the lips, Jewish tradition, drawing upon various
scriptural verses, speaks also of the need, in the case of
repentance, of a feeling of shame for one's sins,[106] of a feeling
of remorse [107] and of a feeling of chastisement in the heart.[108]
Reflecting all these Jewish traditions, Philo describes re-
pentants as those who "feel shame" (καταιδεσθέντες), "re-
proach themselves" (κακίσαντες), and "openly confess and

---

[103] *Virt.* 33, 177; cf. above, I, 451, on this qualification with regard to a "divine
man." *Fragmenta*, Richter, VI, 222 (M, II, 662): "I think it absolutely impossible
that no part of the soul should become tainted, not even the outermost and lowest
part of it, even if the man appeared to be perfect among men."

[104] *Sifra, Aḥre, Pereḳ* I, p. 80d, on Lev. 16: 6; *Pereḳ* II, p. 81a, on Lev. 16: 11;
cf. the same expression in Maimonides in *Sefer ha-Miṣwot*, Positive Commandment
73; *Mishneh Torah, Teshubah* I, 1.

[105] Hos. 14: 3; cf. *Pesiḳta Rabbati*, 47, p. 189b.   [107] *Ḥagigah* 5a.

[106] *Berakot* 12b.   [108] *Berakot* 7a.

acknowledge all their sin, first within themselves . . . secondly with their tongues." [109] Again, in Jewish tradition, repentance and confession avail only in the case of sins between man and God; in the case of sins between man and man, in addition to repentance and the asking for forgiveness, reparation for the injury caused in the commitment of the sin must be made. [110] So also Philo says that in cases of sin between man and man, besides confession of the wrong and the asking for forgiveness, the repentant must give evidence of the truth of his repentance by actions, by restoring what he has taken from the other unlawfully. [111]

There are more such striking similarities. According to both Jewish tradition and Philo, there had been an idea of repentance before the repentance of an individual human being, Adam in the case of the rabbis and Enoch in the case of Philo, actually came into existence. [112] Again, in Jewish tradition, Enoch is represented as one whose life has not always been perfect [113] and hence as one who is "an example of repentance to all generations." [114] So also in Philo Enoch is represented as a repentant. [115] In Scripture as well as in Jewish tradition repentance is described as a "healing." [116] So also in Philo repentance is compared to the recovery from a disease. [117] In Jewish tradition repentance is said to cause redemption to come to Israel. [118] So also Philo says that Israel will be redeemed as a result of repentance. [119] In Scrip-

[109] *Praem.* 28, 163.
[110] *M. Yoma* VIII, 9, and *M. Baba Kamma* VIII, 7.
[111] *Spec.* I, 43, 235–236.
[112] Cf. above, I, 185.
[113] *Genesis Rabbah* 25, 1.
[114] Sirach 44: 16.
[115] *Abr.* 3, 17 ff.; *Praem.* 3, 15 ff.
[116] Isa. 6: 10; *Rosh ha-Shanah* 17b; Hos. 14: 5; *Yoma* 86a–b.
[117] *Abr.* 4, 26; *Virt.* 33, 176.
[118] *Yoma* 86b.
[119] *Praem.* 28, 163–164. Cf. below, pp. 411 f.

ture it is said that God, who is "merciful and gracious . . . forgiving iniquity and transgression and sin," [120] does not deal with us "according to our sins" nor does He retribute to us "according to our iniquities," [121] and the rabbis similarly say that "there is no creature that is not indebted to God, but He is gracious and merciful and forgives the sins of the past." [122] So also Philo says that God is "merciful and forgiving" [123] and that through His "gracious nature" He "sets forgiveness before chastisement." [124] Finally, in native Jewish tradition, as contrasted with the "repentant" there is what is called the "perfectly righteous," and there is a question whether the "perfectly righteous" or the "repentant" is of a higher rank. Rabbi Abbahu of Caesarea, who held the view that the "repentant" is of a higher rank, expresses himself in the statement that "in the place where the repentant stand the perfectly righteous do not stand." [125] Philo similarly compares "repentance" with "perfection" or with "perfect guiltlessness" and expresses his view, which happens to be that the perfectly righteous is of a higher rank, in the statement that "repentance holds the second place to perfection" [126] or that repentance is "the younger brother of perfect guiltlessness." [127] Though it is not impossible that Rabbi Abbahu (third century A.D.) uttered his statement in direct opposition to Philo, for he is reported to have had a knowledge of Greek [128] and to have even visited Alexandria, [129] the problem itself as to relative merit of the repentant and the perfectly righteous undoubtedly reflects an old Jewish tradition which is the common

[120] Exod. 34: 6–7; cf. Ps. 78: 38.
[121] Ps. 103: 10.
[122] *Exodus Rabbah* 31, 1.
[123] *Spec.* III, 21, 121.
[124] *Ibid.* II, 32, 196.
[125] *Berakot* 34b.
[126] *Abr.* 4, 26.
[127] *Somn.* I, 15, 91.
[128] Cf. W. Bacher, *Die Agada der palästinensischen Amoräer*, II, p. 97.
[129] *Ibid.*, p. 93.

source of both Philo and the rabbis. The reason given by Philo for the inferiority of the repentant is that just as wounds leave behind them bodily scars so "in the souls of the repentant there remain, in spite of all, the scars and prints of their old misdeeds." [130] So also in Jewish tradition the verse "I will heal your backslidings" [131] is taken to mean that the repentant are compared to those that have been wounded in whom scars remain even after they have been healed. [132]

(c) Study and Teaching

In addition to the virtue of prayer and the virtue of repentance, by which, as we have tried to show, Philo means the commandment of prayer and the commandment of repentance, Philo dwells also upon the study and the teaching of the Law as a religious commandment which he ranges under the virtue of justice. [133] In native Jewish tradition, the religious duty of studying the Law and of teaching it to others is based upon such verses as "ye shall learn them, and observe to do them" [134] and "ye shall teach them your children, speaking of them when thou sittest in thine house, and when thou walkest by the way, when thou liest down, and when thou risest up." [135] The term "thy children" in a parallel verse [136] is taken to mean "thy pupils." [137] Now

[130] Spec. I, 19, 103. See Heinemann, Philos Werke, and Colson, ad. loc., for Greek parallels.
[131] Jer. 3: 22.
[132] Yoma 86a and cf. Rashi, ad loc.
[133] Spec. IV, 26, 136–142.
[134] Deut. 5: 1; cf. Ḳiddushin 29b. In Sifre Deut., § 41, F, p. 80a; HF, p. 87, it is derived from the word "to serve Him" in Deut. 11: 13. Cf. Maimonides, Sefer ha-Miṣwot, Positive Commandments 5 and 11.
[135] Deut. 11: 19; cf. Ḳiddushin 29b.
[136] Deut. 6: 7.
[137] Sifre Deut., § 34, F, p. 74a; HF, p. 61; cf. Ps. 34: 12; Prov. 1: 8; Sirach 2: 1, 17.

Philo does not directly discuss the pentateuchal source of
the religious duty of the study of the Law, but that the study
of the Law is a Jewish duty is assumed by him in the statement that the "holy congregation" is that "in which it is
ever the practice to hold conferences and discussions about
virtue," [138] by which he means, it is ever the practice to
meet for the study of the Law.[139] With the assumption that
the study of the Law is a religious duty, evidently prescribed in the Pentateuch, he tries to find in the Pentateuch
further specifications of this duty in the verse "and ye shall
lay up these my words in your heart and in your soul, and
bind them for a sign upon your hand, that they may be
movably before your eyes." [140] The first of these three figurative expressions, he says, intimates that the learning of the
Law is not to be a matter of mere hearing with the ear but
rather one of understanding with the mind.[141] The second
expression intimates that learning must be reinforced by
action.[142] The third expression intimates that the laws which
we learn must be a vital force within us, moving us to action.[143] When a man has achieved this last stage of the
knowledge of the Law, he says, "he is no longer to be ranked
among learners and pupils but rather among teachers and
instructors." [144] Drawing, therefore, upon the verse [145] from
which the rabbis derive the religious duty to teach the Law
to others and taking also the words "your children" in that
verse to mean "your pupils," he paraphrases it as follows:
"Indeed he must be forward to teach the principles of justice

---

[138] *Immut.* 24, 111.
[139] Cf. below, nn. 174–177.
[140] Deut. 11: 18. σαλευτόν was Philo's reading of the Greek for the Hebrew word
usually translated by frontlets. Cf. Colson VIII, p. 435, § 137.
[141] *Spec.* IV, 26, 137.
[142] *Ibid.* 138.   [144] *Ibid.* 140.
[143] *Ibid.* 139.   [145] Deut. 11: 19.

to kinsfolk and friends and to all young people at home and in the street, both when they go to their beds and when they arise." [146]

There is also in Philo a reflection of the problem raised in rabbinic Judaism as to the relative importance of the study of the Law and the practice of the Law. The generally accepted opinion is that not learning but doing is the main object of the Law,[147] so that even those who claimed that study is the greater thing did so only because "study leads to doing." [148] In rabbinic literature this view is expressed in a comment upon the verses "For if ye shall diligently keep all this commandment which I command you, to do it . . . then will the Lord drive out all the nations from before you." [149] Taking the word "keep" in this verse to mean to "remember" what one has "studied," [150] the rabbis say: "From the first part of the verse I might have inferred that once a man has memorized any precept of the Law he may seat himself down and do nothing, it therefore adds 'to do it,' intimating that you must still do the commandments, so that if a man has studied the Law, he has fulfilled one commandment; if he has studied it and remembered it, he has fulfilled two commandments; if he has studied it and remembered it and practiced it, there is nothing higher than that." [151] In the same way Philo, evidently drawing upon these same verses, in which the Septuagint reads "if ye shall diligently hearken" instead of "if ye shall diligently keep," restates them as follows: "If, he says, you keep the divine commandments in obedience to His ordinances and accept His precepts, not merely to hear them [i.e., to learn

[146] *Spec.* IV, 26, 141.   [148] *Ḳiddushin* 40b.
[147] *M. Abot* I, 17.   [149] Deut. 11: 22–23.
[150] After the analogy of the expression: "And the father kept the saying [in mind]" (Gen. 37: 11).
[151] *Sifre Deut.*, § 48, F, p. 84b; HF, p. 113.

them] but also to fulfill them by the actions of your lives, the first boon you will have is victory over your enemies," [152] for "while the commandments of the Law are only on our lips our acceptance of them is little or none, but when we add thereto deeds which follow in their company, deeds shown in the whole conduct of your lives, the commandments will be as it were brought up out of the deep darkness into light." [153] Reflecting the same verse, the Letter of Aristeas similarly says: "The good life consists in the keeping of the enactments of the Law, and this end is achieved much more by hearing [i.e., by learning them] than by reading." [154]

Sometimes the question as to whether the study of the Law or the practice of the Law is superior is reflected in Philo's treatment of the problem current in the philosophy of his time as to the comparative value of the contemplative and the practical life.

In both Plato and Aristotle the priority of the contemplative life to the practical is assumed. In Plato there are several long passages in which the contemplative life is exalted above the practical life.[155] In Aristotle it is expressed in the statement that happiness is primarily a contemplative activity [156] and that life in accordance with non-contemplative virtue is happy only in a secondary degree.[157] The Stoics, on the other hand, reverse this order of importance, arguing that a speculative life, or rather a scholastic life (σχολαστικὸν βίον), is as bad as a life of mere amusement (διαγωγή) and pleasure (ἧδος).[158]

---

[152] *Praem.* 14. 79; cf. Deut. 30: 10; 11: 22–27.

[153] *Praem.* 14, 82.

[154] Aristeas, 127. Evidently "keeping," "hearing," and "reading" correspond to the rabbinic "practice," "remember" and "study" quoted above. But see H. G. Meecham's edition of *Aristeas*, p. 321, on "hearing" and "reading."

[155] *Theaetetus* 173 c ff.; *Gorgias* 481 ℇ ff.

[156] *Eth. Nic.* X, 7, 1177a, 12–18.

[157] *Ibid.* X, 8, 1178a, 9.　　　　[158] Plutarch, *De Stoicorum Repugnantiis* 2, 3.

Philo does not follow the view of the Stoics. In fact, the Stoics themselves did not follow their own view, and the discrepancy between their teaching of the preference of the practical to the contemplative life and their actual pursuit of the contemplative life in preference to the practical is one of the glaring contradictions that were found in the Stoics.[159] Many of the leading Stoics, it was argued by their opponents, in contradiction to their doctrine of the preferability of the practical life, "left their countries, not because they had anything to complain against them, but in order that they might, while engaged in studying and disputing, pass their life quietly, more pleasantly, and in full leisure."[160] It is no wonder then that Philo in many of his utterances aligns himself with Plato and Aristotle as over against the Stoics in placing the contemplative life over the practical. Thus, in one passage, re-echoing Plato and Aristotle, he describes the contemplative life as "the more excellent way of life, for it is proper to go through the practical life before beginning the theoretical one, as being a sort of rehearsal of the more perfect contest."[161] In another passage, classifying the three kinds of life, the contemplative, the practical, and the pleasurable,[162] he describes the practical life as low (*parva*) when it is close to the pleasurable life, and as high

[159] *Ibid.* 2, 4.
[160] *Ibid.*
[161] *Fug.* 6, 36.
[162] *Qu. in Gen.* IV, 47: *contemplativa, operativa, condecens.* The last term reflects the Greek συμπρεπής but, as required by the context, it should be some Latin term which translates the Greek ἡδύς. Professor Ralph Marcus informs me that the underlying Armenian term here is generally used as a translation of both the Greek πρέπων and the Greek τερπνός. Judging by the context, therefore, we may conclude that the term in the original Greek was undoubtedly the latter, for the term τερπνός is used by Aristotle as the opposite of λυπῶν (*Eth. Nic.* IV, 8, 1128a, 26–27) and hence as the equivalent of ἡδύς. Consequently, while the Armenian translation of this term here is only ambiguous, the Latin translation from the Armenian is incorrect.

(*magna*) when it is close to the contemplative life. It is evidently also because the practical life may degenerate into a life of pleasure that he is led to speak with approval of those who flee society and seek solitude in order to be able to lead a life of contemplation.[163]

But all these statements as to the greater importance of the contemplative life mean nothing more than that statement of the rabbis that the study of the Law is the greater thing, whereby they mean only, as we have seen, that it is greater in the sense that it leads to doing. With his belief that the laws of the Pentateuch are to be obeyed and followed and practiced, Philo believed that they had an intrinsic value, and a practical life based upon these laws, and upon the contemplation or the study of these laws, could not be dismissed as valueless nor even reduced to a secondary position. Accordingly we shall find many passages in which he asserts the equality of the practical life and the contemplative life, provided the practical life is a life in accordance with the Law. Thus in one passage he says that "while virtue contains both contemplation and practice, nevertheless it is of surpassing excellence in each of these two, for the contemplation of virtue is perfect in beauty, and the practice and exercise of it is a prize to be striven for." [164] The intrinsic value of the practical life based on virtue is affirmed by him in his statement that "happiness consists in the practice and enjoyment of virtue, not in its mere possession," [165] or that "happiness results from the practice of perfect virtue." [166] Drawing upon his own experience, he tries to show that to lead a contemplative life one does not necessarily have to escape from the practical life. "For

---

[163] *Abr.* 4, 22–23; *Spec.* II, 12, 44; *Prob.* 10, 63; cf. also *Spec.* III, 1, 1–6.
[164] *Leg. All*, I, 17, 58.
[165] *Deter.* 17, 60.   [166] *Agr.* 36, 157.

many a time," he says, "have I myself forsaken friends and kinsfolk and country and come into a wilderness, to give my attention to some subject demanding contemplating, and derived no advantage from doing so, but my mind scattered or bitten by passion has gone off to matters of the contrary kind. Sometimes, on the other hand, amid a vast throng I can bring my mind into solitude. God has dispersed the crowd that besets the soul and taught me that a favorable and an unfavorable condition are not brought about by differences of place, but by God who moves and leads the ear of the soul in whatever way He pleases." [167] Not only is it not necessary to escape from practical life in order to lead a contemplative life, but the former may serve as a preparation for the latter, for "it is proper to go through a practical life before beginning the contemplative one: as being a sort of prelude to a more advanced contest." [168] His conception of the equality of the practical life and the contemplative life is discerned in his treatment of the Essenes [169] and the Therapeutae.[170] The former are praised by him as an exemplification of the practical life; the latter are praised by him as an exemplification of the contemplative life.[171] Finally, a proof-text for the equality of the practical and contemplative life is found by him in the verses in which the command to rest and to cease work on the seventh day is explained on the ground that on that day God rested from His work of creation.[172] "Always follow God, it says, find in that single six-day period in which, all-sufficient for His purpose, He created the world, a pattern of the time set apart to thee for activity. Find, too, in the seventh day the pattern of the duty to

[167] *Leg. All.* II, 21, 85.   [168] *Fug.* 6, 36.
[169] *Prob.* 12, 75–13, 91; *Hypot.* 11, 1–18 (*Fragmenta*, Richter, VI, 183–185; M. II, 632–634).
[170] *Cont.* I, 1.
[171] *Ibid.*   [172] Exod. 20: 8–11.

study wisdom, that day in which we are told that He sur-
veyed what He had wrought, and so learn to meditate thyself on the lessons of nature and all that in thy own life
makes for happiness. Let us not then neglect the great
archetype of the two best lives, the practical and the contemplative." [173] By the contemplative here he means study
and teaching, for elsewhere he explains that the seventh
day, which is to be devoted to contemplative life, is a day
devoted to study and teaching.[174] This study and teaching
he explains as meaning the study and teaching of "virtue"
or of "philosophy" or of the "duty to God" and the "duty
to men" [175] or of "the philosophy of their fathers," [176] but
by all these he means nothing but what he calls elsewhere
"the sacred laws." [177]

(d) Deeds, Words, Intentions

These three commandments, prayer, repentance, and the
study of the Law, are distinguished from most of the other
commandments in that they are expressed not in actions but
in words. They constitute, therefore, with similar other commandments which are expressed in words, such as the prohibitions of reviling or cursing,[178] of calumniating,[179] and of
swearing falsely,[180] and the command to rebuke one's neighbor,[181] a special class of commandments. But in addition to
these two types of commandments dealing with practical
virtues,[182] there are also, as we have seen above, commandments which deal with intellectual [183] and moral virtues,[184]

[173] *Decal.* 20, 100–101; cf. *Spec.* II, 15, 64.
[174] *Mos.* II, 39, 215–216; *Spec.* II, 15, 61–62; *Fragmenta*, Richter VI, pp. 181–182 (M. II, 630–631).
[175] *Spec.* II, 15, 61–63; *Mos.* II, 39, 215. Cf. above, I, 79–80.   [180] Lev. 19: 12.
[176] *Mos.* II, 39, 216.   [181] Lev. 19: 17.
[177] *Fragmenta*, Richter VI, p. 182 (M. II, 631).   [182] Cf. above, p. 208.
[178] Exod. 21: 17; 22: 27; Lev. 19: 14.   [183] Cf. above, pp. 208 ff.
[179] Exod. 23: 1; Lev. 19: 16.   [184] Cf. above, pp. 218 ff.

that is, with beliefs and feelings, both of which may be regarded as constituting one type of commandment, dealing
with what may be called duties of the heart.[185] Evidently
referring to these three types of commandments and describing the third type by terms meaning "thoughts" and
"intentions," he says that "offenses and right actions exist in
three things: thoughts or intentions (διάνοιαι, βουλαί), words
(λόγοι), and deeds (πράξεις, ἔργα)."[186] He bases this view on a
verse which in the Septuagint reads: "The word is very near
thee, in thy mouth and in thy heart, and in thy hand, to do
it." [187] Commenting upon this verse, he says that the words
"mouth," "heart," and "hand" symbolize respectively
"words," "intentions," and "deeds." [188] In another place,
alluding to the same verse,[189] he restates the same interpretation of it as follows: "For if our words (λόγοι) correspond with our intentions (βουλεύματα) and our actions (πράξεις) with our words, and the three mutually follow each
other, bound together with indissoluble bonds of harmony,
happiness prevails." [190] In the Wisdom of Solomon, similarly, the condition in the pursuit of wisdom is said to be
purity in thought,[191] purity in word,[192] and purity in deed.[193]

This new distinction thus raises Philo's classifications of
the commandments to five: (1) positive and negative; (2)
duties to God and duties to men; (3) as subdivisions of the
ten commandments; (4) according to the classification of
virtues into intellectual, moral, and practical;[194] (5) those
of the hands, those of the mouth, and those of the heart, or
deeds, words, and intentions.

---

[185] Cf. below, p. 309.
[186] *Mut.* 41, 236, and cf. 237.
[187] Deut. 30: 14. In the Hebrew the words "and in thy hand" are omitted.
[188] *Mut.* 41, 237; cf. *Virt.* 34, 183; *Probus* 10, 68.   [189] *Praem.* 14, 80.
[190] *Ibid.*, 81.   [191] Wisdom of Solomon 1: 1–5.   [192] *Ibid.* 1: 6–11.
[193] *Ibid.* 1: 12–16.   [194] Cf. above, pp. 200–201, 208.

268   PHILO

V. The Definition of Virtue

Philo had before him two definitions of virtue. One was
the Aristotelian definition, according to which virtue is "a
mean (μεσότης) between two vices, one of excess and one of
defect." [1] There is an anticipation of this doctrine of the
mean in Plato's statement that a man should always choose
"the life that is seated in the mean (μέσον) and shun the
excess in either direction." [2] The other was the Stoic definition, according to which virtue consists in the complete
exemption from emotion (ἀπάθεια). [3] The difference between
these two definitions may be gathered from the discussions
among the Stoics as to the differences between their own
view and that of the Peripatetics. "Between virtue and
vice," they say, "there is nothing intermediate (μεταξύ),
whereas according to the Peripatetics there is, namely, the
state of improvement (προκοπή)." [4] The difference between
these two definitions of virtue may be illustrated by a dia-
gram in which the area of human conduct is represented by
a quadrangle ABCD, and this quadrangle is divided in the
middle by a line EF which is equidistant from AB and CD.

According to Aristotle, the extremes AB and CD constitute
vices, the mean EF constitutes
virtue, but the entire area of con-
duct between AB and EF or between CD and EF is to be
called neither complete virtue nor complete vice but rather
the field of progressive virtue or progressive vice, wherein
one may move either in the direction of virtue or in the direc-

---

[1] *Eth. Nic.* II, 6, 1107a, 2–3.
[2] *Republic* X, 619 A; *Laws* III, 691 C; V, 728 E; VII, 792 C.
[3] Cf. above, p. 230, n. 24.
[4] Diogenes, VII, 127.

tion of vice. To the Stoics, too, virtue is the line *EF*, but vice to them is not merely the extremes *AB* and *CD* but the entire area of conduct between *AB* and *EF* and between *CD* and *EF*. Consequently, according to them, any deviation from the line on either side is a deviation from virtue into the area of vice, there thus being no progressive virtue nor progressive vice.

As a result of their new definition of virtue the Stoics lay down three principles with regard to emotion.

First, as reported in the names of their chief exponents, in opposition to the Peripatetics, who found some emotions useful, the Stoics argue that none of the emotions are useful. They particularly try to show that there is nothing good or useful in such emotions as anger,[5] pain,[6] and pity.[7] Anger (ὀργή), hatred (μῖσος), pity (ἔλεος), and pain (λύπη) are all described by them as irrational emotions,[8] without any qualification, though in later Stoicism some qualifications are made.[9] To the Stoics, therefore, the wise man is to extirpate all his emotions so as to become free of them, whereas to the Peripatetics the wise man is not to extirpate all his emotions; he is only to indulge in them in moderation.[10]

Second, there is no difference of degree of importance between the various virtues or the various vices. "They hold that the goods (i.e., virtues) are equal and that all good is desirable in the highest degree and admits of no lowering or heightening of intensity"[11] and similarly, "it is one of their tenets that sins are all equal . . . for if one truth is not more

[5] Cicero, *Tusculanae Disputationes* IV, 22, 49 ff.; cf. 19, 43.
[6] *Ibid.*, 23, 51 ff.; cf. 20, 45.
[7] *Ibid.*, 25, 56; cf. 20, 46.
[8] Diogenes, VII, 111, 113.
[9] Cf. Zeller, III, 1⁴, p. 275, nn. 1–3 (*Stoics, Epicureans and Sceptics²*, p. 29, nn. 1–3).
[10] Diogenes, V, 31.   [11] *Ibid.*, VII, 101.

than another, neither is one falsehood more false than another, and in the same way one deceit is not more so than
another, nor sin than sin." [12]

Third, there is no intermediate class of human beings between those who are perfectly virtuous and those who are
perfectly vicious. Men are either virtuous or vicious, and
either of these in an absolute sense, "for, say the Stoics, just
as a stick must be either straight or crooked, so a man must
be either just or unjust." [13]

To all these three points in the Stoic doctrine Philo must
have found the teachings of Judaism in opposition.

First, not all the emotions are bad and useless. With regard to such emotions as anger and hatred and pity and pain
and their like, there are definite statements that under certain conditions they are good and useful. Moses is on many
occasions said to have become angry. [14] In many a place in
Scripture the hating of evil is approved of. [15] The people are
urged by the Prophet Zechariah to "show mercy and compassion every man to his brother." [16] Jacob is said to have
been afraid and distressed. [17] In rabbinic literature, similarly, the moral hero is not he who has extirpated his evil
yeṣer, but rather he who has brought it under control. [18] The
same view is also expressed by the rabbis in the story of
the consequences that followed when for three days the
evil *yeṣer* was imprisoned and was made completely powerless. [19] By the time of Philo, the question whether virtue
means the extirpation of the emotions or only their control
seems to have been a subject of discussion among Hellenistic
Jews who had a knowledge of philosophy. In the Fourth

[12] *Ibid.*, VII, 120.
[13] *Ibid.*, VII, 127.
[14] Exod. 16: 20; Lev. 10: 16; Num. 31: 14 ($\dot{\omega}\rho\gamma\iota\sigma\theta\eta$).
[15] Amos 5: 15; Ps. 45: 8; 97: 10; 139: 21; Prov. 13: 5.
[16] Zech. 7: 9.
[18] *M. Abot* IV, 1.
[17] Gen. 32: 8.
[19] *Yoma* 69b.

Book of Maccabees this question is the principal topic of discussion. Guided by Jewish tradition the author comes out in opposition to the Stoics. The question as posed by him is whether "the Inspired Reason is the supreme ruler over the passions." [20] By passions, as he subsequently explains, he does not mean such mental defects as "forgetfulness and ignorance" but rather moral defects "that are adverse to justice and courage and temperance and prudence," and the view which he upholds is that the action of reason is "not to extirpate the passions, but to enable us to resist them successfully." [21] The prohibition, according to the Law, not to eat the meat of certain animals does not mean that we should extirpate any desire for it but rather that we should control that desire.[22] As proof-text he quotes, among others,[23] the case of Moses who "was angered against Dathan and Abiram" but "governed his anger by his reason." [24]

Second, not all sins and virtues are equal. While indeed all the laws are to be observed with equal scrupulousness, some laws are considered weightier than others. This is implied in Scripture itself, in the fact that different sacrifices are required and different punishments are meted out in cases of violation of different laws. In rabbinic literature the laws are explicitly described as being either "heavy" or "light." [25] Similarly, in the Fourth Book of Maccabees there is a reference to a distinction between a "small sin" and, by implication, a great sin, or between a "transgression of the law" in "small things" and that in "great things,"

---

[20] IV Macc. 1: 1.   [21] Ibid. 1: 5–6; 3: 1–2.
[22] Ibid. 1: 34–35. Cf. Sifra, Ḳedoshim, Pereḳ 11, p. 93d: "A man should not say 'I have no desire to eat swine's flesh.' . . . Nay, he should say 'I have a desire for it, but what can I do seeing that my Father who is in heaven has forbidden me.'"
[23] Ibid. 2: 19–20; 3: 6–16.
[24] Ibid. 2: 17; 3: 3.   [25] M. Abot II, 1.

though in accordance with the teachings of Judaism, it adds, both are to be equally avoided.[26] The emphasis in this book is as much on the distinction between different grades of laws as upon their equality with reference to the observance of them, and it is therefore not in agreement with the Stoic view of the equality of sins, but rather in disagreement with it.[27]

Third, not all men are either perfectly righteous or perfectly wicked. Scripture explicitly asserts that "there is not a righteous man upon earth that doeth good and sinneth not." [28] Among the rabbis it is held that between the completely righteous and the completely wicked there is a class of men, described as intermediate (*benonim*), who are neither completely righteous nor completely wicked.[29]

With these traditionally Jewish conceptions of virtue and the virtuous men in the back of his mind, Philo starts out on his treatment of the philosophic conception of virtue.

To begin with, he adopts the Aristotelian definition of virtue as a mean. In one place, commenting upon the verse, "we will go along the king's highway, we will not turn aside to the right hand nor to the left," [30] he says that "it is better to proceed along the middle road, the road that is truly the royal road, seeing that God, the great and only King, laid it out a broad and goodly way for virtue-loving souls to keep to; hence it is that some of those who followed the mild and social form of philosophy have said that virtues are means." [31] In another place, where he similarly reproduces the definition

[26] IV Macc. 5: 19–20 (18–19); cf. *M. Abot* II, 1; *Jer. Kiddushin* I, 7, 61b.

[27] Cf. Townshend's note on IV Macc. 5: 20 in Charles's *Apocrypha and Pseudepigrapha of the Old Testament*, where he tries to show that these verses in IV Macc. reflect the Stoic view as to the equality of sins.

[28] Eccles. 7: 20; cf. I Kings 8: 46; II Chron. 6: 36.

[29] *Berakot* 61b; *Rosh ha-Shanah* 16b.

[30] Exod. 20: 17.

[31] *Migr.* 26, 146–147.

of virtue as a mean, he adds the Aristotelian statement to the effect that "deviations in either direction, whether of excess or of deficiency, whether they tend to strain or to laxity, are in fault." [32] The implication of the Aristotelian conception of virtue as a mean is also to be discerned in the lesson which he derives from the verse, "Behold I rain upon you bread out of heaven, and the people shall go out and they shall gather the day's portion for a day, that I may prove them whether they will walk in My law or not." [33] This lesson is stated in the form of an apostrophe to the soul. "Gather together, therefore, O soul, what is sufficient of itself and what is suitable, and neither more than sufficient so as to be excessive, nor on the other hand less so as to fall short, that dealing in just measures thou mayest do no injustice." [34] In two other places, he tries to show, in conformity with Aristotle's definition of virtue, and more especially with his statement that "the law is the mean," [35] that the practical virtues or the laws taught by Moses are themselves means. First, speaking of the dietary laws, he says: "He approved neither of rigorous austerity, like the Spartan legislator, nor of dainty living, like him who introduced the Ionians and Sybarites to luxurious and voluptuous practices. Instead he opened up a path midway between the two." [36] Second, commenting on the verse, "Ye shall not add unto the word which I command you, neither shall ye take from it," [37] he explains this injunction on the ground that "each of the virtues is free from all deficiency and is complete, deriving its perfection from itself, so that if there be any adding or taking away, its whole being is changed and transformed into the opposite condition." [38] The implica-

---

[32] *Immut.* 34, 162; cf. 35, 164.
[33] Exod. 16: 4; cf. *Leg. All.* III, 56, 162.
[34] *Leg. All.* III, 57, 165.   [37] Deut. 4: 2; 13: 1 (12: 32).

[35] *Politica* III, 16, 1287b, 4–5.
[36] *Spec.* IV, 17, 102.
[38] *Spec.* IV, 27, 144.

tion is that the Law is a mean between opposites. So also in the Letter of Aristeas, the elders selected by the high priest as translators of the books of the Law are praised in that "they espoused the middle course — and this is always the best course to pursue." [39]

But having aligned himself with Aristotle in his definition of virtue as a mean, he becomes conscious of the traditional Jewish view, which he himself has restated elsewhere, that certain individuals, by the free grace of God, were virtuous by birth.[40] He is thus compelled to admit that there may be some truth also in the Stoic definition of virtue, inasmuch as for the few favored perfectly righteous persons virtue would mean the complete extirpation of the emotions. Accordingly he stages a debate on the question as to what constitutes virtue, with Aaron and Moses as the exponents of the two opposite views. Aaron is the exponent of the Aristotelian view, who believes in the control of emotions, and therefore with regard to his emotion of irascibility "he cures and controls it, first by reason, that being driven by an excellent charioteer it may not get restive; next by the virtues of speech, distinctness, and truth." [41] Moses, on the other hand, is the exponent of the Stoic view, who "thinks that it is necessary completely to extirpate and eradicate anger from the soul, for he is contented not with a moderation of emotion but rather with a complete absence of emotion." [42] But as for his own view on the subject, Philo considers complete exemption of emotions to be possible only for a wise man like Moses who by special grace of God was endowed with "a share of surpassing excellence, even the power to

---

[39] Aristeas, 122.
[40] Cf. above, I, 450 ff.
[41] *Leg. All.* III, 44, 128.
[42] *Ibid.*, 129. Cf. Heinemann, *Philos Werke*, and Colson, *ad loc.*

cut out the emotions," [43] for Moses is one of those individuals who receive virtue "as a gift from God without any toil or difficulty." [44] For the majority of men, who like Aaron make only gradual progress, virtue consists in the moderation of emotion. [45]

For the majority of mankind, then, according to Philo, the cure for the emotions is not their extirpation but rather their control and moderation. Moreover, he argues, an emotion when controlled by reason becomes transformed into a virtue, to which he gives the special name of eupathy ($\epsilon\dot{\upsilon}\pi\dot{\alpha}\theta\epsilon\iota\alpha$) or a good emotional state. Now the term eupathy is of Stoic origin; Philo uses it, however, in a new sense. To the Stoics, to whom virtue consists in complete freedom from emotion or, as they call it, apathy, the term eupathy is used only as a description of certain emotions, such as joy ($\chi\alpha\rho\dot{\alpha}$), caution ($\epsilon\dot{\upsilon}\lambda\dot{\alpha}\beta\epsilon\iota\alpha$), and wishing ($\beta\sigma\dot{\upsilon}\lambda\eta\sigma\iota\varsigma$), which they concede to be of a rational nature ($\epsilon\ddot{\upsilon}\lambda\sigma\gamma\sigma\varsigma$). [46] While these eupathies, to them, are not pure emotions, for pure emotions by definition are the cause of "instability" ($\dot{\alpha}\kappa\alpha\tau\alpha\sigma\tau\alpha\sigma\dot{\iota}\alpha$), [47] whereas eupathies are equable states (*constantiae*) of the soul, [48] still they are not virtues, for virtue by definition consists in complete apathy. They are to them something between pure emotions and virtues. Philo goes further than that. Any emotion that is controlled by reason is a virtue and therefore the Stoic eupathies will according to him be virtues. He therefore very often uses the terms "virtue and eupathy" or "eupathy and virtue" as if they were synonymous. [49] In one place, evidently reflecting Aristotle's differ-

[43] *Ibid.* III, 45, 131.
[44] *Ibid.* III, 46, 135; cf. above, pp. 450 f.   [46] Diogenes, VII, 116.
[45] *Ibid.* III, 45, 132.   [47] *Ibid.*, VII, 110.
[48] Cicero, *Tusculanae Disputationes* IV, 6, 14.
[49] *Leg. All.* III, 7, 22; *Sacr.* 31, 103; *Migr.* 39, 219; *Abr.* 36, 204; *Praem.* 27, 160.

entiation of virtue from emotion in that the former involves choice (προαίρεσις),[50] he says that "the Passover is," that is to say, the attainment of virtue takes place,[51] "when the soul studies to unlearn irrational emotion and of its own free will (ἐκουσίως) experiences rational eupathy (εὔλογον εὐπάθειαν)." [52] Here then he has restated Aristotle's definition of virtue, the chief characteristic of which is that it is an act of choice or free will, by identifying the term virtue with the Stoic term eupathy. When, therefore, he says in another place that "we extol those philosophers who declare that virtue is eupathy,"[53] the reference is undoubtedly not to the Stoics, who have never identified virtue with eupathy, but rather to the Aristotelians, whose definition of virtue Philo himself has rewritten in terms of eupathy.[54]

Then, actuated again by Jewish traditional teachings, he aligns himself with the Peripatetics as against the Stoics in regarding some emotions as good and useful. He thus speaks with approval of "righteous anger" (ὀργὴ δικαία)[55] and of the "severe anger against men-stealers." [56] Similarly, pity (ἔλεος) is considered by him a virtue and a quality of the wise.[57] And so also he approves of the hatred of evil

[50] Eth. Nic. II, 5, 1106a, 2–4.
[51] See Philo's allegorical interpretation of the Passover in Sacr. 17, 63: "For we are bidden to keep the Passover which is the passage from the life of passions to the practice of virtue."
[52] Heres 40, 192.
[53] Mut. 31, 167.
[54] Cf. Colson ad loc. (V, 591): "Who are the philosophers alluded to? Hardly the Stoics. . . . I can hardly think, however, that he speaks without authority." My discussion of Philo's treatment of the term eupathy here will explain this statement, unless some literary source is discovered, and if such happens, I dare say it will be a Peripatetic source.
[55] Fug. 17, 90; Somn. I, 15, 91; II, 1, 7. Cf. Aristotle, Eth. Nic. IV, 5, 1125b, 31–32: "The man who is angry at the right things and with the right people, and, further, as he ought, when he ought, and as long as he ought, is praised."
[56] Spec. IV, 4, 14.
[57] Sacr. 37, 121.

ETHICAL THEORY 277

(μισοπονηρία),[58] an emotion which Chrysippus explicitly declares to have no existence in the experience of any good man.[59] In speaking of the ideal legislator as represented by Moses, he finds that his chief characteristics are "love of humanity, love of justice, love of goodness, and hatred of evil," [60] and of the ideal magistrates to be appointed by a king he says that one of their chief qualifications should be their hatred of arrogance as a thing pernicious and utterly evil.[61]

Then also, in conformity with Jewish tradition, not all vices and not all virtues are of an equal degree of importance. Using the same descriptive terms, light (*kal*) and heavy (*ḥamur*),[62] that are used by the rabbis, he speaks of sin (ἁμάρτημα) as being either lighter (κουφότερον) or heavier (βαρύτερον).[63] Similarly with regard to virtues, he describes some of them, like piety (εὐσέβεια) and holiness (ὁσιότης), as great virtues (μεγάλαι ἀρεταί),[64] and piety and holiness, as well as faith and justice, are described as the queen (βασιλίς) or the leader (ἡγεμονίς) or the chief (ἔξαρχος) of the virtues.[65] That he considers virtues as differing in importance, and that like Aristotle and in opposition to the Stoics he considers the middle course as a virtue, may be also gathered from his statement that, according to Scripture, rewards are offered "for the acquisition of virtue, and to those who cannot reach the highest virtues, even the acquisition of the middle ones (τῶν μέσων) is serviceable." [66]

---

[58] *Mos.* II, 2, 9; *Spec.* I, 9, 55.
[59] Plutarch, *De Stoicorum Repugnantiis* 25.
[62] *M. Yoma* VIII, 8.
[63] *Sacr.* 13, 54; *Mut.* 42, 241, 243; *Spec.* III, 11, 64. Cf. the expression "one of these least commandments" in Matt. 5: 19.
[64] *Plant.* 8, 35.
[65] *Plant.* 28, 122; *Abr.* 5, 27; *Decal.* 23, 119; *Spec.* IV, 25, 135; 27, 147; *Praem.* 9, 53; cf. above, pp. 214, 220.
[66] *Agr.* 27, 121.

[60] *Mos.* II, 2, 9.
[61] *Spec.* IV, 33, 170.

Finally, the majority of men to whom, according to Philo, virtue does not mean the extirpation of emotion, but rather its control, constitute a class of people who are not perfectly righteous nor perfectly wicked, for, reëchoing a fundamental Jewish view, he maintains "absolute sinlessness belongs to God alone, or possibly to a divine man." [67] Between the "virtuous" (σπουδαῖος) or "perfect" (τέλειος) man and the "wicked" (φαῦλος) man there is the man whom Philo, like the rabbis, describes as "the intermediate man (ὁ μέσος), the man who is neither wicked nor virtuous," [68] and "quite naturally, then," he adds, "does God address the recommendations and exhortations before us to the earthly mind which is neither wicked nor virtuous but intermediate." [69] Another reference to the "intermediate" is to be found in a passage in which he says that between the wise (σοφοί) and the bad (κακοί) there are the practicers (ἀσκηταί) of virtue, who are described by him as being "on the boundary (μεθόριοι) between two extremities." [70] In another passage, speaking of "sin" rather than of "sinners," he applies the term "intermediate" to sin committed unintentionally and compares ᶜhis term "intermediate" with the Stoic term "indifferent." [71] "As to sin intentionally," he says, "is unjust, so to sin unintentionally and out of ignorance is not at once justifiable, but perhaps it is something on the boundary (μεθόριον) between the two, that is, between righteousness and unrighteousness, and is what some persons call indifferent (ἀδιάφορον), for no sin can be an act of righteousness." [72] The comparison between unintentional

[67] *Virt.* 33, 177; cf. above, p. 256.
[68] *Leg. All.* I, 30, 93.
[69] *Ibid.*, 95.
[70] *Somn.* I, 23, 151–152.
[71] Cf. Arnim, III, 117–123.
[72] *Fragmenta*, Richter, VI, 205–206 (M, II, 651).

sin described by him as "intermediate" and what the Stoics call "indifferent," it may be remarked, is only in so far as the Stoic "indifferent" is also defined as "those things which are between virtue and vice." [73] The Stoics, however, do not mean to imply by this definition that there is an intermediate class of human beings who are neither perfectly virtuous nor perfectly vicious.

VI. THE REWARD OF VIRTUE

The problem of virtue and its reward presents itself in Greek philosophy and in Judaism after the same pattern. In both of them, it is assumed that in man there is a continuous struggle between two motive forces. In philosophy these forces are called emotion and reason; in Judaism they are called the evil imagination (*yeṣer raʿ*, *yeṣer ha-raʿ*) and the good imagination (*yeṣer tob*). In both of them, man is told what force is best for him to follow. In philosophy, he is told to follow reason; in Judaism, he is told to follow the good imagination. But why should man follow reason or the good imagination with all its demand for self-restraint and self-denial? To this both philosophy and Judaism give the same answer. In philosophy, it is promised that a life of virtue in accordance with reason will be rewarded by happiness, whereas a life of vice in accordance with emotion will be punished by unhappiness, for "virtuous activities are what determine happiness, and the opposite activities its opposite." [1] In Judaism, it is similarly promised that life in obedience to the Law will be rewarded by blessings, whereas life in disobedience to the Law will be punished by curses, for "Behold, I set before you this day a blessing

---

[73] Stobaeus, *Eclogae* II, p. 79, ll. 14-15 (Arnim, III, 118, p. 28, l. 26).

[1] *Eth. Nic.*, I, 10, 1100b, 9-11.

and a curse; a blessing, if you obey the commandments of
the Lord your God . . . and a curse, if you will not obey the
commandments of the Lord your God." [2]

But philosophers were quite fully aware of the common
complaint of mankind that "injustice pays better than
justice, for the most part," [3] and Plato quotes the complaint
of religious-minded Greeks that "the gods themselves assign to many good men misfortunes and an evil life, but to
their opposites a contrary lot." [4] Similarly, Scripture and
rabbis were aware of the fact that not all those who are
obedient receive the promised blessings and not all those who
are disobedient receive the threatened curses, and the
question is therefore raised, "Wherefore holdest Thou thy
tongue when the wicked devoureth the man that is more
righteous than he?" [5] and "Wherefore doth the way of the
wicked prosper?" [6] In post-biblical Judaism the problem is
stated in the form of the question: "Why is there a righteous
man who fares well and another righteous man who fares
badly, and why is there a wicked man who fares well and
another wicked man who fares badly?" [7]

Many answers are given to the question of the suffering
of the righteous and the prosperity of the wicked, but the
main answers fall into four groups.

First, no really righteous man will suffer and no really
wicked man will prosper. If a righteous man appears to us
to suffer, it is because of some sin of his which is unknown to
us, and similarly, if some wicked man appears to us to
prosper, it is because of some meritorious deeds of his which
are unknown to us. Among philosophers, Plato declares that
"the friend of the gods may be supposed to receive from

[2] Deut. 11: 26–28.
[3] *Republic* II, 364 A.
[4] *Ibid.*, 364 B.

[5] Hab. 1: 13.
[6] Jer. 12: 1.
[7] *Berakot* 7a.

them all things at their best, excepting only such evil as is
the necessary consequence of former sins," [8] and in Judaism
a rabbi similarly declares that "the righteous who fares
badly is one who is not perfect in his righteousness" and that
the "wicked who fares well is one who is not wicked throughout." [9]

Second, no real evil will befall the righteous nor will real
good come to the wicked. Real evil and real good are not
those of the body in life but those of the soul after death, and
even in life, what appears to be evil may be a prelude to
something good. Plato expresses this view in his statement
that even when the just man is "in poverty or sickness, or
any other seeming misfortune, all things will in the end work
together for good to him in life and death" [10] and especially
certain is he of "the recompenses which await both just and
unjust after death." [11] Among the Stoics, the evil which
befalls the righteous is itself sometimes said to serve some
good purpose, for "these things which you call hardships,
which you call adversities and accursed are . . . for the good
of the persons themselves to whom they come." [12] The
rabbis similarly declare that the real reward of the righteous
and the real punishment of the wicked are in the world to
come [13] and, as for the evils in this world, they say that
"whatever the Merciful does is for a good purpose." [14]

Third, sometimes the evil which God brings upon the
righteous is merely for the purpose of trying and testing
them. Seneca declares that God "does not make a spoiled
pet of a good man; He tests him, hardens him, and fits him
for His own service," [15] and that "the gods follow the same

[8] *Republic* X, 613 A.

[9] *Berakot* 7a.

[10] *Republic* X, 613 A.

[11] *Ibid.*, 614 A.

[12] Seneca, *De Providentia* III, 1.

[13] *Ta'anit* 11a; *Kiddushin* 39b; 40b.

[14] *Berakot* 60b.

[15] *De Providentia* I, 6.

rule that teachers follow with their pupils; they require most effort from those of whom they have the surest hopes. Do you imagine that the Lacedaemonians hate their children when they test their mettle by lashing them in public?"[16] So also the rabbis, commenting upon the verse "The Lord trieth the righteous,"[17] say: "A potter does not test defective vessels, for he cannot give them a single blow without breaking them. What kind of vessels does he test? Good vessels, for however many blows he gives them, they are not broken. Similarly the Holy One, blessed be He, does not test the wicked but only the righteous. . . . When a flax-worker knows that his flax is of good quality, the more he beats it the more it improves and the more it glistens, but when he knows that it is of inferior quality he cannot give it one knock without its splitting. Similarly the Holy One, blessed be He, does not test the wicked but only the righteous."[18] The analogy of father and son as an explanation of the seemingly unmerited suffering of the righteous occurs in Scripture in the verses "and thou shalt consider in thy heart, that, as a man chasteneth his son, so the Lord thy God chasteneth thee"[19] and "for whom the Lord loveth He correcteth, even as a father the son in whom he delighteth."[20]

Fourth, sometimes the righteous suffer not for their own sins but for those of their ancestors, and similarly sometimes the wicked prosper for the meritorious deeds of their ancestors. Seneca declares, with reference to the prosperity of the wicked, that "some people are treated [by the gods] with greater indulgence because of their parents and ancestors, others because of their grandchildren and great-

---

[16] *Ibid.* IV, 11.
[17] Ps. 11: 5.
[18] *Genesis Rabbah* 32, 3.

[19] Deut. 8: 5.
[20] Prov. 3: 12.

grandchildren and the long line of their descendants, whose qualities are as yet unrevealed." [21] The rabbis declare that "the righteous who fares badly is a righteous man who is the son of a wicked man" and "the wicked who fares well is a wicked man who is the son of a righteous man" [22] and also that "a son can make his father acquire merit." [23]

All these justifications of God's dealings with the righteous and the wicked imply a belief in individual providence. Now in Judaism such a belief was compatible with its conception of God, for its conception of Him was that of a miracle-working God who is not bound by the laws of nature which He himself has implanted in the world. It was also compatible with the conception of the gods in Greek popular religion, who were endowed with human emotions as well as with human qualities. But the god of Plato and of the Stoics as conceived in their respective philosophies could not exercise individual providence in the world. He was a god who could not deviate from certain inexorable laws of nature. If they wished at all to attribute to him providence, it had to be a universal providence, a providence that extends only to the species. They could all say, as indeed the Stoics did say, that "the gods attend to great matters; they neglect small ones." [24] If they do speak of divine providence as if it were individual divine providence and try to find explanations for certain deviation from such individual divine providence, they do not speak as philosophers from their own philosophic premises but rather as statesmen and citizens who believed in the need of bolstering

[21] *De Beneficiis* IV, 32, 1.
[22] *Berakot* 7a.
[23] *Sanhedrin* 104a; cf. S. Schechter, *Some Aspects of Rabbinic Theology*, pp. 196–197.
[24] Cicero, *De Natura Deorum* II, 66, 167; cf. III, 35, 86; Plutarch, *De Stoicorum Repugnantiis* 37, 2.

up popular religion as a valuable sanction for right conduct. Aristotle who kept his philosophy apart from his good citizenship does not commit himself philosophically to individual providence. He cautiously says that "if the gods have any care for human affairs, as they are thought to have, it would be reasonable both that they would delight in that which was best and most akin to them (i.e., reason) and that they should reward those who love and honor this most, as caring for things that are dear for them and acting both rightly and nobly." [25]

To Greek philosophers, then, because of their disbelief in individual providence, there was no problem of divine justice, and hence to them there was no need for any theories as to its vindication. It happens, however, that all of them were interested not only in what they called speculative philosophy but also in practical philosophy, and in practical philosophy, which was to deal with both society and the individual, they were concerned with the problem of how to maintain order in society and also how to make men shun evil and pursue good. Now, for the great mass of men who were still unshaken in their inherited beliefs, these philosophers felt they could justifiably invoke the help of certain notions of popular religion, even though they themselves did not believe in them, and this they did quite profusely. But at the same time they also realized that there were many men, who, though not professional philosophers, had already been deeply affected by the teaching of philosophy, and these could not be expected to relish the pap of popular religion handed out by the philosophers for the consumption of the masses. For such men, they must have felt, the only deterrent from evil that was thus left was the fear of being punished by the laws of the state, and the only incentive for

[25] *Eth. Nic.* X, 8, 1179a, 24–29.

good was the hope of being rewarded by some of the various kinds of external goods. As philosophers, however, they knew full well that mere fear of punishment and hope of reward were not strong enough motives to assure right conduct, for the motives of fear and hope, they could not help feeling, would only invite each man to take a chance on his own calculation as to whether any action contemplated by him would be more likely to bring punishment or to bring reward. As philosophers, too, they felt that it was a part of their business to provide mankind with some universal principle of guidance; but here, again, on the basis of their own philosophy, the only principle of guidance they could provide mankind with was the practical advice that it was for each man to take care not to be caught, if he has committed a punishable crime, and not to be overlooked, if he has done something for which there is a reward. The problem for Greek philosophers, therefore, was to find some universal principle of guidance more effective than the individual calculation of each man as to the outcome of any contemplated action of his, and more lofty than advice for the need of precaution on the part of each man against the possibility of being caught or of being overlooked.

The solution offered by them for this problem is to be found in their common advice that virtue is to be practiced for its own sake. Plato suggests it in his statement that "justice in itself is the best thing for the soul itself"; [26] Aristotle restates it in more general terms when he says that "to do noble and virtuous deeds is a thing worthy of choice for its own sake"; [27] and the Stoics formulate it as a general principle that "virtue is worthy of choice for its own sake." [28]

[26] *Republic* X, 612 B; cf. *Theaetetus* 176 B ff.
[27] *Eth. Nic.* X, 6, 1176b, 8–9.
[28] Diogenes, VII, 89, 127.

Now when closely examined in its various philosophical contexts, it will be found that this advice implies a confession of lack of faith in the rewardfulness of virtue. All those who have used it, whether Plato or Aristotle or the Stoics or any of their followers, seem to argue that, inasmuch as despite every possible calculation there is no certainty as to what, in the form of external goods as a reward or external evils as a punishment, will follow as a result of one's actions, it is advisable for one to take a chance on the practice of virtue rather than on the practice of vice, for, they must have argued, while both virtue and vice may each bring either external goods or external evils, it is quite certain that virtue will always bring internal happiness and vice will always bring internal unhappiness. Underlying this advice is evidently the observation so often stressed by the philosophers themselves that external goods do not constitute happiness,[29] coupled also with the common human experience, in which even the philosophers must have shared, that it is easier for one to induce in himself a feeling of happiness in the misery that may follow a life of virtue than it is to induce in himself such a feeling of happiness in the misery that may follow a life of vice. To philosophers, then, the formula that virtue is to be chosen for its own sake was a counsel of despair, which had grown out of the realization that no other reward can be expected with certainty for the choice of virtue.

The advice that one is to practice virtue for its own sake is given also by the rabbis. As expressed by them, it reads: "Be not like servants who minister to their master in expectation of receiving a reward; but be like servants who minister to their master in no expectation of receiving a reward." [30] It is also expressed by them in the statement

---

[29] *Eth. Nic.* I, 5, 1095b, 14–1096a, 10; 8, 1098b, 9–1099b, 8.   [30] *M. Abot* I, 3.

that only "if thou hast done the words of the Law for their own sake will they be life unto thee." [31] But with the rabbis this advice has a different meaning than with the philosophers. With their belief in individual providence and divine justice, no righteous deed can go unrewarded, even though occasionally, as in the case of those who are not perfectly righteous, the reward for some righteous deeds may be overwhelmed by the punishment for some wicked deeds, and sometimes also, even in the case of the perfectly righteous, the reward for some righteous deed may be of such a nature that it is not evident to the eye. What then do the rabbis mean by saying that man should not serve God in expectation of receiving a reward? They certainly cannot mean thereby that the service of God might not bring any reward at all. Quite obviously what they mean thereby is that, even though a reward, in some form, is sure to come, still one should not serve God in expectation of any reward. Underlying this advice is evidently the belief that rewards are distributed by God according to the principle of justice, and that therefore rewards are to be proportionate to the number of good deeds done and to the manner in which they are done. "All is according to the amount of the work," [32] say the rabbis, and also "greater is he who does the commandments of God out of love than he who does them out of fear." [33] The service of God out of love, then, is of a higher quality than the service of God out of fear and will therefore bring a greater reward. Now the opposite of serving God out of love is not only to serve Him out of fear, as in the passage quoted, but also to serve Him in expectation

[31] *Sifre Deut.* § 306, F, p. 131b; HF, p. 338; cf. *Ta'anit* 7a; *Pesiḳta Zuṭarta* on Deut. 32: 2.
[32] *M. Abot* III, 15. This is the meaning of the statement according to one of its traditional interpretations. Cf. Commentary of Bertinoro *ad loc.*
[33] *Sota* 31a.

of a reward. Thus in another passage, which expresses the same sentiment, the rabbis, commenting upon the scriptural words "to love the Lord your God," [34] derive therefrom the lesson that "whatever you do should be done by you only out of love" and that consequently one should not say "I will study the Torah in order that I may . . . acquire a reward in the world to come." [35] In the light of all this, then, when the rabbis urge men to serve God without the expectation of a reward, they merely mean to emphasize the principle that one is to serve God out of love, and this not because of any doubt as to whether a reward will be forthcoming but because the service of God out of love is intrinsically the highest kind of service.

These two traditions, the philosophic and the Jewish, are combined in Philo in his treatment of the same problem. The continuous conflict that goes on within man between good and evil is usually described by him in philosophic language as a conflict between the irrational soul and the rational soul [36] or between emotion and reason.[37] But it is also described by him in the traditional language of Judaism as a conflict between the evil *yeṣer* and the good *yeṣer*. Explaining the symbolism of Isaac as the father of twins, he says: "For the soul of every man from the first, as soon as he is born, bears in its womb twins, namely, good and evil, having the image ($\phi\alpha\nu\tau\alpha\sigma\iota o\upsilon\mu\acute{\epsilon}\nu\eta$) of both of them." [38] The expression "having the image of both of them" undoubtedly reflects the Hebrew terms 'good *yeṣer*" and "evil *yeṣer*," for "imagination" ($\phi\alpha\nu\tau\alpha\sigma\acute{\iota}\alpha$) is a good rendering of *yeṣer*, even though it is not used as such in the Septuagint. Moreover,

---

[34] Deut. 11: 13.
[35] *Sifre Deut.* § 41, HF, p. 87; cf. F, p. 80a.
[36] Cf. *Spec.* IV, 23, 123–24, 125; *Opif.* 46, 134; *Leg. All.* I, 12, 31.
[37] Cf. below, n. 43.
[38] *Praem.* 11, 63; cf. IV Macc. 2: 21–23.

his statement that the soul of man has this image "from the first, as soon as he is born" undoubtedly reflects the verse saying that "the *yeṣer*-of-the-heart (διάνοια) of man is studiously bent upon evils from his youth" [39] and also the traditional Jewish interpretation of the verse "God formed man of the dust of the ground, and breathed upon his face a breath of life" [40] as meaning that God formed man with the two *yeṣarim*, the good and the evil.[41] Philo himself, in his direct comment on this last-quoted verse, expresses the same view in philosophic language by saying that the man whose creation is described in this verse, unlike the man whose creation is described in a previous verse,[42] is of a

[39] Gen. 8: 21 (LXX), quoted by Philo in *Heres* 59, 296. I take the Greek διάνοια in this verse to represent the Hebrew לב יצר just as the Greek διανοεῖται (Gen. 6: 5) and ἐνθύμημα (I Chron. 28: 9) and διάνοια (I Chron. 29: 18) represent the Hebrew מחשבות יצר. I do not think that Schleusner, in his *Lexicon in LXX*, and Hatch and Redpath, in their *Concordance of the Septuagint*, are right in taking the Hebrew יצר in this verse to be represented by the Greek verb ἔγκειται. In Deut. 31: 21, the Septuagint translates the Hebrew *yeṣer* by πονηρία, indicating that it has taken this term there in the sense of evil *yeṣer* (as the term is so also used in this specific sense in *M. Abot* IV, 1). In Sirach 15: 14, the Hebrew *yeṣer* is reflected in the Greek διαβούλιον.

Evidently it was as difficult to find an exact equivalent of *yeṣer* in Greek as it is in modern languages. Literally the term means "formation," whence "the formation of images or thoughts," "device," "design," "desire," "bent of mind," "inclination," "impulse." Of mediaeval Jewish authors, Saadia in his Arabic version of the Pentateuch translates *yeṣer* in Gen. 6: 5 and 8: 21 by *ḫāṭir*, probably in the sense of "imagination" (see my study on "The Internal Senses in Latin, Arabic, and Hebrew Philosophic Texts," *Harvard Theological Review*, 28 (1935), p. 106). As "imagination" (*fikr*, see again my study, *op. cit.*, pp. 91–92; *ḫāṭir*) it is also translated by Ibn Janaḥ in his Hebrew-Arabic Lexicon *Sefer ha-Shorashim*, *s.v.* Ibn Ezra in his Commentary on the Pentateuch (Gen. 8: 21) explains it by *toladah*, "nature," "inborn quality," "disposition." Ḳimḥi in his Hebrew Lexicon *Sefer ha-Shorashim*, *s.v.*, explains it by *ta'awah*, "desire," *ra'yon*, "thought," "imagination" (see my study as above, *op. cit.*, pp. 130–132).

On the *yeṣer* in general, see Strack and Billerbeck, "Exkurs: Der gute und böse Trieb," in their *Kommentar zum Neuen Testament aus Talmud und Midrash*, IV, pp. 466–483; Schechter, *Some Aspects of Rabbinic Theology*, pp. 242–292; Moore, *Judaism*, I, 479–486.

[40] Gen. 2: 7.

[41] *Genesis Rabbah* 14, 4.   [42] Gen. 1: 27.

double nature, consisting of an earthlike soul which is the
seat of desire and the other irrational emotions and a spiritual
soul which is the seat of reason acting as a restraint upon the
emotions.[43] So also in the Letter of Aristeas this same verse
is rephrased in philosophic language to read: "All men are
by nature intemperate and inclined to pleasure." [44] Men
are therefore urged by Philo, in the language of philosophy,
to follow reason and virtue and, in the language of Scripture, to obey the commandments of the Lord their God, and
as a reward for such a life of reason and virtue and obedience
of the commandments he promises, in the language of philosophy, happiness [45] and, in the language of Scripture, blessings.
In a special treatise he describes the "blessings" and
"curses," [46] or the rewards and punishments, which Scripture holds out to each according to his desert, "as affecting
individual men, families, cities, countries and nations, and
vast regions of the earth." [47]

But, like Scripture and philosophy, Philo was troubled
by the question of the suffering of the righteous and the
prosperity of the wicked. In his treatise on Providence, he
is asked by Alexander: "Are you alone ignorant that to
the worst and vilest of men good things in abundance
come crowding in, wealth, high repute, honors paid to
them by the masses, authority . . . while those who love
and practice wisdom and every kind of virtue are, I may
almost say, all of them poor, obscure, of little repute and in
humble position?" [48]

The answers given by Philo are like those common to

[43] *Spec.* IV, 24, 123; cf. *Opif.* 46, 134; *Leg. All.* I, 12, 31.
[44] Aristeas, 277; cf. 108, 222.   [46] *Praem.* 14, 79; 20, 126.
[45] Cf. above, pp. 165 ff.   [47] *Ibid.* 1, 7.
[48] *Provid.* 2, 1 (Eusebius, *Praeparatio Evangelica* VIII, 14, 386b; Aucher, II, 3).
With the treatment of the subject here, cf. P. Barth, "Die stoische Theodizee bei
Philo," *Philosophische Abhandlungen. Max Heinze . . . gewidmet*, 1906, 14–33.

philosophers and rabbis. In these answers he sometimes deals only with the suffering of the righteous and sometimes he deals only with the prosperity of the wicked, but in each case one may apply the same reasoning to the opposite case.

First, if some righteous men suffer, it is because they are not really perfect in their righteousness. "It does not follow," he says, "if certain persons are considered good by us, they are so in reality, for God judges by standards more accurate than any which the human mind employs." [49]

Second, the good which befalls the wicked is not the real good. "Mayest thou never be so led astray from the truth as to think that happiness is the lot of any of the wicked though he excel Croesus in wealth, Lynceus in keen sight, Milo of Crotona in muscular strength and Ganymede in beauty," [50] for when you have attained to a closer conception of the true and only good, you will laugh at those things which you have for some time admired,[51] for of these things "none ranks of itself in the sight of God as a good." [52] In these particular passages he speaks of real good as the good of the soul in this world, but elsewhere, as we know, he also speaks of the real good of the soul after death as well as the real evil of the soul after death.[53]

Third, the suffering of the righteous may come from God as a trial or test. Drawing upon the verses "and it shall come to pass, because ye hearken to these ordinances . . . the Lord will take away from thee all sickness," [54] he first says: "He promises that those who take pains to cultivate

---

[49] *Provid.* 2, 54 (Eusebius, *op. cit.*, 396b; Aucher, II, 102).
[50] *Ibid.* 2, 7 (Eusebius, *op. cit.*, 387a; Aucher, II, 16).
[51] *Ibid.* 2, 9 (Eusebius, *op. cit.*, 387c; Aucher, II, 17).
[52] *Ibid.* 2, 10 (Eusebius, *op. cit.*, 387d; Aucher, II, 22).
[53] Cf. above, I, 406 ff.
[54] Deut. 7: 12, 15.

virtue and set the laws before them . . . will receive as well
the gift of complete freedom from disease"; but then adds:
"And if some infirmity should befall them it will come not
to do them injury but to remind the mortal that he is mortal,
to humble his over-weening spirit and to improve his moral
condition." [55] The analogy of father and son which Scripture and Stoics use as an explanation for the seemingly
unmerited suffering of the righteous is used by Philo as an
explanation of the seemingly unmerited prosperity of the
wicked. "Just as parents do not lose thought of their
wastrel children . . . and often too they lavish their kindness on the wastrel more than on the well behaved . . . so
God also . . . takes thought even for those who live a mis-
spent life, thereby giving them time for reformation and
also keeping within the bounds of His merciful nature." [56]

Fourth, while in his discussion of divine providence Philo
does not mention the fact that the wicked are sometimes
dealt with kindly by God for the sake of the merit of their
ancestors, we know that in several places of his writings he
discusses this characteristically Jewish doctrine.[57]

In the course of his discussion of divine providence, Philo
also says that individuals may sometimes suffer undeservedly
because God's "care is for the whole human race" or "for
the whole world," [58] for "Providence or forethought is contented with paying regard to things in the world of the most
importance, just as in kingdoms and commands of army it
pays regard to the cities and troops, not to some chance individual of the obscure and insignificant kind." [59] Superficially this statement would seem to be nothing but a

[55] *Praem.* 20, 119.
[56] *Provid.* 2, 4–6 (Eusebius, *op. cit.*, 387a; Aucher, II, 15).
[57] Cf. above, I, 454 f., and below, p. 413.
[58] *Provid.* 2, 44 (Eusebius, *op. cit.*, 394c–d; Aucher, II, 99).
[59] *Ibid.* 2, 54 (Eusebius, *op. cit.*, 396b–c; Aucher, II, 102).

restatement of the Stoic doctrine quoted above that "the gods attend to great matters; they neglect the small ones." But Philo could not have meant by it the same as the Stoics. The Stoics meant by it to deny individual providence and to assert that what they call providence is merely the uniformity and unity and continuity and immutability of the universal laws of nature. Philo, however, did believe in individual providence. This is indirectly implied in his belief in miracles, which to him means that God may upset the universal laws of nature out of his care for certain favored individuals,[60] and it is directly expressed in his statement that God "guides and controls the universe by the law and right of an absolute sway, having a providential regard not only for those which are of greater importance, but also for those which appear to be of less importance." [61] Now, if as he says in this last-quoted statement that God's providential regard is not only for things which are "of greater importance" but also for things which are "of less importance," he certainly could not mean by his previously quoted statement what it would superficially seem to mean, namely, that God sometimes actually neglects the individual because of this primary concern "for the whole human race" or "for the whole world" or for things "of the most importance." What he really means by this previously quoted statement is this: Providence is both universal and individual. Universal providence means the operation of the laws of nature. Individual providence includes among other things, the miraculous suspension of the laws of nature by God for the benefit of some individual. Such a miraculous intervention on the part of God in the order of nature, however, takes place only in the case of individuals who are especially deserving of it. If they are not deserving of it, the

[60] Cf. above, I, 347 ff.   [61] *Migr.* 33, 186.

laws of nature are left undisturbed. It is in this sense that Philo says in the previously quoted statement, that individuals who are not deserving of a miraculous intervention on the part of God in their behalf may sometimes suffer undeservedly by the operations of the laws of nature, inasmuch as in their case God's direct care is "for the whole human race" or "for the whole world" or for things "of the most importance." Philo's belief in individual providence, but his belief also that divine providence acts in accordance with justice and in accordance with the deserts of man, is clearly brought out in the following statement: "It is not possible with God that a wicked man should lose his good reward for a single good thing which he may have done among a great number of evil actions; nor, on the other hand, that a good man should escape punishment, and not suffer it, if among many good actions he has done wickedly in anything." [62] This reflects a view similar to that expressed by rabbis in such statements as "the Holy One, blessed be He, does not withhold the reward of any creature" [63] and "he who says that the Holy One, blessed be He, overlooks any sins of man ought to forfeit his right to the protection of his life by law." [64]

Like the philosophers, Philo also urges men to practice virtue for its own sake. "For," he says, "prudence is itself the reward (ἆθλον) of prudence, and justice and each of the other virtues is its own recompense (γέρας)." [65] The expression of the principle of virtue for its own sake in terms of its being its own "recompense" or "reward" does not

[62] *Fragmenta*, Richter, VI, 203 (M. II, 649).
[63] *Pesaḥim* 118a.
[64] *Baba Ḳamma* 50a. Cf. Sirach 5: 6: "And say not, 'His mercies are great, He will forgive the multitude of mine iniquities,' for mercy and wrath are with him, and His indignation abideth upon the ungodly."
[65] *Spec.* II, 47, 259.

occur in Stoic literature, in so far as it has been preserved, until after the time of Philo,[66] and one may speculate on the question whether Philo's use of the terms "recompense" and "reward" represents an original Stoic version of the principle, or whether it reflects some other source. In the rabbinic equivalent of this principle, formulated long before Philo, the term used, as we have seen above, is "recompense" or "reward."[67] This principle Philo finds implied in the verse "and the people shall go out and gather a day's portion for a day, that I may prove them, whether they will walk in My law, or not."[68] Commenting upon this verse, he says, "the man of worthy aims sets himself to acquire day for the sake of the day, light for the sake of light, the beautiful for the sake of the beautiful alone, not for the sake of something else," and concludes: "this is the divine law, to value virtue for its own sake."[69] The phrase "virtue for its own sake" is, of course, Stoic, but whereas among the Stoics and in Greek philosophy in general, as we have seen, it means an admission that the practice of virtue may not be rewarded, in Philo, as in Judaism, it means that the worship of God

---

[66] Heinemann in *Philos Werke* (II, p. 181, n. 3) quotes Epictetus, III, 24, 51, who uses the term ἔπαθλον, and Colson (VII, 630, § 259) quotes Servius (Arnim, III, 45), who uses the term *praemia*. Cf. also Seneca's use of the terms *merces* and *commodum* in *De Beneficiis* IV, 25, 3.

[67] Cf. *M. Abot* I, 3 (quoted above, p. 286) where the Hebrew term used is *peras*. Cf. also *M. Abot* IV, 2: "For the recompense (*sekar*) of the performance of a commandment is the performance of another commandment." Antigonus of Soko, the author of the maxim in *M. Abot* I, 3, flourished in the third or the second century B.C. No dependence of the rabbis upon the Stoics is to be assumed in such pious utterances as the one under consideration on the mere basis of similarity. Cf. Bergmann, "Die stoische Philosophie und die jüdische Frömmigkeit," *Judaica: Festschrift zu Hermann Cohens siebzigstem Geburtstage*, pp. 145–166, especially p. 161, n. 1, on the maxim under consideration, and p. 165, general conclusion. Cf. also Julius Guttmann, *Die Philosophie des Judentums*, pp. 50–51; A. Kaminka, "Ha-Musar she-be-Sifre Seneca ve-ha-Musar ha-Yehudi," *Moznayim*, 4 (1935), pp. 46–51; Weiss, *Dor Dor we-Dorshaw*, II⁴, p. 27.

[68] Exod. 16 : 4.   [69] *Leg. All.* III, 57, 167.

out of love will bring the highest reward. That this is what Philo means by his restatement of the philosophic principle of virtue for its own sake may be gathered from several places in his writings. In one place he says: "These virtues are said to be chosen for their own sake, but they will assume a grander and loftier aspect if practiced for the sake of honoring and pleasing God." [70] What he quite evidently means is that these virtues, which are urged by philosophers to be chosen for their own sake, will assume a grander and loftier aspect if, as recommended in Judaism, they are practiced for the sake of honoring and pleasing God, that is, for the love of God. In another place, speaking of piety, that is, the worship of God, which to him is one of the virtues,[71] he expresses himself in terms like those used by the rabbis, contrasting the worship of God from fear with the worship of Him from love. "For I observe," he says, "that all the exhortations to piety through the laws refer either to our loving or our fearing the Existent," concluding that while to fear God is quite suitable for some people, to love God implies a higher conception of the nature of God and marks a higher form of the worship of God.[72] A reference to these two modes of worshiping God is to be found also in his contrast between the "lovers (φίλοι) of God," such as Moses, and those who are only "servants (δοῦλοι) of God." [73] In still another place he says that with regard to the worship of God, "there are three classes of human temperaments," [74] and to these three classes of worshipers he makes God address himself as follows: "My first rewards will be set apart for (1) those who worship Me for myself

[70] *Congr.* 14, 80.
[71] Cf. above, pp. 212 ff.
[72] *Immut.* 14, 69; cf. Moore, *Judaism*, II, 99, n. 2.
[73] *Migr.* 9, 45.
[74] *Abr.* 25, 124.

alone, the second for those who worship Me for their own sakes, either (2) hoping to win blessings or (3) expecting to obtain remission of punishments."[75] These three classes, it is quite obvious, refer respectively (1) to those who worship God from love, (2) to those who worship Him in expectation of a reward, and (3) to those who worship Him from fear. Among the rabbis, as we have seen, to worship God from love is contrasted, on the one hand, with worshiping Him in expectation of a reward and, on the other hand, with worshiping Him from fear.[76]

Despite, then, his urging that man should practice virtue for its own sake, Philo believes that the practice of virtue is to be rewarded by a good that is a real good, and that real good is what philosophers call happiness and what Scripture calls blessings. This identification of the real good or happiness with the scriptural blessings has led Philo to throw himself into the philosophic controversy as to what "goods" are and to allow himself to be guided in this question by the scriptural description of what the "blessings" are.

Both Plato and Aristotle divide goods ($\tau \grave{a}$ $\mathring{a} \gamma a \theta \acute{a}$) into three classes, (1) those which they both describe as the goods of the soul, (2) those which they also both describe as the goods of the body, and (3) those which Aristotle describes as external goods.[77] Under the first they put the moral and intellectual virtues, under the second they put health and beauty[78] and similar bodily qualities, and under the third they put what Plato describes as "the so-called

[75] *Ibid.*, 128.
[76] Cf. above, pp. 287 f.
[77] *Laws* III, 697 B; V, 728 E; V, 743 E; cf. I, 631 C; *Philebus* 48 E; *Euthydemus* 279 A–C; *Eth. Nic.* I, 8, 1098b, 12–16; Sextus, *Adversus Ethicos*, 45.
[78] The term "beauty" ($\kappa \acute{a} \lambda \lambda o s$) occurs in *Eth. Nic.* I, 8, 1099b, 3, and in *Rhet.* I, 5, 1360b, 22.

goods of substance (οὐσία) and property (χρήματα)" [79] or
"the possession of property (χρήματα) and chattels (κτή-
ματα)" [80] or wealth (πλοῦτος)[81] or "good birth (εὐγένεια) and
talents (δυνάμεις) and distinctions (τιμαί) in one's own country," [82] and what Aristotle describes as friends (φίλοι),
riches (πλοῦτος), political power (πολιτικὴ δύναμις), good
birth (εὐγένεια), and goodly children (εὐτεκνίαι).[83] In the
Stoic literature, summarizing the views of Plato and Aristotle, under goods of the body are placed "health (ὑγίεια) and
well-being (εὐεξία) and keenness of sense (εὐαισθησία) and
beauty (κάλλος) and everything which is of a similar character," and under external goods are placed "wealth (πλοῦ-
τον), country (πατρίδα), parents (γονεῖς), children (τέκνα),
friends (φίλους), and the like." [84] Both Plato and Aristotle
admit that only the goods of the soul are real goods,[85] but
differ in their statements as to the relation of the bodily and
external goods to the goods of the soul. Plato expresses his
view in the statement that "the human goods (i.e., the
bodily and external goods) are dependent on the divine
(i.e., on the goods of the soul) and he who receives the
greater acquires also the less or else he is bereft of both." [86]
But how bodily and external goods are acquired by one who
possesses the goods of the soul he does not say. Evidently
what he means is that in the long run moral conduct leads
to health and wealth and that without moral conduct
health and wealth will not be permanent. Aristotle expresses
his view in the statement that "happiness also requires external goods in addition, as we said, for it is impossible, or
at least not easy, to play a noble part unless furnished with

[79] *Laws* III, 697 B.
[80] *Ibid.* V, 728 E.
[81] *Ibid.* I, 631 C.
[85] Cf. above, pp. 165 f.
[86] *Laws* I, 631 B. Cf. *Apology* 30 A–B.

[82] *Euthydemus* 279 B.
[83] *Eth. Nic.* I, 8, 1099b, 1–3.
[84] Sextus, *Adversus Ethicos*, 45.

the necessary equipment." [87] Among the Stoics, however, with the exception of Posidonius who retained the Platonic and Aristotelian classification of the goods,[88] some excluded both bodily and external goods from their classification [89] and others excluded only bodily goods.[90] Those things which are excluded by them from their classifications of the goods are described by them as being neither good nor evil (οὐδέτερα)[91] or as being indifferent (ἀδιάφορα),[92] but still they admit that they may contribute to happiness, describing them, therefore, as preferred (προηγμένα).[93]

Now Philo approaches the classification of the goods with certain prepossessions derived from the Law of Moses. In the books of this Law, all those things which in Greek philosophy are described as bodily and external goods, such as health, wealth, and children, are described as blessings which God will grant to those who walk in His commandments.[94] These blessings are described as God's "good treasure" [95] and as "good." [96] Accordingly Philo was bound to reject the Stoic exclusion of bodily and external goods from the classification of goods. He was furthermore bound to accept the Platonic formula that the bodily and external goods depend upon the goods of the soul, but more explicitly than Plato he could say that these bodily and external goods are sure to be given by God as a reward for the observance of the Law. In the light of these remarks, let us see how Philo treats of the classification of the goods.

---

[87] *Eth. Nic.* I, 8, 1099a, 31–33.
[88] Diogenes, VII, 103.
[89] *Ibid.*, 101–102.
[90] Sextus, *Adversus Ethicos*, 46.
[91] Diogenes, VII, 101.
[92] *Ibid.*, 102–104; cf. Sextus, *Adversus Ethicos*, 5 ff.
[93] Diogenes, VII, 105–106; Sextus, *Adversus Ethicos*, 62–63.
[94] Deut. 28: 1 ff.; Lev. 26: 3 ff.
[95] Deut. 28: 12.   [96] Deut. 30: 15.

To begin with, in opposition to the Stoics, with the exception of Posidonius, he follows the Platonic and Aristotelian
classification of the goods. He invariably speaks of three
classes of goods, and describes them as those which pertain
to the soul, as those which pertain to the body, and as those
which are external.[97] Drawing directly upon the writings of
Plato and Aristotle, as well as upon the Stoic restatements of
their views, he describes the goods of the souls as consisting
of the moral and intellectual virtues, of the goods of the
body as consisting of health ($\dot{v}\gamma\dot{\iota}\epsilon\iota a$), keenness of sense
($\epsilon\dot{v}a\iota\sigma\theta\eta\sigma\dot{\iota}a$), power ($\delta\dot{v}\nu a\mu\iota s$), and strength ($\dot{\rho}\dot{\omega}\mu\eta$), and of external goods as consisting of wealth ($\pi\lambda o\hat{v}\tau os$), reputation
($\delta\dot{o}\xi a$), the enjoyment and use of necessary pleasures,[98] and
nobility of birth ($\epsilon\dot{v}\gamma\dot{\epsilon}\nu\epsilon\iota a$).[99] Sometimes he describes the
goods of the body as the virtues of the body, and external
goods· as external advantages ($\dot{\epsilon}\kappa\tau\dot{o}s$ $\pi\lambda\epsilon o\nu\epsilon\kappa\tau\dot{\eta}\mu a\tau a$).[100] The
terms "virtue of the body" and "advantages" are both used
by Aristotle.[101] Like Plato and Aristotle he maintains that
bodily and external goods are not true goods, asserting that
"the true good cannot find its home in anything external,
nor yet in things of the body." [102] In one place, he says that
"it is well to pray on the behalf of him who holds bodily and
external advantages to be goods," [103] by which he evidently
refers not to those who classify bodily and external advantages as goods, which he himself, as we have seen, has
done, but rather to those who classify these as real goods
or the main goods. Still almost in the words of Aristotle he

---

[97] *Deter.* 3, 7; *Sobr.* 12, 61; *Virt.* 35, 187; *Qu. in Gen.* III, 16.
[98] *Sobr.* 12, 61.
[99] *Virt.* 35, 187.
[100] *Sobr.* 12, 61.
[101] *Rhet.* I, 5, 1361b, 3 ($\sigma\dot{\omega}\mu a\tau os$ $\dot{a}\rho\epsilon\tau\dot{\eta}$); *Politica* V, 10, 1311a, 5 ($\pi\lambda\epsilon o\nu\epsilon\kappa\tau\dot{\eta}\mu a\tau a$).
[102] *Virt.* 35, 187; cf. *Deter.* 4, 9.
[103] *Sobr.* 13, 67.

admits that of these three kinds of goods "each is in need of each and all of all, and that the aggregate resulting from taking them all together in a body is a perfect and really complete good," [104] or that "happiness is not peculiarly to be sought for either in the external things, or in the things of the body, or in the things of the soul, taken by themselves ... but it must be looked for in the combination of them all together." [105]

Then, evidently following Plato's formula that bodily and external goods are dependent upon the goods of the soul, he explains in accordance with that formula the blessings for right conduct promised in Scripture.[106] He formally divides these blessings into "blessings of the body" and "external blessings." [107] Under the former he puts "freedom from disease," "health," and "keenness of sense," adding that if some injury should befall the righteous it would be only by way of trial and warning and chastisement.[108] Under the latter he puts riches ($\pi\lambda o\hat{v}\tau o\iota$), honors ($\tau\iota\mu ai$), offices ($\dot{a}\rho\chi ai$) and praises [109] ($\dot{\epsilon}\gamma\kappa\dot{\omega}\mu\iota a$), and goodly children ($\epsilon\ddot{v}\pi a\iota\delta a$).[110] Besides these bodily and external blessings, both of which were promised to the individuals as individuals, he finds in Scripture also three other kinds of promises.

First, there is the promise of a bodily as well as a spiritual good here on earth to the Jewish people as a whole and with it to all mankind. For the Jewish people it is the promise of an ultimate national restoration, which is known as the Messianic ideal. Drawing upon the verse "Though thy dispersion may have been from one end of the earth to the other, thence the Lord thy God will gather thee," [111] he says:

104 *Deter.* 3, 7.
105 *Ibid.* 3, 8.
106 *Praem.* 1, 2; 1, 7; 4, 22.
107 *Ibid.* 20, 118.
108 *Ibid.* 20, 119.
109 *Ibid.* 20, 118.
110 *Ibid.* 18, 110.
111 Deut. 30: 4.

"For even though they dwell in the uttermost parts of the earth, in slavery to those who led them away captive, one signal, as it were, one day will bring liberty to all." [112] With this ultimate liberation of Israel there will furthermore come an age when all mankind will be united by the Law of Moses which is described by him as being based upon democracy and equality by which the whole world will be united as a single city.[113]

Second, there is the promise of a purely spiritual good here on earth to the individuals, for as a result of obedience to the Law God will favor them with that divine grace by which he helps those who try of their own free will to do good.[114] Drawing again upon the verse "Though thy dispersion may have been from one end of the earth to the other, thence the Lord thy God will gather thee," he interprets it allegorically as follows: "And therefore those who would imitate these examples of good living so marvelous in their loveliness, are bidden not to despair of changing for the better or of a restoration to the land of wisdom and virtue from the spiritual dispersion which vice has wrought. For when God is gracious He makes all things light and easy, and He does become gracious to those who depart with shame from incontinence to self-restraint and deplore the deeds of their guilty past, abhor the base sensitive images which they imprinted on their souls and first earnestly strive to still the storm of the passions, then seek to lead a life of serenity and peace." [115]

Finally, there is the promise of a purely spiritual good, not here on earth, but in heaven, and that is the promise of immortality as a reward of good conduct. We have already shown how in common with the Jewish tradition of his time

[112] *Praem.* 28, 164.
[113] Cf. below, pp. 425 f.
[114] Cf. above, I, 445 ff.
[115] *Praem.* 19, 115–116.

he sought and also found scriptural evidence for the belief in the immortality of the soul and how immortality was conceived by him as a reward for righteous conduct during lifetime.[116]

VII. Conclusion, Influence, Anticipation

In common with all philosophers Philo formulates the problem of ethics as a search for the good, identifying the good with happiness and defining happiness as an activity according to virtue, both intellectual and moral. With the philosophers, too, he agrees that intellectual virtue owes its birth and growth to teaching, and moral virtue comes about as a result of habit and that the inculcation of intellectual and moral virtues is the duty of the state, the former by education and the latter by laws, which are called practical virtues. But as to what should constitute the object of education which is to inculcate intellectual virtues and what should be the laws which are to train one in moral virtues Philo differs from the philosophers. To the philosophers the object of the teaching should be those doctrines which philosophers attained by reason, and the practical virtues should be those laws which philosophers similarly worked out by reason and in accordance with virtue. These rational and virtuous laws of the philosophers, being as they are enacted by men, are not what the philosophers themselves call natural laws in the true sense of the term, for by natural laws are meant laws spontaneously arrived at by all mankind by virtue of some common instinct that is inherent in them and they are therefore universal and eternal and immutable. Still these laws, though not natural in the primary sense of the term, are described by the philosopher as being in accordance with nature in a secondary sense, in the sense

[116] Cf. above, I, 396–398, 408–410.

that they are in harmony with certain human impulses or capacities or are calculated to attain certain gifts of nature.

To Philo, however, the intellectual and practical virtues consist respectively of those doctrines and laws which were revealed by God through Moses. These laws of Moses, like the laws of the philosophers, are to be sure enacted laws and not natural laws, but, being enacted by God who is the creator of nature, they are, more than the laws of the philosophers, in accordance with nature, not only in the sense that they are in harmony with human impulses or capacities or that they are best fitted to the attainment of the gifts of nature, but also in the sense of their being universal, eternal, and immutable. With Philo, therefore, the philosophic maxims that happiness is life in accordance with virtue or in accordance with reason or in accordance with nature come to mean life in accordance with the Law. All the philosophic maxims about man's duty to follow God or to imitate God or to be like God come to mean with him that man must act in accordance with the Law. All the philosophic discussions as to whether virtue come to man by learning or habit or nature or divine dispensation comes to mean with him that virtue comes to man by God through nature as a divine grace, or through learning the truths taught in the book of His Law and through training in the performance of the precepts of this Law.

The Law of Moses, therefore, contains a system of law given by revelation which accomplishes all that the philosophers aim to attain by those ideal systems of law which they try to devise by reason. The laws of Moses are therefore what the philosophers call virtues. Being virtues, these Mosaic laws, besides their traditional classification into positive and negative, into ten main headings corresponding to the ten commandments, and into those relating to

God and those relating to men, are also to be divided in accordance with the philosophic classification of the virtues.

Various classifications of the virtues are attempted by Philo, but the classification which he adopts is that of (a) contemplative virtues, by which he means (1) the possession of certain intellectual virtues in the form of beliefs, and (2) the possession of certain moral virtues in the form of good emotions, and (b) practical virtues, by which he means (3) actions corresponding to intellectual virtues and (4) actions corresponding to moral virtues. Accordingly the Law of Moses is held by him to contain these four kinds of virtues, which may be briefly stated as (1) beliefs, (2) virtuous emotions, (3) actions symbolizing beliefs, and (4) actions symbolizing moral virtues.

While the philosophic discussion of virtue has furnished Philo, on the one hand, with a framework for the classification of the commandments, his identification of the commandments with virtues has caused him, on the other hand, to introduce certain innovations into the theory of virtue.

First, under the influence of Judaism he introduces new virtues. "Faith" is added by him as a virtue under intellectual virtues, and "humanity" is added under moral virtues. Under the influence of Judaism, too, he makes "faith" and "piety" and "holiness," and probably also "godliness," leaders among intellectual virtues, and "justice" and "humanity" leaders among moral virtues. Again, under the influence of Judaism, the term faith assumes with him two special meanings: (1) belief in the existence, unity, and incorporeality of God as well as belief in His providence; (2) assent to the truth of Scripture in contradistinction to assent to truths discovered by reason; (3) trust in God. Then also, to the list of practical virtues, under the influence of Judaism, he adds the virtues of prayer, study, and repentance. Moreover, under the influence of Judaism, he considers the emotion of desire as a voluntary emotion and adopts parts of both the Aristotelian and the Stoic definitions of virtue. Finally, in his discussion of the question of the reward of virtue, under the influence of Judaism, he departs from the philosophers in his assertion of individual providence, in his certainty of reward and punishment, and in his classification of the goods.

The essential point in Philo's theory of ethics is the view that the Mosaic Law is a law unique in its kind, unlike any other law. The laws known to Philo were of a threefold kind. There were natural laws, which consisted of common conceptions of right and wrong universal to all men. These were described as general laws. Then there were enacted laws, which consisted of laws enacted by unscientific legislators for the guidance of particular groups of peoples. These laws were not always based upon reason; they were sometimes contrary to nature and not always in accordance with virtue. Finally there were ideal laws enacted by philosophers or scientific legislators which were supposed to be in accordance with reason and nature and virtue. The Mosaic Law, according to Philo, is unlike any of these three kinds of law in its origin, for unlike any of them it is not man-made, being neither the work of human impulse nor of human reason. It is a law revealed by God. In its content, however, it accomplishes what all philosophers aimed to accomplish by their ideal laws. It is in accordance with reason and nature and virtue. Every law in it is a philosophic virtue, every law in it has a rational purpose, every law in it is in accordance with the nature of man and the nature of the world.

From now on in the history of philosophy, whether Jewish, Christian, or Moslem, there will be a conception of a revealed law which is to establish successfully what philosophers aimed to establish by their ideal laws and failed. In Jewish philosophy this claim will continue to be made, as in Philo, on behalf of the Mosaic Law; in Christianity it will be made on behalf of the Mosaic Law as well as on behalf of the teachings of the Gospels; in Islam it will be made on behalf of the Koran. In all of them attempts will be made to identify their respective scriptural doctrines and commandments with philosophic virtues; in all of them attempts will therefore be also made to find reasons for doctrines and commandments. Certain departures from Philo will indeed appear. New classifications of virtues will be made; new rational explanations will be offered. The most radical departure will appear in the rise of the view that not all the revealed laws are laws of reason or of virtue or in accordance with nature; that some of them are of a statutory nature, for which either there is no reason or no reason can be discovered by the human mind.

Directly connected with Philo is the treatment of the Mosaic Law among the Church Fathers, though an additional source for their method of treatment is St. Paul's statement, which in itself reflects Jewish tradition, that "the gentiles, which have not the law, do by nature the things contained in the law," [1] the implication of which is that the revealed Law of Moses contains laws which are in accordance with nature and are known by reason.

Clement of Alexandria, evidently having in mind such passages in Philo as that in which "all His commandments and ordinances and judgments which are written in the book of this Law" [2] are identified with "the laws and statutes of nature," [3] says that "both the law of nature and the law of instruction (i.e., revelation) are one," inasmuch

[1] Rom. 2: 14.   [2] Deut. 30: 10.
[3] *Somn.* II, 26, 174–175; cf. above, p. 193.

as both are of God.[4] Like Philo, too, he identifies the commandments with what philosophers call virtues. Dividing the commandments into four groups, (1) historic, (2) legislative, (3) those which relate to sacrifice, and (4) those which relate to theology, he describes the first two divisions as those "which properly belong to an ethical treatise" and the fourth as that which "Aristotle calls metaphysics," [5] and declares in general that "the Mosaic Law is the foundation of all ethics, and the source of which the Greeks drew theirs." [6] In his description of that class of laws which relate to sacrifice he says that it "belongs to physical speculation." [7] By this he means that these are laws which have an allegorical [8] meaning besides their obvious meaning, without necessarily implying that they were never meant to be observed literally, at least before their abrogation at the advent of Christianity. In this, too, he follows Philo.[9]

Reflecting the same view of Philo that the revealed Law of Moses is identical with the law of nature and is to be contrasted with all other systems of law which are the work of men, Origen contrasts the Law of Moses with all other laws as "the law of nature" with "the written laws of cities," [10] describing the former as the law "of which God would be the legislator," as "the law of God" and as "the laws in harmony with the will of God," [11] and affirming concerning it that "the first who created these laws and delivered them

---

[4] *Stromata* I, 29 (PG, 8, 929 A).

[5] *Ibid.* I, 28 (PG, 8, 921 C–924 A). Aristotle does not call it metaphysics.

[6] *Ibid.* II, 18.

[7] *Ibid.* I, 28 (PG, 8, 924 A).

[8] The term physical (φυσική) is used here in the Stoic sense of a special kind of allegorical interpretation, as distinguished from ethical interpretation, in which sense the term is often used also by Philo, as, e.g., *Leg. All.* I, 13, 39. Cf. Leisegang's note on *Post.* 2, 7, in *Philos Werke*, IV, p. 6, n. 2.

[9] Cf. above, I, 127–131.

[10] *Contra Celsum* V, 37.   [11] *Ibid.*

to Moses was God who was the creator of the world."[12]
Consequently he declares that when various Greek writings
are compared with the laws of Moses, "histories for histories
and ethical discourses with laws and commandments," the
latter "are better fitted to change the character of the
hearers on the very spot."[13] Unlike Philo, however, he
maintains that many laws are irrational and were not
meant to be taken literally.[14]

From the Church Fathers these speculations about the
distinction between a revealed law, on the one hand, and a
natural or rational or legislated law, on the other, and also
the view that the revealed law is either in whole or in part
a law in accordance with nature or in accordance with reason,
had drifted also into Arabic philosophy, both Moslem and
Jewish. Among the Moslems, with reference to the Koran,
and among the Jews, with reference to the Pentateuch, the
view was maintained that the laws within them were in accordance with reason, though the question was debated
whether any of the laws were not in accordance with reason.[15]
Moreover analogous to Philo's interpretation of the scriptural
term "heart" as dealing with commandments which are not
concerned with actions or words is the distinction which appears both in Jewish and Moslem philosophy between duties
of the heart and duties of the body.[16]

The continuity of this Philonic method of dealing with the
Mosaic law may be illustrated by its treatment in Maimon-

[12] *Ibid.* I, 18.   [13] *Ibid.*
[14] *De Principiis* IV, 1, 17.
[15] In Islam, the discussion of this problem is between the Mutazilites and the
Ikhwān al-Safā; among the Jews the discussion is between the author of the *Kitāb
Ma'āni al-Nafs* and Maimonides, on the one hand, and Saadia, for instance, on the
other. Cf. I. Goldziher, *Kitāb Ma'āni al-Nafs, Vorwort*, pp. 22–23.
[16] Cf. Bahya's *Ḥobot ha-Lebabot, Hakdamah*; for Moslem parallels, see A. S.
Yahuda, *Al-Hidāja 'ilā Farā'id al-Qulūb des Bachja ibn Josef ibn Paqūda, Ein-
leitung*, pp. 59–60. Cf. above, p. 267.

ides and St. Thomas, though neither of these authors was directly influenced by Philo.

Maimonides does not use the term natural law in its primary Aristotelian sense of general laws arrived at by all men instinctively by their innate sense of justice.[17] He uses it rather in its secondary sense of laws enacted by wise legislators on the basis of reason — a sense in which, as we have shown, it is used by Aristotle as well as by other Greek philosophers.[18] In his discussion of the revealed law of Moses in its relation to natural law, Maimonides starts with the Aristotelian observation that "man is by nature a political animal, and therefore, men, even when they do not require one another's help, desire to live together," [19] which he paraphrases in the statement "that man is by nature a political animal and that by virtue of his nature he desires to live together with other people." [20] To this observation he adds also the observation that "by its nature the human species shows a greater variation among its individuals than any other species." [21] From these two observations he infers that by nature men require a leader able to "prescribe actions and morals which all would practice always according to the same rule so that the natural diversity would disappear by the great conventional agreement and society would become well ordered." [22] Beneficial laws enacted by wise legislators for the purpose of establishing and maintaining a well-ordered society are thus according to Maimonides to be described as natural laws, on the ground that they ultimately rest upon the fact that men by nature differ from one another and by nature also desire to live in harmony with one another. Now since the laws of

[17] Cf. above, pp. 173 f.
[18] Cf. above, pp. 176, 178 f.
[19] *Politica* III, 6, 1278b, 19–21.
[20] *Moreh Nebukim* II, 40.
[21] *Ibid.*
[22] *Ibid.*

Moses are not human enactments dictated by the natural differences among men and by their natural desire for harmonious living together, they cannot, in respect to their origin, be described as natural laws; they are, strictly speaking, revealed laws. But inasmuch as the purpose of the revealed laws of Moses is like that of the natural laws enacted by wise legislators, namely, to establish and maintain a well-ordered society, they can, in respect to their purpose, be described as being in accordance with nature. "I therefore maintain," says Maimonides, "that the Law, though not natural, is still in accordance with nature." [23] Being in accordance with nature, the laws of Moses are in their entirety what Aristotle would describe as being in accordance with reason. And consequently, in describing the Law as being in accordance with nature and in accordance with reason, Maimonides, just like Philo, makes no distinction between the various ordinances contained therein. All of them are in accordance with nature and reason. All of them, therefore, had they not been revealed, would have been discovered by men themselves, by virtue of the special nature and the special reason which they possess, and now that these laws have been revealed the human mind can discern the reason and purpose of their revelation. There are, however, certain laws which Maimonides admits would not have been discovered by man himself had they not been revealed. Such are the laws which are described in the Pentateuch as statutes (*ḥuḳḳim*).[24] But even in the case of these laws, while they would not have been discovered by mere reason, and the reason for their revelation is not evident to the human mind, there are still good reasons for their existence, reasons which are unknown to us. Even these laws then are in accordance with reason and in accordance with nature.

[23] *Ibid.*   [24] *Ibid.* III, 26 and 31; *Shemonah Perakim*, 6.

With this conception of the laws as being in accordance
with nature and in accordance with reason, Maimonides
describes them also as being in accordance with virtue. The
commandments are thus identified by him with virtues and
are classified in accordance with the classification of the virtues. Several classifications of the commandments are
openly discussed by Maimonides. Of course, he divides them
according to their external form of expression, into the
traditional positive and negative.[25] He divides them according to their contents into those between men and God
and those between men and men,[26] and also into fourteen
classes.[27] More general and more characteristic, however,
is his division of the laws into four classes, namely, (1) those
dealing with principles of belief, (2) those dealing with actions, (3) those dealing with states of moral character, and
(4) those dealing with speech [28] — a classification analogous to that we have found in Philo.[29] But underlying these
fourteenfold and fourfold classifications is the classification
of the laws, as in Philo, in accordance with the classification
of the philosophic virtues. These virtues are divided by
Maimonides into (1) intellectual, (2) moral, and (3) practical,
and consequently all the laws either teach directly (1) intellectual virtues or (2) moral virtues, or else they are (3)
practical virtues, that is, actions, which are intended to
train man in intellectual or moral virtues.[30]

St. Thomas' treatment of the old problem of the relation
of the laws of Moses to laws of nature or reason was determined by his special attitude as a Christian toward those

[25] As for example in his *Sefer ha-Miṣwot*, and *Moreh Nebukim* III, 36.
[26] *Moreh Nebukim* III, 36.
[27] *Moreh Nebukim* III, 35, with which the same fourteenfold division of the laws
in the *Mishneh Torah* is to be compared.
[28] *Sefer hd-Miṣwot*, *Shoresh* 9.
[29] Cf. above, pp. 208, 218, 266–267.   [30] *Moreh Nebukim* III, 27.

laws. On the one hand, he believed that these laws were divinely revealed and hence they had to be perfect, universal and eternal, but on the other hand he believed that they were abrogated with the advent of Jesus and that even before their abrogation they were obligatory only upon the Jews. Consequently he could neither declare, like Philo or Maimonides, that all the laws were in accordance with nature, nor could he declare that none of them was in accordance with nature. To get out of this difficulty he had drawn a distinction between various kinds of law, some of them being in accordance with nature and others not in accordance with nature. The drawing of such a distinction was made possible by him by his adoption of the use of the term natural law in its strict Aristotelian sense.

Unlike Maimonides, therefore, St. Thomas uses the term natural law as it is directly used by Aristotle, in the sense of self-evident principles of ethics which man by his very nature as a rational and social being would arrive at without any act of agreement or convention.[31] "The principles of the natural law," he says, "are to the practical reason what the first principles of demonstrations are to the speculative reason; because both are self-evident principles."[32] How man arrives at these principles of natural law is explained by him in his statement that "there is in man an inclination to good, according to the nature of his reason, which nature is proper to him: thus man has a natural inclination to know the truth about God, and to live in society."[33] This reflects Aristotle's statements that "all men by nature desire to know"[34] and that "men are by nature political animals and, therefore, even when they do not require one another's

---

[31] Cf. above, pp. 173 f.
[32] *Sum. Theol.* I, II, 94, 2 c.
[33] *Ibid.*   [34] *Metaph.* I, 1, 980a, 21.

help, desire to live together." [35] But as in Philo, this nature in man was implanted by God and is in itself divine. [36] Then, like Aristotle, he distinguishes such natural laws from laws which came about by agreement and convention, the latter of which he calls human law, that is, laws "framed by men." [37] But though, unlike Maimonides, he does not include human law under natural law, still he admits that human law, if it is just, is derived from the law of nature, either as a conclusion from premises or by way of determination of certain generalities. [38] The latter kind of human law is likened by him to that "whereby, in the arts, general forms are particularized as to details," [39] thus reflecting Aristotle's distinction between natural law and conventional law as a distinction between general law and particular law. [40] Finally, besides natural law and human law, there is also a divine law, of which there is an old and a new, the Law of Moses and the Gospel. [41]

Now with regard to the Old Law, which is our present subject of study, St. Thomas suggests several classifications. Like Philo and Maimonides, he divides it into positive (*affirmativa*) and negative (*negativa*) [42] and also into laws which direct "men to God" and laws which direct "men to one another." [43] But then he divides them into three classes, moral, ceremonial, and judicial,[44] a classification which is implied in Philo and Maimonides and in all those who have attempted to classify the precepts of the Pentateuch. Under the moral precepts he includes the precepts "Thou shalt love the Lord thy God"[45] and "Thou shalt love thy neighbor,"[46]

[35] *Politica* III, 6, 1278b, 19–21.
[36] *Sum. Theol.* I, II, 91, 2 c and 4 Obj. 1.
[37] *Ibid.*, 95, 1.
[38] *Ibid.*, 2 c.
[39] *Ibid.*
[40] *Rhet.* I, 13, 1373b, 4–6; cf. above, p. 174.
[41] *Sum. Theol.* I, II, 91, 4–5.
[42] *Ibid.*, 100, 4, Obj. 2.
[43] *Ibid.*, 99, 3 c.
[44] *Ibid.*, 2–4; 5 c.
[45] Deut. 6: 5; 11: 1.
[46] Lev. 19: 18.

the ten commandments, and a number of special laws which "are reducible to the precepts of the ten commandments, as so many corollaries." [47] Unlike Philo and Maimonides and all Jewish philosophers who considered all the laws of Moses as eternal, St. Thomas, as a Christian, considers only the moral laws universal and eternal, whereas the ceremonial laws and judicial laws were meant to be binding only upon Jews and were abrogated with the advent of Jesus. In his own restricted use of the term natural law as applying only to self-evident general principles of morality he finds an explanation for his distinction within the laws of Moses, despite their all being divine revelations. The moral precepts are precepts of natural law and hence they were revealed by God to all men and for eternity; [48] the ceremonial and judicial precepts are not precepts of natural law and hence they were revealed only for a particular and temporary purpose. [49] His use of the term "moral precepts" as a description of those laws in the Pentateuch which are natural reflects Aristotle's indirect use of the term "moral" as the equivalent of the term "natural." [50]

Still, despite his use of the term natural laws exclusively as an application to the moral laws of the Pentateuch, St. Thomas describes not only its moral laws but also its judicial laws and ceremonial laws as being in accordance with virtue and hence in accordance with reason. Of the moral laws in the Pentateuch he repeatedly says that they are "about acts of virtue" [51] or "about acts of all the virtues" [52] and that "they accord with reason." [53] Similarly of the judicial

---

[47] *Sum. Theol.* I, II, 100, 11 c; cf. 3.
[48] *Ibid.*, 100, 8 c.   [49] *Ibid.*, 103, 3 c; 104, 3 c.
[50] *Eth. Nic.* VIII, 13, 1162b, 21–23; cf. above, p. 174.
[51] *Sum. Theol.* I, II, 99, 2 c: de actibus virtutum.
[52] *Ibid.*, 100, 2 c: de actibus omnium virtutum.
[53] *Ibid.*, 1 c: rationi congruunt.

laws he says that they "relate to the virtue of justice," [54]
and, while they were not to be eternal, they "directed the
people to justice and equity," [55] and on the whole they are
"fitting," "suitably framed," and are based on reason
(*ratione*).[56] And so also of the ceremonial laws he says that
they are particular determinations of the worship of God,
the latter of which is "an act of virtue," [57] and, while they
were not meant to be eternal,[58] there is a reason for them,
though the reason, as says also Maimonides, is not always
evident.[59]

Their identification of the commandments of the Pentateuch with virtues has led both Maimonides and St. Thomas
to add, like Philo, some new virtues borrowed from the list
of scriptural commandments. Thus to Maimonides, belief
in the existence of God, almsgiving, or what Philo calls
philanthropy or humanity, prayer, repentance, and the
study of Scripture are all commandments [60] and hence are
to be included in the list of virtues. Similarly St. Thomas
explicitly states that faith (*fides*) is a virtue, one of the three
virtues described by him as theological virtues,[61] and this
inclusion of faith among the virtues is based upon a verse
in the New Testament.[62] So also almsgiving is called by him
a virtue. In one place, using scriptural language, he says
that almsgiving (*eleemosyna*)[63] is included under works of
charity (*opera caritatis*), of which he further says that they
are "essential to virtue" (*de necessitate virtutis*) and pertain to the moral precepts of both the Old Law and the
New Law.[64] In another place, using classical language and

[54] *Ibid.*, 104, 3, Obj. 1; cf. 100, 2 c.
[55] *Ibid.*, ad 3.
[56] *Ibid.*, 105, 1–4.
[57] *Ibid.*, 99, 3, ad 2; cf. 101, 1 c.
[58] *Ibid.*, 103, 3 c; cf. above, p. 315.
[59] *Ibid.*, 100, 1, ad 4; cf. 2 c; 3 c.
[60] Cf. *Sefer ha-Miṣwot*, Positive Commandment 1, 195, 5, 73, and 11 respectively.
[61] *Sum. Theol.* I, II, 62, 3 c.
[62] I Cor. 13: 13.
[63] *Sum. Theol.* I, II, 108, 3, Obj. 4.
[64] *Ibid.*, 2 c.

quoting Macrobius [65] and Andronicus of Rhodes,[66] he says that humanity (*humanitas*), which he explains to mean beneficence (*beneficentia*), or liberality (*liberalitas*), which he explains to mean the same as humanity, is a virtue under the virtue of justice (*iustitia*).[67] Repentance (*poenitentia*), too, is explicitly said by him to be a virtue.[68] He does not say directly that prayer (*oratio*) is a virtue, but he does say that it is an act of religion,[69] which means that it is a virtue, for religion is said by him to be a virtue.[70] As for the study or the reading of Scripture, in the early history of Christianity, Scripture was read in the meetinghouses for the same reason as that described by Philo, namely, to inculcate virtue.[71] Says Tertullian: "We assemble to read our sacred writings. . . . With the sacred words we nourish our faith, we animate our hope, we make our confidence more steadfast; and no less by inculcations of God's precepts we confirm good habits." [72] Had this view persisted in Christianity, St. Thomas would have undoubtedly recommended the reading of Scripture as a virtue. But it happens that in the history of Christianity, first in the Greek Church, in the ninth century, and then in the West, toward the end of the twelfth century, from fear of heresy, the reading of Scripture on the part of the people was restricted.[73] The reading of Scripture thus for a time ceased to be a virtue in Christianity, until it was later revived under new conditions.

As true Aristotelians, both Maimonides and St. Thomas

[65] Cf. above, p. 220, n. 146.
[66] Cf. above, p. 237, n. 4.
[67] *Sum. Theol.* II, II, 80, 1, Obj. 2 and 4, and ad 2 and 4.
[68] *Ibid.* I, 95, 3, Obj. 3; III, 85 1 c and 2 c.
[69] *Ibid.* II, II, 83, 3 c.
[70] *Ibid.* II, II, 81 3 c and 4 c.
[71] Cf. above, pp. 259 ff.
[72] Tertullian, *Apologeticus*, Cap. 39.
[73] Cf. K. R. Hagenbach, *History of Doctrines*, § 162, nn. 5 and 6.

define virtue as a mean.[74] But as to what is to be done with the Stoic definition that virtue is the extirpation of emotion, they differ. Maimonides, like Philo, considers the extirpation of the emotions as the guiding principle of the chosen few whom he describes as men of superior piety.[75] St. Thomas, following St. Augustine, tries to show that the difference between the Stoics and the Peripatetics is "one of words rather than of opinions" and that the Stoics by their extirpation of the emotions mean the control of the emotions by reason.[76]

Differences of opinion appear, however, between Philo and Maimonides on the one hand and St. Thomas on the other with regard to the attitude of Judaism toward certain aspects of the commandments and virtues.

First, with regard to the meaning of the tenth commandment "Thou shalt not desire" or "Thou shalt not covet." As we have already seen, the old Tannaitic rabbis,[77] and following them Maimonides,[78] and, reflecting the same old Jewish tradition, also Philo,[79] take this prohibition to refer not only to the external act of desire but also to the mere emotion of desire. Furthermore, as we have seen, the commandment not to desire, both to the rabbis and to Philo, was a prohibition of any kind of emotion which might lead to the violation of any of the ten commandments, such as adultery and murder.[80] With regard to adultery, the rabbinic interpretation of the seventh commandment reads that "also he who commits adultery with his eyes is called

---

[74] Maimonides, *Shemonah Perakim*, 4; St. Thomas, *Sum. Theol.* I, II, 64, 1–5.
[75] *Shemonah Perakim*, 6.
[76] *Sum. Theol.* I, II, 59, 2 c.
[77] Cf. above, pp. 226 f.
[78] *Sefer ha-Miṣwot*, Negative Commandment 266.
[79] Cf. above, pp. 227 ff.
[80] Cf. above, pp. 227, 229.

adulterer." [81] So also the commandments not to "hate thy brother in thine heart" [82] and not to "bear any grudge" [83] are taken as prohibitions of the mere emotion of hatred [84] and of the mere emotion of revenge.[85] But St. Thomas, deriving his knowledge of Judaism from the New Testament, maintains that "the Scribes and Pharisees . . . thought that the prohibition of adultery and murder covered the external act only, and not the internal desire" [86] and also "they thought that desire for revenge was lawful . . . that the emotion of covetousness was lawful . . . that the emotion of hatred was lawful." [87]

Second, with regard to the question as to what is to be the right motive in the worship of God. The rabbis, Philo, and Maimonides, all of whom derived their knowledge of Judaism from an inherited belief and practice — a belief and practice antedating Christianity — proclaim in unison that Judaism as based upon the Old Testament demands that one is to worship God not out of fear but out of love [88] and, in the case of Philo, in addition to expressing himself in rabbinic terms,[89] he expresses himself also in philosophic terms, that virtues are to be chosen for their own sake.[90] St. Thomas, however, insists that "the Jews so distorted the true meaning" of the promises of the Old Testament "as to think that we ought to serve God with these things [i.e., exalted honors and exalted riches] as the end in view," concluding, "wherefore Our Lord set this aside by teaching, first of all, that works of virtue should not be done for human

---

[81] *Pesiḳta Rabbati*, 24, p. 124b; *Leviticus Rabbah* 23, 12. Cf. Strack-Billerbeck, *Kommentar zum Neuen Testament*, Matt. 5: 28.

[82] Lev. 19: 17.

[83] Lev. 19: 18.

[84] *Sifra, Ḳedoshim, Pereḳ* 4, p. 89a.

[85] *Ibid.*, p. 89b; *Yoma* 23a.

[86] *Sum. Theol.* I, II, 108, 3, ad 1.

[87] *Ibid.*, ad 2.

[88] Cf. above, pp. 286 ff.

[89] Cf. above, p. 296.

[90] Cf. above, p. 294.

glory,"[91] or, quoting St. Augustine,[92] he says: "In a word
the difference between the Law and the Gospel is this — fear
and love."[93]

Like the rabbis and Philo and Maimonides, St. Thomas
believes in the reward of virtue. Now the rabbis and Philo
and Maimonides all declare in unison that, according to their
own belief as Jews, a belief based upon the traditional Jewish understanding of the Old Testament — a traditional
Jewish understanding antedating Christianity — the ultimate reward of virtue is eternal spiritual life. The rabbis ask:
What is the meaning of the words "that thy days may be
prolonged, and that it may go well with thee"[94] which
Scripture promises as a reward for the performance of certain commandments? and their answer is: "'that it may go
well with thee' — in a world which is wholly good; 'that thy
days may be prolonged' — in a world which is wholly last-
ing."[95] Philo similarly explains the promises for right conduct to mean either spiritual goods on earth or immortal
life.[96] Maimonides, on the basis of the same scriptural expression quoted above, declares that "the good reserved for
the righteous is life in the world to come."[97] St. Thomas,
however, insists that in the Old Law man was directly ordained to "a sensible and earthly good," whereas in the
New Law, man was ordained to "an intelligible and heavenly
good,"[98] or, quoting St. Augustine,[99] he declares: "The
promises of temporal goods are contained in the Old Testa-

[91] Sum. Theol. I, II, 108, 3, ad 4.
[92] Contra Adimantum Manichaei Discipulum, Cap. 17, 2 (PL, 42, 159).
[93] Sum. Theol. I, II, 91, 5 c.
[94] Deut. 5:16; cf. 22:7.
[95] Kiddushin 39b.
[96] Cf. above, pp. 302 f.
[97] Mishneh Torah, Teshubah VIII, 1.
[98] Sum. Theol. I, II, 91, 5 c.
[99] Contra Faustum Manichaeum IV, Cap. 2 (PL, 42, 217-218).

ment, for which reason it is called old; but the promise of eternal life belongs to the New Testament." [100]

In his grand assault upon traditional philosophy, by his denial of the revealed origin of Scripture, Spinoza has knocked out the main prop of the view commonly held ever since Philo that the doctrines and commandments of the Pentateuch are to be identified with the intellectual and moral virtues of the philosophers. The doctrines of the Pentateuch, contends Spinoza, reflect the beliefs of simple-minded people, from which no knowledge of what philosophers usually call intellectual virtues can be gained. [101] Indeed Scripture teaches what philosophers would call moral virtues, [102] but the moral virtues taught in Scripture are based upon faith and not upon philosophy, [103] and they are not to be identified with philosophic virtues which are based on reason. When therefore he himself sets out to draw up a philosophic system of ethics he returns to Aristotle and partly also to the Stoics. He discusses all the standard problems of ethics, the highest good, the emotions, the virtues, the reward of virtue, all in the manner of Aristotle and without the benefit of scriptural quotations. [104]

[100] *Sum. Theol.* I, II, 91, 5 c.
[101] *Tractatus Theologico-Politicus,* ch. 2 (*Opera,* ed. Gebhardt, III, p. 29, ll. 29–31); cf. ch. 13.
[102] *Ibid.,* ch. 13.
[103] *Ibid.,* ch. 14.
[104] Cf. *Ethics* III–V, and H. A. Wolfson, *The Philosophy of Spinoza,* chapters on "Emotions," "Virtues," and "Love, Immortality, and Blessedness."

CHAPTER XIII

POLITICAL THEORY

I. The Mosaic Constitution

BESIDES the classification of the laws into the ten commandments and into positive and negative and into those which deal with the relation of men to men and those which deal with the relation of men to God, there was in the mind of Philo another classification. His identification of the laws with what Aristotle calls "practical philosophy," has led him also to divide them, after the manner of the Aristotelian division of practical philosophy,[1] into ethics, household management, and state management. "The business of life," that is, practical philosophy, he says, deals with private affairs (ἰδίοις), that is, ethics, and with public affairs (κοινοῖς), and under the latter he includes household-management (οἰκονομική) and state-management (πολιτική).[2] Sometimes using the term "ethic" (ἠθική) in the general sense of a science which "tends to the improvement of human conduct," he says that it takes various forms: "politic, dealing with the state; economic, with the management of a house; sympotic, or the art of conviviality, with banquets and festivities; and further we have the kingly faculty dealing with the control of men, and the legislative dealing with commands and prohibitions."[3]

The component parts of the household, according to Aristotle, are human beings and property,[4] and consequently under the science of household-management he

---

[1] Diogenes, V, 28; cf. also Plato, *Statesman* 258 E.
[2] *Fug.* 6, 36; cf. *Leg. All.* III, 9, 30; *Jos.* 8, 38; *Qu. in Gen.* IV, 165.
[3] *Ebr.* 22, 91.
[4] *Oecon.* I, 2, 1343a, 18.

deals with the family [5] and the manner of procuring and preserving property, including under this latter agriculture, trade and wage-earning employments,[6] slavery,[7] and interest on money.[8] With this general classification of the topics of the science of household-management in mind, Philo challenges the man who would have regard only for his individual advantage to tell him whether he would do away with "honor due to parents, loving care of a wife, bringing up children, happy and blameless relations with domestic servants, management of a house." [9] Here, then, we have an informal classification of the conventional topics under the science of household-management, and all these topics are dealt with by him in his exposition of the laws of the Pentateuch. He deals with laws relating to marriage, divorce, inheritance, parents, children, slavery, free labor, land, animals, personal property, loans, and interest. Philo expounds all these laws in great detail in several of his works.[10]

In his challenge to that man who would have regard only for his individual advantage Philo also asks him to tell whether he would do away with "the government of a city, the firm establishment of laws, the guardianship of morals, reverence towards elders, respect for the memory of the departed, fellowship with the living, piety in words and actions towards the Deity." [11] Here, then, we have a classification of the conventional topics that are usually included under the science of government in the works of Plato and Aristotle and the Stoics. In all of them religion is considered as one of the functions of a state. To Plato, the state is to provide

---

[5] *Ibid.* I, 3, 1343b, 7–4, 1344a, 22.
[6] *Ibid.* I, 2, 1343a, 26–30.　　　　　　　　[8] *Ibid.* II, 1, 1346a, 13.
[7] *Ibid.* I, 5, 1344a, 23 ff.　　　　　　　　[9] *Post.* 53, 181.
[10] *De Vita Mosis* II, 43, 233–242; *De Decalogo*; *De Specialibus Legibus* I–IV; *De Virtutibus.*
[11] *Post.* 53, 181.

priests for the care of the sacred places and the services of the gods [12] and "impiety either by word or deed" is to be punished by the state,[13] in some instances even by death.[14] So also to Aristotle, in the state "there must be a care of religion, which is commonly called worship"[15] and "people who are puzzled to know whether one ought to honor the gods and love one's parents or not need punishment."[16] All those laws which in a purely philosophic treatise would have been included under the heading of the management of the state are treated in his exposition of the special laws of the Pentateuch, arranged under the headings of some of the ten commandments. He deals with laws regulating the office of king, the appointment of magistrates, the administration of justice, the position of strangers within the state, the relation of the state to other states in war, the office of the priest, the regulation of divine worship in the temple and outside the temple.[17] The art of government is described by him as "an art of arts and a science of sciences" and as an art which is to concern itself, in its broadest sense, with the care of "matters private, public, and sacred."[18]

Here, too, in his restatement of the laws of Moses of this group, he does not follow the text of the Pentateuch literally. For his subject-matter he draws upon certain oral Jewish traditions and for his literary form he draws upon terms and expressions familiar to his non-Jewish readers.

Let us, then, see how Philo, on the basis of the knowledge available to him, analyzes the Mosaic constitution.

[12] *Laws* VI, 758 E ff.   [13] *Ibid.* X, 907 D ff.
[14] *Ibid.*, 908 E; 909 A.
[15] *Politica* VII, 9, 1328b, 11–13.
[16] *Topica* II, 11, 105a, 5–7.
[17] Similarly Josephus singles out all the laws which deal with the management of the state and describes them as laws dealing with the form of government (πολιτεία). Cf. *Antt.* IV, 8, 4, 198; IV, 8, 2, 184.
[18] *Spec.* IV, 29, 156.

(a) King

There is nowhere in Scripture a definite statement as to what form of government the Jewish state should take. The verse in Deuteronomy about the appointment of a king is couched in language which suggests that the appointment of a king was permissible if it should happen that, in imitation of all the neighboring nations, the Jews could not resist the temptation of having a king set up over them. "When thou art come unto the land which the Lord thy God giveth thee, and shalt possess it, and shalt dwell therein; and shalt say: 'I will set a king over me, like all the nations that are round about me,' thou shalt in any wise set him king over thee, whom the Lord thy God shall choose." [19] From the story in Samuel about the appointment of the first king, introduced by the words of the elders of Israel to Samuel "make us a king to judge us like all the nations" and followed by God's comment "they have rejected Me, that I should not be king over them" and by Samuel's unfavorable description of kingship,[20] it may be gathered that, according to the author of that story in Samuel, kingship was not considered either as an obligatory form of government nor as the best form of government. In post-Biblical Judaism a difference of opinion existed as to the meaning of the Deuteronomic verse with regard to the appointment of a king. Josephus regards it as optional.[21] In rabbinic sources, some authorities are recorded as considering it as optional, others as obligatory.[22] The latter had to explain the reluctance of Samuel in granting the people's request for a

[19] Deut. 17: 14–15.
[20] I Sam. 8: 4–22; 12: 17.
[21] *Antt.* IV, 8, 17, 223.
[22] *Sifre Deut.*, § 156, p. 105a; *Midrash Tannaim*, on Deut. 17: 14, pp. 103–104; *Sanhedrin* 20b.

king. The explanation offered is that the people were not
yet ripe for the royal form of government or that the ignorant
elements of the population couched their demand for a king
in the wrong term, namely, their desire to have a king "like
all the nations." [23]

Nor is there in the Pentateuch any definite statement as
to the manner in which a king is to come to office. In the
Pentateuch it only says: "Thou shalt in any wise set him
king over thee, whom the Lord thy God shall choose." [24] In
the case of Moses, who according to Jewish tradition based
upon the verse "And he was king in Jeshurun" [25] held the
office of king, there seems to be a difference of opinion as to
the manner in which he came to office.[26] There is one statement in which it is said that he was appointed by God,[27]
but there is another statement in which it is intimated that
he was king by virtue of his election by the assembly of the
seventy elders.[28] In the case of Saul and David, Saul is said
to have been first chosen by God through the prophet
Samuel [29] and then chosen by lot.[30] David, again, is said
to have been chosen by God through the prophet Samuel [31]
and then anointed first by "the men of Judah" [32] and later
again by "all the elders of Israel." [33]

Of these four methods of election of a king, lots, prophet,
all the people, the elders of the people, the first is never mentioned in post-Biblical literature. The other three are men-

[23] *Ibid.*
[24] Deut. 17: 15.
[25] Deut. 33: 5.
[26] Cf. Ginzberg, *The Legends of the Jews*, III, 153–154; 455.
[27] *Exodus Rabbah* 40, 2.
[28] *Midrash Tannaim*, on Deut. 33: 5, p. 213.
[29] I Sam. 9: 15–17.
[30] I Sam. 10: 20–21. According to tradition, lots were also used in the selection
of the seventy elders by Moses (cf. *Sifre Num.*, 95, F, p. 26a; H, p. 95).
[31] I Sam. 16: 1–13.
[32] II Sam. 2: 4.   [33] II Sam. 5: 3.

tioned in various sources. In the First Book of Maccabees, when Simon the Maccabean was made high priest (ἀρχιερεύς) and captain (στρατηγός) and governor (ἐθνάρχης; ἡγούμενος),[34] with all the dignities and honors of a king,[35] though without the title of king, it is said first that "the Jews and priests were pleased"[36] that he should be all these and then that "all the people consented to ordain for Simon"[37] all these, with the proviso, however, "until a faithful prophet should arise."[38] The implication of all this is that, according to the understanding at that time of the scriptural law, such an election had to be made by (a) a prophet and by (b) the people, but, inasmuch as there was no prophet by whom Simon could be chosen, his choice was made by the people "until a faithful prophet should arise."[39] In the Tannaitic literature, one source, using as proof-text the cases of Saul and David, declares that a king is to be chosen by a prophet;[40] another source, evidently dealing with the time after the close of prophecy, declares that a king is to be set up by a council of seventy-one members.[41]

Nor, finally, is there in the Pentateuch any definite statement as to how long the office should be held by the king,

[34] I Macc. 14: 41, 47; 13: 42; 15: 1, 2.

[35] *Ibid.* 14: 43, 44.

[36] *Ibid.* 14: 41.

[37] *Ibid.* 14: 46.

[38] *Ibid.* 14: 41.

[39] Or it may also mean that his rule was to be temporary, as a true ruler of the house of David would ultimately be announced by a faithful prophet. Cf. H. Graetz, *Geschichte der Juden*[5], III, p. 59; S. Krauss, "Simon Maccabaeus," *Jew. Enc.* XI, 371; J. Klausner, *Ha-Ra'ayon ha-Meshiḥi be-Yisra'el*, p. 164.

[40] *Midrash Tannaim*, on Deut. 17: 16, p. 104; cf. *Sifre Deut.*, § 157, F, p. 105a; HF, p. 208.

[41] *Tos. Sanhedrin* III, 4. Maimonides, in *Mishneh Torah: Melakim* I, 3, referring to Biblical time says the election of a king is to be by seventy elders and a prophet. In *Sanhedrin* V, 1, he says the election of a king is to be by a council of seventy-one elders, evidently referring to post-Biblical times. Cf. Ritter, *Philo und die Halacha*, p. 100, n. 2.

and as to whether the office of king should be hereditary. All that is said on this point is that the king should observe the Law "to the end that he may prolong his days in his kingdom, he and his children, in the midst of Israel." [42] This implies lifelong tenure of office and heredity, but both are conditioned on merit. When David became king, however, he was promised by God through Nathan the prophet that his throne "shall be established for ever." [43] This continuity of the Davidic dynasty, as would seem from Scripture, was not to be conditioned on the merits of his successors, for it says that "if his children forsake My law, . . . then will I visit their transgressions with the rod . . . but My mercy will not break off from him, . . . his seed shall endure for ever, and his throne as the sun before Me." [44]

In post-Biblical literature it is generally assumed that the statement in Deuteronomy "to the end that he may prolong his days in his kingdom, he, and his children" [45] means that the office is of lifelong tenure and is hereditary, provided the children are qualified for the office by merit.[46] This conception of the royal office as hereditary, but conditioned on merit, is also implied in the discussion of Joshua's succession to Moses. There are three traditions on this point. First, Moses is represented as having expected his sons to inherit his office of king in accordance with the general law of inheritance, but God told him that Joshua was more deserving than they, for "while thy sons sat idle and neglected the study of the Torah, Joshua attended much upon thee and paid much regard to thee and studied early and late in thy

[42] Deut. 17: 20.
[43] II Sam. 7: 16.
[44] Ps. 89: 31–37.
[45] Deut. 17: 20.
[46] *Midrash Tannaim*, on Deut. 17: 20, p. 106; *Horayot* 11b; *Tos. Shekalim* II, 15; *Sifre Deut.*, § 162, F, p. 106a; HF, pp. 212–213.

schoolhouse and did also arrange the benches and spread the mats." [47] Second, Moses is represented as having desired to be succeeded by his sons as kings, but God told him that kingship was in His design to be given to David and his descendants.[48] Third, Moses is represented as having himself desired that Joshua should succeed him in preference to his own sons.[49] In the case of the dynasty of David, its perpetuity is assumed without any attached condition.[50]

Philo, in his restatement of the Pentateuchal laws with regard to the government of the state, probably assumes, as did some of the exponents of Jewish tradition,[51] that kingship is the prescribed form of government.[52] Following strictly the Mosaic legislation and in conformity with post-Biblical Jewish tradition which passes over in silence the precedent of casting lots in the case of the election of Saul, Philo declares that "Moses does not even mention appointment of rulers by lot, but determines to institute appointment by election" and by the free choice of the "whole multitude" (σύμπασα ἡ πληθύς).[53] This statement is preceded by a diatribe against "some [legislators who] have introduced the system of filling magistrates by lot." [54] Elsewhere he condemns also the election of rulers "by the votes of men for the most part hirelings." [55] His criticism of election by lots is evidently directed against Plato and Aristotle, both of whom recommend that method of elec-

[47] *Numbers Rabbah* 21, 14; *Tanḥuma, Phinehas* 11; cf. Ginzberg, *The Legends of the Jews*, III, 398.

[48] *Exodus Rabbah* 2, 6.

[49] *Sifre Zuṭa*, on Num. 27: 18, 22; *Sifre Num.*, § 140, F, p. 526; H, p. 186; cf. Ginzberg, *The Legends of the Jews*, III, 400; VI, p. 142, n. 837.

[50] Cf. Sirach 47: 11, 22; 48: 15; I Macc. 2: 57; Psalms of Solomon 17: 5 (4).

[51] Cf. above, p. 325.

[52] *Spec.* IV, 30, 157. Cf. Ritter, *Philo und die Halacha*, p. 100; Heinemann, *Bildung*, p. 184.

[53] *Ibid.*   [54] *Ibid.*, 29, 151–156; cf. *Mut.* 28, 151.   [55] *Mut.* 28, 151.

tion.[56] His mention of election "by votes of men for the most part hirelings" undoubtedly refers to events in the Roman principate to which he refers also elsewhere in his statement that Moses was "invested with this office of kingship, not like some of those who thrust themselves into position of power by means of arms and engines of war and strength of infantry, cavalry, and navy, but on account of his goodness and nobility of conduct and the universal benevolence which he never failed to show." [57] His emphasis upon the fact that the king is to be elected by the *"whole multitude"* is obviously in criticism of those views which would restrict the right of electing rulers only to some of the citizens,[58] to be determined by qualifications of property or of birth. His omission, however, to mention the council of elders as being intrusted with the power of electing a king is due to the fact, as we shall see later,[59] that according to his conception of the Mosaic constitution no specific provision was made by it for the continued existence of a council of seventy elders. Again, like one of the two Tannaitic sources referred to above,[60] he makes no mention of the election of kings by a prophet.

Still the divine element is not missing in the election of kings. Drawing evidently upon the wording of the verse "thou shalt in any wise set him king over thee, whom the Lord thy God shall choose," [61] he declares that even though the election of the king is done by the people, "God himself will add His vote in favor of such an election and set His seal to ratify it," [62] that is to say, the choice of the people is an expression of the will of God. In another place, drawing

---

[56] Plato, *Laws* VI, 759 B; Aristotle, *Politica* IV, 9, 1294b, 7–8.

[57] *Mos.* I, 27, 148; cf. S. Tracy, *Philo Judaeus and the Roman Principate* (Williamsport: 1933), p. 50.   [60] Cf. above, p. 327.

[58] Aristotle, *Politica* IV, 15, 1300a, 15.   [61] Deut. 17: 15.

[59] Cf. below, p. 350.   [62] *Spec.* IV, 30, 157.

upon the verse "thou art a king from God among us," [63] he rephrases it in philosophic language, declaring that rulers are "appointed for ever by nature herself," [64] that is to say, by God himself. The king selected by the people is to be assumed he says, to "have been judged worthy to fill the highest and most important office." [65] What he means by this divine element in the vote of the people is explained by him in his statement with regard to the manner in which Moses was elected to the office of king. Combining the two Jewish traditions, one that Moses was appointed by God and the other that Moses was elected by the people through their representatives in the assembly of the seventy elders, [66] he says that "he was appointed by God with the free consent of those who were to be governed by him, for God wrought in his subjects a willingness to make such a voluntary choice," [67] but in order to show that his recognition of a divine source for royal authority is not to be confused with the common pagan conception that the king in person is divine and is to be worshiped, [68] he says that "in his material substance a king is equal to every man, but in the power of his authority and rank he is like the God of all, for there is nothing on earth that is higher than he." [69]

Similarly in accordance with native Jewish tradition is his treatment of the problem of the length of the king's tenure of office and the problem of succession.

The office of king is to be held for life, and he criticizes those who elect rulers only "for a short time," [70] evidently

[63] Gen. 23: 6 (LXX).
[64] *Mut.* 28, 151–152.
[65] *Spec.* IV, 33, 170.
[66] Cf. above, p. 326.
[67] *Praem.* 9, 54.
[68] Cf. above, I, 14, 29.
[69] *Fragmenta*, Richter, VI, pp. 235–236 (M. II, 673); cf. Goodenough, *The Politics of Philo Judaeus*, pp. 98–99. On the traditional Jewish conception as to the divine element in kingship, see Ch. Tchernowitz, *Toledoth ha-Halakah* I, ii, pp. 14–17.
[70] *Mut.* 28, 151.

referring to the office of royalty of ancient Hellas which, according to Aristotle, was sometimes held "until certain fixed limits of time." [71] He is silent on the question whether the office is to be hereditary or not. In his comment on the verse "to the end that he may prolong his days in his kingdom, he and his children, in the midst of the children of Israel," [72] he interprets it allegorically, maintaining that the verse does not mean to teach that God "grants him long years of life in presiding over the state, but to teach the ignorant that the law-abiding ruler, even when deceased, lives an age-long life through the actions which he leaves behind him as immortal, monuments of high excellence which can never be destroyed." [73] In this allegorical interpretation, then, the phrase "and his children" is evidently taken by him to mean "the actions which he leaves behind him." But, as in all his allegorical interpretations of legal passages, the literal meaning is not wholly to be discarded. Literally the law means to him, as it does in native Jewish tradition, that the office is hereditary, but conditioned on merit. This may be gathered from the address to Moses which he puts in the mouth of an imaginary person. In that address Philo makes the imaginary person say to Moses: "Master, what do you mean, have you not lawful sons, have you not nephews? Bequeath the sovereignty to your sons as first choice, for they naturally take precedence as heirs, or, if you reject them, at least to your nephews." [74] The meaning of this would seem to be that lawfully the office

---

[71] *Politica* III, 14, 1285a, 34–35.

[72] Deut. 17: 20 (LXX).

[73] *Spec.* IV, 32, 169. Cf. rabbinic non-literal interpretation of the words "that thou mayest prolong thy days" (Deut. 22: 7) as referring to the hereafter (*Ḳiddushin* 39b; *Ḥullin* 142a) and also the statement "no monuments are set up for the righteous; their words are their monuments" (*Genesis Rabbah* 82, 10; *Jer. Sheḳalim* II, 7, 47a).

[74] *Virt.* 10, 59.

belonged first to his sons and next to his nephews. This corresponds exactly to the view of the rabbis that "kingship passes as an inheritance to sons, and he who has precedence in inheritance in general has precedence in the inheritance of the office of king." [75] Philo seems to treat Moses' bequeathal of his office to Joshua rather than to his sons or nephews as a case of disinheritance, and the reason for that, as suggested by Philo, is the possibility that "the claims of his sons were under suspicion" [76] and that Joshua was more worthy than they on the ground that he was "the imitator of his amiable characteristics." [77] This, again, is exactly like the expression used by the rabbis, namely, "provided the son conducts himself in the manner of his fathers." [78] This native Jewish view that no man is elected to the office of king or inherits the office of king unless he is worthy of it is expressed by Philo also in a statement, couched in philosophic language, that "no foolish man is a king even though he is invested with supreme power by sea and land, but he only is a king who is a virtuous and God-loving man." [79] No reference is made by Philo to the hereditary dynasty of David, evidently because he was writing on the ideal state as it was outlined in the laws of Moses and not on the history of the Jewish state. David is once mentioned by him by name and is referred to as "psalmist" only,[80] and when the psalms are quoted David is referred to as "a prophet" [81] or a "divinely inspired man" [82] or "a member of Moses' fellowship." [83] Similarly Solomon, who is also mentioned by

[75] *Midrash Tannaim*, on Deut. 17: 20, p. 106; *Tos. Shekalim* II, 15.
[76] *Virt.* 9, 53.   [77] *Ibid.* 11, 66.
[78] *Tos. Shekalim* II, 15; cf. *Midrash Tannaim*, on Deut. 17: 20, p. 106.
[79] *Fragmenta*, Richter, VI, 215 (M. II, 657). Heinemann (*Bildung*, p. 183) uses this quotation as proof of the influence of Hellenic culture upon Philo's conception of kingdom.
[80] *Conf.* 28, 149.   [82] *Plant.* 7, 29.
[81] *Agr.* 12, 50.   [83] *Ibid.* 9, 39.

him only once by name, is referred to only as the author of Proverbs and is described as "one of the disciples of Moses" [84] or "some one of the men of the divine company." [85] The duties and powers of a king as conceived in Jewish tradition rest upon the Mosaic laws in Deuteronomy and upon Samuel's address in which, in answer to the people's request for a king, he undertook to describe for them "the prerogative of the king who shall reign over them." [86] The powers enumerated by Samuel are those of levying taxes in money and in forced labor. The people themselves mentioned that the king was to judge them and to lead them in war. [87] In post-Biblical Jewish law, based upon the statements in the Book of Samuel, taxation and leadership in war are considered the chief prerogatives of a king. [88] Neither of these two prerogatives is dwelt upon by Philo, evidently because they are not mentioned in the Pentateuch, for, as we have already seen, his purpose was to describe the Mosaic constitution and not the actual working of that constitution in Jewish history. The duties and functions which he does ascribe to a king are fourfold: (1) He is to rule and judge the people in accordance with the law. [89] (2) He is to appoint subordinates to act in his place in minor matters. [90] (3) He is to rule the people for their benefit and judge them with righteousness. [91] (4) He is to defer in doubtful cases to legal authorities. [92] Though none of these four duties is definitely said in the Pentateuch to be the duties of a king,

[84] *Congr.* 31, 177.
[85] *Ebr.* 8, 31.
[86] I Sam. 8: 9 ff. On the powers of a king, see Ch. Tchernowitz, *Toledoth ha-Halakah* I, ii, pp. 113 ff.
[87] I Sam. 8: 20.
[88] *M. Sanhedrin* II, 4; *Sanhedrin* 20b; cf. Maimonides, *Mishneh Torah, Melakim* IV, 1; V, 1.
[89] *Spec.* IV, 32, 160–169.
[90] *Ibid.*, 33, 170–175.
[91] *Ibid.*, 35, 183–187.
[92] *Ibid.*, 36, 188–192.

still Philo, we shall try to show, was not without justification
in describing them as royal duties.

The first duty ascribed by Philo to the king, that of acting
as judge, would seem to have been derived by him from the
verse in which the king is ordered, upon his assumption of
office, to write out a copy of the Law and to have it with him
and to read therein all the days of his life in order "that he
may learn to fear the Lord his God, to keep all the words
of this law and these statutes, to do them." [93] In the Septuagint the last part of the statement reads: "and to keep all
these commandments (ἐντολὰς) and to do (ποιεῖν) all these
statutes (δικαιώματα)." We have translated the Greek δικαιώματα here by "statutes" on the basis of its underlying Hebrew ḥuḳḳim, of which it occurs as a translation also in
other places in the Septuagint. But it is not impossible that
Philo took this term here in its original Greek sense of
"acts of justice" or "just claims," in which sense the term
is also sometimes used in the Septuagint.[94] The last words
of the statement accordingly meant to him that the king
was to administer justice. For such an understanding of
the verse he could have derived support from the fact that
Moses, David, and Solomon, all in their capacity as kings,
were also judges.[95] He could have also derived support
from the verses "O house of David, thus saith the Lord,
administer justice (κρίμα) in the morning" [96] and "the king
that faithfully judgeth the poor, his throne shall be established for ever." [97] Similarly when the rabbis interpret the
verse commanding that a copy of the book of the Law "shall

[93] Deut. 17: 18–19.
[94] Cf. Deut. 10: 18; I Kings 8:45, 59, as a translation of the Hebrew mishpat,
and Jer. 11: 20, as a translation of the Hebrew rib.
[95] Exod. 18: 13; II Sam. 14: 5 ff.; 15: 2; I Kings 3: 16 ff.
[96] Jer. 21: 12.
[97] Prov. 29: 14.

be with him" [98] to mean that "when he sits in judgment it
shall be with him," [99] the implication is that they understood the verse to mean that the king acts as judge. This,
we may assume, was the original law. It was only during
the time of Alexander Jannaeus that a new law was enacted, according to which non-Davidic kings were not to
act as judges.[100] This scriptural and traditional Jewish view
about the judicial function of the king is often expressed by
Philo in words, which reflect a similar Greek conception of
kingship, namely, that "it is a king's duty to command
what is right and forbid what is wrong" [101] or that the royal
power "is the root of the punishing and the law-making
power." [102]

The other three duties ascribed by him to the king are
based upon verses in the Pentateuch which do not directly
deal with kings. The verse upon which the second duty
rests only reads: "Judges and officers shalt thou make thee

---

[98] Deut. 17: 19.   [100] Sanhedrin 19a; M. Sanhedrin II, 2.
[99] M. Sanhedrin II, 4.   [101] Mos. II, 1, 4.
[102] Qu. in Exod. II, 68.

Heinemann's view is that Philo's attribution of judicial power to kings is of
non-Jewish origin, for the following reasons: (1) Philo had but little acquaintance
with the books of Samuel, Kings, and Proverbs, where kings are described as
judges. (2) Deuteronomy does not confer upon kings judicial powers. (3) The
statement in M. Sanhedrin II, 2 that a king cannot be a judge represents the old
tradition; the distinction between non-Davidic kings and Davidic kings is a later
innovation. (4) Philo quotes Greek sayings in support of the judicial function of
kings (cf. Bildung, pp. 183–184).

In answer to all these points, it may be said: (1) No one knows how much Philo
was acquainted with the books of Samuel, Kings, and Proverbs. All these books,
we know, are quoted by him. (2) In Deuteronomy, as we have shown, Philo could
have found a direct statement as to the judicial power of a king. (3) That kings,
according to Deuteronomy, are judges is definitely stated in M. Sanhedrin II, 4,
and consequently the statement in II, 2 that kings cannot be judges must inevitably
refer, as is explained in the Talmud, to a later act of legislation (cf. J. Juster,
Les Juifs dans l'Empire Romain, II, p. 127, n. 2). (4) Philo's quotations of Greek
sayings about the judicial function of kings is in accordance with his general practice
of quoting Greek authorities in support of scriptural teachings.

[103] Deut. 16: 18. Cf. below, pp. 345–348.

in all thy gates."¹⁰³ The verse upon which the third duty rests reads only: "Ye shall do no unrighteousness in judgment: thou shalt not respect the person of the mighty. In righteousness shalt thou judge thy neighbor. Thou shalt not go about with deceit among thy people."¹⁰⁴ The verse upon which the fourth duty rests only reads: "If there arise matters too hard for thee in judgment . . . thou shalt come unto the priests, the levites, and unto the judge that shall be in those days."¹⁰⁵ In none of these laws is the word king mentioned. But inasmuch as in the first duty which he assigns to the king Philo assumes that the king is to act as judge, it was quite natural for him to interpret all those verses dealing with the administration of justice to apply to the king.

(b) High Priest

The conception of high priesthood with which Philo started and upon which he based his own discussion of the subject is that which one may gather from the Pentateuch and post-scriptural native Jewish tradition. Moses, according to Jewish tradition, supported by the verse "Moses and Aaron among his priests,"¹⁰⁶ was not only king but also priest. Originally, so the tradition runs, it was God's design that Moses should be priest and Aaron only a levite, but as a punishment for Moses' hesitation to undertake his mission to Egypt the priesthood was transferred to Aaron. Moses officiated as high priest during the week of the installation of Aaron, but even after that, according to one view, he continued to officiate together with Aaron.¹⁰⁷ The priesthood is explicitly said to descend to the sons of Aaron.[108] From among these priests a high priest is elected by a court of seventy-one members.[109] The office of the high priest is hereditary, the order of succession following the regular law of inheritance, but this is conditioned upon the qualifications of the son in piety.[110]

Philo follows the same outline. Moses, besides being king, was also high priest, and in this capacity he built the tabernacle and its equipment and designed the vesture of the high priest and of the ordinary priests, all of these, of course, by the direction of God.[111] Then, when he was about to select permanent priests to perform the service in the Tabernacle, he did not select his sons, because "neither of his sons, of whom he had two, did he judge worthy of this distinction." [112] He selected Aaron as high priest "because of his superior virtue" and he appointed Aaron's sons as priests also because of "the piety and holiness which he observed in their characters." [113] But having selected them, naturally by the order of God, "he installed them in office with the consent of the whole nation." [114] During the seven days of installation, Moses himself, as is told in the Pentateuch, officiated as priest.[115] Whether he continued to officiate as priest even after that Philo does not say. The reason, according to Philo, why the sons of Aaron, who were found morally worthy to be priests and hence could not be assumed to be unworthy to be kings,[116] were not selected by Moses to succeed him as kings is that "very likely he

[108] Exod. 40: 15.
[109] *Tos. Sanhedrin* III, 4.
[110] *Sifra, Sav, Perek* 5, pp. 31d–32a; *Aḥre, Perek* 8, p. 83b; *Midrash Tannaim*, on Deut. 17: 20, p. 106.
[111] *Mos.* II, 15, 71 ff.
[112] *Ibid.*, 28, 142.
[113] *Ibid.*
[114] *Ibid.*, 143.
[115] *Ibid.*, 28, 143–30, 152; cf. Lev. 8: 30–9: 24.
[116] *Virt.* 9, 53.

considered that it was impossible for the same persons to do justice to both offices, the priesthood and the royal authority, one of which professes the service of God, the other guardianship of men." [117] There is in these words the unmistakable ring of a criticism of a theory or a practice to combine these two offices, and the theory or practice alluded to may be that of ancient Greece and Egypt or of Rome in his own time. [118] He, himself, refers to such non-Jewish theory and practice when he speaks of "ancient kings" who "were at the same time also priests." [119] Or perhaps it may be a repercussion of the smoldering criticism that prevailed among certain Jews in Palestine against the Maccabees for combining the royal and priestly office. [120]

With the appointment of Aaron and his sons to the priesthood, the office was to remain within that family to eternity, [121] which means that it is to be hereditary. Accordingly in his summarization of the laws of marriage which are to govern priests he says that they provide for the "pure descent from a noble stock." [122] No rules for the appointment and succession of high priests are mentioned by him. But indirectly we may gather from his writings his view as to at least one rule governing the succession of high priests. In his comment on the verse with regard to Phinehas, "and it shall be unto him, and to his seed after him, the covenant of an everlasting priesthood," [123] he paraphrases the last

[117] *Ibid.*, 9, 54.

[118] But see Goodenough, *By Light, Light*, p. 190; *The Politics of Philo Judaeus*, pp. 97 ff.

[119] *Qu. in Exod.* II, 105; cf. below, p. 344.

[120] Concerning which, see V. Aptowitzer, *Parteipolitik der Hasmonäerzeit*, 1927, pp. 49–63.

[121] *Mos.* II, 34, 186; cf. Badt in *Philos Werke* and Colson, both *ad loc.*, on the question whether this verse is to be taken literally as referring to the priestly tribe of Aaron or symbolically as referring to Israel or the soul.

[122] *Spec.* I, 16, 82.   [123] Num. 25:13.

words to mean "complete possession (παγκρατησία) of the
priesthood, a heritage to himself and his family which none
could take from them." [124] The substitution of the words
"complete possession of the priesthood" for the original
word "priesthood" is undoubtedly meant by Philo to interpret the verse as meaning that the high priesthood is to
belong to the family of Phinehas, and this evidently in order
to obviate the difficulty that the priesthood had already belonged to Phinehas by virtue of his being a son of Aaron.
Similarly in Palestinian literature, in order to obviate this
difficulty, one of the explanations given is that the reference
here is to the high priesthood, and to prove this it is added
that eighteen high priests during the period of the first
Temple were descendants of Phinehas. [125] So also Ben-Sira
takes the "covenant of an everlasting priesthood" promised
to Phinehas to refer to the high priesthood [126] and prays on
behalf of the high priest Simeon: "May His mercy be established with Simeon, and may He raise up for him the covenant of Phinehas." [127] Philo does not explicitly say that un-
fitness with reference to piety would disqualify one from
succeeding his father in the office of high priesthood. But
virtuous perfection is set up by him as a moral, if not a legal,
requirement even for the subordinate priests. Commenting
upon the laws of bodily perfection which are to govern
priests, he says that "all these seem to me to symbolize perfection of soul" [128] and to provide for the perfection of
priests "both of body and soul." [129] When, therefore, he

---

[124] *Mos.* I, 55, 304.
[125] *Sifre Num.*, § 131 on Num. 25: 13, F, p. 48b; H, p. 173. The other explanation is that Phinehas, owing to his absence at the time of the installation of Aaron
and his sons in the priesthood, was not made priest until after he had shown his zeal
for God; cf. *Zebaḥim* 101b.
[126] Sirach 45: 23–24.   [128] *Spec.* I, 16, 80.
[127] Sirach 50: 24.   [129] *Ibid.*, 82.

says that the "true priest" is "advanced to the service of the Truly Existent not more by birth than by virtue,"[130] he does not mean to deny the principle of heredity in priesthood. All he means to say is that, inasmuch as the first priests were chosen on the ground of their superior virtue and inasmuch also as the later hereditary priests are to be perfect in virtue, the true priest may be said to attain to his office not merely by birth but also by virtue.

In the Pentateuch priests are presented as having a twofold function. Primarily they are to be in charge of the sacred rites in the sanctuary.[131] But secondarily they are also to be the interpreters of the Law both as teachers and judges.[132] In the post-Biblical period, after the restoration from the Babylonian exile, with the rise of lay scribes and scholars, the priests still continued to dominate whatever organized bodies existed for the interpretation of the Law until shortly before the time of the Maccabean uprising. In Palestine, from that time on the function of the priests as the custodians of the Law and as its interpreters disappeared. In Alexandria, however, where the Jewish community was established by Palestinian Jews at a time when in Palestine the priests were still the interpreters of the Law, the priests would seem to have continued to function in that capacity until a much later time. In his own community, during his own time, Philo reports that priests, together with others who were not priests, read and interpreted the laws to the people on Sabbaths.[133] In accordance with all this, Philo describes the function of priests as being twofold, that of

---

[130] *Ibid.* IV, 36, 192.
[131] Exod. 28: 1 ff.
[132] Deut. 17: 8–9; 21: 5; 33: 10; Isa. 28: 7; Jer. 2: 8; 18: 18; Ezek. 7: 26; Hos. 4: 6; Micah 3: 11. On priests as judges, see Ch. Tchernowitz, *Toledoth ha-Halakah* I, ii, pp. 64 ff.
[133] *Fragmenta*, Richter VI, pp. 181–182 (M. II, 630–631).

having charge of the sacred rites [134] and that of being the
interpreter of the law.[135] The first function belongs to them
by right of birth and inheritance and cannot therefore be
transferred to non-priests; the second function, however, belongs to them only by virtue of their special training and
may therefore be transferred to non-priests who possess a
knowledge of the law. The second function is assigned to
priests, says Philo, for two reasons. First, they are especially
trained for it.[136] Second, "the true priest is necessarily a
prophet, advanced to the service of the Truly Existent not
more by birth than by virtue, and to the prophet nothing is
unknown." [137] What he means to say is that the priest is
more likely to have a knowledge of the Law in cases where
the question cannot be decided by reasoning, for, owing to his
virtuous character, he may receive knowledge by divine inspiration. Prophet here is used in the sense of scholar, and
perhaps especially in the sense of a scholar who is aided in the
acquisition of knowledge by divine inspiration.[138]

The functions of the king and the high priest are according
to Mosaic law so clearly delimited that in the words of Philo
the high priest "professes the service of God," whereas the
king professes "guardianship of men." [139] Theoretically,
therefore, in matters of the government of the state, the two
offices should not come into conflict with one another and
there should be no question of precedence between them.
Still, with regard to matters of dignity and honor, different
opinions are expressed in post-Biblical Jewish literature as to
which one of these offices is prior to the other.

---

[134] Cf. *Mos.* II, 1, 5; 15, 71 ff.; *Praem.* 9, 56.   [135] *Spec.* IV, 36, 190.
[136] *Ibid.*, 191.   [137] *Ibid.*, 192; cf. above, p. 14, n. 31.
[138] Cf. above, p. 53. So also Josephus, in *Antt.* IV, 8, 14, 218, substitutes for
"the judge" in Deut. 17: 9 the words "the prophet and the council of elders," evidently using the term "prophet" in the sense of one trained in the Law.
[139] *Virt.* 9, 54; cf. below, p. 344.

In the Testament of Judah it is said that the Lord "set the kingdom beneath the priesthood," for to the former "He gave the things upon the earth" and to the latter "the things in heaven" and, "as the heaven is higher than the earth, so is the priesthood of God higher than the earthly kingdom, unless it falls away through sin from the Lord and is dominated by the earthly kingdom." [140] In a Baraita, with reference to the ransom of captives, the order of priority is scholar, king, high priest, and prophet [141] and the proof-text for the priority of king to high priest is the verse wherein David says to Zadok the priest and Nathan the prophet "take with you the servants of your lord," [142] David thus calling himself the lord of the high priest. In a Tannaitic Midrash, however, in a comment upon the verse "and he (i.e., Joshua) shall stand before Eleazar the priest," [143] it is said: "the Holy One blessed be He has apportioned such dignity to Eleazar that even a king (i.e., Joshua) is to stand before him." [144] The implication of the priority of high priesthood to kingship is also to be noticed in the order in which the terms are arranged in the statement of the Mishnah that "there are three crowns: the crown of Torah, the crown of priesthood, and the crown of royalty." [145] In Philo, the words of the Testament of Judah as to the priority of high priesthood to royalty is put into the mouth of Agrippa I, when he is made to say that his ancestors thought that "the high priesthood is as much superior to the power of a king as God is superior to man, for the one is occupied in render-

---

[140] Testament of Judah 21: 2–4.　　　[142] I Kings 1: 33.

[141] *Horayot* 13a; *Jer. Horayot* III, 7, 48b.　　　[143] Num. 27: 21.

[144] *Sifre Zuṭa*, on Num. 27: 21; Maimonides, *Mishneh Torah: Melakim* II, 5; cf. commentary *Ambuha de-Sifre* by Jacob Ze'eb Joskowitz on *Sifre Zuṭa, ad loc.*, p. 477, n. 31; Ch. Tchernowitz, *Toledoth ha-Halakah*, I, ii, pp. 56–59.

[145] *M. Abot* IV, 13; the order in a corresponding passage in *Yoma* 72b is priesthood, Torah, and royalty, or literally, altar, ark [of the Law], and [royal] table.

ing service to God, and the other has only the care of governing men." [146] Again, commenting upon the fact that the high priest is to wear a miter,[147] Philo says that "in setting a miter on the priest's head, instead of a diadem, he expresses his judgment that he who is consecrated to God is, during the time of his exercising his office, superior to all others, not only the ordinary laymen, but even kings." [148] Note the qualification "during the time of his exercising his office." Similarly in his explanation of why Aaron and his sons themselves are ordered to light the lamp,[149] he says that it is "because nothing is more pleasant and agreeable or glorious than to devote one's attention to God, which service surpasses even great royal power," and to show the importance of performing this service to God personally, without entrusting it to others, he refers to the ancient custom among non-Jews of having kings officiate as priests: "To me, however, it seems that the ancient kings were at the same time also priests, in order publicly to show by their service that it is necessary that they who rule others should themselves respectfully worship God." [150] Previous to that in the same passage, trying to explain the meaning of this order to Aaron and his sons to light the lamp by themselves, he says that it is meant to be a censure of "the negligence of their successors in later times who on account of their indolence entrusted the service of the holy things to their second and third assistants." [151] The reference is

[146] *Legat*, 36, 278; cf. above, p. 342.
[147] Exod. 28: 4.
[148] *Mos.* II, 26, 131.
[149] Exod. 27: 21.
[150] *Qu. in Exod.* II, 105.
[151] *Ibid.* Goodenough takes this passage to mean that Aaron and his sons became kings, and paraphrases it as follows: "Aaron and his sons have been initiated for the divine ministry and have become greater kings than the Great King; like all kings they must thus be priests and serve God if they are to rule others" (*By Light, Light*, p. 113). I cannot accept this interpretation for the following reasons. First, in *Virt.* 9, 53, Philo definitely says that the sons of Aaron were only priests

undoubtedly to the actual practice in the Temple of Jerusalem, as Philo himself observed it there, of assigning the task of lighting the perpetual lamp to one of the subordinate priests by means of lots.[152]

(c) Judges and Officers

In the constitution established by Moses there is also a provision for two classes of officers described in the Pentateuch by two terms: (1) *shofeṭim*, "judges," and (2) *shoṭerim*," [153] "officers," the latter term of which in this place is translated in the Septuagint by γραμματοεισαγωγείς, and elsewhere simply by γραμματείς, terms which in Egyptian Greek mean "officers." [154] From the few places where the function of the *shoṭerim* is described we may gather that they made proclamations [155] and conveyed orders [156] to the people in time of war and that during the sojourn of Israel in Egypt they were Israelite officers subordinate to Egyptian taskmasters supervising the forced labor of the Israelites.[157] In rabbinic tradition *shoṭerim* are said to be "the managers that lead or rule the community" [158] or those who enforce the law.[159] As to who appoints these judges and these community rulers who enforce the law, the Pentateuch does not

---

and did not succeed Moses as kings. Second, this is quite obviously not the meaning of the passage. The passage begins with the following statement: "He received Aaron as one initialed by divine influence and as one endowed with prophetic spirit, reprehending the negligence of priests following afterwards, who on account of their indolence entrusted the service of the holy things to their second or third assistants." Then follows the passage quoted in the text. It is quite evident that the example of ancient kings is brought in only to show the importance of personally serving God on the part of those who rule others. The criticism of priests of later generations refers to the actual practice in the Temple.

[152] M. *Tamid* III, 1 and 9; M. *Yoma* II, 3. On Philo's pilgrimage to the Temple, see above, p. 242.

[153] Deut. 16: 18.

[154] Cf. G. A. Deissmann, *Bible Studies*, 1901, p. 110.

[155] Deut. 20: 5, 8, 9.

[156] Josh. 1: 10; 3: 2.   [158] *Tanḥuma, Shofeṭim*, § 2.

[157] Cf. Exod. 5: 6, 10, 14–16.   [159] *Pesikta Rabbati*, § 33, p. 149b.

say. The commandment on this point simply reads: "Judges and officers shalt thou appoint thee in all thy gates." [160] In the Pentateuch, we are told that the first judges and officers were appointed by Moses himself,[161] who, according to native Jewish tradition and Philo, was king.[162] Who appointed the judges from the time of the death of Joshua to the establishment of the kingdom Scripture does not say. During the existence of the kingdom there is mention of two kings who appointed "judges and officers," David [163] and Jehoshaphat.[164] Upon the restoration from Babylon, when there was no king, Ezra is said to have been empowered by the Persian king to appoint "officers (*shofeṭim*, γραμματεῖς) and judges (*dayyanin*, κριτάς)." [165] With the reëstablishment of the kingdom under the Hasmoneans it is not unlikely that judges were again appointed by the king. The Talmudic expression "the court of the Hasmoneans" may not refer to a court which supported the Hasmoneans at the beginning of their insurrection [166] or to "the leaders of the nation and the elders of the country" mentioned at the time Simon was elevated to the office of "prince of the people of God," [167] but rather to a court appointed by Simon after his having acquired princely or kingly power.[168] Accordingly, judges were appointed by a king whenever there

---

[160] Deut. 16: 18.

[161] Deut. 1: 15; Exod. 18: 25–26.

[162] Cf. above, pp. 337, 338.

[166] Frankel, *Darke ha-Mishnah*, ed. 1923, p. 43.

[163] I Chron. 23: 4; 26: 29.

[164] II Chron. 19: 4–11.

[165] Ezra 7: 25.

[167] Weiss, *Dor Dor we-Dorshaw* I⁴, p. 162; cf. I Macc. 14: 28.

[168] Cf. above, p. 327. The appointment of the judiciary by the king continued also under the Herodians, as may be gathered from *Antt.* XX, 9, 6, 216, where the Levites are said to have urged King Agrippa II to "assemble a sanhedrin" which would allow them to wear linen garments like the priests. The king's prerogative to "assemble" a court of justice was nothing but an extension of his scriptural prerogative to appoint judges. And since it was the king's prerogative to assemble the sanhedrin, it was also his prerogative to adjourn it, as may be gathered from the action of Hyrcanus II during the trial of Herod (*Antt.* XIV, 9, 5, 177).

was a king, but they were appointed in some other way, whenever there was no king. In Tannaitic tradition, therefore, the law of the appointment of judges is restated as a duty which rests upon the people, without making any mention as to who has the appointive power.[169]

In the light of these historical and traditional views, we may study the passages in which Philo undertakes to describe the institution of "judges and officers." He deals with conditions when there is a king. The "judges and officers" are therefore to be appointed by the king. Being appointed by the king, they are therefore the king's "lieutenants" (διάδοχοι;[170] ὕπαρχοι[171]). The use of this term reflects the description of the first judges and officers as having been appointed by Moses to act as his lieutenants, and more particularly the description of the officers, including the *shoṭerim*, appointed by David as those "who serve the king" (λειτουργοῦντες)[172] as well as the use in the Septuagint of the term διάδοχος as a description of those servants of the king who are next to him in rank.[173] Then, following tradition, he defines the duty of the *shoṭerim*, γραμματοεισαγωγεῖς, as that of governing together with the king (συνάρξουσι),[174] as distinguished from the duty of the *shofeṭim*, κριταί, in his own language δικασταί,[175] which is that of judging together with the king (συνδικάσουσι).[176] The terms ἄρχοντες (implied in συνάρξουσι) and δικασταί used here by Philo for the pentateuchal *shofeṭim*, κριταί, and *shoṭerim*, γραμματοεισαγωγεῖς, are taken from the Athenian constitution.[177] But whereas in Athens the judges and magistrates were elected by the general assembly from among themselves, in the Mosaic con-

---

[169] *Sanhedrin* 16b.
[170] *Spec.* IV, 33, 170.
[171] *Ibid.*, 174.
[172] I Chron. 27: 1; 28: 1.
[173] I Chron. 18: 17; II Chron. 26: 11; II Chron. 28: 7.
[174] *Spec.* IV, 33, 170.
[175] *Ibid.*, 174; cf. below, p. 351.
[176] *Ibid.*, 170.
[177] Cf. Aristotle, *Politica* III, 1, 1275a, 22–31.

stitution they were appointed by the king. Following also his conception of the state as it existed under the reign of Moses, he limits the duties of these judges and officers to cases of lesser importance; cases of higher importance are to be attended to by the king himself,[178] as was the custom under the reign of Moses.[179] Again following the example of Moses who appointed "rulers of thousands, and rulers of hundreds, rulers of fifties, and rulers of tens," [180] he prescribes for future kings to choose officers "to act as second and third to themselves." [181]

(d) Council of Elders

Besides the institution of "judges and officers" which was established under the reign of Moses and for the continuation of which there is a special law, there is also mention of a body of "seventy men," selected by Moses from among "the elders of the people, and officers over them," the function of that body being described in the words that "they shall bear the burden of the people" with Moses.[182] There is no special law in the Pentateuch, for the continuation of that body of seventy elders. But bodies of elders continue to be mentioned throughout the books of the Hebrew Scripture. Sometimes they are the elders of the city [183] or of the gate [184] or of a particular place [185] or of a particular tribe [186] or of the priests,[187] but sometimes they are also the elders of Israel,[188] the elders of the people,[189] or the elders of the land,[190] and once there is mention of "seventy men of the elders of

[178] Spec. IV, 33, 171.
[179] Exod. 18: 22.
[180] Exod. 18: 21.
[181] Spec. IV, 33, 175.
[182] Num. 11: 16–17.
[183] Deut. 21: 3.
[184] Deut. 25: 7.

[185] Judges 11: 5.
[186] Deut. 31: 28; II Sam. 19: 12.
[187] II Kings 19: 2.
[188] Exod. 3: 16.
[189] Num. 11: 16.
[190] I Kings 20: 7.

the house of Israel." [191] Sometimes the "elders" are bracketed with "officers," without any mention of "judges," [192] sometimes they are bracketed with "judges," without any mention of "officers," [193] but sometimes they are bracketed with both "officers" and "judges," [194] all of which shows that "elders" as distinguished from "officers" were "judges" and as distinguished from "judges" were "officers" but as distinguished from both were something else altogether. That something else is described in Scripture as their acting in the capacity of counselors. "Counsel" ($\beta o v \lambda \dot{\eta}$), according to Scripture, is sought from "elders," [195] and Rehoboam, on becoming king, seeks counsel from the elders.[196] After the restoration from the Babylonian exile, with the emergence of various governing bodies which continued to exist under various names and with constantly changing powers, throughout the period of the second commonwealth, both at the time when there was no king and during the Hasmonean and Herodian kings, the members of these governing bodies were also known as "elders" [197] and one of these bodies, during the Hellenistic and Maccabean periods, is known in Greek sources as *gerusia*, council of elders, a term which was used also as a designation of the governing body of the Jews of Alexandria at the time of Philo.[198] During the Roman period all such governing bodies among the Jews in Palestine came to be known, even among Jews who did not speak Greek, by the Greek name Synedrion, or, in its Hebraized form, Sanhedrin.

[191] Exod. 8: 11.
[192] Num. 11: 16; Deut. 31: 28.
[193] Deut. 21: 2.
[194] Josh. 8: 33; 23: 2.
[195] Ezek. 7: 26; Ezra 10: 8.
[196] I Kings 12: 6–8; II Chron. 10: 6–8.
[197] Ezra 5: 5, 9; 6: 7, 14; 10: 8; Judith 6: 16; 7: 23; 8: 10; 10: 6; 13: 12; I Macc. 7: 33; 11: 23; 12: 35; 14: 20; II Macc. 1: 10; 4: 44; 11: 27; Matt. 28: 41; Mark 11: 27; Acts 4: 23.
[198] *Flac.* 10, 74.

This is the picture which we have reason to believe Philo has formed in his mind of the institution of elders, and this picture could have been formed in his mind out of the books available to him at his own time as well as out of a knowledge of conditions in Palestine at his own time. It is in the light of this that we shall try to understand the full meaning of his brief references to the institution of elders. That he does not directly describe this body in his delineation of the Mosaic constitution can be explained on the ground that no special law for its continuation is laid down in the Pentateuch. But he does not overlook the fact that such a body of seventy elders was established by Moses. He refers to these seventy elders of Moses in several places,[199] in one of which he describes them as *synedroi* (σύνεδροι)[200] of Moses. His description of them as *synedroi* would seem to suggest a conscious effort on the part of Philo to connect the Synedrion of Jerusalem at his own time with the seventy elders of Moses, thus reflecting the native Jewish tradition that the Synedrion of Jerusalem had a continuous history, under various names, from the council of the seventy elders of Moses.[201]

What Philo considered as the functions of these seventy elders gathered together by Moses, whom he calls *synedroi*, is not clear. In Palestine during Philo's own time the function of the Sanhedrin was primarily that of a court of justice,

---

[199] References to these seventy elders of Moses are to be found in *Gig.* 6, 24; *Sobr.* 4, 19; *Migr.* 36, 199, and 201. His mention of the seventy γενάρχαι of the nation in *Mos.* I, 34, 189, does not refer to the seventy elders of Moses but rather to the seventy souls with which Jacob came to Egypt (Gen. 46: 27; Deut. 10: 22), to which reference is made by Philo also in *Migr.* 36, 201. Cf. *Fug.* 33, 187, where the seventy palm-trees (Exod. 15: 27) are different from the seventy elders of Moses (Num. 11: 16) and also *Mos.* I, 34, 188–189, where the seventy γενάρχαι are said to be symbolized by the seventy palm-trees.

[200] *Sobr.* 4, 19.

[201] *M. Sanhedrin* I, 6; *Jer. Sanhedrin* I, 5, 19b.

though it had also other functions, and it is used interchangeably with the term *bet din*, court of justice.[202] In the
same sense is the term *synedrion* also used in the Septuagint
where it quite evidently reflects the reading *bet din* [203] in the
Hebrew text upon which it is based. In Greek, however, the
primary meaning of *synedrion* is that of a council and
not many years after Philo in a work written probably in
Alexandria it is contrasted with the term δικαστήριον, court
of justice.[204] As for Philo, the term *synedrion* is sometimes
used by him in the sense of council [205] and sometimes in the
sense of court.[206] Similarly with regard to the term *synedros*, it is used by him both in the general sense of coun-
selor and in the specific sense of an officer in a court of
justice.[207] Philo's double use of the term *synedrion* is brought

[202] *Jer. Sanhedrin* I, 6, 19c.

[203] Prov. 22: 10; cf. Commentaries of Paul de Lagarde, 1863, Ant. J. Baum-
gartner, 1890, and C. H. Toy, 1899, *ad loc.*; cf. also Schürer, *A History of the Jewish
People in the Time of Jesus Christ*, II, i, p. 169, n. 461.
    The use of the term *synedrion* in the sense of court of justice is implied in the
verse "sit (*synedreue*) not in judgment with sinners" (Sirach 11: 9) and also in the
verses stating that the profane man who sits in "the *synedrion* of the pious . . . is
severe in speech in condemning sinners in judgment, and his hand is first upon the
sinner as though acting in zeal" (Psalms of Solomon 4: 1–3). The last statement,
moreover, quite evidently refers to Deut. 13: 10 and 17: 7, which deal with the
execution of the judgment of a court of justice. Undoubtedly the term *synedrion*
here is a translation of the Hebrew *'edah*, which means not only "assembly" but
also a "court of justice" (cf. Num. 35: 24). So also in the verse "In the synagogues
(συναγωγαῖς) he will judge the peoples" (Psalms of Solomon 17: 48), the word
"synagogues" is undoubtedly also a translation of the Hebrew *'edot* in the special
sense of "courts of justice." Professor Louis Ginzberg has called my attention to
the term *'edah* in Num. 25: 7, which in *Targum Jonathan* and *Jer. Sanhedrin* X,
2, 28d, is translated by *sanhedrin*.

[204] Pseudo-Aristotle, *De Mundo* 6, 400b, 15–18. However, the use of the Greek
term *synedrion* in the sense of a court occurs in a papyrus of 120 B.C. (cf. Moulton
and Milligan, *The Vocabulary of the Greek Testament*, 1914–1929, *s.v.*).

[205] *Conf.* 18, 86; *Somn.* I, 34, 193; *Legat.* 31, 213.

[206] *Probus* 2, 11. In this passage, speaking of men who are not guided by reason,
Philo says of them figuratively that their "unstable *synedrion* is always open to
bribes from those who are brought to trial (κρινομένων)."

[207] Compare *Legat.* 33, 244, and 34, 254, where the term *synedros* is used simply

out in two passages, in one of which he connects it by the conjunction "and" with the term court ($\delta\iota\kappa\alpha\sigma\tau\acute{\eta}\rho\iota\text{o}\nu$)[208] and in the other with the term council ($\beta\text{o}\nu\lambda\epsilon\nu\tau\acute{\eta}\rho\iota\text{o}\nu$).[209] Now, if the conjunction "and" ($\kappa\alpha\acute{\iota}$) is used in both passages to join two contrasting terms, then in the first passage the term *synedrion*, being used in contrast to the term *dikasterion*, is definitely a council, but in the second passage, being used in contrast to the term *bouleuterion*, the term *synedrion* is definitely a court of justice. And if the conjunction "and" is used to join two terms of the same meaning, then in the first passage the term *synedrion* is definitely a court of justice, whereas in the second passage it is definitely a council. It was quite natural for Jews, in whose own form of government the same body of elders acted both as council and as court, to attach to the Greek term *synedrion* primarily the meaning of court.

(e) The People: Native-born and Proselytes

The "whole multitude"[210] which, according to Philo, is to elect the king corresponds to what Scripture calls "the people"[211] or "the congregation of the Lord"[212] or "the assembly of the Lord."[213] But when Philo substitutes for these scriptural terms the term "the whole multitude" ($\sigma\acute{\nu}\mu\pi\alpha\sigma\alpha\ \acute{\eta}\ \pi\lambda\eta\theta\grave{\nu}s$), he had in mind what Aristotle calls the "political multitude" ($\pi\lambda\tilde{\eta}\theta\text{o}s\ \pi\text{o}\lambda\iota\tau\iota\kappa\grave{\text{o}}\nu$),[214] that is to say, the multitude of citizens. Now, according to Aristotle, "a mul-

---

in the sense of counsellor, with 44, 350, where Philo complains that Caligula acted not as a judge ($\delta\iota\kappa\alpha\sigma\tau\acute{\eta}s$) sitting with his *synedroi*, but as an accuser ($\kappa\alpha\tau\acute{\eta}\gamma\text{o}\rho\text{o}s$). The terms "judge" and "accuser" quite clearly show that the term *synedroi* in this last passage is used in the sense of members of a court of justice.

[208] *Praem.* 5, 28. [211] Exod. 18: 10.
[209] *Cont.* 3, 27. [212] Deut. 23: 2–4; cf. below, p. 394.
[210] *Spec.* IV, 30, 157; cf. above, p. 329. [213] Num. 27: 17.
[214] *Politica* III, 13, 1283b, 2–3; VII, 6, 1327b, 18; 10, 1329b, 24–25.

titude of citizens" (πολιτῶν πλῆθος) constitutes a state (πόλις),[215] and a citizen (πολίτης) in the strictest sense of the term is defined by his right "to participate in the administration of justice and in office," [216] for a citizen, according to him, must possess the ability not only to be ruled but also to rule.[217] But as to who is to have these rights whereby he is to be a citizen is a question which causes Aristotle some difficulty. Some maintain, he says, that a citizen is he whose both parents are citizens; others maintain that his ancestors to the second or third preceding generation, or even further, must be citizens; still others wonder how these remote ancestors came to be citizens.[218] Then, in addition to citizens by birth, Aristotle finds that in every state there are also those who have been adopted as citizens.[219] But concerning these adopted citizens Aristotle finds that the manner in which they acquire their citizenship is purely arbitrary, and he suspects that not all who are usually admitted to citizenship deserve to be admitted.[220] He himself, however, fails to suggest any definite method by which aliens are to be admitted to citizenship. Moreover, in view of the fact that a citizen must be able to rule, Aristotle raises the question whether certain classes of the native-born population should not be excluded from citizenship on account of the occupations in which they happen to be engaged, and he answers this question in the affirmative.[221] Finally, besides these two classes of citizens, native-born and adopted, Aristotle also finds that among the inhabitants of various states there are aliens (ξένοι) and resident aliens (μέτοικοι).[222] The legal

[215] Ibid. III, 1, 1274b, 41.   [217] Ibid., 4, 1277a, 26–27.
[216] Ibid., 1275a, 22–23.   [218] Ibid., 2, 1275b, 21–26.
[219] Ibid., 1, 1275a, 6.
[220] Ibid., 2, 1275b, 34–39; cf. V, 3, 1303a, 38 f.
[221] Ibid., 5, 1277b, 33–1278b, 5; VII, 6, 1327b, 8–15; VII, 9, 1328b, 39–41.
[222] Ibid. III, 5, 1277b, 38–39.

354   PHILO

status of these, however, he finds, is nowhere definitely established, for, as he observes, the rights of resident aliens
differ in different places.²²³

Philo, therefore, undertakes to treat that "assembly
(ἐκκλησία) of the Lord" or "congregation (συναγωγή) of the
Lord" as a polity (πολιτεία),²²⁴ as a political state governed
by a constitution embodied in the laws of Moses, and to
show how the constitution of that state defines with clearness and precision as well as with fairness the status of the
various classes of inhabitants.

Without any direct reference to other constitutions, he
describes the status of the various classes of inhabitants
under the Mosaic constitution in such a way as to be indirectly a criticism of their status under other constitutions.
Under the man-made constitutions discussed by Aristotle,
he would seem to argue, a citizen must have the ability not
only to be ruled but also to rule, and it is because of this
conception of citizenship that Aristotle demands that certain native-born inhabitants should be excluded from citizenship on account of their occupation and it is probably
also because of this conception of citizenship that no definite
law for the admission of aliens to citizenship is offered by
him. Citizenship, according to Aristotle, could be conferred
on aliens only by the good will of the people. Under the
divinely ordered constitution, however, Philo would seem
to say, a citizen is he who is willing to be ruled by the
Law. No one born under the Law can be excluded from
citizenship; no alien who is willing to accept the Law can be
refused citizenship. Moreover, under the divinely ordered
constitution the rights of temporary aliens and resident
aliens are well defined by law.

²²³ *Ibid.*, I, 1275a, 11 ff.
²²⁴ Cf. below, pp. 374 ff.

In the Mosaic state, as in the states dealt with by Aristotle, there are two classes of citizens. The first class consists of native-born Jews. These, says Philo, form a nation (ἔθνος), composed of twelve tribes (φυλαί), being descendants of twelve tribal ancestors (ἡγεμόνες), who were connected not by being merely members of the same household (οἰκία) or by mere kinsmanship (συγγένεια) but by being all brothers (ἀδελφοί) having one and the same father.[225] Native-born Jews are therefore described by him as fellow-nationals (ὁμοεθνεῖς)[226] or fellow-tribesmen (ὁμόφυλοι)[227] or kinsmen (συγγενεῖς),[228] or simply as native-born (αὐτόχθονες),[229] which term is generally used in Scripture.[230] Members of the assembly of this kind are all equal before the law: every one of them is eligible to any office and is excluded from no privilege. Wealth or birth or occupation is no barrier. Even the so-called Hebrew slave is only a hired laborer,[231] with all his duties and privileges of the law remaining intact. The only discrimination between native-born Jews is to be found in the laws regarding priests and bastards, but for these discriminatory laws Philo offers explanations both rational and allegorical.[232]

Members of the assembly of the second kind are described by Philo by the Septuagint term proselytes (προσήλυτοι), that is, those who have come over, and also by the term

[225] *Praem.* 10, 57. With all these terms used by Philo, compare the Greek terms *ethnos, genos, patra, phratria,* and *phyle,* for groups in the city-state.

[226] *Spec.* II, 17, 73; 25, 122; *Virt.* 19, 101; 20, 102; *Legat.* 31, 212; cf. also *Spec.* I, 9, 54: τῶν ἀπὸ τοῦ ἔθνους τινές. Cf. below, pp. 359, 360, 363.

[227] *Spec.* IV, 31, 159. Cf. below, p. 359.

[228] *Ibid.* But see S. Zeitlin, "The Jews: Race, Nation or Religion," *Jewish Quarterly Review,* N.S., 26 (1936), pp. 333–336, who argues that the terms ὁμόφυλοι and ἔθνος, in their application to Jews, are always used by Philo in a religious sense. Cf. below, pp. 400–402.

[229] *Ibid.* I, 9, 52, *et passim.*   [230] Exod. 12: 49.

[231] *Spec.* II, 18, 79–85; *Virt.* 24, 121–123.

[232] *Spec.* I, 15, 79–22, 111; 60, 326–329, and *Decal.* 24, 128–130.

epelytes (ἐπηλύται), that is, those who have come in. "These Moses calls proselytes," he says, "because they have come over to the new and God-loving polity,"[233] and the "epelytes," he says, are those who "have taken a journey to a better home, from idle fables to the clear vision of truth."[234] With the exception of certain restrictions in the case of Amonites, Moabites, Edomites, and Egyptians,[235] all aliens are accepted at once into the Mosaic polity on equal terms with the native-born Jew. Drawing upon the verse which in the Septuagint reads "the proselyte who cometh to you shall be as one born among you, and thou shalt love him as thyself,"[236] he says, "thus, while giving equal rank to all incomers with all the privileges which he gives to the native born, he exhorts the old nobility to honor them not only with marks of respect but with special friendship and with more than ordinary good will"[237] and "he commands all members of the nation to love the in-comers, not only as friends and kinsfolk but as themselves both in body and soul."[238]

The admission of proselytes on equal terms with native-born Jews into the Jewish polity indicates, according to Philo, that the basis of that polity is not common descent but rather the common heritage of the Law which was revealed by God to the people of Israel. Even the native-born Jew is a member of that polity, in the full sense of the term membership, not only because he is a descendant of the stock that founded that polity but also, and primarily so, because he remained loyal to the Law which is the heritage of that stock. "The native-born Jews," he says, "obtain the approval of God not because they are members of the God-loving polity from birth (ἐξ ἀρχῆς) but because they were

---

[233] *Spec.* I, 9, 51.
[234] *Virt.* 20, 102; cf. *Spec.* IV, 34, 178.
[235] Deut. 23: 4–9; cf. *Virt.* 21, 108.
[236] Lev. 19: 34; cf. Deut. 10: 19.
[237] *Spec.* I, 9, 52.
[238] *Virt.* 20, 103.

not false to the nobility of their birth (εὐγένειαν)"; the prose-lytes obtain His approval "because they have thought fit to make the passage to piety." [239] It is for this reason, he says, that the latter, who have left "their country, their friends (φίλους), and their kinsfolk (συγγενεῖς) for the sake of virtue and holiness," are not to be denied "other states (πόλεων) and other households (οἰκείων) and other friends (φίλων)," for "the most effectual love-charm and the chain which binds indissolubly the good will which makes us one is to honor the one God." [240] These statements, while Jewish in sentiment, are couched in language in which one may discern an echo of Aristotle's statements that "friendship (φιλία) seems to hold states (πόλεις) together" [241] and friendship may be either that of fellow-citizens (πολιτικαί) or that of kindred (συγγενικήν),[242] the former being based on a sort of compact (ὁμολογία)[243] and the latter being based upon the same blood (ταὐτὸν αἷμα) or the same stock (ῥίζαν),[244] but "per-fect friendship is the friendship of men who are good and alike in virtue." [245]

The superiority of a kinship which is based upon a common belief to that which is based upon a common descent is re-peatedly asserted by Philo in other passages. In contrast to "the so-called kinships (συγγένειαι) which have come down from our ancestors and are based on blood-relationships" the relationship based upon common belief is called by him "kinships of greater dignity and sanctity" [246] and it is this latter kind of kinship which, according to him, is meant when

---

[239] *Spec.* I, 9, 51. Similarly, according to rabbinic law, an apostate Jew is not allowed to eat of the paschal lamb, whereas a proselyte is allowed to eat of it (*Pesaḥim* 96a; *Yebamot* 71a; *Sifre Num.*, § 71, F, p. 18b; H, p. 67).

[240] *Ibid.*, 52.

[241] *Eth. Nic.* VIII, 1, 1155a, 22–23.

[242] *Ibid.* VIII, 12, 1161b, 12–13.

[243] *Ibid.*, 13–14.

[244] *Ibid.*, 32.

[245] *Ibid.* VIII, 3, 1156b, 7–8.

[246] *Spec.* I, 58, 317.

Scripture describes all those who do what is pleasing to
nature, that is, to God, as "sons of God." [247] Such a kinship
is established by one's "willingness to serve God." [248] By
the expression "to serve God" he means here, as he does
elsewhere, to serve God in the manner prescribed by the
Law of Moses,[249] for, speaking of the law about resting on
the Sabbath, to observe which the proselyte is explicitly commanded,[250] Philo says "He commanded those who should
live in this polity to follow God in this as in other matters." [251] The superiority of the kinship based upon the service of God to that based upon blood relationship is also
asserted by him in his comment upon the verse "The
proselyte who is with thee shall rise higher and higher; but
thou shalt fall lower and lower." [252] The proselyte, he says,
will be exalted "because he has come over to God of his own
accord . . . while the nobly born who had falsified the sterling
of his high lineage will be dragged down to the lowest depths
. . . in order that all men who behold this example may be
corrected by it, learning that God received gladly virtue
which grows out of ignoble birth, utterly disregarding its
original roots." [253] It is not impossible that his use of the
terms "he has come over to God of his own accord" (αὐτο-
μολῆσαι)[254] and "they have thought fit (ἠξίωσαν) to make the
passage to piety" [255] and that any stranger may become a
proselyte "out of an excess of virtues" (ὑπερβολαῖς ἀρετῶν)[256]
all imply that a proselyte is he who has accepted Judaism
out of pure and disinterested motives, thus corresponding to
the rabbinic teaching that the "righteous" or "true"

---

[247] *Ibid.*, 318; cf. Deut. 14: 1; Wisdom of Solomon 9: 7; 12: 19, 21; 16: 10, 26;
18: 4.   [252] Deut. 28: 43 (LXX).
[248] *Ibid.*, 317.   [253] *Praem.* 26, 152.
[249] Cf. above, pp. 51–52.   [254] *Ibid.*
[250] Exod. 20: 10.   [255] *Spec.* I, 9, 51.
[251] *Decal.* 20, 98.   [256] *Ibid.* II, 17, 73; cf. below, p. 417.

proselyte is he who embraces his new religion "for the sake
of heaven"[257] or "for the sake of the holiness of Israel"[258]
or "for the sake of covenant,"[259] and without any ulterior
motive.

With this conception of the Mosaic polity as being based
upon a common law but within which there are two kinds
of citizens, one descendants of the original founders of the
polity and the other those who have joined it later, the
question may be raised as to what is meant by the term
"thy brother" in those laws where it is explicitly mentioned that they apply only to "thy brother." Is this term
to apply only to a brother by race or also to a brother by
religion? In answer to this question we shall examine the
passages in which Philo happens to comment upon those
laws in which the term "thy brother" is mentioned.

First, there is the law with regard to the election of a king
in which it is specified that the king is to be elected from
among "thy brethren" and that "thou mayest not set a
stranger over thee, who is not *thy brother.*"[260] In his discussion of this law, Philo defines the term "thy brother" as
meaning "one who was their fellow-tribesman (ὁμόφυλον) and
fellow-kinsman (συγγενῆ),"[261] that is, a Jew by birth, adding,
however, that this Jew by birth must also share "in that
relationship which brings the highest kinship (συγγένειαν) —
and that highest kinship is one citizenship (πολιτεία) and the
same law (νόμος) and one God who has taken all members of

---

[257] *Jer. Ḳiddushin* IV, 1, 65b.
[258] *Ibid.*   [259] *Tos. ʿAbodah Zarah* III, 13.
[260] Deut. 17: 15. This, according to tradition, excludes a proselyte from kingship. A Jewish mother, however, qualifies his descendants for the office (*Midrash
Tannaim*, on Deut. 17: 15, p. 104).
[261] Both these terms here, we take it, are used in their original racial sense, as
above, nn. 227–228. The passage under consideration reads literally as follows:
"A fellow-tribesman and fellow-kinsman, who had a share in the relationship
which makes for the highest kinship."

the nation (ἔθνους) for His portion," [262] that is, this Jew by birth must also be a Jew by religion. In this passage, then, Philo takes the term "thy brother" to mean both a Jew by descent and a Jew by loyalty to his religion. This is in agreement with the traditional Jewish interpretation of this law that one to be chosen as king must not only be worthy of the office by his manner of life [263] but also by his descent, thus disqualifying a proselyte from the office of king.[264] Whether Philo would extend this law, as do the rabbis, to include all other offices of magistrates and judges [265] is not certain. In Athens a naturalized citizen was not allowed to become an archon or to hold a priesthood,[266] the latter of which was a state office. Though, following the Septuagint, Philo calls the king *archon*, he does not include other officers under it, for he does not require their election by the people.[267]

Second, in connection with the Hebrew slave who is to be set free on the year of the jubilee or on his seventh year of service, Philo explains the terms "thy brother" [268] and "thy brother, a Hebrew man" [269] to mean "a fellow-tribesman" (ὁμόφυλον)[270] or "of the same nation (ἔθνους), perhaps also of the same tribe (φυλέτης) and of the same family (δημό-της)." [271] All these terms imply kinship based upon descent.[272] The implication then is that the laws regulating

[262] *Spec.* IV, 31, 159; for the last part of the quotation, cf. *Post.* 25, 89–90; *Mos.* II, 35, 189.

[263] Cf. above, p. 328.   [264] Cf. above, n. 260.

[265] *Midrash Tannaim, loc. cit.; Jer. Ḳiddushin* IV, 5, 66a.

[266] Cf. P. Gardner and F. B. Jevons, *A Manual of Greek Antiquities*, 2nd ed., 1898, p. 456.

[267] Cf. above, p. 347. But see Heinemann, *Bildung*, p. 189; Belkin, *Philo and the Oral Law*, p. 185.   [268] Lev. 25: 39.

[269] Deut. 15: 12.   [270] *Spec.* II, 18, 80.   [271] *Ibid.*, 82.

[272] The last two terms in this list, φυλέτης and δημότης, undoubtedly correspond respectively to the Hebrew *shebet*, tribe, and *mishpaḥah*, family, (cf. Num. 36: 3, 6, 12. 1: 20, 22; 2: 34) and do not refer to contemporary classifications of citizens in Alexandria (cf. Colson, *ad loc.*).

the Hebrew slave do not apply to a proselyte. This corresponds exactly to the rabbinic view, according to which a proselyte sold into slavery does not come under the laws of a Hebrew slave; the reason given is that on his release he cannot return, as the verse says, "unto his own family," [273] inasmuch as he has no family.

Third, in connection with the law about restoring lost property which in one place reads "If thou meet thy enemy's ox or his ass going astray, thou shalt surely bring it back to him again," [274] and in another place reads, "Thou shalt not see thy brother's ox or sheep go astray, and hide thyself from them: thou shalt in any case bring them back unto *thy brother*," [275] Philo describes the term "thy enemy" in a rather general way, without indicating whether he takes it to refer to a Jew or to a non-Jew,[276] and similarly in his description of the term "thy brother" he says that it refers to "one of your relations (οἰκείων) or friends (φίλων), or in general a person you know," [277] without indicating whether he takes it to refer only to a native-born Jew, or also to a proselyte, or even also to a heathen. One may reasonably assume, however, that Philo takes this law to apply not only to a proselyte but also to a heathen. In rabbinic literature a proselyte is definitely included under the term "thy brother" in this case, for the term is said to exclude only "a heathen." [278] But even with regard to a heathen there seems to be a difference of opinion, for among the various interpretations of the term "thy enemy," there is one interpreta-

---

[273] Lev. 25: 41; cf. *Baba Meṣiʿa* 71a; but see opposite view in *Mekilta, Nezikin* 1 (F, p. 75a; W, p. 81b; L, III, p. 5).

[274] Exod. 23: 4.   [275] Deut. 22: 1.

[276] *Virt.* 23, 117; cf. 116.

[277] *Ibid.*, 18, 96.

[278] *Midrash Tannaim*, on Deut. 22: 3, p. 134; *Jer. Baba Meṣiʿa* II, 5, 8c; *Baba Ḳamma* 113b.

tion which takes it to mean "a heathen," [279] thus making the laws about the restoring of lost property apply even to the property of a heathen. Moreover, even those who on strictly legal grounds exclude a heathen from the benefit of this law maintain that on higher moral grounds he is to be included within this law.[280]

Fourth, in connection with the law about the release of debts in the seventh year, Philo, commenting upon the verse "of an alien thou mayest exact what may be due to thee from him but to *thy brother* thou shalt make a release of what he oweth thee," [281] says that "He does not allow them to exact their money from their fellow-nationals (ὁμοεθνῶν), but does permit the recovery of dues from the others," for "the condition of being an alien excludes any idea of partnership, unless indeed any alien (τις) out of an excess of virtues should transform that condition of being an alien (ταύτην) into a kinship of relationship, since it is a general truth that the [best] polity rests on virtues and laws which propound the morally beautiful." [282] In this passage Philo quite evidently wishes to say that the term "thy brother" used in this law is to include a proselyte. An "alien" (ἀλλότριος), he argues, is not a fellow-national (ὁμοεθνής) of the Jews, and consequently Scripture excludes him explicitly from the law of the release of debts in the seventh year. But should such an alien through an excess of virtue, that is, through "the willingness to serve God" or "to follow God" in the observance of the Sabbath and the

---

[279] *Mekilta, Kaspa* 2, F, p. 99a; W, 104b; HR, p. 324; L, III, p. 163. Other interpretations are that it means a proselyte who reverted to heathenism, or a Jew who became a heathen, or simply a Jew by descent and religion with whom the finder of the lost property happens to be on unfriendly terms.

[280] *Midrash Tannaim,* on Deut. 22: 3, p. 134; *Jer. Baba Meṣi'a* II, 5, 8c; *Baba Kamma* 113b.

[281] Deut. 15: 3 (LXX). [282] *Spec.* II, 17, 73.

other laws, join the "holy polity" which is based upon "one
manner of life and the same law and one God," then he is
brought into "the highest kinship" with the rest of the Jews
and thereby becomes entitled to the benefit of this law.
Similarly in the Tannaitic law, the term "thy brother" in
this verse is taken to include a proselyte [283] and to exclude a
resident alien (*ger toshab*).[284]

Finally, in connection with the law about not lending
money on interest, Philo commenting upon the verses "thou
shalt not lend upon interest to *thy brother*" [285] but "unto
an alien thou mayest lend upon interest," [286] says that the
term "thy brother" means "not merely a child of the same
parents, but anyone who is a fellow-townsman (ἀστός) and
fellow-tribesman (ὁμόφυλος)." [287] Now while the term "fellow-
tribesman" may mean here, as it does in its original sense,
a native-born Jew, the term "townsman" (ἀστός) usually
means in Greek the same as the term "citizen" (πολίτης),[288]
and consequently at least the term "fellow-townsman," if
not also the term "fellow-tribesman," is undoubtedly to be
taken here as referring to a proselyte, who, as we have seen,
is a member of the Jewish polity (πολιτεία).[289] His statement
here that the term "thy brother" includes "anyone who is a
fellow-townsman and a fellow-tribesman" means, therefore,
that it includes both native-born Jews and proselytes. His
inclusion of proselytes in this prohibition is further em-
phasized by him in his statement that "he absolutely commands those who shall be members of his holy polity to

---

[283] *Midrash Tannaim*, on Deut. 15: 2, p. 80.
[284] *Sifre Deut.*, § 112, F, p. 97b; HF, p. 173; cf. below, p. 362.
[285] Deut. 23: 20.
[286] Deut. 23: 21.   [287] *Virt.* 14, 82.
[288] Cf. Aristotle, *Politica* III, 7, 1279a, 34–36; Philo, *Mos.* I, 7, 35; cf. below,
p. 399.
[289] Cf. above, p. 356.

discard such methods of profit-making." ²⁹⁰ Proselytes, as
we have seen, are members of the holy polity. In this latter
statement, Philo tries to emphasize the fact that just as it is
prohibited for a Jew to lend money on interest to a proselyte,
so it is prohibited for a proselyte to lend money on interest
to a Jew or to another proselyte. In rabbinic law it is similarly assumed that the proselyte is included in the law prohibiting interest, both to be exacted interest by a Jew and to
exact interest from a Jew.²⁹¹

From all this it may be gathered that, with the exception
of certain laws regarding king and slave, Philo, like the
rabbis, took the term "thy brother" to include a proselyte.

(f) Aliens, Resident Aliens, and Spiritual Proselytes

Within this Mosaic polity, in which citizens are those who
are "sons of God" in the sense of their willingness to serve
God and to follow Him in the observance of His laws, there
is also room for three other classes of people who are neither
native-born Jews nor proselytes.

First, there is the alien who in the Septuagint is described
by the term ἀλλογενής or ἀλλότριος, which translates the
Hebrew *ben nekar* or *nokri*. He is mentioned in the legal
portions of the Pentateuch as one (1) who is not allowed to
eat of the passover,²⁹² (2) to whom a Jew is not allowed to
sell his Jewish maidservant,²⁹³ (3) to whom anything that
dies of itself is to be sold,²⁹⁴ (4) whose debt is not to be re-
leased in the seventh year,²⁹⁵ (5) who cannot be made king,²⁹⁶
and (6) to whom money may be lent on interest.²⁹⁷ Of these
six laws in which the alien is specifically mentioned Philo

²⁹⁰ *Virt.* 14, 87.
²⁹¹ *Baba Meṣi'a* 72a.
²⁹² Exod. 12: 43.
²⁹³ Exod. 21: 8.

²⁹⁴ Deut. 14: 21.
²⁹⁵ Deut. 15: 3.
²⁹⁶ Deut. 17: 15.
²⁹⁷ Deut. 23: 21 (20).

happens to deal with him only in his discussion of the laws about the release of debts in the seventh year [298] and the office of king.[299] In his discussion of the alien in connection with both these laws the assumption is that they are confessing as well as practicing heathen.

Second, there is the resident alien who in the Septuagint is called πάροικος. This term translates the Hebrew *toshab*, who is mentioned in the Pentateuch as one (1) who is not allowed to eat of the passover,[300] (2) who, if he lives with a priest, is not allowed to eat of the consecrated things,[301] (3) who is to eat of the after-growth of the harvest and of the grapes of the undressed vine in the sabbatical year,[302] (4) who is to be helped if he is poor,[303] (5) who may be bought as a slave,[304] (6) from whom a Hebrew slave is to be redeemed, [305] and (7) who is among those for whose benefit the six cities of refuge were to be built.[306] In addition to these usages of the term *paroikos* as a translation of the Hebrew *toshab*, this term is used in the Septuagint also as a translation of the Hebrew term *ger*, (8) to whom anything that dies of itself is to be given.[307] Of these eight laws about a *paroikos*, Philo happens to reproduce only one, that of the verse that "the *paroikos* of a priest, or an hired servant, shall not eat of the holy things." [308] But in this case, he does not take the term *paroikos* in the sense of a resident alien but rather in the sense of neighbor, that is, a Jewish neighbor (γείτων) who happens to live with a priest.[309] So also in rabbinic law the term *toshab* in this verse is taken to refer

[298] *Spec.* II, 17, 73.
[299] *Ibid.* IV, 30, 157–31, 158.
[300] Exod. 12: 45.
[301] Lev. 22: 10.
[302] Lev. 25: 5–6. In this verse the expression "thy settler that sojourn with thee" is taken to include a heathen (cf. *Sifra, Behar, Perek* 1, p. 106c).
[303] Lev. 25: 35.
[304] Lev. 25: 45.
[305] Lev. 25: 47 ff.
[306] Num. 35: 15.
[307] Deut. 14: 21.
[308] Lev. 22: 10.
[309] *Spec.* I, 24, 120.

to a Jew who happens to live with a priest, or more particularly to a Hebrew slave of a priest who on the completion of his years of service has preferred to have his ear bored [310] and to remain with his master.[311] None of the other laws dealing with the *paroikoi* or resident aliens is discussed by him; nor does he give any clear indication whether he considered these "resident aliens" as heathen who differed from "aliens" only by their permanence of residence among Jews, or whether he considered them as differing from "aliens" also in their religious beliefs and practices. Now in Tannaitic law, the "resident alien" (*ger toshab*), the equivalent of the *paroikos* of the Septuagint, is not a heathen but rather one who, while uncircumcised, has abandoned idolatry or, in addition to his abandonment of idolatry, is also practicing certain Jewish laws generally referred to as the Noachian laws.[312] According to Tannaitic law, then, the "resident alien" of the Pentateuch, while not a full proselyte, was not a practicing idolater. Among later rabbis, moreover, probably as a result of this Tannaitic conception of the "resident alien" of the Pentateuch, the question was debated whether practicing idolaters were allowed at all to establish permanent residence in Palestine under Jewish rule.[313] While Philo does not discuss either of these two problems directly, there are three passages in his writings which may have a bearing upon them.

First, there is his reference to the non-Jewish population of Jamnia. "There is a city called Jamnia," he says, "one of the

---

[310] Cf. Exod. 21: 5–6.

[311] *Sifra, Emor, Perek* 4, p. 97a; *Yebamot* 70a.

[312] *'Aboda Zarah* 64b; cf. below, p. 373, and above, p. 185.

[313] Cf. Maimonides, *Sefer ha-Miṣwot*, Negative 51; *Mishneh Torah: 'Akum* X, 6, and *Rabad, ad loc.*; *Sefer Miṣwot Gadol (Semag)*, Negative 49; *Sefer ha-Ḥinnuk* 94; *Rashi* on *Giṭṭin* 45a. The question turned on the meaning of the verse "They shall not dwell in thy land" (Exod. 23: 33), whether it referred only to the original seven nations or to heathens in general.

most populous cities in Judea, which is inhabited by a promiscuous multitude, the greatest number of whom are Jews; but there are also some persons of other tribes from the neighboring nations who have mischievously made their way in, who are in a manner residents (μέτοικοι) among the original native citizens (αὐθιγενέσι), and who do them a great deal of injury and cause them a great deal of trouble, as they are constantly undoing (παραλύοντες) some of the ancestral national customs of the Jews." Then he goes on to tell how during the reign of Caligula, "thinking that they have now an admirable opportunity for attacking them themselves, they have erected an extemporaneous altar of the most contemptible materials, having made clay into bricks, for the sole purpose of plotting against their fellow citizens; for they knew well that they would never endure to see their customs transgressed; as was indeed the case." [314]

Now in this passage, it will be noticed, he describes the heathen population in Jamnia as being "in a manner *metoikoi*," and he complains of their being "constantly undoing some of the ancestral national customs of the Jews." We take it that Philo uses the Athenian term *metoikos* as synonymous with the Septuagint term *paroikos*,[315] and consequently what he means to say is that these non-Jews in Jamnia have enjoyed among the Jews the privilege of what the Septuagint calls *paroikoi*, which "in a manner" is the equivalent of what the Athenians call *metoikoi*. His complaint against them, it will be noticed, is not that they themselves do not observe Jewish customs but rather that they are constantly "undoing," that is to say, trying to destroy, Jewish customs, and that at the time of Caligula they openly joined with those who tried to force the Jews to violate their law. The inference to be drawn from this

[314] *Legat.* 30, 200–201.   [315] Cf. below, n. 317.

passage is that practicing idolaters were allowed to establish residence among Jews in Palestine and, in accordance with the prescription of the Mosaic Law, were treated as "resident aliens."

Second, there is his interpretation of the verse "thou shalt not abhor an Egyptian because thou wast a resident (πάροικος, Hebrew *ger*) in his land." [316] Commenting upon this verse, he says that "residents" (μέτοικοι) [317] in a foreign land should "pay some honor (τινὰ τιμήν) to those who have accepted them." [318] The implication is that "residents in a foreign land" in general, that is, both Jews in the diaspora and non-Jews in Palestine, are legally bound to "pay some honor to those who have accepted them." Now with reference to the honor to be paid by the Jews to those who have accepted them, Philo makes it clear that he means by it prayer offered for the welfare of the government under whose rule they happen to live. Speaking of his own native city, he says that the Jews of Alexandria pay honor (τιμή) to the Augustan house by setting forth their gratefulness (εὐχάριστον) in the synagogues,[319] that is, by praying for it. It is quite reasonable to assume that the "some honor" which he expects of non-Jewish residents in Palestine is of a similar nature, and nothing more.

Finally, there is his interpretation of the verses "Whosoever curses god shall be guilty of sin" [320] and "Thou shalt not revile the gods" [321] as referring generally to "the gods of the different cities who are falsely so called" [322] or to "the

---

[316] Deut. 23: 8 (7); cf. *Virt.* 21, 106.

[317] On the interchangeability of the terms πάροικος and μέτοικος, see M. Engers, *Klio* 18 (1923), p. 83, n. 4.

[318] *Virt.* 21, 105; cf. Jer. 29: 7.

[319] *Flac.* 7, 48–49.

[320] Lev. 24: 15 (LXX).

[321] Exod. 22: 27 (LXX).   [322] *Mos.* II, 38, 205.

gods whom others acknowledge." [323] The reason given by him for this law is that, by speaking insultingly of these other gods, one might "get into the habit of treating lightly of the word 'God' in general." [324] Inasmuch as this Mosaic law was meant primarily for the Jews residing in Palestine, we may assume that according to Philo heathens were to be allowed by the Mosaic law to live among Jews in Palestine.

All these passages would thus seem to indicate that the "resident alien," according to Philo's conception of the Mosaic Law, was, unlike the rabbinic *ger toshab*, a practicing idolater who was allowed to live among Jews in Palestine under the Pentateuchal laws regarding a *toshab*.

But, besides the "alien" and the "resident alien" Philo, in one single passage, speaks of a third type of non-Jewish resident in the Mosaic polity. He calls him "proselyte," but unlike the proselyte who has adopted all the practices and beliefs of Judaism and is a full member of the "congregation of the Lord," this new kind of proselyte is like the *ger toshab* of the rabbis, who, while he has not undergone circumcision and has not adopted all the Jewish practices and beliefs, has renounced polytheism and idolatry and has given up certain other heathen practices. We shall refer to this kind of proselyte as the "spiritual proselyte" instead of the more common name "semi-proselyte" to which objection has been raised. [325] A reference to such spiritual proselytes is found by Philo in the verses which in the Septuagint are translated "A proselyte (*ger*) shall you not wrong, neither shall you oppress him, for you were proselytes (*gerim*) in the land of Egypt" [326] and "A proselyte (*ger*) shall you not op-

---

[323] *Spec.* I, 9, 53. Cf. G. Allon in *Tarbiz*, 6 (1934–35), p. 30, n. 1.
[324] *Mos.* II, 38, 205; cf. *Spec.* I, 9, 53; *Qu. in Exod.* II, 5.
[325] Cf. Moore, *Judaism*, I, 339. [326] Exod. 22: 20 (21).

press, for you know the soul of a proselyte (*ger*), for you were proselytes (*gerim*) in the land of Egypt." [327] Commenting upon these verses, Philo tries to show that the term proselyte in them does not refer to a proselyte in the technical sense of the term, namely, one who is circumcised and follows all the laws. His reason for this interpretation of the term "proselyte" in these verses is its comparison to the term "proselytes" applied to the Jews in Egypt. According to Philo, the Jews, during their servitude in Egypt, did not practice circumcision,[328] and consequently, he argues, the proselyte who is not to be wronged must also refer to one who has not undergone circumcision. Still, while not circumcised, the "proselyte" in question is assumed by Philo to have accepted certain principles of Judaism.[329] What

[327] Exod. 23: 9. Cf. Belkin, *Philo and the Oral Law*, pp. 46–48.

[328] This view of Philo is based upon the Septuagint version of Joshua 5: 4, which reads: "All who had been born on the way, and all who had been formerly uncircumcised when they came out of Egypt, all these Joshua circumcised." So also according to native Jewish tradition none but the tribe of Levi practiced circumcision while in Egypt. *Sifre Num.*, § 67, F, p. 17b; H, p. 62; *Exodus Rabbah* 19, 5; cf. Ginzberg, *The Legends of the Jews* III, 211; VI, p. 78, n. 409; cf. also *Kimḥi* on Josh. 5: 5.

[329] The reasoning employed by Philo to show that the term "proselyte" in the two verses in question is to be taken in the sense of a "spiritual proselyte" because of its comparison to the Jews who were "proselytes" in Egypt is not followed out by him in his interpretation of the term "proselyte" in two other similar verses. In the verse "The proselyte who cometh to you shall be as the native-born among you, and thou shalt love him as thyself" (Lev. 19: 34), the term "proselyte" is taken by him, as by the rabbis, to refer to a full proselyte (*Spec.* I, 9, 52; *Virt.* 20, 103; cf. *Sifra, Ḳedoshim, Pereḳ* 8, p. 91a), though the verse concludes with the clause "for you were proselytes in the land of Egypt." Similarly in the verse "He administereth justice to the proselyte and the orphan and the widow, and loveth the proselyte in giving him food and raiment (Deut. 10: 18), the term "proselyte" is taken by him to refer to the full proselyte (*Spec.* I, 57, 308–309; *Virt.* 20, 104), even though it is followed by the verse "Love ye therefore the proselyte, for you were proselytes in the land of Egypt" (Deut. 10: 19). Evidently in these verses he takes the term "proselyte," which is applied to the Jews while they were in Egypt, merely in the general sense of one who is a newcomer, a stranger, and not a native. In one place the Jews in Egypt are described by him as aliens (ξένοι) (*Mos.* I, 7, 34) and in another place this term "alien" is taken by him to mean the

those principles are he does not specify. He only describes them as (a) a circumcision of "the pleasures and the desires and the other passions of the soul" and (b) "an estrangement (ἀλλοτρίωσις) from the opinions of the worshipers of many gods, and establishing a relationship (οἰκείωσις) with those who honor the one God, the Father of the universe." [330] Why such an uncircumcised gentile should be described as "proselyte" when this term in its technical sense means circumcision and the acceptance of all the laws is explained by Philo on the ground that the term "proselyte" is used here figuratively in two senses. First, as he himself has already indicated, such a gentile, while he is not circumcised in the flesh and has not fully joined the "holy polity," has "circumcised" his "pleasures" and "desires" and "other passions of the soul" and has become a stranger (ἀλλοτρίωσις) to polytheists and a relation (οἰκείωσις) to those who believe in one God. Second, referring to "some persons," he says that they explained the figurative use of "epelyte," which to Philo means the same as "proselyte," on the ground that the term "epelytes" in its literal sense means any aliens (ξένοι) "who have newly arrived (ἐπήλυδες) in the country," even though they have not been established in it as citizens, and consequently in its figurative sense it may be applied to "aliens who have come over to the truth" of some beliefs, even though they have not become fully converted.

In connection with Philo's interpretation of the term "proselyte" in the commandment about not wronging and not oppressing a "proselyte," it is interesting to note that in native Jewish tradition this commandment is similarly taken to refer to what is called a "resident alien" (ger toshab),

---

same as the term πάροικος, which in Deut. 23: 7, is applied to the Jews in Egypt (Virt. 21, 106).
[330] Qu. in Exod. II, 2; Fragmenta, Richter, VI, pp. 241–242 (M. II, 677).

which is the equivalent, as we have seen, of what we have called for Philo a "spiritual proselyte." This native Jewish interpretation of the law may be inferred from the rabbinic interpretation of the verses "Thou shalt not deliver unto his master a slave that escaped from his master unto thee; he shall dwell with thee, in the midst of thee, in the place which he shall choose within one of thy gates, where it liketh him best; thou shalt not wrong him." [331] Commenting upon these verses, the rabbis say that the laws contained in them apply not only to a fugitive slave but also to a "resident alien" (*ger toshab*).[332] The inference to be drawn is that the last words in these verses, "thou shalt not wrong him," are taken by the rabbis, as the similar words in other verses are taken by Philo, to include a "spiritual proselyte."

Whatever the value of Philo's interpretation of the term "proselyte" in the verses in question, his reference to what we have called spiritual proselytes reflects the actual ex-

[331] Deut. 23: 16–17.

[332] *Sifra, Behar, Perek 7*, on Lev. 25: 40, p. 109c; *Sifre Deut.*, § 259, F, p. 121a; HF, p. 282; *Midrash Tannaim*, on Deut. 23: 16, p. 149; *Gittin* 45a; *'Arakin* 29a. In a homiletical interpretation of the law in question, however, the term "proselyte" is explicitly taken by the rabbis in the sense of a full proselyte. Thus, commenting upon the verses "If a proselyte sojourn with thee in your land, ye shall not do him wrong; the proselyte that sojourneth with you shall be unto you as a native-born among you, and thou shalt love him as thyself, for ye were proselytes in the land of Egypt" (Lev. 19: 33–34), they say as follows: "'As a native born': just as the 'native-born' is he who has accepted the entire law, so also the 'proselyte' is he who has accepted the entire Law" (*Sifra, Kedoshim, Perek* 8, p. 91a; *Megillah* 17b; *Yebamot* 46b). In another homiletical passage, commenting upon the verse "Thou shalt not wrong a proselyte" (Exod. 22: 20), the rabbis say: "Thou shalt not wrong him with words . . . Thou shalt not say to him: Yesterday thou wast worshipping Bel, bowing down [to] Nebo (cf. Isa. 46: 1) and behold swine's flesh is still between thy teeth, and now thou darest to say things against me" (*Mekilta, Nezikin* 18, F, p. 95a; W, p. 101a; HR, p. 311; L, III, p. 137). In this passage, it is not clear whether the expression "and behold swine's flesh is still between thy teeth" should be taken literally, the reference thus being to one who is not a full proselyte, or whether it should be taken figuratively and the reference would thus be to a full proselyte. Legally, however, as we have seen, the law in question is taken by the rabbis, as it is by Philo, to apply also to a spiritual proselyte.

istence at his time of a class of gentiles who, while uncircumcised, had renounced idolatry and otherwise led a
virtuous life. In the literature of a time shortly after Philo
there are specific references to the existence of such spiritual
proselytes in all parts of the Jewish world. They are called
by the name of "God-fearers" (οἱ φοβούμενοι or σεβόμενοι τὸν
θεόν),[333] derived from a similar scriptural expression.[334] A
reference to such "God-fearers" occurs also in Tannaitic
literature, where they are explicitly distinguished from
"righteous proselytes," that is, full proselytes.[335] These
"God-fearers" in that Tannaitic passage, in so far as they
are distinguished from the full proselyte, are probably
identical with the "resident alien" who observes the seven
Noachian laws, or, at least, they belong to the same class
of gentiles who have adopted certain Jewish beliefs and
practices. Identical with these "God-fearers" and "resident
aliens" are probably also what the rabbis call "righteous
gentiles" or "pious gentiles," concerning whom they say
that they have a portion in the world to come.[336] In the
light of this application of the term "righteous" or "pious"
to gentiles who have adopted a certain number of Jewish
beliefs, called by the rabbis "resident aliens," who are
identical with Philo's spiritual proselytes, it is not impossible
that when Philo speaks of the "blameless life of pious men
(ὁσίων ἀνθρώπων) who follow nature and her ordinances" [337]
and of "all who practice wisdom either in Grecian or bar-

333 Cf. J. Klausner, *From Jesus to Paul*, pp. 29 ff., for a general survey of the subject, with bibliography.
334 Cf., e.g., Ps. 15: 4.
335 *Mekilta*, *Nezikin*, 18, F, p. 95b; W, p. 101b; HR, p. 312; L, III, p. 141;
Maseket Gerim IV, 5 (ed. Higger, p. 79). Cf. J. Klausner, *op. cit.*, p. 58.
336 *Tos. Sanhedrin* XIII, 2. Maimonides identifies the "pious of the nations"
with the "resident alien" (*Mishneh Torah: Issure Bi'ah XIV*, 7; *Melakim* VIII,
10–11).
337 *Spec.* II, 12, 42.

barian lands, and live a blameless and irreproachable life,"[338] the reference, in so far as it includes non-Jews, is to his spiritual proselytes. The expression "nature and its ordinances" which these "pious men" are said by him to follow, includes, as we have shown above,[339] five laws which are characteristically similar to laws generally described by the rabbis as Noachian. Similarly when he includes among "the wise and just and virtuous"[340] not only the Jewish Essenes[341] but also the seven wise men of Greece,[342] the Magi among the Persians,[343] and the Gymnosophists in India,[344] he would call them all spiritual proselytes. The "spiritual proselytes" of Philo are, therefore, not only those gentiles who have acknowledged the Jewish God and accepted certain Jewish laws of conduct but also those gentiles who by the power of their own reason have arrived at a philosophic conception of God and a philosophic life of virtue.

II. THE IDEAL CONSTITUTION

In Philo's delineation of the Mosaic constitution there is nothing the like of which we do not find in the constitutions of the various states analyzed and examined by Aristotle. There is a king, there are judges and magistrates and a council of elders, there are citizens, both native and naturalized, and there are aliens and resident aliens. In his analysis and description of the Mosaic constitution, however, it was not Philo's purpose to bring to the knowledge of his Greek readers a constitution which had been overlooked by Aristotle. Nor was it his purpose to show that this constitution was like all other constitutions. His purpose was to show that

[338] Ibid., 44.
[339] Cf. above, pp. 185–187.
[340] Probus 11, 72.
[341] Ibid., 12, 75.

[342] Ibid., 11, 73.
[343] Ibid., 74.
[344] Ibid.

it was unlike any of the other known constitutions; it was better than any of them; in fact, it was the ideal constitution which philosophers had been looking for.

In Greek philosophy the question is raised whether any of the existing forms of government can be characterized as the ideal form of government. Both Plato and Aristotle answer it in the negative.

Plato divides all forms of government into what he describes as right (ὀρθή) and not right (οὐκ ὀρθή),[1] the former being those which rule according to law and the latter those which rule without law. Under the former he places (1) kingship, (2) aristocracy, and (3) democracy; under the latter he places (1) tyranny, (2) oligarchy, and (3) a lawless democracy.[2] Still, no form of government which is based upon a fixed law, though called by him a right form of government, is according to him, in his *Statesman* and *Republic*, an ideal form of government. And the reason why he does not consider any such form of government as ideal is that no fixed law, according to him, can be perfect, complete, eternal, immutable, and operating in the interest of all the people. Plato clearly expresses this view in his statements that "law could never, by determining exactly what is noblest and most just for one and all, enjoin upon them that which is best; for the differences of men and of actions and the fact that nothing, I may say, in human life is ever at rest forbid any science whatsoever to promulgate any simple rule for everything and for all time,"[3] and that "each form of government enacts the laws with a view to its own advantage, a democracy democratic laws and tyranny autocratic, and the others likewise."[4]

Aristotle similarly divides all forms of government into

---

[1] *Statesman* 302 B–C.
[2] *Ibid.*
[3] *Ibid.* 294 B.
[4] *Republic* I, 338 E.

what he describes as faultless (ἀναμάρτητος) or right (ὀρθή) and faulty (ἡμαρτημένη) or perverted (παρεκβεβηκυῖα),[5] the former being those which rule "with a view to the common interest" and the latter those which rule "with a view to the private interest."[6] Under the former he places (1) kingship, (2) aristocracy, and (3) polity, that is, what Plato calls democracy; under the latter he places (1) tyranny, (2) oligarchy, and (3) democracy,[7] that is, what Plato calls lawless democracy. Still, none of the right forms of government is regarded by him as an ideal form of government, and the reason for this again is ultimately to be traced to the fact that the laws in accordance with which these forms of government are supposed to rule for the common interest are imperfect laws and often they operate in the interest of only certain groups of people. Aristotle indirectly expresses this view in his statements that while laws "are rules according to which the magistrates should administer the state,"[8] laws vary in accordance with the forms of government, and, while indeed true forms of government will of necessity have just laws,[9] faulty forms of governments will have unjust laws, for laws are made by those who are empowered to legislate by what happens to be the constitution of the state, and therefore they cannot be more ideally just than the men themselves who constitute the ruling class in the state and make its laws.

The reason, then, why both Plato and Aristotle despaired of an ideal state is that there is no ideal law. An ideal state, therefore, according to Plato, would be one in which "the rulers are found to be truly possessed of science, not merely to seem to possess it, whether they rule by law or without law,

---

[5] *Politica* III, 1, 1275b, 1–2; 7, 1279a, 24–25.
[6] *Ibid.* III, 7, 1279a, 28–31.
[7] *Ibid.* 1279a, 32–1279b, 10.
[8] *Ibid.* IV, 1, 1289a, 19–20.
[9] *Ibid.* III, 11, 1282b, 10–13.

whether their subjects are willing or unwilling . . . so long as they act in accordance with science and justice and preserve and benefit it by making it better than it was," [10] and he is looking forward to the coming of a "scientific law-maker" to establish such an ideal state. [11] In his *Republic* he himself sketches the constitution of such an ideal state, wherein philosophically trained guardians would rule the people in accordance with science and justice. When later in the *Laws*, he conceived of another type of state, wherein the people are to be ruled by fixed laws, that state is described by him not as the best but as the second best. [12] Similarly, Aristotle, while disagreeing with Plato's earlier view that a government without fixed laws can be the best government, provided it is ruled by wise men, and while also maintaining that the best form of government is that which is based on law, for "he who bids the law rule may be deemed to bid God and reason alone rule, but he who bids man rule adds an element of the beast," [13] still does not think that any government that is devised by man can be the absolutely best government, "for the best," he says, "is often unattainable," [14] and any government called best is best only "relatively to given conditions." [15] And the reason for this is again that he does not believe there can be an ideal law upon which an ideal state is to be based, for "what are good laws has not yet been clearly explained" [16] and the law everywhere is made and will always have to be made by men, and consequently he rightly asks, "What if the law itself be democratical or oligarchical, how will that help us out of our difficulties?" [17]

[10] *Statesman* 293 C–D.
[11] *Ibid.* 295 E.
[12] *Laws* V, 739 A; 739 E; *Statesman* 297 E.
[13] *Politica* III, 16, 1287a, 28–29.
[14] *Ibid.* IV, 1, 1288b, 25.

[15] *Ibid.*, 26.
[16] *Ibid.* III, 11, 1282b, 6–7.
[17] *Ibid.* III, 10, 1281a, 36–38.

Taking his cue from both Plato and Aristotle, Philo seems to argue as follows: Suppose we have a "scientific lawgiver" who is even better than the scientific lawgiver of Plato, and that that scientific lawgiver produces a law which is, as Plato says, "in accordance with science and justice," which is "noblest and just for one and all," which takes into cognizance "the differences of men and of actions" and which promulgates a "simple rule for everything and for all time." [18] Suppose also that that law, unlike all the laws with which Aristotle was acquainted, was not promulgated by legislators in an established government which happened to be of a certain form, but rather by a legislator who was neither "democratic" nor "oligarchic." [19] Such a law would undoubtedly be admitted by both of them to be a perfect law, and a form of government founded on the basis of such a law would also be admitted by both of them to be a perfect form of government. Now such a law, contends Philo, is the Law of Moses. Unlike the man-made constitution and laws framed by Plato which are only the second best and suitable only to certain conditions of place and time, and unlike also all the man-made laws envisaged by Aristotle which are relative to the constitution of the state, this Law of Moses is God-given and hence suitable to all conditions of place and time and is not relative to the constitution of a state. In this view of the exceptional character of the Mosaic law he must have confirmed himself by his knowledge of its internal development whereby it was possible for it to function as a living law for the Jews of his own time both in Palestine and in the various lands of the diaspora, and this despite the vast changes in the condition of the life of the people. In one place he explicitly argues for the future eternity of the Law on the ground of past experience, for in

[18] Cf. above, n. 3.   [19] Cf. above, n. 17.

the past, "though the nation has undergone so many changes, both to increased prosperity and the reverse, nothing, not even the smallest part of the ordinances, has been changed."[20] The last statement would seem to be rather strange, especially in view of the fact that his own exposition of the Mosaic laws as they were practiced at his own time shows many changes from the original form in which they are recorded in the Pentateuch. But these changes, according to Philo, came about as a result of the operation of the oral law, and, with his conception of the oral law as implicit within the written law,[21] it was quite natural for him not to consider the many changes wrought in the Mosaic Law by means of interpretation and enactment as innovations in the Law. He rather considered them, after the rabbis, as the unfoldment of the true meaning of the Law.

This argument which we have put in the mouth of Philo may be discerned in the introductory statement to his exposition of the laws of Moses. Referring to those whom he describes as thinking themselves "superior legislators," he says that those superior legislators, "having first founded and established a city in accordance with reason, have then, by framing laws, adapted to it the constitution which they thought most agreeable and suitable to the form in which they had founded it." [22] The reference is primarily to Plato, but it applies also to Aristotle. When Plato wished to establish, not an ideal state, but the next best to an ideal state, he found it necessary to try his experiment in a new colony to be established on a deserted site and to have a constitution and laws prepared for the colony by a committee of ten.[23] The constitution and the laws in Plato's next best to the ideal state are thus man-made and are thus particularly

[20] *Mos.* II, 3, 15.
[21] Cf. above, I, 194.
[22] *Mos.* II, 9, 49.
[23] *Laws* III, 702 b ff.

devised to meet the requirements of a particular city, of a special size, built on a special site and inhabited by a special kind of population. They are not a universal constitution and universal laws suitable for all men, and for all time, and for all places. The same criticism would apply also to the relatively best state in Aristotle's *Politics*, for according to Aristotle, too, laws are always relative to constitutions [24] and constitutions are best only relatively to circumstances,[25] and, as in Plato, therefore, any system of law presupposes a special kind of state inhabited by a special kind of population.[26]

The laws of Moses, argues Philo, are different. They are not laws framed by men for a "city made with hands"; they are laws revealed by God, "too good and too divine to be limited as it were by any circle of things on earth"; they are laws suitable for all cities within this "Great City" created by God, for they are veritable laws of nature, being "a faithful image of the constitution of the whole world." [27] Why were the laws of Moses promulgated "in the depths of the deserts instead of in cities?" asks Philo, and his answer is that it was for three reasons: first, because in the desert the people could be convinced through a variety of miracles that the laws were "not the inventions of a man but quite clearly the oracles of God"; [28] second, because also these laws, not being the work of legislators in a society already established, or, at least, conceived of according to a certain form of government, but rather the revelation of God to be served as the foundation of a society as yet to be estab-

---

[24] *Politica* III, 11, 1282b, 10–11.
[25] *Ibid.* IV, 1, 1288a, 24–27.
[26] *Ibid.* VII, 4, 1325b, 35 ff. There is no ground for Colson's statement (VI, 473, note) that "Aristotle's *Politics* hardly fits the case." Philo's essential criticism, as herein presented, will apply to any ideal state conceived by philosophers.
[27] *Mos.* II, 9, 51.   [28] *Decal.* 4, 15.

lished, had to be revealed in the desert before the people organized themselves into a form of government;[29] third, because the people among whom this law was to be established were to start as new-born babes, free from the wrong opinions and the passions acquired by them during their life in the cities of Egypt, and therefore they had to undergo a period of purgation in the desert.[30] These laws, continues Philo, consist of "just principles" ($\tau\hat{\omega}\nu$ $\delta\iota\kappa\alpha\acute{\iota}\omega\nu$) prepared for the people from beforehand,[31] which are complete, perfect, suitable for all men, in all places, and under all circumstances, "firm, unshaken, immovable," that "will remain for all future ages as though immortal."[32] And so the law of Moses is presented by Philo as the ideal law sought after by all philosophers, to serve as the basis of a new constitution in a new state to be established by a new people in a new country.

Such a state ruled by a law revealed by God has its source of authority in God, and should therefore be described as a state ruled by God. There is in it, indeed, a king, but that king, though elected by the people, rules by virtue of his having been chosen by God.[33] God is, then, according to the Pentateuch, the real ruler; the king rules only when he is chosen by God. The same view is directly expressed in other parts of Scripture. When Gideon refused the kingdom it was because, as he said, "the Lord shall rule over you,"[34] and when the elders of Israel asked Samuel to give them a king, God is made to say concerning this request: "They have rejected me, that I should not be king over them."[35] On the basis of scriptural terminology, then, the constitution

[29] *Ibid.* 3, 14.
[30] *Ibid.* 1, 2–3, 13.
[31] *Ibid.* 3, 14.
[32] *Mos.* II, 3, 14.

[33] Cf. above, pp. 326, 330.
[34] Judges 8: 23.
[35] I Sam. 8: 7.

of the state as outlined by Moses should be called a government by God. For such an appellation Philo could have
found philosophic support in Aristotle's statement that
"he who bids the law rule may be deemed to bid God and
reason alone to rule." [36] In fact, Josephus suggests that the
Mosaic constitution "may be termed a theocracy, placing
all sovereignty and authority in the hands of God." [37] This
term is indirectly suggested also by Philo when he describes
the people of the tower of Babel as those who "enroll themselves as rulers and kings, making over the undestroyable
rule of God (τὸ θεοῦ κράτος) to creation that passes away and
perishes" [38] and when he also explains that as a retribution
for their attempt to destroy "the eternal kingship" in the
world, God has punished them with the destruction of government among them.[39] It is also suggested in his constant
description of God as exercising "monarchical rule," as
being "ruler" and "king," [40] and especially in his description of God as the ideal king after whom the human king
is to model himself.[41]

Philo, however, wished to describe the Mosaic form of
government in terms familiar to Greek readers. But how
should he describe it? Certainly it is not to be described as
a tyranny or an oligarchy or a lawless democracy. It would
have to be one of the three forms of government which Plato
and Aristotle characterize as good, and of these three it
would have to be that which is the best among them. But
which is the best among the three good forms of government? There is no definite answer for that in either Plato

[36] *Politica* III, 16, 1287a, 28–30; cf. Quotations from Plato above.
[37] *Apion.* II, 16, 165.
[38] *Somn.* II, 43, 290.
[39] *Ibid.*, 285–286.
[40] *Decal.* 29, 155; for more references see Leisegang, *Indices*, sub θεός, p. 368.
[41] *Spec.* IV, 34, 176 f.

or Aristotle. Plato in one place says that "monarchy, when bound by good rules, which we call laws, is the best of all the six" forms of government enumerated by him,[42] but in other places he says that aristocracy is the best form of government.[43] Similarly Aristotle maintains that monarchy and aristocracy are the two best forms of government,[44] though, under certain conditions, he considers aristocracy preferable to monarchy.[45] But then, again, even though democracy is considered by them less desirable than monarchy and aristocracy as a form of government, still both of them describe democracy by a term which is laudatory. The chief characteristic of democracy, according to both Plato and Aristotle, is equality,[46] and, concerning equality, Plato quotes what he terms "an old and true saying" that "equality produces amity" [47] and Aristotle says that "when men are equal they are contented." [48] Moreover, among the Peripatetics and Stoics there was a tendency to find the best form of government in a combination of monarchy, aristocracy, and democracy. The Peripatetic Dicaearchus is said to have held such a view.[49] The Stoics are reported to have maintained that the best form of government is "a mixture of democracy, kingship, and aristocracy." [50] Such also was the view of Polybius [51] and Cicero.[52] With all this in the back of his mind, Philo is trying to show that the

---

[42] *Statesman* 302 E.
[43] *Republic* IV, 445 c; VIII, 544 E.
[44] *Politica* IV, 2, 1289a, 31–33.
[45] *Ibid.* III, 15, 1286b, 3–7.
[46] *Republic* VIII, 558 c; *Politica* IV, 4, 1291b, 30–31.
[47] *Laws* VI, 757 A.
[48] *Politica* V, 7, 1307a, 18.
[49] Zeller, II, 2³, p. 893, n. 1 (*Aristotle* II, p. 441, n. 5).
[50] Diogenes, VII, 131.
[51] Polybius, VI, 3, 7.
[52] Cicero, *De Re Publica* I, 29, 45.

Mosaic constitution contains the best features of all the good forms of government.

In the first place, the Mosaic form of government contains the best feature of the monarchical form of government. According to Plato, as we have seen, "monarchy, when bound by good written rules, which we call laws, is the best of all the six" [53] forms of government which he has enumerated. Philo therefore tries to show that the scriptural form of government is in part a monarchy bound by good written rules. In that scriptural monarchical form of government, the duty of the monarch is not only to be law-abiding himself but also to enforce the rule of the law. The injunction that the king is to write out with his own hand the Sequel to the laws [54] and to read it and to familiarize himself with it is all for the end "that he may have a constant and unbroken memory of ordinances, so good and profitable to all," [55] for by knowing these laws he will follow them.[56] "Other kings," he says, "carry rods in their hands as scepters but my scepter is the book of the Sequel to the law." [57] It is because the king rules by law that Philo contrasts king-rule with ochlocracy and oligarchy, both of which stand for lawless rule.[58] He does not contrast it, however, with aristocracy or democracy, and this undoubtedly because he considered either of these two forms of government as compatible with kingship, for as says Aristotle, kingship according to law may be found either in an aristocracy or a democracy.[59] And so Philo will next try to show how the monarchical form of government of the Mosaic constitution is at the same time also an aristocracy and a democracy.

---

[53] *Statesman* 302 E.
[54] Deut. 17: 18–20. By the "Sequel" Philo means the Book of Deuteronomy.
[55] *Spec.* IV, 32, 161.
[56] *Ibid.*, 165–169.
[57] *Ibid.*, 164.
[58] *Decal.* 29, 155; *Fug.* 2, 10.
[59] *Politica* III, 16, 1287a, 3–6.

In the second place, he therefore says, it contains also the best features of the aristocratic form of government. By definition an aristocracy is a government in which "the rulers are the best" or "they have at heart the best interests of the state and of the citizens." [60] In his contention that rulers must be men of merit and of special equipment for their task, Plato is fond of drawing upon the illustration of physicians and steersmen. [61] These two kinds of illustration are also drawn upon by Aristotle. [62] In accordance with these conceptions of aristocracy, Philo tries to show that the Mosaic government, though a monarchy in form, insists upon the rule of the best and for the best interest of the state and of the citizens. The head of the government, though a king, is to be chosen on the ground that he "has been judged worthy to fill the highest and most important office." [63] The king is to have as his lieutenants, "to share with him the duties of governing, giving judgment, and managing all the matters which concern the public welfare," [64] men who are "all chosen according to their merit (ἀριστίνδην) in good sense, ability, justice, and godliness." [65] He reproduces with great embellishment Plato's favorite example of the physician and the steersman to illustrate the wisdom of scriptural law with regard to its insistence upon merit in the appointment of kings and magistrates. [66] The king together

---

[60] *Ibid.* III, 7, 1279a, 35–37.

[61] Cf. *Statesman* 293 A; 295 B; 296 B; 297 E; *Laws* XII, 963 A; *Gorgias* 464 B ff.; *Republic* VI, 488 A.

[62] *Politica* III, 6, 1279a, 3–5; 11, 1281b, 38–1282a, 7; 1282a, 10; VII, 2, 1324b, 29–31.

[63] *Spec.* IV, 33, 170.

[64] *Ibid.*

[65] *Ibid.*

[66] *Ibid.*, 29, 153–156; *Jos.* 12, 63. It is in this sense that Philo also says that "it is advantageous to submit to one's betters" (*Fragmenta*, Richter, VI, 207; M, II, 652).

with the magistrates appointed by him is to manage everything which is for the "common advantage" (κοινωφελής)[67] of
all the citizens, not only of those who are "distinguished" or
"rich" or are "men in high office" but also of "the com-
moner or the poor or the obscure," [68] for the commands of
the Law are "good and profitable to all." [69]

In the third place, the Mosaic form of government contains also the best features of democracy. Now both Plato
and Aristotle, as we have seen, identify democracy with
equality [70] and both of them speak highly in praise of equality,[71] and yet both of them repudiate democracy as an un-
desirable form of government. What is wrong then with
democracy? The answer which they both give is that
equality in democracy is not always the right kind of equality. Equality (ἰσότης), they say, may be either numerical or
proportional.[72] The former means the distribution of things
equally among all men irrespective of merit, that is, all men
by virtue of their being citizens have a right to vote and to
determine policies of state, and are entitled also to hold any
kind of office to administer affairs of the state; the latter
means the distribution of things among all men according to
their individual merits, that is, no man is to be excluded from
voting or from holding office if he has the proper technical
qualifications for the performance of his duties. Now, in
democracy, they argue, the equality on which it is based often

[67] Ibid., 33, 170.
[68] Ibid., 172.   [70] Cf. above, n. 46.
[69] Ibid., 32, 161.   [71] Cf. above, nn. 47, 48.
[72] Plato, (1) Laws VI, 757 B–C; (2) V, 744 C; (3) Gorgias 508 A–B; Aristotle,
(4) Politica V, 1, 1301b, 29–1302a, 8; (5) Eth. Nic. V, 3, 1131a, 29–32; (6) VIII,
7, 1158b, 29–36.
    Terms for numerical equality are: ἀριθμῷ (1, 4); κατ' ἀναλογίαν ἀριθμητικήν (5);
μέτρῳ (1); σταθμῷ (1); πλήθει (4); μεγέθει (4); κατὰ ποσόν (6).
    Terms for proportional equality are: κατὰ λόγον (1); λόγῳ (4); ἀνίσῳ ξυμμέτρῳ
(2); γεωμετρική (3); κατ' ἀναλογίαν γεωμετρικήν (5); κατ' ἀξίαν (4, 6).

degenerates into numerical equality and, when that happens, then the democracy becomes what Aristotle describes as a form of government "in which, not law, but the multitude (πλῆθος), have the supreme power, and supersede the law by their decrees." [73] This lawless sort of democracy, Aristotle says further, "becomes despotic" and "is relatively to other democracies what tyranny is to other forms of monarchy." [74] In such a democracy there is disorder (ἀταξία) and anarchy (ἀναρχία), which ultimately lead to revolution and ruin.[75]

With all this in the back of his mind, Philo tries to show, on the one hand, how numerical equality is denounced in Scripture, how it is really inequality and not better than oligarchy and tyranny and despotism, and how it is disorder, anarchy, and lawlessness; but, on the other hand, how proportional equality is true democracy which makes for harmony, order, and stability, and how such true democracy is embodied in the Mosaic constitution.

The denunciation of numerical equality is found by him in two places in Scripture.

First, alluding to the verse, "Take heed to thyself that thou be not snared by following them . . . saying, How did these nations serve their gods? even so will I do likewise," [76] he says: "Some people suppose that what the many think right is lawful and just, though it be the height of lawlessness; but they do not judge well, for it is good to follow nature, and the headlong course of the multitude runs counter to what nature's leading would have us do." [77]

---

[73] *Politica* IV, 4, 1292a, 4–6.   [74] *Ibid.*, 15–18.
[75] *Ibid.* V, 3, 1302b, 27–30; VI, 4, 1319b, 14–17; cf. *Republic* VIII, 557 E–558 C; 562 B–E.
[76] Deut. 12: 30.
[77] *Spec.* IV, 8, 46. I take Sections 45–47 to allude to Deut. 12: 30, for the Sections immediately following, 48–50, quite evidently refer to Deut. 13: 2–6.

388 PHILO

Second, drawing upon the story of the uprising of Korah against Moses,[78] he says that at the root of the uprising was the issue whether the few who are qualified by merit should rule, or whether the rule should be entrusted to the many irrespective of their qualification. The lower temple attendants, under the leadership of Korah, says Philo, "puffed with pride over their own numerical superiority over the priests, despised their fewness, and combined in the same deed two trespasses, by attempting on the one hand to bring low the superior, on the other to exalt the inferior," thereby overthrowing "that most excellent promoter of the common weal, order." [79]

Then taking numerical equality, which Aristotle describes as a form of democracy "in which, not the law, but the multitude, have the supreme power," [80] he describes it as ochlocracy,[81] characterizing the latter as "the counterfeit of democracy." [82] Like Aristotle, who says that in a democracy based upon numerical equality the multitude "supersede the law by their decrees" [83] and that in such a democracy there is "disorder" (ἀταξία) and "anarchy" (ἀναρχία), which ultimately lead to "sedition" (στάσις),[84] he says that in ochlocracy "lawlessness" is paramount,[85] that "disorder" (ἀταξία) prevails in existing things as a result of ochlocracy,[86] that "anarchy" (ἀναρχία) is the mother of ochlocracy,[87] and that through being infected with ochlocracy "we

[78] Num. 16: 1 ff.   [79] Mos. II, 50, 277.
[80] Politica IV, 4, 1292a, 4–6.
[81] The use of the term "ochlocracy" as a description of lawless democracy occurs in Polybius, VI, 4, 6, and 10; VI, 57, 9.
[82] Agr. 11, 45; cf. Conf. 13, 108.
[83] Politica IV, 4, 1292a, 6–7.
[84] Ibid. V, 3, 1302b, 27–30; cf. VI, 4, 1319b, 14–17; Republic VIII, 557 E–558 C; 562 B–E.
[85] Conf. 23, 108.
[86] Fug. 2, 10.   [87] Agr. 11, 46.

pass our lives forever amid tumults, and commotions, and intestine seditions (ἐμφυλίοις στάσεσιν)." [88] Again, like Aristotle, who says that this sort of lawless democracy "is relatively to other democracies what tyranny is to other forms of monarchy" [89] and compares it also to that one of the three forms of oligarchy which is lawless,[90] Philo also adds tyranny to ochlocracy as another form of lawless government [91] and brackets "oligarchy and ochlocracy" as two "mischievous forms of government, which arise among the vilest of men, produced by disorder and covetousness." [92] Finally, like Aristotle, who tries to show that democracy which is based upon numerical equality is a perversion of "proportionate equality" and "justice," [93] Philo says that ochlocracy "admires inequality." [94] It is in this sense of numerical equality that Philo says that "to give equal things to unequal people is an action of great injustice." [95]

In contradistinction to all these evils of numerical equality, when made a principle of government, is proportional equality. Speaking for himself as well as for Plato, Aristotle says, "the only stable principle of government is equality according to proportion, and for every man to enjoy his own" [96] and this stable principle of government, as may be gathered from his discussion, is not confined to any particular form of government; it may be found in any form of government, especially in those forms of government which he calls constitutional governments (πολιτεῖαι) and which he describes as inclining more to the side of the "multitude" (πλῆθος)[97] and to "democracy" (δῆμος).[98] Indirectly thus

---

[88] *Ibid.*, 45.
[89] *Politica* IV, 4, 1292a, 17–18.
[90] *Ibid.*, 1292b, 7–9.
[91] *Agr.* 11, 46.
[92] *Decal.* 29, 155.
[93] *Politica* V, 1, 1301a, 25 ff.
[94] *Conf.* 23, 108.
[95] *Fragmenta,* Richter, VI, 206 (M, II, 651).
[96] *Politica* V, 7, 1307a, 26–27.
[97] *Ibid.*, 16.
[98] *Ibid.*, 21–22.

Aristotle suggests that proportional equality is to be described as a tendency to democracy, even if it is not to be described by the term democracy itself.[99] Such proportional equality, according to Aristotle, constitutes justice, for, as he says, "all men think justice to be a sort of equality"[100] and "proportional equality"[101] at that. But to be just means also to act in accordance with law.[102] Consequently, democracy means to Aristotle not only equality but also a government of law.

With all these statements on proportional equality in the back of his mind, namely, that it is the only stable principle of government, that it is to be found especially in those forms of government which incline more to the side of democracy and that it is the basis of justice and of law, Philo designates it by the simple term democracy, contrasting it with numerical equality which he calls ochlocracy. The term democracy is thus not used by him in the sense of any particular form of government; it is rather used by him in the sense of that general principle of justice according to which each man enjoys that which is justly due to him under any form of law-abiding government, be it monarchic or aristocratic or democratic. This use of the term democracy as meaning a certain principle of government rather than any particular form of government seems to have been common at the time of Philo. Thus Dio Cassius quotes Maecenas to the effect that the change by Augustus of the Roman form of government into what is "strictly speaking" a monarchy[103] will result in that "all will gain the true democracy and freedom which does not fail."[104] To the

---

[99] *Ibid.* V, 1, 1301a, 28–30.   [100] *Ibid.* III, 12, 1282b, 18.
[101] *Ibid.* V, 1, 1301a, 27; 1301b, 35–36; *Eth. Nic.* VIII, 7, 1158b, 30–31.
[102] *Eth. Nic.* V, 1, 1129b, 11 ff.   [103] Dio Cassius, LII, 1, 1.
[104] *Idem*, LII, 14, 4; cf. Goodenough, *The Politics of Philo Judaeus*, p. 88, nn. 11, 12. For various explanations of why Philo calls the Mosaic state democracy, see

mind of Philo, associated as democracy was with the principle of proportional equality, democracy meant, as proportional equality did to Aristotle, the principle of justice.
Quoting therefore in the name of "the masters of natural
philosophy," that is, the Pythagoreans, that "the mother of
justice is equality," [105] he elaborates this statement, evidently on the basis of statements culled from Plato, to show
how proportional equality, democracy, and justice all mean
the same. Says Plato: "It is of the nature of proportion
(ἀναλογία) to accomplish this [unity] most perfectly"; [106]
"justice imparts harmony and friendship"; [107] "heaven and
earth and gods are held together by communion and friendship, by orderliness, temperance, and justice; and it is this
reason, my friend, why they call the whole of this world by
the name of cosmos"; [108] without justice "states cannot
be"; [109] "what health and disease are in the body justice and
injustice are in the soul"; [110] virtue is a harmony of the
soul.[111] With all these Platonic statements in his mind,
and in addition to this his general use of the term democracy
in the sense of proportional equality, he says that "all that
keeps its due order is the work of equality, which in the
universe as a whole is most properly called the cosmos, and
in cities is democracy, the best legally regulated and most
excellent of constitutions, in bodies is health and in souls
virtuous conduct." [112] The term democracy, in this passage,
described by him as "the best legally regulated and most

F. Geiger, *Philon von Alexandreia als sozialer Denker*, 1932, pp. 52-57; E. Lang-
stadt, "Zu Philos Begriff der Demokratie," *Occident und Orient . . . [Moses] Gaster
Anniversary Volume*, 1936, pp. 349-364; Goodenough, *op. cit.*, 1938, pp. 86-90;
Colson, 1939, VIII, 437-439.
[105] *Spec.* IV, 42, 231. Cf. Heinemann (*Philos Werke*) and Colson, *ad loc.*
[106] *Timaeus* 31 C.
[107] *Republic* I, 351 D.   [110] *Republic* IV, 444 C.
[108] *Gorgias* 508 A.   [111] *Phaedo* 93 E.
[109] *Protagoras* 323 A.   [112] *Spec.* IV, 42, 237.

excellent of constitutions," is, as we have seen, not used in the sense of a particular form of government which is opposed to that of monarchy or aristocracy, but rather in the sense of any form of government which is based upon just laws and in which all men are equal before the law, for, as he has said, it is equality of this kind that keeps things in due order. Descriptions of proportional equality as making for peace and harmony and order are also to be found in his statements that "equality of measurement (ἰσόμετρον) is the cause of the most perfect blessings," that "equality is free from all annoyances and contributes to unite men for advantageous ends," and that "obedience to the law and equality are the seeds of peace and the causes of safety and continued durability." [113]

It is equality in this sense, the equality of proportion, which means, as Aristotle says, "for every man to enjoy his own," [114] and which he himself refers to as democracy, that Philo finds embodied in the Mosaic constitution. That constitution, as he has already shown, is a mixture of monarchy and aristocracy: at the head of the state is a king, who is elected to the throne or inherits it, but only on the basis of merit; judges and officers are appointed by the king, but again only on the basis of merit; the law is fixed and it changes only by the interpretation of competent authorities and not by the vote of the multitude. Still this constitution has also an ingredient of democracy in it, not democracy in the perverted sense of a government "in which the multitude and not the law has supreme power," [115] but rather democracy in the true sense of the term, in the sense of a government based upon law and upon the principle of proportional equality, wherein each man gets what he de-

[113] *Fragmenta*, Richter, VI, 226 (M, II, 665).
[114] Cf. above, n. 96.   [115] *Politica* IV, 4, 1292a, 5–6.

serves. "According to the law of such a democracy," says
Aristotle, "equality implies that the poor are to have no
more advantages than the rich." [116] Philo similarly says
that the Law, in its insistence upon justice, by which is
meant equality, despite its many injunctions to show pity
and kindness to the poor, explicitly admonishes "not to
show pity to the poor man in giving judgment." [117] "Our
law," he says again, "exhorts to equality when it ordains
that the penalties inflicted on offenders should correspond to
their actions." [118] The principle of equality of proportion is
found by him also in the verse in which three different kinds
of repentance are prescribed for the sinner.[119] His comment
thereon is that "small offenses do not require great purifications, nor are small purifications fit for great offenses, but
they should be equal and similar and in due proportion." [120]
He also finds the same principle in the verse in which the
king is enjoined to copy and read and memorize the Law in
order "that his heart be not lifted up above his brethren." [121]
His restatement of this verse is as follows: "And if I always
keep the holy laws for my staff and support I shall win . . .
the spirit of equality, and no greater good can be found than
this." [122] So also in the Letter of Aristeas one of the elders
counsels the king that in governing his subjects he should
punish those who deserve punishment "in accordance with
their deserts" [123] and maintain "a just bearing towards
all" [124] and be "equally fair (ἴσος) in speech to all" [125] — in
other words, he should act in accordance with what Philo
calls the spirit of equality.

The Mosaic polity thus embodies within itself all the best

[116] Ibid., 1291b, 31–33.
[117] Spec. IV, 13, 72; cf. Exod. 23: 3.
[118] Spec. III, 33, 182.
[119] Lev. 5: 7–11.
[120] Mut. 41, 235.
[121] Deut. 17: 20.
[122] Spec. IV, 32, 165.
[123] Aristeas, 188.
[124] Ibid., 189.
[125] Ibid., 191.

elements of the various good forms of government that could
be devised by philosophers. Moreover, like any good state
which, according to the philosophers, is not to exist for the
sake of mere companionship [126] or for the sake of merely
supplying the necessaries of life [127] but rather for the sake
of the highest good,[128] of virtue,[129] of noble actions,[130] of the
most eligible life,[131] and of the best life possible,[132] the Mosaic state exists for the purpose of establishing a life in accordance with the Law, which to Philo is identical with life
in accordance with virtue and the best life. But inasmuch
as the Law of Moses, as distinguished from the laws devised
by the various legislators and philosophers, is God-given,
it is the ideal law, for it implants the highest virtues and
leads to the best kind of life, and therefore the Mosaic state
based upon that law is the ideal state. In contradistinction
to every other form of government which he describes by
the general name of the "human polity" (ἀνθρωπίνη πολιτεία),[133] he describes the Mosaic state as the holy polity
(ἱερὰ πολιτεία),[134] the God-loving polity (φιλόθεος πολιτεία),[135]
the best polity (ἀρίστη πολιτεία),[136] and the irreproachable
polity (πολιτεία ἀνεπίληπτος); [137] or, drawing upon the scriptural expressions the "ecclesia or church (ἐκκλησία) of the
Lord" [138] and "congregation or synagogue (συναγωγὴ) of
the Lord," [139] he calls it "divine ecclesia (ἐκκλησία) and
congregation (σύλλογος)" [140] or "holy congregation and ec-

---

[126] *Politica* III, 9, 1281a, 3–4.
[127] *Ibid.* IV, 4, 1291a, 17–18.
[128] *Ibid.* I, 1, 1252a, 3–6.
[129] *Ibid.* III, 9, 1280b, 6–7.
[130] *Ibid.*, 1281a, 2–3.
[131] *Ibid.* VII, 1, 1323a, 15–16.

[132] *Ibid.* VII, 8, 1328a, 36–37.
[133] *Somn.* I, 38, 219.
[134] *Spec.* IV, 9, 55, *et passim.*
[135] *Ibid.* I, 9, 51.
[136] *Ibid.* III, 30, 167.

[137] *Ibid.*, 4, 24; cf. Wisdom of Solomon 10: 15: "a holy people and a blameless
(ἄμεμπτον) seed."
[138] Deut. 23: 2–4.
[139] Num. 7: 17.   [140] *Leg. All.* III, 25, 81.

clesia" [141] or "holy congregation." [142] What he means by ecclesia is explained by him in the statement that Scripture "called them no longer multitude (*multitudinem*) or nation (*gentem*) or people (*populum*) but ecclesia (*ecclesiam*)," and this because they were united not only "in body" (*corpore*) but also "in mind" (*mente*). [143] In contrast with man-made political constitutions which may be at variance with truth, [144] the divinely revealed constitution of the Mosaic state is described by him as "a polity which is eager for the truth" [145] or "a polity which is full of true life and vitality." [146] Finally, this "divine ecclesia" was established on earth, "because God wished to send down from heaven to earth an image of His divine virtue, out of His compassion for our race, that it might not be destitute of a more excellent portion, and that He might thus wash off the pollutions which defile our miserable existence, so full of dishonor." [147]

III. The Messianic Age

Such, then, is Philo's conception of the ideal state. It is a state in which every individual has his primary allegiance to God and to the Law revealed by God. Whatever human authority exists in it, such as the king in governing the relations of man to man and the high priest in presiding over the temple and governing the relations of man to God, that authority is derived from the Law and functions only as an instrument in the application of the Law or in the interpretation of the Law. This ideal polity was to exist in Palestine and the temple was to exist only in Jerusalem, for, loyal to the Deuteronomic law, Philo adhered to the principle of

[141] *Somn.* II, 27, 184; cf. *Immut.* 24, 111.
[142] *Spec.* I, 60, 325; 63, 344.
[143] *Qu. in Exod.* I, 10.
[144] *Deter.* 3, 7; 9, 28.
[145] *Spec.* III, 33, 181.
[146] *Virt.* 39, 219.
[147] *Fragmenta*, Richter, VI, 231 (M, II, 669).

the centralization of sacrificial worship, and even tried to explain rationally why there should be only one temple.[1] No mention is made by him of the temple which existed in Egypt at Leontopolis. When urged by a desire to worship God by means of sacrifices as prescribed by the Law, he made a pilgrimage to the Temple in Jerusalem.[2]

But Philo could not help feeling that the reality of the Jewish polity in Palestine in his own time fell short of the ideal pattern as described by Moses. There were still there the external trappings of a state. There was a king, there was a high priest, there were judges and magistrates, and there were also elders sitting in council. But the founder of the then reigning dynasty, Herod, had not come into power through an election by "the whole multitude" and certainly God did not "set His seal to ratify" him, and, though Agrippa I is presented by him sympathetically as a devoted Jew,[3] the succession of Herod's rule to his children was certainly not because they were worthy of it. Nor were the high priests under the Herodian dynasty always elected for their superior virtue. There were indeed native-born Jews and proselytes and aliens and resident aliens in that Jewish polity in Palestine. But often these aliens were in control of historically Jewish cities, acted as masters of them, and treated the Jews as aliens, sometimes even denying them the hospitality due to aliens. During his own time, under Caligula, the non-Jewish settlers in Jamnia openly outraged the religious feelings of their Jewish hosts.[4]

Then there was the diaspora. By the time of Philo the Jewish polity transcended the boundaries of Palestine. Jew-

[1] *Spec.* I, 12, 67. Cf. Deut. 12: 5–7, 11–14, 17–18.
[2] *Provid.* 2, 64 (Eusebius, *Praeparatio Evangelica* VIII, 14, 398b; *Fragmenta*, Richter VI, 200; M. II, 646); Aucher, II, 107.
[3] *Legat.* 35, 261–42, 333.
[4] *Ibid.* 30, 200–201.

ish polities, governed by the laws of Moses, as much as it was possible for these laws to be practiced outside of Palestine, existed throughout the Roman-Hellenistic world as well as throughout the Parthian world. How Philo looked upon these widespread Jewish polities in their relation to the Palestinian polity may be gathered indirectly from scattered passages in his writings.

The Jews in the diaspora are described by him as colonies (ἀποικίαι) of the Jewish population in Judea, and these colonial Jews, he says, while "holding the Holy City where stands the sacred Temple of the most high God to be their mother city (μητρόπολις)," still account each city in which they have been born and brought up as their native city (πατρίς),[5] just as Jerusalem is the native city (πατρίς) of the Jews born therein.[6] The Jews of Palestine and of all these colonies constitute to him one whole nation (ἄπαν ἔθνος), of which the Jews in each locality are a part (μέρος).[7] That whole nation of the Jews forms a polity which, in comparison with the local polities of each individual Jewish locality, is described by him as the more universal polity (ἡ καθολικωτέρα πολιτεία), which bears the general name of the nation (τὸ κοινὸν τοῦ ἔθνους ὄνομα), that is, the name Israel, and which depends for its existence upon the existence of the Temple.[8]

In Alexandria the Jews are said by him to have a polity

5 *Flac.* 7, 46; *Legat.* 36, 281.
6 *Legat.* 36, 278, and 281.
7 *Ibid.* 29, 184.
8 *Ibid.*, 194. That by this "general name of the nation" he refers to the name of Israel may be gathered from the full statement that in the destruction of the Temple Caligula "will also order the general name of the whole nation to be blotted out (συναφανισθῆναι)." This undoubtedly reflects such scriptural expressions as "Thou wilt not blot out (ἀφανιεῖς) my name" (I Sam. 24: 22) and "he will surname himself by the name of Israel" (Isa. 44: 5) and "who are called by the name of Israel" (Isa. 48: 1), and especially the verse "And the Lord said not that he would blot out (ἐξαλείψαι) the name of Israel" (II Kings 14: 27) in which, however, the Septuagint has "seed" (σπέρμα) for "name."

(πολιτεία),⁹ which, from his description of it, entitles them to the pursuit of "ancestral customs and the enjoyment of political rights." ¹⁰ The term "ancestral customs" quite clearly describes the Jewish *politeia* in Alexandria as a religious organization. The second term, "the enjoyment of political rights," is not so clear, but it is quite certain, on the evidence of the Claudine letter to the Alexandrines, that the Jews were not full citizens of Alexandria.¹¹ When Philo, therefore, speaks of the Jews of Alexandria as well as of other Hellenistic cities as citizens (πολῖται),¹² he does not mean that they were full citizens; he uses that term only in the sense of their being members of the Jewish *politeia*. Accordingly, Philo describes the Alexandrian Jews in their relation to each other as "their own fellow-citizens" (τῶν ἰδίων πολιτῶν), whereas Alexandrian gentiles in relation to Alexandrian Jews are described as belonging to a different tribe (ἀλλόφυλοι),¹³ and are contrasted with "us", and "our people" as "them" and "Alexandrians." ¹⁴ Still, being residents of Alexandria, the Jews there are described by him as "Alexandrians" (Ἀλεξανδρεῖς).¹⁵

This conception of the Jews in Alexandria as "citizens" of the Jewish *politeia* but not of the city of Alexandria itself is expressed by him in a statement which evidently refers to conditions in Alexandria at his own time. In that state-

⁹ *Flac.* 8, 53; *Legat.* 44, 349; 45, 363.

¹⁰ *Flac.* 8, 53.

¹¹ H. I. Bell, *Jews and Christians in Egypt* (1924), pp. 23–29; cf. pp. 11–13 for a summary of earlier views on the problem; cf. also M. Radin, *The Jews among the Greeks and Romans* (1915), pp. 109–110; A. Tscherikower, *Ha-Yehudim we-ha-Yevanim ba-Tekufah ha-Hellenistit* (1930), pp. 314–339.

¹² *Flac.* 7, 47.

¹³ *Legat.* 31, 211. The term "tribe" here may perhaps also have the additional reference to the "tribes" into which full citizens of Alexandria were enrolled (cf. above, p. 360, n. 272).

¹⁴ *Flac.* 6, 43; 10, 78–79.

¹⁵ *Legat.* 29, 194.

ment he pleads on behalf of strangers in the following words: "For strangers (ξένοι), in my judgment, must be regarded as suppliants of those who receive them, and not only suppliants but settlers (μέτοικοι) and friends, eagerly seeking equality of privilege with burgesses (ἀστῶν) and already being near in status to citizens (πολίταις), differing but little from natives (αὐτοχθόνων)."[16]

In this passage, it will be noticed, Philo contends that "strangers" are to be regarded as "settlers" and the condition of the latter is described by him in its relation to that of three other classes of the population, namely, "burgesses," "citizens," and "natives." Now the term "burgesses" is technically applied to the most privileged class of the Alexandrian population, the Greeks, for Alexandria, like Athens, strictly speaking, was a town or burg (ἄστυ) and the privileged Greeks there, again strictly speaking, were burgesses,[17] though they are also called citizens (πολῖται). The term "natives" refers to the native Egyptians, known as the λαοί, whom Strabo and Josephus call ἐπιχώριοι.[18] The term "citizens" which in this passage stands between "burgesses" and "natives," is used by Philo, as we have already seen, as a description of the Jews of Alexandria. Thus the Jews in Alexandria were not included among the "burgesses." His description of "settlers" as "eagerly seeking equality of privilege with burgesses" implies that there was an opportunity for them of becoming "burgesses" and that they were availing themselves of that opportunity. From the Claudius letter to the Alexandrines we gather that settlers had the

---

[16] *Mos.* I, 7, 35.

[17] H. S. Jones, "Claudius and the Jewish Question in Alexandria," *The Journal of Roman Studies*, 16 (1926), p. 28. For a more precise definition of this term see E. Bickermann, "A propos des ἀστοί dans l'Égypte Gréco-Romaine," *Revue de Philologie*, 3e Série, 1 (1927), pp. 362–368.

[18] Strabo, XVII, 1, 12; Josephus, *Bell. Jud.* II, 17, 7, 487.

opportunity of becoming burgesses, or, as he would say, of becoming Alexandrian citizens, by joining the *ephebi* and that during his reign many have availed themselves of that opportunity.[19] His description of settlers as "differing but little from natives" undoubtedly refers to the fact that both of them were subject to the payment of a poll tax,[20] from which "burgesses" and Jewish "citizens" were exempt.[21] His description of settlers as "already being near in status to citizens" probably means that settlers enjoy the privileges of religious autonomy like those enjoyed by Jews.[22]

From all this it may be gathered that the unity of all the scattered Jews rested, according to Philo, on two facts: first, their common racial origin, on which account he describes them by the term "nation" (ἔθνος);[23] second, their common religion, on which account he describes them as a "universal polity" or a "divine ecclesia,"[24] that is to say, a number of individual communities, geographically and politically dispersed, but united by a common law, a common form of organized life and a common way of living. Inasmuch, however, as at the time of Philo there was no group of racial Jews who did not confess Judaism, and inasmuch also as the prose-

[19] Cf. Bell, *op. cit.*, p. 24, ll. 53–57; p. 28 (9); Jones, *op. cit.*, p. 28. No special term is used by Claudius as a description of those settlers whom he confirmed as citizens because of their having joined the *ephebi*. But we take it that it is settlers of the same kind that Philo means by his *metoikoi*. On Philo's use of the term *metoikoi*, see above, pp. 367, 368.

[20] There is no explicit statement that those settlers whom Philo describes as *metoikoi* were subject to poll-tax, but from the list of those who were exempt from such a tax it may be inferred that all "settlers" who were not "citizens" had to pay it. Cf. L. Mitteis und U. Wilcken, *Grundzüge und Chrestomathie der Papyruskunde*, I, 1, pp. 57 and 189; Laum, Λαογραφία, Pauly-Wissowa, 23, col. 733, ll. 54–65; S. L. Wallace, *Taxation in Egypt from Augustus to Diocletian* (1938), pp. 116 ff.

[21] Cf. Tscherikower, *op. cit.*, p. 322.

[22] Cf. H. A. Wolfson, "Philo on Jewish Citizenship in Alexandria," *Journal of Biblical Literature*, 63 (1944), pp. 165–168.

[23] Cf. above, p. 355.

[24] Cf. above, pp. 394–395.

lytes at that time were as a rule absorbed individually in the
Jewish community and did not constitute a distinct group of
Jews by religion only, the term "nation," and similarly the
terms designating subdivisions of a nation, such, for instance,
as "tribe" (φυλή), came to have also a religious connota-
tion, expressed by him in his description of proselytes as being
related to Jews by "kinships of greater dignity and sanctity"
than kinships of blood and in his interpretation of the
scriptural term "sons of God" as applying also to proselytes.[25] In this conception of Jews as constituting a nation
which transcends race and local citizenship, Philo thus formulates a new conception of nationality, one expressed not in
terms of race or territory or political government, but rather
in terms of religion or culture. Native-born Jews constituted a nation in both these senses; proselytes were part
of the Jewish nation in the second sense, which to Philo
was the more important sense. Palestine, symbolized by its
capital city Jerusalem, was looked upon as the mother
country of all the Jews, and this because it was the home

[25] *Spec.* I, 58, 317–318; cf. above, p. 357, nn. 246, 247; p. 363, nn. 288, 289; cf.
also above, p. 364, Philo's interpretation of the scriptural term "thy brother."
   With regard to the term "Israel," which he considers as "the general name of
the nation" (cf. above, p. 397), it may be assumed that in his allegorical interpretation of it as meaning "the race endowed with vision" (τὸ ὁρατικὸν γένος) (*Immut.*
30, 144), he applies it also to proselytes. But when he singles out Israel as the
people especially favored by God with the highest grade of prophecy, namely,
prophecy by the voice of God, such as manifested itself on Mount Sinai (*Mos.*
II, 35, 189), he would seem to exclude proselytes. Cf. above, pp. 51–52.
   Corresponding to the change in the term Israel or Jew from a racial to a spiritual
conception in Philo as well as in Judaism in general is a similar change in the term
Hellene among the Greeks (cf. J. Jüthner, *Hellenen und Barbaren*, 1923, pp. 34
ff.; Heinemann, *Bildung*, pp. 567 f). Expression to the change of conception
among the Greeks is given by Isocrates in his statement that "Athens has brought
about that the name Hellenes suggests no longer a race but an intelligence, and
that the title Hellenes is applied rather to those who share our culture than to
those who share a common blood" (*Panegyricus* 50). So also Aristotle is reported
to have said of the Jew he had met that "he was Hellenic not only in speech but
also in soul" (*Apion.* I, 22, 180).

from which the various Jewish colonies in diaspora had originally migrated and because it had the Temple which was the
recognized center of Jewish religious worship and also because it was the place to which they hoped to return ultimately, when the looked-for redemption came. If we find
that no mention is made by Philo of any political unity of the
Jews, it is because no political unity existed then among
Jews. Again, if we find that Palestine as the seat of a
Jewish government under Agrippa I is not spoken of by
him as a political center of the Jews, it is because at that
time Palestine exercised no political authority upon the Jews
abroad. Agrippa I is described by him as ruling by an appointment from Rome over part of Palestine, as was his contemporary Flaccus over Egypt, except that the former was
favored by Rome with the title of king.[26] In short, Philo
describes the Jews of his time as a nation either in the sense
of a people connected by ties of blood or in the sense of a
people having like beliefs and institutions or in both these
senses. If he does not describe them as a nation in the sense
of a people united under a single government, it is for two
reasons: first, the Jews of his time were not united under a
single government; second, the term nation had not yet
acquired that strictly political sense. Philo, as all the Jews of
his time, however, considered the diaspora only as a temporary
stage in Jewish history—a stage which was to be terminated
with the coming of the Messianic age when all the exiles
would become reunited under one government of their own.

To Philo as a student of Greek literature and one who undoubtedly knew the works of the historians, especially the
Histories of Polybius, on the rise and growth of states, the
spread of the Jewish population and the establishment of
Jewish colonies outside of Palestine would not by itself pre-

[26] *Flac.* 5, 25–30.

sent any anomaly. He undoubtedly looked upon it as the natural growth of the Palestinian Jewish polity analogous to that of the Roman empire. Both of them, starting from a single country, spread out to other countries, the one through being conquered by others, the other through conquering others. But as a student of Scripture he could not help looking upon the dispersion of the Jews as a divine punishment for their sin. The Jewish polity in Alexandria, despite its external semblance of a self-government, still represented to him what Scripture calls captivity. The existence of that Jewish polity in Alexandria was made possible as a result of new political conceptions which arose after the conquests of Alexander out of the necessity to organize the heterogeneous conquered populations into political unities. But these new political conceptions never struck root into the hearts of those who carried within them the ancient political traditions of the Greeks. According to the new political conceptions of the founders of Alexandria, the city was to be a confederacy of autonomous religious polities, but the Greek inhabitants of Alexandria could not help thinking of their city as a city of the old Greek type based upon a common religion. The classical Greek political philosophy upon which the cultivated Greeks of the Hellenistic age were brought up recommended as its example of an ideal polity the city-state of the old Greek type with a population which, though made up of different kinds of men,[27] was still united by living together in the same place, by continuous intermarriage, by common religious sacrifices, and by common amusements.[28] The newer political theory, that of the Stoics, reflected indeed the changed conditions of the new Hellenistic cities and later of the Roman empire. It spoke of a world polity in

[27] Aristotle, *Politica* II, 2, 1261a, 22–24.
[28] *Ibid.* III, 9, 1280b, 35–38.

which there was no distinction of race and nations and religions, but that universal polity was in fact nothing but the
ancient Greek city magnified, in which Zeus and the other
traditional Greek deities continued to be worshiped under
the new guise of cosmic forces. It was a universal polity of
the old pagan world. In this new universal polity the Jews,
with their own beliefs and worship and practices, were considered as strangers just as much as in the old pagan cities.
The poets, statesmen, and historians of that period, all of
them inspired by the Stoic teachings, could find a philosophic rationalization for old Greek religious beliefs and a
social sanction for old Greek religious customs, but they
could see nothing but superstition in Jewish beliefs and inhospitality in Jewish customs.[29]

When Caligula forgot that he was a Roman emperor and
acted like a Hellenic hero, demanding to be worshiped by his
subjects, and when also popular feeling and thinking in
Alexandria threatened the existence of the autonomous Jewish polity, Philo did his best to defend it. First, he appeals
to the Jewish constitutional rights, which have been confirmed by the Roman emperors.[30] Second, he condemns
popular agitation against the Jews as falsely masquerading
under the guise of patriotism, or, as he expresses himself,
under the guise of wishing "to do honor to the Emperor." [31]
Third, he dwells upon the antiquity of the Jews in Alexandria and elsewhere, arguing that in some places they were
among the original founders.[32] Fourth, he parades Jewish
patriotism, maintaining that the Jews are bound by their
religion to pay honor ($\tau\iota\mu\dot{\eta}$) to the ruler of the country

[29] Cf. Th. Reinach, *Textes d'Auteurs Grecs et Romains relatifs au Judaïsme*, 1895,
"Index" under "Superstitions des Juifs" and "Misoxénie."
[30] *Legat.* 23, 153–24, 161.
[31] *Flac.* 7, 51.
[32] *Ibid.*, 47.

which treats them hospitably,[33] evidently having in mind his own interpretation of the verse "thou shalt not abhor an Egyptian because thou wast a sojourner in his land" [34] as constituting a commandment that "settlers" in a foreign land should "pay some honor ($\tau\iota\mu\dot{\eta}\nu$) to those who have accepted them." [35]

This was his formal defense. But he knew that by such arguments one can win a debate, but one cannot change a social situation. He knew that the root of the problem was too deep to be overcome by such palliative arguments. The root of the problem, as he himself states it, was to be found in the peculiar laws ($\nu\dot{o}\mu o\iota$ $\dot{\epsilon}\xi\alpha\dot{\iota}\rho\epsilon\tau o\iota$) practiced by the Jews.[36] Many before Philo, and Philo himself, had tried to convince the world of the intrinsic merits of these laws. But he knew that the world was offended by these laws not because they were harmful, but because they were different; more so if it were constantly told that these laws were superior; and still more so if it actually felt that these laws were superior. These laws, says Philo, "are necessarily grave and severe, because they inculcate the highest standard of virtue; but gravity is austere, and austerity is held in aversion by the great mass of men because they favor pleasure." [37] Indeed one might argue, as Josephus later did argue,[38] that similar religious differences exist also among non-Jews themselves. But Philo felt that the differences between the Jews and non-Jews are unlike the differences that may exist between various religious groups of non-Jews. The former are more fundamental. They place the Jews as a group apart from the totality of non-Jews, with all the varieties of religions and sects among the non-Jews themselves. Whenever any hos-

---

[33] *Ibid.*, 49-50.
[34] Deut. 23: 8 (7).
[35] *Virt.* 21, 105; cf. Jer. 29: 7; and above, p. 368.

[36] *Spec.* IV, 34, 179.
[37] *Ibid.*
[38] *Apion.* II, 6, 65.

tility breaks out between two groups of non-Jews, he says, the hostile groups do not stand alone, for "by reason of their frequent intercourse with other nations, they are in no want of helpers who join sides with them." Not so, however, is the case of the Jews. "The Jewish nation has none to take its part" and "one may say that the whole Jewish nation is in the position of an orphan compared with all other nations in other lands." [39]

What, then, is the solution of the problem? Long before Philo, when for the first time Jews became conscious of the gulf created between themselves and non-Jews by reason of their Law, we are told, "there came forth out of Israel lawless men, and persuaded many, saying: 'Let us go out and make a covenant with the nations that are round about us, for since we separated ourselves from them many evils have come upon us,'" [40] and this covenant which they advocated to be made with the nations, we are told, resulted in that "they repudiated the holy covenant; yea, they joined themselves to the gentiles." [41] Individual Jews at the time of Philo in Alexandria undoubtedly offered the same solution for the Jewish problem of their own time. His own nephew, Tiberius Julius Alexander, thus solved the Jewish problem for himself in that way. He forsook Judaism and henceforth found no difficulty in rising to high office, and in his subsequent behavior toward his own people, both in Alexandria and Palestine,[42] showed that he succeeded in completely emancipating himself from what was then called Jewish "inhospitality," the common opprobrium of that time for the natural desire on the part of the Jews to preserve their own existence. He must have been looked upon by his non-

---

[39] *Spec.* IV, 34, 179.
[40] I Macc. 1: 11.   [41] I Macc. 1: 15.
[42] Cf. *Bell. Jud.* II, 18, 8, 494; *Antt.* XX, 5, 2, 102.

Jewish contemporaries as an example of what they considered as the better kind of Jew, the desirable Jew, the Jew against whom they had no prejudice. There must undoubtedly have been in Alexandria other Jews like him who, alienated from the spiritual and intellectual sources of Judaism, came to look upon their heritage as a heap of meaningless customs and beliefs and thus sought to emancipate themselves from Jewish "inhospitality" and "superstition" and "atheism" by learning to relish swine's flesh, to idle on a week-day instead of resting on the Sabbath, and to see piety in the worship of images rather than in the worship of the imageless Jehovah. But, having torn themselves away from Judaism, they were evidently contented to enjoy their newly discovered liberties privately, and did not exhibit themselves to the world as examples of an ideal solution of a vexatious problem.[43]

The solution found by Philo for the Jewish problem of his time was the revival of the old prophetic promises of the ultimate disappearance of the diaspora. Without mentioning the term Messiah, he deals in great detail with what is known in Jewish tradition as the Messiah and the Messianic age. His discussion of these topics is to be discerned in his comments on various passages in the Pentateuch.

In his comments upon the blessings of Moses before his death, in which the future of each of the twelve tribes is foretold,[44] he says: "Some of these have already taken place, others are still looked for, since confidence in the future is assured by fulfillment in the past." [45] Those blessings which have not as yet been fulfilled are described by him as "exhortations for the future expressed in hopeful words of comfort which needs must be followed by their fulfillment," [46]

43 Cf. above, I, 82 ff.   45 *Mos.* II, 51, 288.
44 Deut. 33.   46 *Virt.* 11, 75.

for, he concludes, "that these blessings will be fulfilled we must believe." [47] Similarly in the Tannaitic literature some of these blessings of Moses are also taken to refer to the Messianic age. [48]

Then in his comment on the blessings promised for obedience to the commandments, [49] he describes in great detail his conceptions of the Messianic age, which on the whole reflect what in his time were already common conceptions of the Messianic age.

First, there will be a reunion of the exiled. Alluding to the verses that "the Lord thy God . . . will gather thee again out of all the nations among which the Lord hath dispersed thee; though thy dispersion may have been from one end of the earth to the other . . . thence thy God will bring thee, into the land which thy fathers possessed, and thou shalt possess it," [50] he says that "when they have gained the unexpected liberty, those who but now were scattered in Greece and the outside world over islands and continents will arise and post from every side with one impulse to the one appointed place." [51]

Second, this reunion of the exiled will be followed by national prosperity in the homeland to which they will have returned. Drawing on the verse "and He will do thee good and will make thee abundant beyond thy fathers," [52] he says: "When they have arrived, the cities which but now lay in ruins will be cities once more; the desolate land will be inhabited; the barren will change into fruitfulness; all the prosperity of their fathers and ancestors will seem a tiny

[47] *Ibid.* 12, 77.
[48] *Sifre Deut.*, § 352, on Deut. 33: 12, F, p. 145b; HF, p. 410; *Midrash Tannaim*, on Deut. 33: 3, p. 212.
[49] Lev. 26: 3–13; Deut. 28: 1–14; 30: 1–10.
[50] Deut. 30: 3–5; cf. *Praem.* 28, 164.
[51] *Praem.* 29, 165.   [52] Deut. 30: 5.

fragment, so lavish will be the abundant riches in their possession, which flowing from the gracious bounties of God as
from a perennial fountain will bring to each individually
and to all in common a deep stream of wealth leaving no
room for envy." [53] In another place, in contrast to the condition of the Jews in his own times, of which he says that
"our nation has not prospered for many years," [54] he describes the Messianic age as a time when "a fresh start is
made to brighter prospects" and as a period of "national
prosperity." [55]

Third, following the reunion of the exiled and the establishment of national prosperity there will be a reign of peace
between men and men and between men and beasts. Drawing upon such verses as "And I will give peace in the land,
and ye shall lie down, and none shall make you afraid; and I
will cause evil beasts to cease out of the land, neither shall
the sword go through your land," [56] he describes in great
detail the blessing of victory over enemies and the establishment of peace between men and men and between men and
beasts.[57] Now there is nothing in this verse to indicate that
it refers to the Messianic age nor is there in Philo's comment
upon it any direct indication that he has taken it to refer to
the Messianic age. But in his description of the pacification
of animals he says: "For this is one war where no quarter or
truce is possible; as wolves with lambs, so all wild beasts
both on land and water are at war with all men. This war
no mortal can quell; that is done only by the Uncreated,
when He judges that there are some worthy of salvation.
. . . But a very necessary preliminary to this is that the
wild beast within the soul shall be tamed . . . when that

[53] *Praem.* 29, 168.
[54] *Mos.* II, 7, 43.
[55] *Ibid.*, 44.
[56] Lev. 26: 6; cf. Deut. 28: 1, 7.
[57] *Praem.* 14, 79–16, 94.

time comes I believe that bears and lions and panthers . . .
will no longer as heretofore be roused to ferocity by the sight
of man . . . then too the tribes of the scorpions and serpents
and the other reptiles will have no use for their venom. . . .
Among all these the man of worth will move sacrosanct and
inviolate because God has respected virtue and given it the
privilege that none should imagine mischief against it." [58]
This passage bears the unmistakable evidence of the influence of the Messianic verses in Isaiah: "And the wolf shall
dwell with the lamb, and the leopard shall lie down with the
kid; and the calf and the young lion and the fattling together; and a little child shall lead them . . . and the suckling
child shall play on the hole of the asp, and the weaned child
shall put his hand on the basilisk's den. They shall not hurt
nor destroy in all my holy mountain; for the earth shall be
full of the knowledge of God." [59] Peace between men and
men and between men and beasts is thus a third characteristic
feature of the Messianic age.

These three features of the Messianic age described by
Philo reflect common conceptions of the Messianic age current in Jewish tradition.[60] But then Philo dwells upon a
fourth characteristic feature, and that is the divine punishment of the unrepented enemies of Israel. Thus, drawing
upon the verse "and the Lord thy God will put all these
curses upon thine enemies, and on them that hate thee, that
persecuted thee," [61] he says: "Everything will suddenly be

---

[58] *Praem.* 15, 87–90.

[59] Isa. 11:6, 8, 9. Heinemann (*Bildung*, p. 419), thinks that in the passage of
Philo there is no direct allusion to Isaiah. Colson (VIII, 455, § 87), on the other
hand, asserts that there is such an allusion. Cf. Z. Frankel, "Alexandrinische
Messiashoffnungen," *Monatsschrift für Geschichte und Wissenschaft des Judenthums*,
8 (1859), 328–329; J. Kroll, "Posidonios und Vergils vierte Ekloge," *Hermes*, 50
(1915), 139–141.

[60] Cf. J. Drummond, *The Jewish Messiah*, chs. xviii, xx; J. Klausner, *Ha-Ra'ayon
ha-Meshiḥi be-Yisra'el*, pp. 146–148.   [61] Deut. 30:7.

reversed, God will turn the curses against the enemies of these penitents, the enemies who rejoiced in the misfortunes of the nation and mocked and railed at them [62] . . . who have mocked at their lamentations, proclaimed public holidays on the days of their misfortunes, feasted on their mourning, in general made the unhappiness of others their own happiness." [63] The description of what the enemies had done to the Jews before the liberation undoubtedly reflects local conditions in Alexandria in the relation between Jews and non-Jews,[64] and it is quite understandable why Philo, whose God in mercy and forgiveness remembers justice, should look forward toward divine punishment of these enemies. Still, while punishment of enemies is characteristic of the Messianic age as depicted in Jewish tradition, especially characteristic as a feature of the traditional conception of the Messianic age is the uprising of the heathen nations under the leadership of Gog and Magog and their ultimate defeat either by God or by the Messiah.[65] This statement in Philo may therefore be a description in terms of local Alexandrian experience of the war of Gog and Magog. That it should take place after the gathering of the exiled and the reëstablishment of national prosperity reflects the verses in Ezekiel according to which Gog will make war on the Jewish people after they have been "gathered out of the nations" and after they have established themselves in quiet and safety.[66]

The condition that will bring about the Messianic age is repentance. Drawing upon the verses that the gathering of the people from the lands of their exile will take place when

[62] *Praem.* 29, 169.   [63] *Ibid.*, 171.

[64] Cf. *Flac.* 5, 25–11, 96; *Legat.* 18, 120–20, 135.

[65] Drummond, *op. cit.*, ch. xii; Klausner, *op. cit.*, pp. 323–325; Moore, *Judaism*, II, 333, n. 3.

[66] Ezek. 38: 11–12; Zech. 12 and 14; cf. Klausner, *op. cit.*, pp. 80, 124; Moore, *op. cit.*, II, 344, n. 4.

"they will confess their iniquity"[67] or when "thou shalt
return to the Lord thy God,"[68] he describes this confession
of iniquity and return to God in terms of what, as we have
seen, constitute repentance in Judaism, consisting of a feeling of shame and of self-reproach and of a confession and
acknowledgment of sin both within one's self and with one's
tongue.[69] Accordingly he describes those who are to return
as those who have repented ($\mu\epsilon\tau\alpha\nu\epsilon\nu\omega\eta\kappa\delta\tau\epsilon s$),[70] thus reflecting
the double meaning of the Hebrew *shabim*. Now, accord-
ing to Scripture, even when man is slow in his repentance,
God in his mercy, by special grace, may sometimes forgive his sin, for "God is merciful and gracious . . . forgiving
iniquities and transgression and sin"[71] and "He hath not
dealt with us according to our sins, nor retributed to us
according to our iniquities."[72] Moreover, forgiveness and
redemption are promised to Israel for the sake of the merit
of the Patriarchs, for "I will remember my covenant with
Jacob, and also my covenant with Isaac, and also my covenant with Abraham will I remember; and I will remember
the land."[73] Reflecting all these, Philo says that "three
intercessors ($\pi\alpha\rho\acute{\alpha}\kappa\lambda\eta\tau\sigma\iota$) they have to plead for their reconciliation with the Father. *One* is the clemency and kindness
of Him to whom they appeal . . . the *second* is the holiness
of the founders of the nation [74] . . . the *third* is one which
more than anything else moves the loving kindness of the
other two to come forward so readily, and that is the improvement [i.e., repentance] working in those who are being
brought to make a covenant of peace."[75] So also in native
Jewish tradition, using the Hebraized Greek term *praklit*
($\pi\alpha\rho\acute{\alpha}\kappa\lambda\eta\tau\sigma s$), the very same Greek term that is used by

[67] Lev. 26: 40.
[68] Deut. 30: 2.
[69] *Praem.* 28, 163; cf. above, p. 256.
[73] Lev. 26: 42.   [74] Cf. *Spec.* IV, 34, 181.

[70] *Ibid.*, 9, 169.
[71] Exod. 34: 6–7; cf. Ps. 78: 38.
[72] Ps. 103: 10; cf. above, p. 258.
[75] *Praem.* 29, 166–167.

Philo, in the sense of an intercessor who pleads in favor of man before God, and using also the Hebrew term *zekut*, merit, in the sense of that on account of which God acts in favor of man, the rabbis say that (1) God confers merit on men and acts in their favor through His "mercy," [76] that (2) He also confers merit on the Jewish people and acts in their favor through the merit of the Patriarchs,[77] and that (3) "repentance and good deeds" are "man's paracletes" to plead for him before God.[78] Again, as in Philo, repentance is considered by the rabbis as the chief condition in the coming of the final redemption of Israel.[79] But redemption may also come, according to them, through the merit of the Patriarchs or by the mercy of God. It is because of the merit of the Patriarchs, they say, that God knew that He would have to redeem Israel from Egypt [80] and by the same token, we imagine, He knows that because of the merit of the Patriarchs He will have to bring about their ultimate redemption. Again, it is argued, on the basis of many verses, that, even without their repentance, God by His own initiative will bring about the redemption of Israel.[81] Ezekiel expresses this view in the verse: "Thus saith the Lord God: I do not this for your sake, O house of Israel, but for my holy name."[82] In the Testament of Asher, the same view is expressed in the statement: "But the Lord will gather you together in faith through His tender mercy, and for the sake of Abraham, Isaac, and Jacob." [83]

Whether Philo believed that the final redemption will take place under the leadership of a particular person such as is known in Jewish tradition as the Messiah is not clear. No-

---

[76] *Sanhedrin* 12a; cf. above, n. 71.
[77] Cf. above, I, 455.
[78] *Shabbat* 32a.
[79] *Yoma* 86b.
[80] *Exodus Rabbah*, 1, 36, on Exod. 2: 25.
[81] *Sanhedrin* 97b–98a.
[82] Ezek. 36: 22; cf. Klausner, *op. cit.*, p. 74.
[83] The Testament of Asher 7: 7.

where in his writings is there any explicit mention of a personal Messiah. There are two vague statements, however, which may refer to such a Messiah.

First, in the course of his discussion of the blessings promised to those who obey the commandments, he quotes from the prophecy of Balaam the verse which in the Septuagint reads: "There shall come forth a man" [84] and then paraphrases the rest of the verse in his statement "and leading his host to war he will subdue great and populous nations." [85] Among students of Philo there is a difference of opinion as to whether this refers to a personal Messiah or not.[86] But inasmuch as in native Jewish tradition this verse in its Masoretic reading, "He shall pour forth water out of his buckets," is sometimes taken as referring to the Messiah,[87] there is no reason why we should not assume that Philo has also taken it in this sense Moreover, in describing that "man" who shall "come forth," Philo says that "God has sent to his aid the reinforcements that befit the godly, and they are dauntless courage of soul and all-powerful might ($\iota\sigma\chi\dot{\nu}s$) of body."[88] Now, in Isaiah's description of the Messiah, it is said: "And the spirit of God will rest upon him . . . a spirit of counsel and might ($\iota\sigma\chi\dot{\nu}os$)." [89] In the light of this, when Philo describes the "man" who "shall come forth" as one to whose aid God will send "dauntless courage of soul and all powerful might ($\iota\sigma\chi\dot{\nu}s$)," he undoubtedly means by that "man" the Messiah of the prophecy of Isaiah.

Second, in his discussion of the ultimate return of the scattered exiled to their home land, he says that the return-

---

[84] Num. 24: 7.   [85] *Praem.* 16, 95.
[86] Cf. Drummond, *The Jewish Messiah*, p. 272; Klausner, *From Jesus to Paul*, pp. 197–198.
[87] Cf. *Targum pseudo-Jonathan* and *Targum Yerushalmi, ad loc.*
[88] *Praem.* 16, 95.
[89] Isa. 11: 2; cf. Bréhier, p. 5, n. 1.

ing exiles will be "guided by some vision, more divine than is compatible with its being of the nature of man, invisible indeed to everyone else, but manifest only to those who were saved." [90] With regard to this passage, too, there is a difference of opinion among students of Philo as to whether it refers to the Messiah or not.[91] According to one interpretation, it refers to the Messiah as well as to the Logos, thus identifying the two. According to another interpretation, it refers to the Logos but not to the Messiah. According to a third interpretation, it refers to something like the cloud by which the people were guided in their first deliverance from Egypt.

As in native Judaism so also in Philo the Messianic age is conceived not only as an age of national deliverance and national prosperity but also as an age during which Judaism will become a universal religion. The Mosaic Law, which he has declared to be eternal,[92] will, as in native Judaism,[93] continue to exist during the Messianic age, in a form, of course, evolved through a continuous process of interpretation. But more than that. With the restoration and the renewed prosperity of the Jewish people, he says, "I think that each nation would abandon its peculiar ways, and, throwing overboard their ancestral customs, turn to honoring our laws alone, for, when the brightness of their shining is accompanied by national prosperity, it will darken the light of the others as the risen sun darkens the stars." [94]

[90] *Praem.* 29, 165.

[91] Dähne, I, pp. 437–438; Gfrörer, I, 528–530; Drummond, *The Jewish Messiah*, pp. 271–272; L. Cohn, *Philos Werke*, II, 382; Colson, VIII, 418, n. 9; F. Gregoire, "Le Messie chez Philon d'Alexandrie," *Ephemerides theologiae lovanienses*, 12 (1935), 28–50.

[92] *Mos.* II, 3, 14; cf. above, I, 187–188.

[93] Cf. discussion on this point, Drummond, *op. cit.*, pp. 326–327; Klausner, *op. cit.*, pp. 287–289; 333–334. M. Higger, *The Jewish Utopia* (The Lord Baltimore Press, 1932), pp. 106–109; Moore, *Judaism*, I, 271–274.   [94] *Moses* II, 7, 44.

On the whole this reflects such Messianic prophecies as
that in which it is predicted that "it shall come to pass in
the end of days, that the mountain of the Lord's house shall
be established as the top of the mountains, and shall be exalted above the hills; and all nations shall flow unto it; and
many peoples shall go and say: Come ye, and let us go up to
the mountain of the Lord, to the house of the God of Jacob,
and He will teach us of His ways, and we will walk in His
paths, for out of Zion shall come forth the law." 95 Similar
hopes, couched almost in the same language as used by Philo
and reminiscent again of the scriptural verses quoted, are expressed also in the Sibylline oracles: "Then again all the
sons of the great God shall live quietly around the temple,
rejoicing in those gifts which He shall give, who is the
Creator, and sovereign righteous judge. . . . Free from war
shall they be in city and country . . . and then all the isles
and cities shall say, How doth the Eternal love these men!
For all things work in sympathy with them and help them.
. . . A sweet strain shall they utter from their mouths in
hymns. Come, let us fall upon the earth and supplicate the
Eternal King, the mighty everlasting God. Let us make
procession to His Temple, for He is the sole Potentate, and
let us ponder the law of the most high God, who is the most
righteous of all on earth. But we had gone astray from the
path of the Eternal, and with foolish heart worshiped the
work of men's hands, idols and images of men that are
dead." 96 Comparing, however, the Sibylline passage with
the Philonic passage, we notice one striking difference. In
the Sibylline passage, despite its reference to the "law," and
the reference in other lines to "sacrifices," 97 the main emphasis is upon the abandoning of idolatry. In Philo it is

95 Isa. 2: 2–4; Micah 4: 1–2.
96 Sibylline Oracles III, 702–722.   97 *Ibid.*, 573–579.

clear that in the Messianic age the gentiles will not only abandon idolatry and polytheism but they will also abandon their "peculiar ways" and "their ancestral customs" and will honor our "laws." In short, in the Messianic age, according to Philo, the gentiles will become full proselytes, and not merely "God-fearers." A similar view is expressed also in the Talmud by various Amoraim, who, from the verse, "For then will I turn to the people a pure language, that they may all call upon the name of the Lord, to serve Him with one consent," [98] inferred that in the Messianic age [99] gentiles will not only abandon idolatry but will also become full proselytes.[100]

The motive for the conversion of the gentiles during the Messianic age is outrightly said by Philo, as will have been noticed, to be the splendor and glory and prosperity which the Jewish people will come into. This is avowedly not a purely religious motive, such as Jewish tradition and Philo himself would require of a proselyte.[101] Now in native Jewish tradition there is a question as to the status of those who become converted to Judaism for motives other than purely religious. The question is especially raised with reference to those who became converted to Judaism during the prosperous reigns of King David and King Solomon and also those who will wish to become converted during the prosperity of the Jewish people in the Messianic age. From the various opinions expressed, it may be gathered that while those who wish to become proselytes for ulterior motives are not to be accepted, those who have already become proselytes for such ulterior motives have the legal status of proselytes.[102] The

[98] Zeph. 3: 9.
[99] Literally: "in the future age" (*le-'atid la-bo*).   [100] *'Abodah Zarah* 24a.
[101] Cf. above, pp. 358 f.
[102] *Yebamot* 24b; *'Abodah Zarah* 3b and 24a; cf. Maimonides, *Mishneh Torah*, *Issure Bi'ah*, XIII, 15 and 17.

same view seems to be reflected also in Philo's statement about the conversion of gentiles during the Messianic age.

In native Jewish tradition the abolition of war during the Messianic age, and the establishment of peace, does not mean the abolition of the existence of distinct nations and governments. In the prophecies of Isaiah and Micah, the peace to be established in the end of days means that "nation shall not lift up sword against nation," [103] which implies that nations will still exist. In the vision of Daniel, the Messiah is depicted as one to whom was given "dominion and glory and a kingdom, that all people, nations, and languages should serve him." [104] There will thus still be different peoples and nations and languages. The Sibylline oracles predict that "neither shall there be any sword throughout the land nor battle din . . . but there shall be a great peace throughout all the earth and king shall be friendly with king till the end of the age, and a common law for men throughout all the earth shall the Eternal perfect in the starry heaven." [105] Kings and states over which they rule will thus still continue to exist. The rabbis in their utterances about the days of the Messiah predict that "no nation or language shall be able to have dominion over them." [106] National and linguistic differences will thus still continue to exist. This is also the conception of the Messianic age in Philo. The peace which will be ultimately established will be a peace among nations, and a peace established by "a man" who shall come forth and subdue those great and populous nations who out of their lust for war started an attack.[107] The nations who will abandon their "peculiar ways" and "ancestral customs"

[103] Isa. 2: 4; Micah 4: 3.
[104] Dan. 7: 14.
[105] Sibylline Oracles III, 751–758.
[106] Megillah 11a; cf. Klausner, Ha-Ra'ayon ha-Meshiḥi be-Yisra'el, p. 326.
[107] Praem. 16, 93–95.

and turn to honor our "laws" will indeed be united, as the Sibyl says, by "a common law," but they will continue to exist as nations.

By the time of Philo, corresponding to the Jewish ideal of a Messianic age, there existed a Stoic ideal of a Messianic age. In this Stoic Messianic ideal all differences of nationality or of historic states will disappear. There is to be a universal state governed by universal law in which peace is to reign and no distinction of race or creed is to exist. Their aim was, as it is recorded in their name, that "all the inhabitants of this world of ours should not live differentiated by their respective rules of justice into separate cities and communities, but that we should consider all men to be of one community and one polity, and that we should have a common life and an order common to us all, even as a herd that feeds together and shares the pasturage of a common field." [108] In the empire established by Alexander contemporary historians and philosophers saw the beginning of that universal empire and in the Roman empire they saw its completion.[109] Now the depiction of the Messianic age in Philo is quite evidently colored with Stoic phraseology, but upon a close examination we shall find it to be really in opposition to the Stoic conception of a Messianic age. There is to be indeed a universal state, as the Stoics say, but that state has not yet been established; it is yet to come into being with the fulfillment of the ancient prophetic promises to the Jewish people. That universal state will indeed be governed by a universal law, but that universal law will be the "laws" of Moses, as Philo calls it, or "a common law for men" which "the Eternal shall perfect in the starry heaven," as the Sibyl describes it. There will indeed be a cosmopoli-

[108] Plutarch, *De Alexandri Magni Fortuna aut Virtute* I, 6.
[109] *Ibid.*; Strabo, *Geography* I, 4, 9; Polybius, *Histories* I, 2, 7; VIII, 2 (4), 3-4.

tanism, a world-citizenship, as the Stoics preach, but this will be due to the fact that all mankind will honor the laws of Moses and thereby become citizens of that polity which Philo describes as "holy," "God-loving," "best," "irreproachable" and "divine." Finally, within that universal state, based upon a common law, there will still continue to exist all the various historic states and the various ethnic and linguistic groups of mankind.

It is in the light of this conception of the Messianic age that we are to understand another Messianic passage in Philo, one of a more general nature, in which the Jewish people is not mentioned. In that passage Philo begins with a reference to the rise and fall of states and nations, mentioning Greece and Macedonia, Persians and Parthians, Egypt, the Ethiopians, Carthage, the kingdoms of Libya, the kings of Pontus, Europe and Asia.[110] Then he concludes with the following reflection: For cyclewise moves the revolution of that divine Logos which most people call fortune ($\tau \acute{v} \chi \eta$). And then, as it continually flows on among cities and nations and countries, it allots what some have to others and what all have to all, changing the affairs of individuals only in point of time, in order that the whole world may, as one city, enjoy the best of polities, a democracy."[111] From the last part of the passage it may be inferred that just as history shows the rise and fall of states so it also shows the rise and fall of various forms of governments, culminating in a world state having democracy as its form of government.

The sentiment expressed in this passage is based upon certain statements of Polybius.[112] In one place Polybius speaks

---

[110] *Immut.* 36, 173–175; cf. *Jos.* 23, 135–136, where he mentions also the successors of Alexander and the Ptolemies.

[111] *Immut.* 36, 176.

[112] The general connection between this passage of Philo and Polybius has been pointed out by R. von Scala, *Die Studien des Polybios* (1890), I, 177, n. 2, who sug-

of the rise and fall of states, mentioning Illium, Assyria, Media, Persia, and Macedonia.[113] In another place he attributes this rise and fall of states to fortune (τύχη).[114] In still another place he shows how forms of governments, such as monarchy, aristocracy, oligarchy, democracy, and then again monarchy, follow one another in a cycle,[115] concluding with the general observation: "This is the cycle of political revolutions (πολιτειῶν ἀνακύκλωσις), the course appointed by nature (φύσεως οἰκονομία) in which constitutions change, disappear, and finally return to the point from which they started." [116] This cycle of political revolutions dwelt upon by Polybius, it has been shown by students, is nothing but the application of the Stoic theory of cycles in the course of the natural history of the universe to the political history of human society.[117]

The analogy between Polybius and Philo in their respective statements is quite striking. Still, when we scrutinize the statements of Philo in the light of what we know about his philosophy and compare them with the statements of Polybius in the light of what we know about the Stoic philosophy which is reflected in them, we notice certain fundamental differences between them.

In Polybius it is fortune which causes this rise and fall of states and the changes in forms of government. Fortune is often presented in Greek literature as a divine agency. In

gests that Philo knew Polybius through Posidonius. Leisegang (*Philos Werke*, IV, 109, n. 1) rejects this suggestion about Posidonius. Cf. also F. Geiger, *Philon von Alexandria als sozialer Denker*, pp. 81–82.

[113] Polybius, *Histories* XXXVIII, 22, 2.
[114] *Ibid.* XXIX, 21, 3–6.
[115] *Ibid.* VI, 6, 1–9, 9.
[116] *Ibid.* VI, 9, 10.
[117] Cf. R. Hirzel, *Untersuchungen zu Cicero's philosophischen Schriften* (1882), II, 871; R. v. Scala, *Die Studien des Polybios* (1890), I, 236–246; E. Täubler, *Tyche* (1926), p. 92.

Plato fortune is said to "co-operate with God in the government of human affairs." [118] Polybius himself speaks of the "gods" and "fortune" as if they were related terms.[119] But this fortune which Polybius describes as causing the rise and fall of states is nothing but what he himself calls "the course appointed by nature" [120] which he similarly describes as causing the rise and fall of forms of government. Now this "course appointed by nature" is described by him as taking place "necessarily (ἀναγκαίως) and naturally (φυσικῶς)." [121] Consequently the "fortune" of Polybius is nothing but what the Stoics would call God or nature or universal law or fate or providence or the Logos of the world, all meaning nothing but the fixed immutable order of nature or the concatenation of cause and effect.[122] Philo, however, significantly says that the changes in states and governments are due to "that divine Logos which most people call fortune." What he means by this locution is this: It is not fortune in the sense of fate or a fixed order of things or even in the sense of God or providence or the Logos of the world as these terms are commonly used in philosophy, and especially in the Stoic philosophy, that is the cause of changes in state governments; it is rather what he himself, Philo, calls the "divine Logos," namely, the providence of a God who is not bound by any fixed laws of nature, but who can upset these laws of nature fixed by himself.[123] All this is a corollary of his belief in the individual providence of God. So also St. Augustine, as a corollary of the belief in individual provi-

---

[118] *Laws* IV, 709 B; cf. above, I, 330.   [120] Cf. above, n. 116.
[119] *Histories* X, 9, 2.   [121] *Histories* VI, 10, 2.
[122] Cf. above, I, 327, 329, and Arnim, Index, under *theos*, p. 70, col. 2. On the relation between "fortune" and "fate," see H. R. Patch, *The Goddess Fortuna in Mediaeval Literature*, 1927, pp. 10–11; V. Cioffari, *Fortune and Fate from Democritus to St. Thomas Aquinas*, 1935, pp. 33–53.
[123] I think that W. Bousset has overlooked the special significance of Philo's phraseology in this passage when in his *Die Religion des Judentums im neutestament-*

dence, argues that "the cause, then, of the greatness of the Roman empire is neither fortuitous nor fatal. . . . In a word, human kingdoms are established by divine providence, and if any one attributes their existence to fate, because he calls the will or the power of God itself by the name fate, let him keep his opinion, but correct his language." [124] This view that fortunes of states and nations are directly guided by God reflects the many scriptural prophecies about the rise and fall of nations [125] and such verses as "For I will rise up against them, saith the Lord of hosts, and cut off from Babylon the name, and remnant, and son and nephew. . . . I will break the Assyrian in my land." [126] "Thus saith the Lord to his anointed, to Cyrus, whose right hand I have holden, to subdue nations before him." [127] "Who smote great nations, and slew mighty kings . . . and gave their land for an heritage, an heritage unto Israel his people." [128] In the Wisdom of Solomon the same view is expressed in the statement, "Because your dominion was given you from the Lord, and your sovereignty from the Most High." [129]

Second, to Polybius the most perfect state was already produced, and that was Rome. Fortune, he says, has accomplished the most surprising feat "in our own times, that is, to bring all the known parts of the world (οἰκουμένης) under one rule and dominion, a thing absolutely without precedent." [130] Philo, who lived under Roman rule during the

---

lichen Zeitalter[2], p. 509, he restates it as follows: "Gott trägt nicht mehr mit mächtiger Hand die Geschichte der Völker und seines Volkes, er greift nicht mehr lohnend und strafend in sie ein. Nach dem ehernen Gesetze einer vernünftigen Notwendigkeit bewegt sich, immer gleichmässig und in derselben Weise, das Weltall."

[124] *De Civitate Dei* V, 1.

[125] Cf. Isa. 13; 17–19; Jer. 46–51; Ezek. 27–28; 35; 38–39; Obad.; Nah. 1.

[126] Isa. 14: 22, 25.

[127] Isa. 45: 1. [128] Ps. 135: 10, 12.

[129] Wisdom of Solomon 6: 3.

[130] *Histories* VIII, 2 (4), 3–4; cf. I, 4, 5.

PHILO

period of its greatness, does not say that Rome is that ideal state aimed at by "the divine Logos." Roman rule is indeed praised by him, its sovereignty indeed extended over all land and sea, and peace and harmony and prosperity and happiness indeed reigned throughout it,[131] but still it was not the ideal state aimed at by the divine Logos. The divine Logos has not as yet accomplished its revolution, it is still to bring about its desired purpose "that the whole world should be as one city, enjoying that best of constitutions, democracy."[132]

Third, to Polybius the cycles of states and constitutions, like the cycles of worlds in the Stoic doctrine, are eternal. To eternity will states rise and fall; never will that process stop; never will a state rise not to fall again. To eternity will monarchies change into aristocracies, aristocracies into oligarchies, oligarchies into democracies, and democracies again into monarchies; never will there evolve a best form of government which will remain stable for ever. Rome indeed is to him the greatest state ever produced by fortune, but Scipio, impressed by the Stoic teaching of the eternal cycle, could not help saying to Polybius at the moment of Rome's triumph over Carthage: "A glorious moment, Polybius; but I have dread foreboding that some day the same doom will be pronounced upon my own country,"[133] and to this Polybius adds: "It would be difficult to mention an utterance more statesmanlike and more profound."[134] Again, Rome to him had the best form of government; still, impressed by the Stoic theory of the eternal cycle, he could not help feeling that in the Roman form of government a change for the worse was sure to follow some day, for, he says, "This state, more than any other, has been formed and has

[131] *Legat.* 2, 8–14.
[132] *Immut.* 36, 176.

[133] *Histories* XXXVIII, 21, 1.
[134] *Ibid.*, 2.

grown naturally, and will undergo a natural decline and change to its contrary." [135] For Philo, however, though he says of the revolution of the Logos that it moves "cycle-wise," there is no eternal cycle of the rise and fall of states, or of the perfection and decline of forms of government. The reason for his rejection of an eternal cycle in social history is the same as that for which he rejects it in cosmic history.[136] An eternal cycle in either of them, according to him, implies a process of events driven on by a blind necessary fate. But to him it is not blind fate but an intelligent and wise God who guides the destinies of the world and nations. The divine Logos which in this passage he substitutes for fortune or fate is the individual providence of God, and this works according to a certain plan. The plan of God is to bring about in due time a perfect state of society which should remain perfect. After various states have attained power and fallen, after various forms of government have been tried and found wanting, ultimately one state will emerge which will not fall, and that state will have the best form of government which will not become corrupt. This is the Messianic state which will be governed by the Law of Moses, a Law described by him elsewhere as being based upon democracy and equality.[137] This view reflects such Messianic predictions as that expressed in the book of Daniel, where the dominion established in the Messianic age is said to be "an everlasting dominion, which shall never pass away." [138]

Finally, while the Mosaic Law will be universally accepted during the Messianic age, there will still exist, as according to native Jewish tradition, many distinct national states. The "one city," after the analogy of which Philo visualizes the "whole world" in the future, is the city as

---

[135] *Ibid.* VI, 9, 12–13.
[136] Cf. above, I, 299–300.
[137] Cf. above, p. 392.
[138] Dan. 7: 14, 27.

he has known it, his own native Alexandria, a confederacy of many distinct polities. The "whole world," then, will be a confederacy of many polities, united into one general polity, and that one general polity will be based upon the principle of democracy or proportional equality or justice, which, according to him, is embodied in the Law of Moses.

IV. Conclusion, Influence, Anticipation

When Philo identified the laws of the Pentateuch with what in philosophic literature was called "practical philosophy," it was quite natural for him to identify the laws dealing with rulers and subjects to that branch of practical philosophy called politics. Accordingly he presents all the laws of this kind in terms of political theories derived from the writings of Plato, Aristotle, and the Stoics. The entire body of such laws is presented by him as a constitution dealing with the form of organization of the inhabitants of the state planned by Moses. In that state there are citizens and non-citizens. Citizens are all those who live according to the Law, whether they are native-born Jews or strangers who came over to the Law, called proselytes. Among the non-citizens there are aliens, resident aliens, and those who may be called spiritual proselytes. Besides these various classes of inhabitants there are rulers. The two chief rulers are the king and the high priest. The manner in which the king and high priest are to be chosen, their qualification for office, the length of their tenure of office, and the functions of their office are all discussed by him. The two offices, according to him, are independent of each other, the king being charged with the administration of justice and the high priest with the administration of temple service and the interpretation of the Law. In a moral sense, however, he evaluates the high priesthood as being superior to kingship.

The king in his capacity as administrator of justice is also to appoint judges and officers. In addition there is also a council of elders.

Philo's delineation of the Mosaic constitution does not contain directly any criticism of other institutions, except on two points, the election of rulers by lot and the short tenure of office. But indirectly his entire presentation of that constitution is aimed as a criticism of certain Greek theories of state. To begin with, as a criticism of Plato in his *Statesman* and *Republic*, he tries to emphasize that the Mosaic constitution is opposed to any form of personal government; the government which the Mosaic constitution sets up is one of fixed laws. Then, as a criticism of Plato in his *Laws* and Aristotle in his *Politics*, he tries to show that the fixed laws upon which the Mosaic state is to be based, in contradistinction to the laws upon which the Platonic and the Aristotelian state are to be based, are not man-made but divinely revealed. Finally, in criticism of both Plato and Aristotle who, because they believed that no man-made law can be an absolutely ideal law, argued that there can be no absolutely ideal state, Philo maintains that the Mosaic state, because it is based upon a divinely revealed and hence an ideal law, is an absolutely ideal state. In this ideal state, citizenship means obedience to the Law revealed by God, and authority means only the authority of the Law. The power which king and high priest enjoy is only that of administering the Law or of interpreting it. The ultimate ruler is then God, who is the author of the Law. Philo almost coined the term theocracy, by which later Josephus described the Mosaic state. In political terms of his own time, however, Philo describes the Mosaic state as combining the best features of kingship, aristocracy, and democracy, the term democracy being used by him not in the sense of the government of the many but rather in the sense of a government in which each one enjoys his own in accordance with law.

The Law was revealed originally to Israel, and the state to be established on the basis of that Law was originally meant to be the state of a single people in a single country under a single ruler. But it is not to be confined to one single people or to one single country or to one single ruler. The state envisaged by Moses is an ideal concept of a society of various peoples in various countries under various rulers living under the same Law according to the principles of democracy and equality. Such a society is described by him as the "holy polity," the "best polity," the "irreproachable polity," the "ecclesia of the Lord," or the "holy ecclesia." This ideal society is ultimately to be realized in the Messianic age, when, besides the reunited Jewish polity, there will be other polities recognizing the Mosaic Law, and all these polities will constitute what Philo would probably call a "universal ecclesia" or a "catholic church."

The identification of the commandments with virtues on the part of mediaeval Jewish philosophers and also their philosophic explanation of some or all of the commandments would naturally lead us to expect that they would also attempt to explain the laws regarding rulers and subjects in terms of political theories known to them. No such attempt, on a large scale and in a systematic way, is, however, made by them. Maimonides, in one place, reproduces the conventional classification of the sciences, in which, under practical philosophy, he enumerates the topics of politics; [1] in another place he discusses philosophically the source of inspiration of "statesmen"; [2] in still another place he discusses again philosophically the origin of the state [3] and the

---

[1] *Millot ha-Higgayon*, ch. 14.
[2] *Moreh Nebukim* II, 37.   [3] *Ibid.* II, 40; cf. above, p. 14, n. 29.

function of the king in it.[4] But no attempt is made by him
to present the Mosaic form of government in terms of political theories of his time. The form of the Mosaic state and
its institutions are dealt with by him in his code of Jewish
law,[5] and there he confines himself to a logical and systematic arrangement of traditional material. It was not until
toward the end of the fifteenth century that Isaac Abrabanel,
under the influence of Christian authors, made a faint effort
to discuss the institution of kingship in Scripture in terms of
current political theory.[6]

More in line with Philo's treatment of the Mosaic constitution is the treatment of it in Christian literature. St.
Thomas, in his fourfold division of what he calls the judicial
laws of the Pentateuch, describes two of its divisions in terms
suggesting two of Aristotle's branches of practical philosophy, namely, political management and household management.[7] Suggesting the former is his description of one
division of judicial laws as dealing with the relation "of the
people's sovereign to his subjects" and "of the citizens to
foreigners"; suggesting the latter is his description of another division as dealing with the relations "of members of
the same household, such as the relations of the father to
his son; of wife to her husband; of the master to his servant."[8]
With regard to the Mosaic form of government in general,
he describes it again in terms of current political theory and,
like Philo, he finds that it is a mixture of kingship, aristocracy, and democracy, which mixed form of government he
describes as "the best form of the organization of rulers . . .

---

[4] *Ibid.* II, 40.

[5] *Mishneh Torah: Sanhedrin* and *Melakim*.

[6] Isaac Abravanel, Commentary on I Sam. 8: 4; cf. L. Strauss, "On Abravanel's
Philosophical Tendency and Political Teaching," *Isaac Abravanel, Six Lectures,*
Cambridge University Press, 1937, pp. 93–129.

[7] Cf. above, p. 322, n. 1.   [8] *Sum. Theol.* I, II, 104, 4 c.

in a state or kingdom" (*optima ordinatio principum . . . in aliqua civitate vel regno*).[9] It was a kind of kingship, "for Moses and his successors governed the people in such a way that each of them was ruler over all"; there was an element of aristocracy in it, for "seventy elders were chosen, who were elders in virtue"; "but it was a democratical government in so far as the rulers were chosen from all the people" and "by the people."[10] It will be noticed that, unlike Philo, he uses the term democracy here loosely in the general sense of the rule of the people.[11] With his belief that these judicial laws were divinely revealed, he considered those laws concerning rulers and foreigners and the members of the household as having been all suitably (*convenienter*) ordered,[12] and with regard to laws concerning rulers, in so far as it was a mixture of kingship, aristocracy, and democracy, as being "the best form of organization" (*optima ordinatio*).[13] But still the Mosaic form of government was not meant to be an ideal form of government and one which was to exist forever and to serve as a model for all future forms of governments, for "the judicial laws did not bind forever, but were annulled by the coming of Christ," so that "when the state of the people changed with the coming of Christ, the judicial precepts lost their binding force."[14] Still St. Thomas makes a distinction between the abrogation of the ceremonial laws and the abrogation of the judicial laws. The former are not only "dead" (*mortua*) but also "deadly" (*mortifera*) and the observance of them is a sin; the latter are only "dead" but not "deadly" and consequently "if a sovereign were to order these judicial precepts to be observed in his kingdom he

---

[9] *Ibid.*, 105, 1 c.

[10] *Ibid.*

[11] Cf. *Statesman* 291 D; *Politica* IV, 4, 1290a, 30 ff.

[12] *Sum. Theol.* I, II, 105, 1, 3, 4.

[13] *Ibid.*, 1 c.

[14] *Ibid.*, 104, 3 c.

would not sin: unless perchance they were observed, or
ordered to be observed, as though they derived their binding force through being institutions of the Old Law." [15]
The traditional Christian view with regard to the Mosaic
state, namely, that it is good but not the best, had been
summed up long before St. Thomas by Clement of Alexandria in his statement that Moses "furnished a good
polity, which is the right discipline of men in social life" [16]
and also in his statement that of the three forms of polity
that of the Greeks is brass, that of the Jews is silver, and
that of the Christians is gold.[17] It is because of this attitude
toward it that the Mosaic constitution, as well as subsequent
Biblical history in general, continues to be frequently
quoted by Christians as proof-text in political controversies,
especially in the problem of the relation of church and state,
in the Middle Ages [18] and also later in Protestantism.[19] This
general Christian view that the Old Testament, though no
longer binding, is still, by reason of its divine origin, to be
used as a source of good examples in political theory is expressed by Petrus Cunaeus in his description of the Mosaic
state as a "commonwealth than which no commonwealth
on earth was ever holier and richer in good examples . . .
for, by Hercules, as its author and founder it has not man
foredoomed by reason of his mortal frame but rather the immortal God himself." [20]

[15] *Ibid.*

[16] *Stromata* I, 26 (PG, 8, 916 B).   [17] *Ibid.*, V, 14 (PG, 9, 145 B).

[18] Cf. C. H. McIlwain, *The Growth of Political Thought in the West* (Macmillan
Co., 1932), pp. 147, 206, 212.

[19] Cf. A. F. S. Pearson, *Church and State: Political Aspect of Sixteenth Century
Puritanism* (Cambridge University Press, 1928), pp. 11, 32, 27, 81, 107, 125.

[20] Petrus Cunaeus, *De Republica Hebraeorum*, Leyden, 1631, Praefatio, p. *2a:
"offero Republicam, qua nulla unquam in terris sanctior, nec bonis exemplis ditior
fuit . . . quoniam illa hercle non hominem quenquam mortali concretione fatum,
sed ipsum deum immortalem, autorem fundatoremque habet."

But while the Mosaic state with its particular laws and institutions was declared in Christianity to have been abolished with the coming of Christ, whose coming was the fulfillment of the promise of a Messianic age, its essential character as described by Philo and Jewish tradition was taken over by Christianity and perpetuated in the Church. Just as in Philo the expression "divine ecclesia" is used as a description of the entire body of professing Jews,[21] so also in Christianity the entire body of professing Christians is described as constituting an "ecclesia of God."[22] Just as in Philo all those who profess Judaism, whether native-born Jews or converts, are called the "sons of God,"[23] so also in Christianity all those who "are led by the Spirit of God" are called the "sons of God."[24] Just as in Philo all those who profess Judaism are called Israel,[25] so also Christianity, considering itself the heir of Judaism,[26] calls itself "the Israel of God."[27] Just as Philo describes the whole body of professing Jews as the "universal polity" ($\dot{\eta}$ $\kappa\alpha\theta o$-$\lambda\iota\kappa\omega\tau\epsilon\rho\alpha$ $\pi o\lambda\iota\tau\epsilon\acute{\iota}\alpha$),[28] by which he means "universal ecclesia"[29] or "catholic church" so in Christianity the whole body of professing Christians came to be called the "universal ecclesia" or "catholic church" ($\dot{\epsilon}\kappa\kappa\lambda\eta\sigma\acute{\iota}\alpha$ $\kappa\alpha\theta o\lambda\iota\kappa\acute{\eta}$).[30]

But there is the following fundamental difference. In Christianity, with the abrogation of the Law, Christ takes the place of the Law and fulfils the functions of the Law. Just as in Judaism God is the ruler of the Mosaic state through His Law, so in Christianity God is the ruler of the

---

[21] Cf. above, p. 394.
[22] Acts 20: 28.
[23] Cf. above, pp. 358, 359.
[24] Rom. 8: 14.
[25] *Legat.* 29, 194; cf. above, p. 401, n. 25.
[26] Gal. 3: 29.
[27] Gal. 6: 16.
[28] Cf. above, p. 397.
[29] Cf. above, p. 358.
[30] This expression first occurs in about the year 169 (cf. Hagenbach, *History of Doctrines*, § 71, n. 2).

Church through His Son. As the Law provides for two in-struments of its rule, king and high priest, so Christ com-bines in his person two functions, that of king [31] and that of high priest.[32] Consequently, in the history of Christian-ity, those who came to be recognized as the vicars of Christ were in theory to combine in their person the same two func-tions. They were to be kings and they were to be also high priests.

Christianity, however, did not appear in a desert among roving Bedouins. It appeared in a world already organized in states, governed by established laws, and headed by kings, and in this world it had to make its way, largely by accommodating itself to existing conditions. Accordingly it did not try to abrogate Roman law, nor did it dare set up kings in defiance of the Roman emperor. It had the prec-edent of its founder, who had taught to render "unto Caesar the things which are Caesar's," [33] as a justification for not trying the former, and it had the memory of the crucifixion of its founder on the charge that he claimed to be the king of the Jews as a justification for not daring the latter. And so when Christianity became the religion of Rome it was willing to leave to the emperor the power of kingship and to claim for itself only the power of high priesthood. It was similarly willing to recognize all the Roman laws in matters relating to men and to claim for itself only the power to legislate in matters relating to God.

In theory, however, he who was recognized as the vicar of Christ was to succeed to all the powers of Christ. He was to be both king and high priest. And hence the protracted conflict between church and state throughout the Middle Ages. In that conflict the Old Testament, as a rule, was the

[31] Matt. 25: 34.
[32] Heb. 4: 14.   [33] Matt. 23: 21.

great arsenal for arguments in favor of the independence of these two officers. This, as we have seen, was also Philo's view in his analysis of the Mosaic constitution.[34]

A new mode of treatment of the Mosaic constitution appears with Spinoza. In his grand assault upon traditional philosophy, with his denial of the divine origin of the Mosaic Law, Spinoza treats of the Hebrew state as a state founded by men like all other states. He feels himself free to dwell upon its defects, though he does not hesitate to mention some good features it contained.[35] Analyzing it like any other human institution, he describes it, like others before him, as a theocracy.[36] During the lifetime of Moses, he finds, it contained elements of democracy, kingship, and aristocracy. "As in a democracy," he says, "all surrendered their rights equally," and "all were equally bound by the covenant" and "all had an equal right to consult the Deity, to accept and to interpret His laws, so that all had an exactly equal share in the government." [37] But then the people "absolutely transferred to Moses the right to consult God and interpret His commands." [38] Thus, through his election by the people,[39] Moses became "supreme judge" [40] and "held the supreme authority." [41] Then there was also, he says, an aristocratic element in the Mosaic state, for Moses chose from among the elders of the tribes "his seventy coadjutors, who formed with himself the supreme council," [42] and these seventy elders, as may be judged from his subsequent description of the captains of

---

[34] Cf. above, pp. 342, 344.
[35] *Tractatus Theologico-Politicus*, ch. xvii (*Opera*, ed. Gebhardt, III, p. 212, l. 4–p. 217, l. 13); cf. ch. iii (p. 47, ll. 33–34).
[36] *Ibid.* ch. xvii (p. 206, l. 17; p. 211, l. 29–p. 212, l. 3).
[37] *Ibid.* (p. 206, ll. 24–29).   [40] *Ibid.* (p. 207, ll. 7–8).
[38] *Ibid.* (p. 207, ll. 2–4).   [41] *Ibid.* (p. 207, l. 9).
[39] *Ibid.* (p. 207, ll. 14–15).   [42] *Ibid.* (p. 211, ll. 17–18).

each tribe, are conceived by Spinoza as having been "not superior to others in nobility or birth, but only . . . by reason of age and virtue." [43] It will be recalled that also Philo and St. Thomas found in the Mosaic states elements of these three forms of government.[44] After the death of Moses, throughout the existence of the republic under the Judges, he finds, the state was "neither monarchic, nor aristocratic, nor popular," [45] for "affairs were not all managed by one man, nor by a single council, nor by popular vote, but partly by one tribe, partly by the rest in equal shares." [46] Another reason why it was neither a monarchy nor an aristocracy nor a democracy is that "the right of interpreting the laws and of communicating God's answers was vested in one man, while the right and power of administering the state according to the laws thus interpreted and the answers thus communicated was vested in another man." [47] This division between those who interpreted the law and those who administered the state continued to exist even after the establishment of the monarchy, and it is this division between civil and religious authority that led to many dissensions and ultimately to the fall of the state.[48] The object lesson to be drawn from scriptural history, concludes Spinoza, is not to allow ministers of religion to participate in affairs of the state and to establish the supreme authority of the state over matters religious.[49] Thus, unlike all religious philosophers before him, who saw in scriptural history examples of good government which are to be

[43] *Ibid.* (p. 214, ll. 3–5).
[44] Cf. above, pp. 383 ff.; 429 f.
[45] *Tractatus Theologico-Politicus*, ch. xvii (p. 211, ll. 27–28).
[46] *Ibid.* (p. 211, ll. 24–27).
[47] *Ibid.* (p. 208, ll. 3–6).
[48] *Ibid.* (p. 217, l. 3–p. 220, l. 30).
[49] *Ibid.*, ch. xviii (p. 225, ll. 12–17; p. 226, ll. 7–13).

followed, Spinoza found in it examples of bad government which are to be avoided.

With his abandonment of the belief in the divine origin of the Mosaic constitution, Spinoza also abandoned the belief in a divinely designed Messianic age, whether yet to come or whether already come. Though he succumbed sufficiently to the influence of the environment to repeat the conventional distinctions drawn by Christian theologians between the prophetic gift of Moses and that of Christ,[50] he did not consider the coming of Christ as the fulfillment of the promise of a Messianic age. With his denial of the belief in a God who acts by design in natural as well as in human history, he could not with any show of consistency affirm the belief in the coming of an ideal age by the design of God. Men to him were to be saved neither by a revealed Law nor by a revealed Messiah; the only source of salvation for them was to be found in their own reason. But while he had faith in the saving grace of reason and while he also urged men to live in accordance with it, he held out to mankind as a whole no hope of an ideal age of reason. For the future of mankind as a whole, he, like Aristotle, saw only an improved form of government, guided by reason, to be sure, but by no means ideal, and he himself tinkered with the mechanism thereof.

But though Spinoza did not envisage a Messianic age in its universal aspect, as taught by Philo and Jewish tradition in general, he still retained a belief in the old Messianic ideal in its limited aspect, which he undoubtedly must have understood to be its original sense, and that is the redemption of the people of Israel. Speaking of the future of the Jews, he says: "If the foundations of their religion have not enfeebled their spirits, I would go so far as to believe that, with the

[50] *Ibid.*, ch. iv (p. 64, l. 2–p. 65, l. 1).

opportunity offered, for so changeable are human affairs, they may raise their government again and God may elect them anew." [51]

The enfeeblement of their spirits which Spinoza feared might stand in the way of the redemption of the Jews was the suspension of reason in the guidance of human affairs, which to him was the greatest weakness of man and the source of his bondage. The strength and freedom of man to him consists in a life according to reason, and to live according to reason, as defined by him, after Aristotle, means first to understand our own nature, our own particular virtue or excellency, and then to act intelligently toward its preservation. For groups no less than for individuals he lays down the general rule that our highest good is "to act, to live, and preserve our being in accordance with the dictates of reason," [52] and just as the being of the individual is not his physical existence but the identity of his personality so also the being of the group is not its biological continuity but rather its social inheritance. [53] In the erstwhile experience of his own people, the Jewish exiles of Spain and Portugal, he could not help but see the working of a native conatus or striving for the self-preservation of a group, unguided by what he would consider as reason. By the blind working of that conatus these Spanish and Portuguese Jews had chosen a life of exile as Jews in preference to a life of ease no longer as Jews. But without thoughtful planning for the future, they allowed themselves to become scattered in all the havens of refuge that happened to be open to them at that time, where they only exposed themselves to the dangers of new exterminations and banishments in the future. Had

---

[51] *Ibid.*, ch. iii (p. 57, ll. 3–6).
[52] *Ethics* IV, Prop. 24.
[53] Cf. chapter on "Virtues," in my *The Philosophy of Spinoza*.

they let reason guide their desires, emotions, hopes, and beliefs, then, with their young and with their old, with their
sons and with their daughters, with their flocks and with
their herds, they would all have sped homeward toward the
land of their fathers, to rebuild its wastes, to fasten themselves as a nail in a sure place, and thus to secure their future.
Instead they entrusted their future to what in the philosophy
of Spinoza was the height of credulity, the care of a miracle-
working Deity who, they believed, in His own good time
would gather together the exiles and bring to them redemption. Spinoza himself witnessed the actual manifestation of
that belief when the descendants of those exiles flocked to
the banner of a self-proclaimed Messiah, Shabbethai Zebi.

In his belief in the power of reason, Spinoza visualized the
possible fulfillment of the Messianic promises of the ultimate redemption of Israel. The time would come, he believed,
when reason would guide the affairs of nations as it did
already guide to some extent the affairs of individuals. Then
all nations in their natural striving for the preservation of
their own being would consider it also their duty to help
the preservation of the being of those who are small and
powerless and homeless and unable to help themselves — and
they would do so even at the sacrifice of some of their own
overabundance of wealth and territorial possessions. Should
such a change in the affairs of nations take place, says
Spinoza, — "for so changeable are human affairs" — then,
if there should still be a surviving remnant of Jews to take
advantage of the opportunity offered to them, "they may
raise their government again." And, unconsciously perhaps,
slipping into the traditional vocabulary of Messianic promises, he concludes: "and God may elect them anew."

CHAPTER XIV

WHAT IS NEW IN PHILO?

WE ALL have a feeling that between ancient Greek philosophy which knew not Scripture and the philosophy which ever since the seventeenth century has tried to free itself from the influence of Scripture there was a philosophy which placed itself at the service of Scripture and was willing to take orders from it. As to what this intervening period in the history of philosophy should be called, historians offer us two choices. Sometimes they call it "Mediaeval Philosophy" and start it with the Church Fathers in the second century,[1] even though in political history the mediaeval period is generally supposed to start many centuries later, either with the death of Theodosius in 395 or with the fall of Rome in 476. Sometimes, however, they call it "Christian Philosophy"[2] and reserve the term mediaeval as a description of that part of Christian philosophy which begins with St. Augustine (354–430) or with Boethius (480–524),[3] both of whom lived close enough respectively to the dates which are generally considered as the beginning of the mediaeval period politically.

But scholarship likes to adorn itself with footnotes and to garnish itself with appendixes. And so the main text of the history of philosophy is generally annotated by, or has appended to it, two philosophical incidents. The first of these incidents is the philosophy of Philo, which is introduced

[1] Cf. J. H. Erdmann, *A History of Philosophy*, I, 225 ff.
[2] Cf. F. Ueberweg-B. Geyer, *Die patristische und scholastische Philosophie* (1928), pp. 1, 3, and 141; E. Gilson and Ph. Böhmer, *Die Geschichte der christlichen Philosophie* (1937).
[3] Cf. M. De Wulf, *History of Mediaeval Philosophy*[3], I, 1–23; 77–82; 105–114.

as a postscript to ancient Greek philosophy. The second incident is Arabic Moslem and Jewish philosophy, which is introduced as a prefatory note to the scholasticism of the thirteenth century. The value of these two philosophic incidents, it must be admitted, is not entirely overlooked; in their subordinate position they are dutifully evaluated; but whatever value is attached to them is that of furnishing certain ingredients in the reconstruction of the background of two periods in Christian philosophy — in the case of the former that of the Church Fathers and in the case of the latter that of the scholasticism of the thirteenth century.

On the whole, this treatment of the history of philosophy reflects that prevailing conception of history in general which, as theologically formulated by Eusebius and St. Augustine, maintains that everything that came before Christianity is to be considered only as preparatory to it and everything that happened outside of Christianity is to be considered only as tributary to it. In Hegel's metaphysical restatement of this theological conception of history, the particular application of this view to the history of philosophy is bluntly stated without any circumlocution. "The history of philosophy," he says, "falls into three periods — that of Greek philosophy, the philosophy of the Middle Ages and modern philosophy," [4] the first of which "has found its place in the religion of the heathen," whereas the second and third have their sphere "within the Christian world," [5] for the philosophy of the Middle Ages, in which the scholastics are to be included, "mainly falls within the Christian Church," [6] and similarly modern philosophy, which is essentially "Teutonic philosophy," is also "philosophy within Christendom." [7] Though "Arabians and Jews

[4] Hegel, *History of Philosophy*, I, 109.
[5] *Ibid.*, III, 1; cf. I, 101.
[6] *Ibid.*, I, 110.
[7] *Ibid.*, I, 101.

are also historically to be noticed," [8] they "have only to be noticed in an external and historic way." [9] As for Philo, he says, "we must make cursory mention of" him, before we enter upon our discussion of "the Neo-Platonists," [10] the latter of which are to be considered as being "closely connected with the revolution which was caused in the world by Christianity" [11] though only as a sort of precursor to its philosophy, for, as he adds, while the Neo-Platonists had some adumbration of "the Idea of Christianity," [12] they "still had not proved their doctrine that the Trinity is the truth." [13]

There is much to be said on this conception of the history of philosophy, both for it and against it. One could go on and argue endlessly whether historical facts, and facts in the history of philosophy in particular, are to be studied — to use the language of Aristotle — as *known to us* or as *known by nature*, and consequently one could also go on and argue endlessly whether in our attempt to break up the continuity of historical events into periods we should look at all for any differentiating characteristics other than those which are visibly known to us and which have palpably proved themselves of consequence in the experience of a great part of mankind who share common beliefs and a common way of life. But such speculative arguments would lead us nowhere. They would be as useless as the old-fashioned speculations as to how to classify species, when species were held to be unalterably and firmly fixed from creation and their classifications were only half-intuitive generalizations based upon inadequate data superficially studied. When, however, as a result of a century's research, beginning with Linnaeus and ending in Darwin's voyage on H. M. S. Beagle, investigators began to base their speculations concerning

---

[8] *Ibid.*, I, 110.　　[10] *Ibid.*, II, 387.　　[12] *Ibid.*, III, 1.
[9] *Ibid.*, III, 1.　　[11] *Ibid.*, I, 374.　　[13] *Ibid.*, III, 2.

species on extensive accumulations of specimens and the study of the internal structures of those specimens, the various attempts at their classification from then on were based upon a solid foundation of reality, even though the boundary lines between species were no longer firmly fixed. Let us also set sail on some Beagle of our own in search of philosophic specimens and, after we have found them, let us study their internal structures and then, from their internal structures, let us try to learn something about the origin and classification of their species, which species we commonly call periods in the history of philosophy or systems of philosophy. It is also possible that as a result of such an investigation so-called periods and systems of philosophy might prove to be not so distinctly and deeply separated from each other as they are generally assumed to be.

The specimens which we bring back from the voyage on our own Beagle are in the form of books, printed books and manuscript books, books preserved in their entirety and books of which only fragments have been preserved in other books, and books of which only the titles have been preserved. In our study of our specimens, we begin, as every scientific study of a subject usually begins, with a classification of them. Taking first as the basis of our classification that which externally differentiates them from one another, namely, language, we find that they fall into five groups, Greek, Latin, Syriac, Arabic, and Hebrew. The Greek specimens date from the fragments of pre-Socratic philosophers to the fifteenth century, falling short by about a century of the reputed end of mediaeval philosophy. The Latin specimens date from Cicero and continue to the end of mediaeval philosophy. The Syriac specimens, the smallest of the five groups, date from the fifth to about the end of the thirteenth century. The Arabic specimens date from the eighth to the end of the twelfth century. The Hebrew specimens date from the tenth century and continue to the reputed end of the medieval period of philosophy.

Continuing then to examine the contents of these specimens, we discover that these five linguistic groups are not independent of each other. To begin with, the last four of them are all dependent upon the Greek specimens. In all of them Greek works are translated, names of Greek philosophers are quoted, certain Greek terms are transliterated in their own respective alphabets, many more Greek terms are translated literally in their own respective languages, and problems of Greek philosophy invariably form the starting point of discussions. Then, the last four of these five groups have certain relations among themselves. Some philosophic specimens are translated from the Syriac into Arabic or are Syriac paraphrases of Arabic works; Some are translated from the Arabic into Hebrew and a few from Hebrew into Arabic; some are translated from both Arabic and Hebrew into Latin; some are translated from the Latin into Hebrew; and together with these translations there go also the adoption of terminology, both in transliterated and translated forms, the quotation of names, and the borrowing of ideas.

Studying our philosophic specimens still more closely, we notice that all of them are streaked through with material drawn from another type of literature, namely, the religious literature. But with respect to this streak of religious literature which runs through the entire field of philosophy, we notice that not long before the rise of Christianity a sudden change takes place in the type of literature drawn upon. Before that time in Greek and also Latin philosophy, and for some time after that in a certain part of Greek and Latin philosophy, the religious literature drawn upon, in the form of quotations, references, or allusions, is pagan Greek literature. But beginning with that time the religious literature drawn upon is that of Scripture in its threefold division, the so-called Old and New Testaments and the Koran. This scriptural streak in its threefold division is variously distributed in our five groups of philosophic specimens. In the Greek philosophic specimens, those dating from before the middle of the first century of the Christian era are Jewish and quote the Old Testament, but those dating after that period are all Christian and quote both the Old and the New Testament. The Latin specimens, beginning with Tertullian toward the end of the second century, are all Christian, and the quotations are from both the Old and the New Testament. The Syriac specimens are Christian, and the quotations in them are from both the Old and the New Testament. The Arabic specimens are both Moslem and Jewish and to a lesser extent also Christian. The Moslems quote only the Koran, the Jews only the Old Testament, and the Christians both the Old and the New Testament. The Hebrew specimens are only Jewish and the Scripture quoted is only the Old Testament. Not only, however, is this break from ancient pagan philosophy marked by a change in the quotations from religious literature, but it is also marked by a new form of philosophic literary expression. Before that time the forms of philosophic literary expression were the gnomic saying, the dialogue, the poem, the diatribe, and the formal discourse. From now on a new form of exposition appears in philosophic literature, the homily on some scriptural text or the running commentary upon some scriptural books.

This change in the type of religious literature drawn upon and in literary form, we discover upon still further study, is not a mere matter of externality; it marks a fundamental break in philosophic doctrines, which break ushers in a fundamentally new period in the history of philosophy, that intermediate or mediaeval period which we all feel intervenes between ancient philosophy which knew not Scripture and modern philosophy which began with an attempt to free itself from Scripture. Mediaeval philosophy, so defined and delimited, is thus the common philosophy of three religions — Judaism, Christianity, and Islam — consisting of one philosophy written in five languages — Greek, Latin, Syriac, Arabic, and Hebrew. It is indeed a continuation of pagan Greek philosophy but at the same time also a radical revision of that philosophy, stressing certain doctrines by which it is distinguished from ancient pagan philosophy. From its very beginning in its original language, even before its spread into other languages, it formed a new school of Greek philosophy, more distinct in fundamental problems from the totality of all the pagan Greek schools of philosophy than those pagan schools are distinct from one another. When we speak of Christian philosophy, and for that matter also of Jewish or Moslem philosophy, and the question is raised as to what we mean thereby apart from Greek philosophic problems dealt with by Christians or Jews or Moslems, or apart from the employment of certain concepts or a certain form of reasoning from Greek philosophy in defense of certain religious doctrines borrowed from Scripture,[14] the answer to be given is that it is a fundamental revision of Greek philosophy on the basis of certain principles common to these three religions, resulting in the introduction of new elements into every branch of pagan Greek philosophy — its epistemology, its metaphysics, its physics, and its ethics.

Let us then take a fleeting glance at these common principles which constitute the common characteristics of that

---

[14] See the collection of forty-seven opinions as to the meaning of Christian philosophy in E. Gilson, *L'Esprit de la Philosophie Médiévale* (1932), I, 297–324, and Gilson's own discussion on the subject in chs. i and ii.

mediaeval philosophy and let us invent a synthetic mediaeval philosopher, made up of all the common elements of the Christian, the Moslem, and the Jewish philosopher, and let us follow in the track of his reasoning as he proceeds to revise Greek philosophy.

Our synthetic mediaeval philosopher begins with the belief that there is one infallible source of truth, and that is revelation, and that revelation is embodied in Scripture, be it Old Testament or New Testament or Koran. In Scripture he finds a description of the world, perhaps not so full as he would have liked to have, but he finds in it enough references to water and earth and air and fire and heavens and stars and minerals and plants and living beings to furnish him with enough materials for an orderly description of the world as he knows it. He also finds in it an explanation of those things which he wants to know about the world, how it came into being and how it is governed. Finally, he finds in it rules for the guidance of man in his various relations to his fellow men, both as an individual to other individuals and as a member of society to the society of which he is a part.

But the God who furnished certain men with certain truths directly by revelation has also equipped men with reason. Thus equipped, certain men were able by their own effort to discover some of those truths which God made known to other men directly by revelation — to discover the nature of the world, to describe it, to explain it, and to lay down rules for the conduct of mankind. And just as the truths of revelation are embodied in the threefold Scripture, written in Hebrew, Greek, and Arabic, so the truths discovered by reason are embodied in a philosophic literature written primarily in Greek. Two bodies of literature thus contain all human wisdom: one the wisdom made known through revelation; the other the wisdom discovered by reason.

Since God is the author both of the truths made known by revelation and of the truths discovered by reason, there can be no conflict between them. If a conflict should appear to exist between them, it must be no real conflict. Any such conflict must be due either to our misunderstanding of Scripture or to the vagaries of human reason which has gone astray. For revelation must of necessity be communicated to man in the language commonly spoken by man, and such a language does not always convey to the ordinary man the real meaning intended by the revelation. Similarly, human reason must of necessity be encased in a human body and function through a human body, and thus, hemmed in by a body, reason sometimes is led astray and errs. Scripture, to our synthetic mediaeval philosopher, is always true, if only its language could be properly understood; reason would always be true, if only it were not misguided by the body in which it is encased. In the proper study of the relation of Scripture to reason, therefore, Scripture has to be interpreted in the light of what is most evidently true in reason, and reason has to be corrected in the light of what is most evidently the true teachings of Scripture. There may be differences of opinion, among those who make up our synthetic philosopher, as to what is most evidently true in reason as well as to what is most obviously the true teaching of Scripture, but they all agree that this is the proper method of procedure.[15]

And so our synthetic philosopher begins to compare the teachings of Scripture with the teachings of philosophy.

Among the teachings of Scripture our synthetic philosopher finds principles which he assumes to constitute what

[15] Cf. above, I, 155-163, 194-199.

Scripture considers as essential to any true religion, namely, the existence of God, the unity of God, creation of the world, divine providence, and the divine origin of the rules for human conduct.[16] He then begins to look into the writings of the philosophers to see what reason has discovered about these principles.

He finds that with the exception of one school of philosophers, the Epicureans, reason has guided all the philosophers to the discovery of the existence of God.[17] He is delighted with the arguments advanced by reason in proof of the existence of God; he appropriates them and makes use of them. He makes a few changes in some of them, especially in the argument which maintains that the existence of God is an innate idea, but on the whole he is willing to follow the pagan philosophers in the proofs they have discovered by reason.[18]

He also finds that reason has led philosophers to discover that God is numerically one and, like Scripture, to come out against popular polytheism. Reason has also led some philosophers, like Plato and Aristotle, to discover that God is internally one, in the sense that He is incorporeal, though some philosophers, like the Stoics, have been led astray by reason to think that God is himself corporeal and never leaves the inwards of the corporeal world. Similarly, reason has led philosophers to discover that God is one in the sense of His being self-sufficient and in need of nothing outside himself,[19] though they do not exploit that property of God to its full extent.

But he finds that reason has failed to guide philosophers to the discovery of two other phases of the unity of God.

First, unlike Scripture, reason has failed to see the unity

---

[16] Cf. above, I, 194.

[17] Cf. above, I, 177–180.

[18] Cf. above, pp. 92–93.

[19] Cf. above, I, 172.

of God as implying His uniqueness in the sense of His being the only one who is both uncreated and a creator. In Plato, God is indeed spoken of as a creator, but by the side of God there are to Plato also ideas, concerning which he sometimes says that they are uncreated and that they possess a creative power of their own. In Aristotle, God is spoken of mainly as a mover, not as a creator, and the world, which is not God, is spoken of as being uncreated. Our synthetic philosopher, in opposition to all this, does not admit by the side of God anything that possesses a creative power of its own and anything that is uncreated; and, if he is occasionally inclined to admit the existence of something coeternal with God, he will try to show that its eternity does not mean uncreatedness.[20]

Second, unlike Scripture, reason has failed to conceive of the unity and unlikeness of God as implying the unknowability and indescribability of His essence. Neither Plato nor Aristotle, despite their belief in the immateriality and simplicity and indivisibility of God, had any conception of the unknowability of God's essence and its indescribability. Indeed our synthetic philosopher will be unable to make up his mind as to what extent God is unknowable and indescribable, and in what sense one is to understand the terms by which as a rule God is described. But he starts his philosophy with a principle of the unknowability and the indescribability of God; and, while he is conscious of the difficulties that this principle may give rise to, he debates these difficulties in his own mind and finds some kind of solution for them without giving up that principle.[21]

Less satisfactory to our synthetic philosopher and requiring correction by him is the finding of reason with regard to the problem of the origin of the world. While reason has

[20] Cf. above, I, 172, 195.   [21] Cf. above, pp. 153 ff.

led some philosophers to regard our present world as having been created out of some preëxistent matter, it has led others to regard it as eternal. For himself, our synthetic philosopher is unable to make up his mind as to the real meaning of the teaching of Scripture with regard to the beginning of the world, though he is inclined to favor the view, never envisaged by reason, that the world came into being *ex nihilo*. But of one thing he is certain: however the world came into being, its coming into being must be so conceived as to make God the cause of its being. Of one other thing is he certain: however the world came into being, it came into being by the will of God, which will of God is to be understood in such a way as to lead to the conclusion that had God willed it He could have created a different kind of world.[22]

Still less satisfactory to our synthetic philosopher and requiring correction by him is the finding of reason with regard to divine providence. On the whole, reason has led philosophers to believe that the world is governed by certain laws, laws which make for order and stability, for permanence and preservation, as if some wise being were presiding over it and supervising it and caring for it. Philosophers even speak of the laws of nature as being the work of God. In Plato they are said to be implanted in the world by the Demiurge at the time of His creation of the world. In Aristotle they are said to be the immutable movements imparted to the world by the prime mover who is God. In the Stoics they are said to be the working of the primordial fire, out of which the world unfolded itself but which continues to abide in the world as an internal Reason. The philosophers also sometimes describe these laws of nature as divine

[22] Cf. above, I, 322–324.

providence. But their divine providence is fated; more often and more correctly do they describe it by the term fate. The laws of nature which they trace to their respective gods are absolutely unchangeable, inexorable; even their gods cannot change them. There is no room in their systems for miracles and individual providence.

Now our synthetic philosopher, on the whole, agrees with the finding of reason that there are immutable laws of nature. God to him is not only the creator of the world but also the cause of its preservation and its governance and its orderly processes. God it is who has implanted in the world that order and regularity of the recurrence of events which we call laws of nature. Because God is unchangeable, these laws of nature which He has implanted in the world are also unchangeable. Still, with all their unchangeability, God has reserved to himself the right of a free agent to change these laws of His own making. The possibility of miracles is a fundamental belief which our synthetic philosopher will insist upon. He may offer different explanations of miracles; he may not be quite certain what extraordinary events reported in the various religious Scriptures and traditions are to be regarded as miracles; but he does not question the principle that God is a free agent who can change the order of nature and perform miracles. This principle is the basis of our synthetic philosopher's belief that divine providence is individual. To him, God's implanting of laws of nature in the universe is a token of His universal providence, for these laws of nature are for the purpose of the preservation of the world as a whole and of all the kinds of genera and species within it. But the upsetting of these laws of nature by God through the working of miracles is to our synthetic philosopher a token of God's individual providence, for these miracles have for their purpose the preservation of

individuals or groups of individuals when all the forces of
nature are lined up against them for their destruction.[23]

As a corollary to the conception of freedom in God is the
conception of freedom in man, and on this point, too, our
synthetic philosopher finds that reason has gone astray and
failed to attain to the truth of the matter. Man, say the
philosophers, is a part of nature, and as everything in nature
is determined so also everything in human nature is determined. There is no such thing as freedom, by which man
can break the chain of causes which have led him up to the
point of being faced with the making of a decision. If Plato
and Aristotle and the Stoics do speak of a distinction in
human actions between actions which are voluntary and
actions which are compulsory, they mean by voluntary
actions only actions that are performed without ignorance
and without external compulsion. To the philosophers, all
the forces that bear upon human action are divided into
forces of emotion and forces of reason. When man is faced
with a choice between two alternative modes of action, the
choice, according to them, will be determined, as in the case
of any physical conflict in nature between opposing forces,
by the relative strength of the forces of reason and the
forces of emotion. If the forces of reason are stronger, the
victory will be that of reason; if the forces of emotion are
stronger, the victory will be that of the emotions. Will itself is merely a description of that choice determined either
by reason or by the emotions; there is no such thing as a will
which is free and independent of these forces of reason and
emotion. If philosophers urge man to act in accordance with
the dictates of reason, it does not mean that they believe
that at the crucial moment which calls for a decision man is
free to choose whether to follow the dictates of reason or the

[23] Cf. above, I, 356–359.

dictates of the emotions. It is only an exhortation to man that he should continually, throughout his lifetime, cultivate and strengthen his reason, by the only means by which reason can be cultivated and strengthened, and that is by the acquisition of knowledge, so that when the crucial moment arrives reason will be found the stronger force and will dominate the emotions.

Our synthetic mediaeval philosopher is opposed to this. Man, indeed, may be considered as part of nature and as subject to its laws. But just as the laws of nature may be upset by God's freedom, so also the laws which govern human action, as part of nature, may be upset by man's freedom. Our synthetic philosopher is indeed conscious of the many difficulties which this belief in human freedom gives rise to and in his attempt to solve all these difficulties he may make all kinds of qualifications as to the nature and exercise of this freedom, but despite all this he will cling strenuously to the belief that the human soul is endowed by God with part of His own power of freedom, to work miracles in man as He himself works miracles in the world. When man is faced with a decision and the forces of his own nature are all set so as to determine his decision in one particular way, he can by the freedom with which he is endowed by God decide to act contrary to all those determining forces. Only external obstacles or forces can defeat the free human decision, for by these external obstacles or forces man may be prevented from acting according to his own free choice or he may be forced even to act contrary to his own free choice, but even these external obstacles and forces may be miraculously removed by God, if man is found worthy of such a direct divine intervention.[24]

Another corollary to the belief in God's freedom and hence

[24] Cf. above, I, 456–462.

also to human freedom is the belief that the immortality of the soul depends by the will of God upon one's individual conduct, so that while each soul can be immortal it can also be destroyed. Now our synthetic philosopher is ready to admit that reason also has led some pagan philosophers, and especially Plato, to a belief in the immortality of the soul, and he may perhaps be also ready to admit that it was the teachings of pagan philosophy that led him to discover the full meaning of this principle in the pages of his Scriptures, but he will insist that reason has failed to discover the full truth of that belief. To those pagan philosophers, even when they have that belief, immortality is assumed to belong to the soul by the necessity of its very nature and hence not only may it be immortal but it must be so. Even to those pagan philosophers who happen to speak of a certain kind of destructibility of the soul, this destructibility also comes to it by a necessary process of nature; it is not the result of individual divine providence. To our synthetic philosopher, however, immortality is a special gift of God and an exercise of individual divine providence. The soul, which is assumed by him to have an existence of its own in the human body, is endowed by God not only with freedom but also with immortality, for by its own nature, like anything else created by God, it cannot be immortal. Of this gift of immortality man must prove himself worthy, and he can prove himself worthy of it only by the exercise of his freedom in a manner approved of by God. If man does not prove himself worthy of immortality, he forfeits it; his soul may suffer destruction. Our synthetic philosopher is perhaps not always quite certain as to how the soul remains immortal as an individual entity and as to how it suffers destruction. But after all his debating with himself on the problem, he comes out with a confession of a belief that each man's soul may by God's grace survive in some sense as an individual entity but of itself it is subject to some kind of destruction.[25]

Finally, a third corollary of divine freedom and hence also of human freedom is the divine origin of morality. To our synthetic mediaeval philosopher the efforts of pagan philosophers to attain by human reason perfect rules for the conduct of men, both as individuals and as members of society, have by their own confession proved to fall short of perfection. To him, the only rule of conduct which is perfect is that which has been revealed by God, for if, as the pagan philosophers maintain, perfect rules of conduct must be in accordance with nature and in accordance with reason, they cannot be discovered by reason, for reason itself never attains perfection in its knowledge of nature; they can be perfect only when revealed by God who is the creator of both reason and nature. In his study of the laws revealed by God, carefully comparing them with the teachings of the pagan philosophers, our synthetic philosopher finds in the divine laws the perfect fulfillment of all that the pagan philosophers have vainly striven to attain. Indeed our synthetic philosopher may debate with himself whether that divine law was to continue eternally to be the Law revealed to Moses, or whether the Law of Moses was to be replaced in part by the law of the Gospels and the Apostles, or whether even this latter law was to be replaced by the law of the Koran; but whatever decision he may arrive at on this particular question he remains firm in his belief that man's conduct is to be guided by a divine law.[26]

These are the main principles of our synthetic mediaeval philosopher. The endless discussions to be found in the voluminous literature of the various languages in which mediaeval philosophy is embodied are only elaborations upon

[25] Cf. above, I, 416–417.   [26] Cf. above, pp. 306 ff.

these principles — explanations of these principles in their manifold implications, discussions of various difficulties arising from these principles, homilies on various scriptural proof-texts advanced in support of them, and discourses on various philosophical passages which appear to be either in agreement or disagreement with them. Taken altogether, these principles of mediaeval philosophy constitute a radical departure from ancient pagan Greek philosophy — they radically change its theory of knowledge, by introducing into it a new source of knowledge; they radically change its metaphysics, by introducing a new conception into the nature and causality of God, who is the main subject of metaphysics; they radically change its physics, by introducing a new conception into the working of its laws; they radically change its ethics, by introducing a new source of morality. The changes thus introduced by our synthetic philosopher into Greek philosophy are as great as those introduced into it by Plato and greater than those introduced into it by any other philosopher after Plato. Our synthetic mediaeval philosopher, indeed, has not introduced anything radically new into what he learned from pagan Greek philosophic works about the description of the structure and composition of the physical universe. He was quite willing to follow Aristotle in his description of the heavens, of the earth, of growing and living things, of the human body, of the human soul, and of the rules of human reasoning, though not without an occasional grumble and not without an occasional excursus into the writings of some other Greek philosophers. He assiduously studied the works of Aristotle as well as those of other Greek philosophers dealing with these subjects, commenting upon them, paraphrasing them, epitomizing them, questioning and disputing about them, and even making some slight original contributions in the course of his study of them — but all this in harmony with those fundamental principles which set off his own philosophy from that of the Greek philosophers. Similarly, when toward the end of mediaeval philosophy, in the sixteenth century, new conceptions of nature and of the physical universe began to make their appearance, exponents of mediaeval philosophy, among whom Descartes is to be included, tried to show how easy it was for them to adjust their inherited principles of mediaeval philosophy to their new conception of nature and the physical universe.

This fundamental departure from pagan Greek philosophy, if the facts of the history of philosophy are to be presented as they are actually *known by nature* and not as they merely happen to be *known to us*, appears first in Hellenistic Judaism,[27] where it attains its systematic formulation in Philo. Philo is the founder of this new school of philosophy, and from him it directly passes on to the Gospel of St. John and the Church Fathers, from whom it passes on to Moslem and hence also to mediaeval Jewish philosophy. Philo is the direct or indirect source of this type of philosophy which continues uninterruptedly in its main assertions for well-nigh seventeen centuries, when at last it is openly challenged by Spinoza.

Historically, a certain nibbling at this type of philosophy, which is properly to be called the Philonic philosophy, started before Spinoza; and historically, too, Philonic philosophy did not completely disappear even after Spinoza. But Spinoza it was who for the first time launched a grand assault upon it, and if the Philonic philosophy did not completely disappear as a result of that assault, it no longer held a dominant position. Henceforth, in order to gain attention at all, it had to disguise its meaning and adopt a new vocabu-

[27] Cf. above, I, 26–27.

lary. It is only recently that Philonic philosophy, through the increasing influence of one of its most distinguished Mediaeval Christian exponents, began to gain vogue and currency in quarters where it is not an inherited tradition, but that is due only to the breakdown of philosophy as a learned discipline, from which some inquiring minds try to seek escape in scholasticism as a substitute for scholarship.

In his grand assault upon Philonic philosophy, Spinoza starts with an attack upon its chief basis, the belief in revelation. This part of his assault he makes in his *Tractatus Theologico-Politicus*,[28] a work written in the Philonic manner, in the form of homilies upon scriptural texts. With his denial of revelation, he then undertakes to restore philosophy to the status in which it was prior to the Philonic revolution. Like most Greek philosophers, he does not deny the existence of God, if by God is meant what the Greek philosopher meant by the principle of causality in the world.[29] Like the Greek philosophers, he similarly does not deny the unity of God, understanding by unity not only the numerical oneness of the cause of the world but also its self-sufficiency and simplicity. Moreover, like Aristotle in the Neoplatonized form in which he understood him, he takes the unity of God to mean His uniqueness as an uncaused cause. He denies, however, with some qualification, the Philonic tradition that the simplicity of God means also His unknowability and indefinability.[30] But, in this particular instance, going beyond the Philonic tradition, he comes out even against the Platonic and Aristotelian tradition which takes the simplicity of God to mean His incorporeality.[31] Then, going back

[28] Cf. above, I, 163.

[29] Cf. the present writer's *The Philosophy of Spinoza*, chapters on "Proofs of the Existence of God" and "The Causality of God."

[30] Cf. above, pp. 162 f.

[31] Cf. above, pp. 161 f.

to general classical Greek philosophy, he denies God that supposed freedom of the will by which He can change the order of nature, though by a special definition of the term freedom he calls the necessity of God's action by the name of freedom.[32] Again going back to general classical Greek philosophy, he denies man that vaunted freedom of his with which Philonic philosophy has endowed him as a gift of God.[33] With Aristotle, he also denies the separability of soul from body,[34] though by following the Neoplatonized form of Aristotelianism he speaks of the immortality of the soul, and even of an individual immortality, without resorting to the Philonic view of the destructibility of the soul.[35] Finally, without a belief in revelation, he goes back to the classical tradition of Greek philosophy in restoring to reason its paramount position as the source of morality.[36]

This, then, is the new period in the history of philosophy, ushered in by Philo and ushered out by Spinoza. If we still choose to describe this period as mediaeval, for after all it comes between a philosophy which knew not of Scripture and a philosophy which tries to free itself from Scripture, then mediaeval philosophy is the history of the philosophy of Philo. For well-nigh seventeen centuries this Philonic philosophy dominated European thought. Nothing really new happened in the history of European philosophy during that extended period. The long succession of philosophers during that period, from among whom various figures are selected by various historians for special distinction as innovators, have only tried to expound, each in his own way,

[32] Cf. *The Philosophy of Spinoza*, chapters on "The Causality of God" and "Necessity and Purposelessness."
[33] Cf. *ibid.*, same chapters and also chapter on "Will."
[34] Cf. above, I, 420–421.
[35] Cf. above, I, 421–423.
[36] Cf. above, p. 321.

the principles laid down by Philo. To the question, then, what is new in Philo? the answer is that it was he who built up that philosophy, just as the answer to the question what is new in Spinoza? is that it was he who pulled it down.[37]

[37] Cf. *The Philosophy of Spinoza*, chapter on "What is New in Spinoza?"

BIBLIOGRAPHICAL NOTE

REFERENCES to the works of Philo are by both chapters and sections, the former being those introduced in the Richter edition and the latter those introduced in the Cohn and Wendland edition, both of which are reproduced in the Colson and Whitaker edition of the Loeb Classical Library. For the sake of simplicity, the enumeration of chapters in each of the four books of *De Specialibus Legibus* and in *De Virtutibus* and *De Praemiis et Poenis* runs continuously as in the Colson edition. But in the Index of References the Richter chapter numbers in these books, which are also those of Cohn and Wendland in their edition, are added within parentheses.

The quotations from Philo are from the Colson and Whitaker translation in the Loeb Classical Library, with occasional verbal changes. Use has also been made, however, of Yonge's English translation as well as of the German translation under the editorship of Cohn, Heinemann, and Adler.

Quotations from Greek and Latin works already published in the Loeb Classical Library are from the English translations published together with the texts of those works. In the case of Plato's *Timaeus*, use has also been made of the translations by R. D. Archer-Hind and F. M. Cornford, and, in the case of Aristotle, of the Oxford translation of his works under the editorship of W. D. Ross.

Quotations from the Apocrypha and Pseudepigrapha are from the English translation under the editorship of R. H. Charles.

References to the Mishnah, Midrash, and Talmud are to the standard editions. Special editions referred to by page are as follows: *Mekilta*, F = Friedmann, M.; W = Weiss, I. H.; HR = Horovitz, H. S.–Rabin, I. A.; L = Lauterbach, J. Z. *Sifra*, ed. I. H. Weiss. *Sifre on Numbers*, F = Friedmann, M.; H = Horovitz, H. S. *Sifre on Deuteronomy*, F = Friedmann, M.; HF = Horovitz, H. S.–Finkelstein, L. *Midrash Tannaim*, ed. D. Hoffmann. *Pesikta de-Rab Kahana, Pesikta Rabbati,* and *Midrash Tehillim,* ed. S. Buber. English translations: *The Mishnah,* by H. Danby, Oxford, 1933. *The Babylonian Talmud,* under the editorship of I. Epstein, London, 1935–. *Midrash Rabbah,* under the editorship of H. Freedman and M. Simon, London, 1939.

A classified list of books and other types of literature on Philo is to be found in *A General Bibliography of Philo,* by H. L. Goodhart and E. R. Goodenough, in *The Politics of Philo Judaeus,* by E. R. Goodenough, New Haven, Yale University Press, 1938. The books and articles referred to in the present study are fully described whenever reference to them is made.

ABBREVIATIONS OF WORKS CITED

PHILO'S WORKS

Abr. = *De Abrahamo.*
Aet. = *De Aeternitate Mundi.*
Agr. = *De Agricultura.*
Cher. = *De Cherubim.*
Conf. = *De Confusione Linguarum.*
Congr. = *De Congressu Eruditionis Gratia.*
Cont. = *De Vita Contemplativa.*
Decal. = *De Decalogo.*
Deter. = *Quod Deterius Potiori Insidiari Soleat.*
Ebr. = *De Ebrietate.*
Flac. = *In Flaccum.*
Fug. = *De Fuga et Inventione.*
Gig. = *De Gigantibus.*
Heres = *Quis Rerum Divinarum Heres.*
Hypoth. = *Hypothetica.*
Immut. = *Quod Deus Sit Immutabilis.*
Jos. = *De Josepho.*
Leg. All. = *Legum Allegoria.*
Legat. = *Legatio ad Gaium.*
Migr. = *De Migratione Abrahami.*
Mos. = *De Vita Mosis.*
Mut. = *De Mutatione Nominum.*
Opif. = *De Opificio Mundi.*
Plant. = *De Plantatione.*
Post. = *De Posteritate Caini.*
Praem. = *De Praemiis et Poenis.*
Probus = *Quod Omnis Probus Liber Sit.*
Provid. = *De Providentia.*
Qu. in Exod. = *Quaestiones et Solutiones in Exodum.*
Qu. in Gen. = *Quaestiones et Solutiones in Genesin.*
Sacr. = *De Sacrificiis Abelis et Caini.*
Sobr. = *De Sobrietate.*
Somn. = *De Somniis.*
Spec. = *De Specialibus Legibus.*
Virt. = *De Virtutibus.*

ABBREVIATIONS OF WORKS CITED

OTHER AUTHORS

Arnim = *Stoicorum Veterum Fragmenta*, collegit Ioannes ab Arnim, Lipsiae, 1903–1924, 4 vols.

Aucher = Latin translation from the Armenian of the *Quaestiones, De Deo*, and *De Providentia*, by J. B. Aucher, in Richter's edition of *Philonis Judaei Opera Omnia*, Lipsiae, 1828–1830, vols. 6–8.

Bréhier = *Les idées philosophiques et religieuses de Philon d'Alexandrie*, par Émile Bréhier, 2nd ed., Paris, 1925.

Colson = Philo with an English Translation, by F. H. Colson and (vols. I–V) G. H. Whitaker, 1929–1941, vols. I–IX. The Loeb Classical Library.

Dähne = *Geschichtliche Darstellung der jüdisch-alexandrinischen Religions-Philosophie*, by August Ferdinand Dähne, Halle, 1834, 2 vols.

Drummond = *Philo Judaeus; or, the Jewish-Alexandrian Philosophy in Its Development and Completion*, by James Drummond, London, 1888, 2 vols.

Gfrörer = *Philo und die alexandrinische Theosophie, oder vom Einflusse der jüdisch-ägyptischen Schule auf die Lehre des Neuen Testaments*, by August Gfrörer, Stuttgart, 1831, 2 vols.

Heinemann, *Bildung* = *Philons griechische und jüdische Bildung*, by Isaak Heinemann, Breslau, 1932.

Leisegang, *Indices* = *Indices ad Philonis Alexandrini Opera*, composuit Ioannes Leisegang, Berolini, 1926–1939, 2 vols.

Philos Werke — *Die Werke Philos von Alexandria in deutscher Übersetzung*, edited by L. Cohn (vols. I–III), by I. Heinemann (vols. IV–V), and by I. Heinemann and M. Adler (vol. VI), Breslau, 1909–1938.

Richter — *Philonis Judaei Opera Omnia*, edited by [C. E. Richter], Lipsiae, 1828–1830, 8 vols.

Siegfried — *Philo von Alexandria als Ausleger des Alten Testaments*, by Carl Siegfried, Jena, 1875.

Zeller — *Die Philosophie der Griechen*, by Eduard Zeller. Editions used indicated in the references.

INDEX OF REFERENCES

Grouped under five headings: I. Philo; II. Greek and Latin Authors; III. Jewish Works and Authors; IV. Christian Works and Authors; V. Moslem Works and Authors.

I. PHILO

II. GREEK AND LATIN AUTHORS

III. JEWISH WORKS AND AUTHORS

IV. CHRISTIAN WORKS AND AUTHORS

INDEX OF TERMS

A. GREEK

B. LATIN

C. HEBREW

D. ARABIC

Son of God, first-born, i, 234
Sons of God, i, 384, 385; ii, 358, 364, 432
Sophists — in relation to Philo, i, 93, 108; on law and nature, ii, 170; early Greek use of the term, i, 28; Philo's use of the term in the sense of the sages of the Law, i, 28, 58, 59
Sophocles, i, 94
Soul — terms *psyche*, *nous* and *pneuma*, i, 102; terms soul, habit, and nature, i, 361; loose use of term soul, i, 362; Philo's outline of the problem of the soul, i, 153; general statement of Philo's view on the soul, i, 413–416; the irrational soul, i, 385–389; preëxistent idea of the irrational soul, i, 214, 360, 390; how the irrational soul was created, i, 269–270, 360, 386–387; its constituent element, i, 204, 387–388; its faculties, i, 389; ii, 4; earthlike, i, 387, 426; corruptible, i, 395; mortal, i, 395; rational souls: various types of rational souls, i, 361, 366–367; ii, 31–32; preëxistent idea of the rational soul, i, 204, 214, 360, 390, 410; how the human soul was created, i, 270, 389–390, 396; its location in the human body, i, 392; its faculties, i, 392; described as: breath, i, 393–394; copy of the Logos, i, 393; divine, i, 392; effulgence of the nature of God, i, 395; eternal, i, 392; ether, i, 394–395; fragment of the Logos, i, 390, 394–395; God, a sort of, to the body, i, 346–347; good and evil souls, i, 383; image, i, 360, 390; immortal, i, 393, 396; impression of the Logos, i, 395; incorporeal, i, 345–346, 391; incorruptible, i, 396; Logos, i, 393; mind, i, 393; rational part, i, 393; ray of the Logos,

i, 395; spirit, i, 393–395; supreme part of our soul, i, 393; its immortality, i, 395–413; relation between rational and irrational souls, i, 392–393, 425–427; ii, 3–4, 100; soul of the universe, i, 213, 325–326, 328, 345–347, 360–361, 390; souls of stars, i, 154, 363–366; the soul in post-Philonic philosophy, i, 416–423
Space, i, 309, 317
Spinoza — overthrow of Philonic philosophy, ii, 457–460; faith and reason, i, 163; existence of God, i, 198; ii, 93; unity of God, i, 198; ii, 160; properties and attributes of God, ii, 161–162; indefinability of God, i, 162–163; the prayer of Moses, ii, 163–164; ideas, i, 294; soul, i, 420–421; immortality, i, 421–423; origin of the world, i, 199; ii, 324; there could not have been another kind of world, ii, 324; providence, i, 199; laws of nature and miracles, i, 395, 420; free will, i, 461–462; revelation, i, 199; prophecy, i, 420; ii, 68–72; angels, i, 419–420; the Mosaic Law, ii, 321; the Mosaic form of government, ii, 434–436; the restoration of the Jews, ii, 436–438. *See also* Index of References
Spirit. *See* Breath
Spirit of God. *See* Divine Spirit
Spiritual proselytes, i, 179–180; ii, 369–374
Stars — problems concerning them, i, 154; made of fire, i, 400; whether they are living and rational beings, i, 154, 363–366, 417–418; gods, i, 38, 173
Stein, M., i, 65, 90, 92, 96, 123, 165, 189, 224
Stewart, J. A., i, 145, 326; ii, 210
Stinespring, W. F., i, 70
Stobaeus. *See* Index of References